REMARKS.

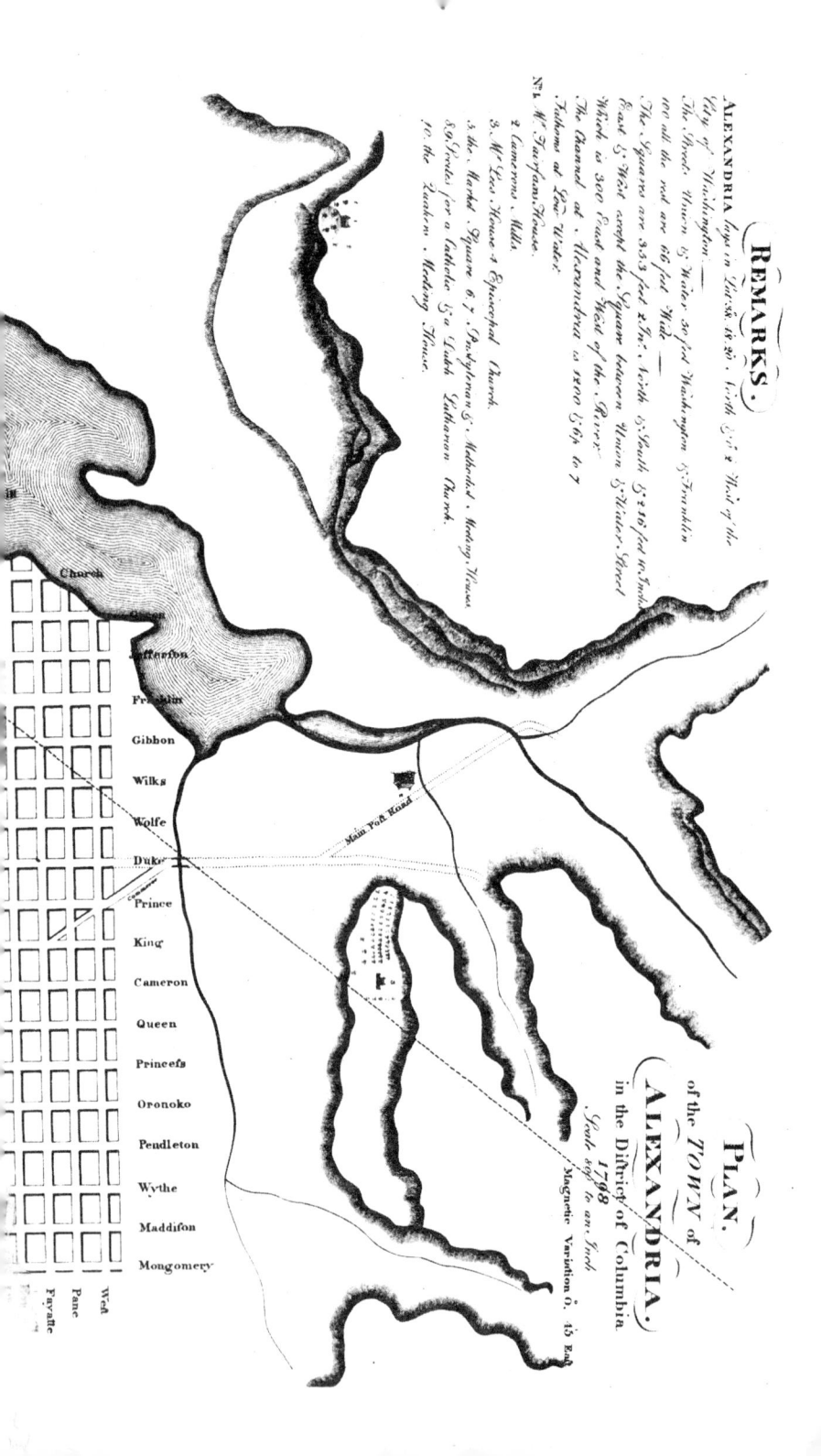

ALEXANDRIA lays in Lat. 38° 49′ North 31′ 2″ West of the City of Washington.

The Streets Run N° & Water 50 feet Washington & Franklin are all the rest are 66 feet Wide.

The Squares are 353 feet 2 Ins. North & South 5210 feet in Ins. East & West except the Squares between Union & Water Street Which is 300 feet and West of the River.

The Channel at Alexandria is 1800 5% to 7 fathom at Low Water.

N° 1. M. Fairfaxs House
2. Camerons Mills
3. M. Lees House & Episcopal Church
4. the Market Square 6, 7 Presbyterian & Methodist Meeting Houses
8, 9 Ground for a Catholic & a Dutch Lutheran Church
10, the Quakers Meeting House.

PLAN of the TOWN of ALEXANDRIA, in the District of Columbia.

1798

Scale 600 ft. to an Inch
Magnetic Variation 0° 45′ East

Church
Queen
Jefferson
Franklin
Gibbon
Wilks
Wolfe
Duke
Prince
King
Cameron
Queen
Princefs
Oronoko
Pendleton
Wythe
Maddifon
Mongomery

West
Pane
Fayatte

ALEXANDRIA. Published by I. V. THOMAS.

POTOMACK RIVER

GREAT HUNTING CREEK

Thomas Ferry

Alfred
Columbus
Washington
St Asaph
Pitt
Royal
Fairfax
Water
Union

ALEXANDRIA, VIRGINIA

ALEXANDRIA HUSTINGS COURT

DEEDS 1783 - 1797

Compiled By

James D. Munson

HERITAGE BOOKS, INC.

Copyright 1990 By

James D. Munson

Published 1990 By

HERITAGE BOOKS, INC.
1540E Pointer Ridge Place, Bowie, Maryland 20716
(301)-390-7709

ISBN 1-55613-329-4

A Complete Catalog Listing Hundreds of Titles on
History, Genealogy & Americana
Free on Request

DEDICATED

TO

Marsha Wilkins Munson

whose counsel led me to
American Studies
and thus to
Alexandria's cultural history

TABLE OF CONTENTS

Plan of the Town of Alexandria in the District of Columbia, 1798 (by Colonel George Gilpin)	*frontispiece*
Preface	vii
Abbreviations & Notes	ix
Deed Book A - 1783-1785	1
Deed Book B - 1785-1787	10
Deed Book C - 1787-1789	32
Deed Book D - 1789-1793	49
Deed Book E - 1793-1794	79
Deed Book F - 1793-1796	114
Deed Book G - 1795-1796	147
Deed Book H - 1795-1797	185
Index	220

PREFACE

As a cultural historian, I am essaying a re-creation of Alexandria in its colonial and early national setting. Faced with a scarcity of material, I decided to read every line of some 7000 pages of deeds, from the time the town got its own court of record, to 1801 when it was incorporated into the District of Columbia. I found a treasure of primary evidence for a reliable reconstruction of town thoroughfares, public and private buildings, commerce, finances, cultural undertakings, change and growth. I learned about individual Alexandrians--not just their properties, but their public and private character, accomplishments, relationships, residences, religions, ethnic groups, and means of livelihood. Here in these abstracts Alexandria emerges as a unique community of people in a special time, in their own distinctive streets and structures.

We can chart the town's growing by annexation and by private additions and developments, extending old streets and opening new ones, and banking out into the Potomac. We can sketch the waterfront's docks and other commercial uses. People improve their real estate holdings by leasing vacant parts, and requiring would-be tenants to build--with their own funds. Real estate values rise swiftly, both the cause and effect of a whirlwind of speculation in the 1790s. Changes in currency rates of exchange reflect the national inflation spiral.

More and more of the town's Old Guard have places within Alexandria, but prefer to live at their country seats in Fairfax. Brick becomes the material of choice. Space between buildings shrinks until at last the Federal town house streetscape (so prized today) emerges. Entrepreneurs offer developments with provisions for courtyards, sidewalks, and community wells.

Cutting up Alexandria's squares into ever smaller lots requires dozens of alleys and passageways. The town begins mandatory street paving and regrades its streets to provide for draining off standing water. Paved "pedestrian ways" (sidewalks) make their debut. Neighbors, with a care for appearance and convenience, put in writing agreements on building styles and placement, even about sharing their necessaries.

People appear in surprising detail. We find out how they were known among the other townspeople--both their honorifics and their nicknames. The use of middle names begins; George Washington--as most of his earlier generation--had none. Now middle names become common. Germans and French anglicize their family names. Some women begin signing their first, maiden, and married names. And we see who is literate and who is not.

Women's property rights increase. Slaves are still bought, sold and used as collateral--but the first manumissions appear. So do ethnic and religious groups other than the familiar English and Scots: French, Irish and German; Presbyterian, Methodist, and Quaker. Artisans who in the town's early days bought property and built upon it, now more and more work in rented shop space. The deeds in these books include some household and business inventories, and along the way also report marriages, remarriages, hard times and deaths.

This close reading of the deeds has met many of my research needs, and happily exceeded my hopes. When I told Laird Towle [Heritage Books, Inc.] all this, he felt my abstracts--on which the above summary descriptions are based--deserved a wider audience. This volume, half the abstracts, runs from 1783-1797. A second volume follows. In fact, the remaining half of the abstracts requires all that second volume to encompass the near frenzy of Alexandria's boom years: 1797-1801.

The Alexandria Hustings Court deed books contain more than property transfers. They give insight and detail of a special community, its people, and their times--from the end of the Revolution to the beginning of the new century.

James D. Munson
Arlington, Virginia
April 1990

ABBREVIATIONS

/	shilling(s): 5/ = five shillings
//	parallel: W//Prince 90' = West parallel Prince St. for a distance of ninety feet
adj	adjacent to, adjoining
admr	administrator of an estate
ALX	Alexandria
atty	attorney
CMN	Commissioners appointed by the court to "examine" (determine in private with) a wife that a transfer of property in which she has a vested interest does also have her free and willing consent
cmv	current money of Virginia
contig	contiguous to
Cwl	Commonwealth: CwlVA = Commonwealth of Virginia
dau	daughter
do, -do-	ditto
exxr	executor of an estate
exxx	executrix of an estate
decd	(also: dec'd) deceased
f/	for
Ffx	Fairfax: FfxCo = Fairfax County
fm	from
gent/gentn	gentleman/gentlemen
int	intersection: int Duke-Lee = intersection of Duke & Lee Streets
JP	Justice of the Peace
Loudon	as always spelled in these deeds; later spelled Loudoun
p	perch (a surveyor's unit of measurement)
p/atty	power of attorney
PG Co	Prince George's County, MD
PW Co	Prince William County, VA
pwt	penny weight
rptd	reported: Rptd back same day = Reported back the same day.
rqmt	requirement
StMD	State of Maryland
StVA	State of Virginia
tobo	tobacco
Twn	town: TwnALX = Town of Alexandria
w/	with; N w/alley = North with the alley
WTT	witness(es)

NOTES

Boiler plate--standard contract clauses regarding procedures in event of non-payment, for re-entry, for repossession, and the like--are noted but not abstracted.

Currency types are here always reported as specified in the deed: Spanish milled dollars, current money of Virginia, etc.

Date Ordered Recorded of a deed has not been abstracted.

Dwellings--under that heading in the index--may in fact not have been used as residences, but as a store house, ware house, etc. Structures named in the deeds as store house/ware house/bake house, etc. have been indexed as such. Similarly, a deed may state a structure is "now in the occupation of John Doe"; this means that John Doe is entitled to the use of the premises--not necessarily that Doe _lives_ under its roof.

Mortgage is here used only when the original text does.
Tripartite/Quadripartite/Cinquepartite Deeds frequently are mortgages, as are deeds of trust. Some mortgages used no special title of any kind.

Names, full or abbreviated, with and without punctuation, are as written by the clerk.

Plats drawn onto the deed book pages could not be reproduced in these abstracts, but are both noted where they appear and indexed.

Surveyors recorded **compass readings** as shown in these abstracts: southwest eighty degrees was recorded S80W; north west six degrees was recorded N6W, and so on.

Water Street is always here abstracted as Water _Street_ or Water _St_ to ensure the reader does not mistake it as the water's edge, water front, the river, the harbor, etc. (For economy's sake, these abstracts frequently omit the words "Street" or "St." with the other streets: King, Oronoco, Washington, Queen, etc.)

ALEXANDRIA HUSTINGS COURT

Deed Book A, 1783-1785

1 20Feb83
Fm William & Christiana Hunter, **Merchant** of ALX
To William Brown, **Physician,** ALX: sale @ £160 of part LOT 66, adj Ffx & Prince Streets:
BEGIN at/near middle of lot, on W side of Ffx (lot line of lot conveyed 19Aug75 by Christopher Bealer to Wm Hunter) ... W// Prince-Duke 90'... N//Ffx & Royal 15' 6"... E//P & D 90' to Fairfax ... S on W side Ffx to BEGIN--this parcel sold 23 Oct75 by George & Mary Keyger to Wm Hunter w/annual ground rent remitted by release 01Dec78.   WTT: Saml Arell, Dennis Ramsay

5 20Feb83
Fm William & Christiana Hunter, **Merchant** of ALX for £5
To William Brown, **Physician,** ALX: part LOT 66 on Fairfax St:
BEGIN at/near middle of the front of said lot on Ffx (at line separating this fm another part sold to Hunter by Geo & Mary Keyger 23 Oct75) ... W//Prince & Duke 90'... S//Ffx & Royal 14' 6"... E//Prince & Duke 90'... N on W side Ffx to BEGIN.
--plus right for an alley 8' wide, running 90' westward, fm Ffx parallel and adj S side of this parcel;
--this parcel conveyed by Christopher Bealer to Wm Hunter 19Aug75 w/annual rent, remittable if w/in 20 years WH pays CB £91.16.8 in "Currency of ALX Dollars at Six Shillings".   WTT: Saml Arell, Dennis Ramsay

10 01Jul82
Fm Richard & Mary Conway, TwnALX, FfxCo, CwlVA
To John Lomax   -do-   : annual lease from 01 July for £14.2.6 of part LOT 22 on Ffx & Princess:
BEGIN NW corner of lot sold by Lucas & Ann Garvey to Lawrence Sanford (part LOT 22 on Ffx) ... N up & w/Ffx 56' 6"... E// Prince & Queen 98'... S//Ffx & Water St 56' 6"... W w/Pr & Qn and w/ N line of lot bought by Sanford to BEGIN;
--rent remittable by paying w/in 20 yrs £282.10.0 in silver $ @ 6/ and Half-Johannes @ 48/   WTT: Saml Arell, Wm Duvall, John Lomax

18 22Jan84
Fm William & Susanna Hartshorne, TwnALX, CwlVA
To Christian Slimmer   -do-   : for 5/ part LOT 111 WH bought fm William & Sarah Carlin 22Mar79 (recorded Lib N, folio 140, Clerk's Office, Ffx Co.):

BEGIN on Prince 49' fm SW corner of LOT 111 ... N//Pitt 94' ... E//Pr 24' 5"...
S//Royal 94'... W//Pr to BEGIN.
WTT: Richard Arell, Gurden Chapin, George Hollingsworth

21 22Jan84
Fm Christian & Mary Slimmer TwnALX, FfxCo, CwlVA
To William Hartshorne of -do-: Sale for 5/ cmv, part LOT 6.
BEGIN E side Royal, 59' fm Prince & Royal ... S w/ Royal 29' 4 1/2"... E//Pr 93' 4"...
N//Royal 29' 4 1/2"... W//Pr to BEGIN--this w/ other adjacent land fm Christopher
Beeler to George & Mary Keyger 09Aug75, and from the Keygers to Chr. Slimmer 18
Oct83 [?], recorded in FFX Co.
WTT: Richard Arell, Gurden Chapin, George Hollingsworth

26 24Dec82   Power of Attorney
Fm Marian Lockhart, relict of Mr. John Campbell, **Minister** of the Gospel at Barr
AND Jean Campbell (dau of John), relict of John Spiers, **Writer**, at Killbarchen;
AND Marian Campbell, (also dau of John);
--BEING the mother and sisters of Matthew Campbell of Fawsfarm, Loudon Co.,
Province of VA, deceased;
WHEREAS M.C. died "about the Month of March last" and no will is known we--his
only relatives--assign p/atty:
To John Ballendine of Nomini, Westmoreland Co., VA AND
To Robert Adam "present or late of ALX, FfxCo.", AND
To William Hunter of ALX, "all **Merchants**"
--Signed at Ayr (Royal Burgh of Ayr, County of Ayr)
WTT: George Dunlop, **Merchant**, Ayr; Anthony MacHarg, **Writer**, Ayr

29 28Feb84
Fm William & Agniss Hepburn, TwnALX, FfxCo, StVA
To John Lomax of   -do-: sale for £400 cmv, part LOT 15, W side Water St, N side
Princess St:
BEGIN int Water-Princess Sts ... N w/ Water St 88'... W//Princess 43' 8"... S//Water St
88'... E w/ Princess to BEGIN--LOT 15 "originally granted by the Trustees...unto
Hugh West the elder."   ["Agniss" signs herself **Agnes**]
WTT: Adam Lynn, William Ward, Roger Chew, John Gretter

33 01Jan84
Fm William & Agniss Hepburn, TwnALX, FfxCo, StVA
To John Lomax of   -do-: lease part LOT 15 for 80 silver $ specie each Jan 1st,
remittable on paying 1600 silver $:
BEGIN N side Princess 43' 5" W of intersection w/Water St ...
?W w/ Water 80' to line between LOTS 15 & 16 ... ?N w/ the line 88' //Water St ...
?E//Princess 88'... ?S//Water St 88' to BEGIN. [Water St. runs N-S, making directions
suspect.]--LOT 15 originally conveyed by the Trustees to Hugh West the elder and by
sundry conveyances to Robert Rutherford, and by RR to Wm Hepburn on 30May80.
["Agniss" signs self **Agnes**]   WTT: Willm Ward, John Wise, James Adam

38 01Mar84
Fm William Ramsay, **Gentleman**, & Ann, TwnALX, FfxCo, CwlVA
To William Duvall of -do-: lease part LOT 38 [fronting on Ffx] fm 01Mar85 for £20
cmv annually, remittable if w/in 20 yrs Duvall pays £400 cmv:
BEGIN upper/north corner of part of same lot belonging to James Hendricks ... N
along Ffx 58'... W 41' to part belonging to Duvall bought fm Adam Lynn ... S 58'
w/Duvall's lot line ... E 41' to BEGIN.   WTT: John Bredin, Hiram Chapin

42 01Mar84
William Ramsay assigns the above annual £20 rent from Duvall to Robert Allison & Dennis Ramsay, **Merchants**, ALX, in trust for wife Ann Ramsay; £10 to each trustee.

44 01Jan84
Fm William & Agniss Hepburn, TwnALX, FfxCo, StVA
To James Adam of -do-: lease part LOT 15 for 88 1/2 silver $ in specie each Jan 1st: BEGIN W side Water St 88' N of int Wtr-Prince Sts... N along Wtr St 88' 6" to division between LOT 15 & LOT [blank] "one of the Lotts whereon the public warehouses for inspecting Tobacco stand"... W w/lot line betw the lots and // to Princess 123' 5"... S //Water St 88' 6" to line of lot granted by WH to John Lomax this same date ... E w/that line, parallel Princess 123' 5" to Water St... and BEGIN.
--LOT 15 originally fm the Trustees to Hugh West the elder, by him to Robert Rutherford, by RR to WH 30May80.
--rent remittable if w/in 20 years JA pays 1770 silver $.
WTT: Willm Ward, John Wise, John Lomax

49 20Dec83
Fm Robert McLeod, Frederick Co, MD (son/heir of James McLeod, formerly of ALX)
To James Kirk, FfxCo, CwlVA: for £180 VA currency in specie, all of LOT 109, bounded by Pitt & Prince as by platt & survey made 10Mar63 by George West, Surveyor of Ffx Co.
WTT: Thomas Fleming, Bety [also "Betey"] Fleming, Betty Fleming Junr, George Darling

53 09Nov84
Fm Baldwin & Catharine Dade, **Merchant**, FfxCo, StVA
To David Griffith, **Clerk**, -do-
WHEREAS 25Aug84 Thomas West sold to Baldwin Dade a tract: BEGIN 123' 5 1/2" fm NW corner of Pitt & Queen, adj LOT 124 of William Hepburn ... S80W w/ N side of Queen 89 perches "crossing the present Georgetown Road to the Old Georgetown Road"... N20W 51 perches along the Old Gtwn Rd to line between land of Alexander & West ... N80E //first course 80 perches to the old [ALX] Town Line ... S10E 50 perches along old Town Line to BEGIN: 26 acres and 98 poles in the tract; EXCEPTING the following earlier sold by Thomas West:
- 1/2A to Thomas Reed, adjac to Wm. Hepburn's LOT 124;
- 1/2A to John Robinson, N side Queen, W side St. Asaph;
- 1/2A to John Bryce, adjac to John Robinson's;
- 1/4A to Wm. Hepburn, N side Princess & W side of St. Asaph as those "streets have been extended from their respective terminations in ALX";
- 1/2A "unto the people called Quakers for a Burying Ground and one other piece of Ground adjoining the last mentioned containing five Acres sold unto William Paton and John Butcher."
AND since buying from Thos. West, Baldwin Dade has sold:
- 1/2A to Charles Lee on N side Princess & W side of Washington ("a new Street lately laid out by him the said Baldwin Dade"), 123' 5" on Princess and 176' 7" on Wshgtn;
ALSO, six 1/2A parcels to Henry Lee:
- 1/2A S side Oronoko & E side Washington adj Charles Lee's Lee's lot ... 176' 7" on Washington ... 123' 5" on Oronoko;
- the others: W of Wash, S of Oro/binding on Oronoko, each extending on Oro 123' 5" & S toward Princess 176' 7";

AND Dade reserved f/his own use:
- 1/2A on N side Princess, E side St. Asaph: on St. A 176' 7" ... on Princess 123' 5";
NOW Dade leases to Griffith the remainder, on these terms: on 01Dec86 £100 cmv;
01Dec87 £200 cmv; from 01Dec88 £300 per yr; (Dade will accept for £50's worth
"warrants for Interest due on Military Certificates until [they] shall be Redeemed or
cancelled by the Assembly.")   WTT: Robert Adam, R.T. Hooe, W. Brown
CMN: [Commissioners to query Mrs. Dade to confirm her consent to this transaction.
This is the first instance of a new format by the Clerk. Other wives have been
"examined privately" but commissioners, dates of appointment and date of their
reporting back to the court were not given.] Abstracted thus:
CMN: William Ramsay, Robert Adam, R.T. Hooe aptd 09Nov84 to examine Catharine Dade. Rptd back [blank]Nov84.

60 07Jun84
Fm Robert & Ann Allison, TwnALX, FfxCo, StVA
To John Harper of -do-: sale for £300 cmv part LOT 89 on Ffx & Wolfe Sts.
BEGIN on N side Wolfe, 43' E of int Wolfe-Ffx ... E w/ Wolfe 60' ... N//Ffx 100' to 10'
alley laid out by RA & "by him denominated Allison's Alley" ... W w/alley line //Wolfe
60' ... S to BEGIN--"which...LOT...89 originally conveyed by the Trustees to the said
Anne while Sole by the Name of Ann Ramsay Junior daughter of William Ramsay"
21 Oct65.
--Robert & Anne agree that the alley is to be forever open, beginning on Ffx, thence
E //Wolfe, and 10' wide fm Ffx "quite across the said Lott No. 89 to the Eastern
Limits thereof."   WTT: James Hendricks, Jesse Taylor, John Short, James Keith
CMN: John Fitzgerald, James Keith, Twn of ALX, **Gentlemen**, aptd 17Jun84 to
examine Ann. Reported back same day.

66 01May84
Fm Robert & Ann Allison, **Merchant**, TwnALX
To James Holliday, **Cordwainer** of -do-: sale for £120 current money of part LOT 89:
BEGIN on Wolfe 23' fm corner Ffx & Wolfe ... E w/Wolfe 20' ... N//Ffx 100' to a 10'
alley "called Allison's Alley" ... W w/alley //Wolfe 20' ... thence to BEGIN.
--w/free use of alley, which the Allisons will keep open.
WTT: James Hendricks, Wm. Hepburn, Jn. Kleinhoff
CMN: John Fitzgerald, William Herbert, Twn of ALX, **Gentlemen**, aptd 23Sep84 to
examine Ann. Rptd back 21Jan85.

71 19Jan85   Mortgage
Fm James Meyler, Berkley Co, StVA
To William Sydebotham, Bladensburg, PG Co, StMD
10,000 lbs inspected tobacco against JM's Negroes Sarah, Moses, and Jack
Terms: JM owes WS. If tobo paid by 19Jan86, slaves remain property of JM.
WTT: Adam Lynn, Roger Chew

74 20Jun85
Fm Hugh & Susanna Finley, Orange Co, State No. Carolina
To John Hickman, TwnALX, FfxCo, StVA: for £50 cmv part LOT on E side St.
Asaph, N side of Wolfe "in that part of...ALX.. lately laid out & added to by John
Alexander & conveyed by JA to John Garner Hamilton." That lot: BEGIN SW
corner LOT 104 ... thence w/ LOT 104 to its NW corner ... W 123' 5" ... S//first line ...
E to BEGIN.
BEGIN [this sale] on St. A 136' 5" N of int w/Wolfe ... thence w/St.A 20' ... E//Wolfe
113' 5" ... S//St.A 20' ... W to BEGIN--the original lot conveyed by John Garner

Hamilton to John Finley; JF died intestate & property went to Hugh Finley as Heir-at-Law.
--Hugh Finley will lay out, 106' 5" N of int Wolfe-St. A, a 10' alley from St. A: E and //Wolfe across to the lot's E boundary AND another 10' alley from the first alley along the E boundary to the North line.
WTT: James Lawrason, Edw. Sanford, Edward Ramsay, John Reynolds, John B. Ford

79   16Jun84
[As above, Finleys (Orange Co, NC) to Hickman] for £70 cmv & 20/ annual rent:
Part LOT [blank] to E of St.Asaph & N of Wolfe:
BEGIN on St. A 116' 5" N of int w/Wolfe and on N line of 10' alley laid out by HF ... E w/alley line //Wolfe 113' 5" to W line of another alley laid out by Finley ... N w/alley line //St.A 20'... W //Wolfe 113' 5" to St.A ... S w/St.A to BEGIN--the whole lot fm John Alexander, **Gent**, to John Garner Hamilton 19Dec74, and by JGH to John Finley 05Nov79. H. Finley = JF's heir-at-law. [HF repeats the two-alley plan as at p. 74.]   WTT: James Lawrason, John Saunders, John Reynolds, John B. Ford

84   10Jun85
Fm Hugh & Susannah Finley, [blank] County, North Carolina
To John Reynolds, TwnALX: for £75 & 23/ annual rent
part of LOT [blank]:
BEGIN at int of Wolfe-St.A ... N on St.A 106' 5" to 10'alley
... E w/alley //Wolfe 23' 5"... S //St.A 106' 5" to Wolfe ...
thence along Wolfe to BEGIN. [Two-alley plan per pp.74,79]
WTT: John Saunders, James Lawrason, John Hickman, John B. Ford

89   16Jun85
Fm Hugh & Susannah Finley, Orange Co, North Carolina
To Joseph Janney, TwnALX, **Merchant,** AND to Samuel Pleasants & John Field, City of Philadelphia, **Merchants,** as Tenants in Common: for £245 cmv & £4 annual rent part LOT [blank], E of St.A & N of Wolfe Sts:
?BEGIN on Wolfe, 23' 5" E of int w/ St. Asaph ... ?E along Wolfe 80'... ?N //St.A 106' 5" to 10' alley ... ?W w/alley //St.A 80'... ?S to BEGIN. [? = questionable, but as written]--recites Alexander to Hamilton to Finley chain of title, and two-alley plan per pp.74,79. WTT: John Dunlop, Philip Marsteller, Joseph Mandeville, James Lawrason

95   10Nov83
Fm Thomas & Sarah May, Cecil Co, MD, **Ironmaster**
To William Herbert, TwnALX, FfxCo, CwlVA, **Merchant**
Chain of title, LOTS 31 & 32, bounded by Ffx-Queen-Potomac River: 20Sep49: Trustees to Gerrard Alexander;
--09Aug60: via GA's will to wife Mary Alexander;
--10 & 11Mar67: Mary & son Philip & Philip's wife Catharine to John Glassford & Archibald Henderson [G&H];
__¦__¦76: Alexander Henderson (G&H's attorney) to John Gibson;
__¦__¦76: Gibson to Alexander Henderson in his own right;
--01Jan78: Alexander Henderson to William Herbert;
--18Feb78: Wm. & Sarah Herbert to Thomas May.   .
NOW for £1300 the Mays sell 1/3 interest in the land and in the improvements of the two-lot parcel to the Herberts
WTT: John Potts, Junr; Js. McCubbin Lingan [whose signature as witness to the Mays' receipt of the £1300 the clerk renders "Jo. McCubbin Linglar"]

5

101 11Dec84
Fm John & Susannah Conway, Somerset Co, MD;
AND Joseph Conway, Northumberland Co, VA
AND Robert & Mary Conway
AND Cuthbert & Mary Elliston
AND Hannah Webb [these last five also possibly of Northumberland County]
To James Rattle, TwnALX, StVA: for £511 cmv part LOT 110, S side of Prince, W side of Pitt.
BEGIN int Prince-Pitt ... W w/Prince 51' 5"... S//Pitt 100' to 9-foot alley ... W w/alley //Prince 51' 5" to Pitt ...
N w/Pitt to BEGIN--plus privilege of the alley 9' wide beginning on Pitt 100' S of Pitt & Prince, thence //Prince across LOT 110 to west lot line.
--LOT 110 originally fm Trustees to James Lowrie who died intestate; thence to heirs in Great Britain; in 1780 seized by Hector Ross--Escheator of Ffx Co--and sold to Thomas Conway, of Northumberland Co. TC's will devised it to these sellers. [John Conway signs self as John **Span** Conway]
WTT: Jas Keith, Cyrus Copper, James Parsons to Robert & Joseph Conway; ALSO John Rogers, Thomas Edward, Edward Coles, John Coles & Cuthbert Elliston, Jr; ALSO John Stewart, Henry Jackson to John & Susannah Conway

109 11Dec84
Fm same Conway heirs as above
To John Murray & Thomas Porter, TwnALX, StVA: for £360 cmv part LOT 110.
BEGIN on Pitt 109' S of Pitt & Prince and southern corner of the 9-foot alley laid out by the Conways ... W w/alley //Prince 123' 5"... S//Pitt 45'... E//Prince 123' 5" to Pitt ...
N on Pitt 45' to BEGIN--plus use of the 9-foot wide alley from Pitt along N boundary of this parcel to the west lot line. [Conway chain of title and alley layout recited as above.] WTT: as above

119 11Dec84
Fm Conway heirs, as above
To John Saunders, TwnALX, StVA: for £180, part LOT 110.
BEGIN on Prince 99' 5" W of int w/Pitt ... W along Pitt 24' to John Saunders' lot line ... S w/Saunders' line //Pitt 100' to 9-foot alley ... E w/alley //Prince 24'... N //Pitt 100' to BEGIN. [Chain of title and alley layout recited as above.] WTT: as above

133 14Dec84
Fm Conway heirs, as above, [ADDING: Thomas Conway's will was dated 25Sep84; that Hannah Webb = relict of John Webb.]
To Charles Lee of FfxCo: for £676.10.0 lawful money of Virginia, part LOT 110:
BEGIN on Prince 51' 5" from Prince & Pitt ... W along Prince 24'... S//Pitt 100' to 9-foot alley ... E along alley//Prince 24'... N//Pitt to BEGIN.
ALSO part LOT 103: BEGIN SW corner Wolfe & Pitt ... N along Pitt 116' 6"... E//Wolfe 82' 3"... S//Pitt 116' 6" to Wolfe ... thence along Wolfe to BEGIN.
WTT: Jas Keith, Cyrus Copper, James Parsons to Robert & Joseph Conway; ALSO John Rogers, Thomas Edward, Edward Coles, John Coles & Cuthbert Elliston, Jr; ALSO John Stewart, Henry Jackson to John & Susannah Conway

144 11Dec84
Fm Conway heirs, as above
To George Richards, TwnALX, StVA: for £180 cmv, part LOT 110:
BEGIN on Prince 75' 5" W of int w/Pitt ... W along Prince 24'

... S//Pitt 100' to 9-foot alley ... E along alley //Prince 24'... N//Pitt 100' to BEGIN--plus privilege of the alley, described as above. [Conway chain of title recited as above.] WTT: as above

158 11Dec84
[Recites the Conway heirs, as above. Then, of them--]
Fm John Spann Conway [earlier, Span w/one "n" at pp. 101ff.]
To Joseph Conway, Northumberland Co, VA: for £120 part LOT 110
BEGIN on Pitt 154' S of int w/Pitt ... W//Prince 123' 5"... S//Pitt 22' 6"... E//Prince 123' 5"... N on Pitt 22' 6" [to the western limit of LOT 110]. [Note no alley cited.]
[Recites Conway chain of title, as above.]
WTT: John Stewart, Henry Jackson, Thos. Edwards, John Coles; Cuthbt. Elliston, Jr.

169 19Jan85
Fm William Hunter, Jr. of TwnALX, FfxCo, StVA
To William Wilson of -do-: for £650 part LOT 33, W of Ffx, S of Queen Sts:
BEGIN on Ffx at line of LOTS 33 & 38 ... W w/ line 123' 5"... N//Ffx 39' 1 3/4"... E//first line & Queen 123' 5" to Ffx ... S w/Ffx to BEGIN--formerly part of 1/4A of Colin Dunlap Son & Company--escheated & sold 19 Oct80 to Wm Hunter, Jr.
--ALSO use of alley laid out by WHjr: BEGIN on Ffx at N property line, thence W w/property line 10' wide to W line of LOT 33, to be forever free & open to use.
WTT: none

176 21Feb85
Fm John Hunter, FfxCo, StVA
To Michael Madden of TwnALX: lease fm 05Aug next for £50 cmv per annum; money to be in Spanish milled $ at 6/ each, Half-Joes weighing 9 pennyweight at 48/ each: part LOT 86, E of Water St, N of Wolfe:
BEGIN on Wolfe at line between this and LOT [blank], being 123' 5" E of int Wolfe-Water Sts ... N w/ this line //Water St 10 poles, 17 1/2 links to northern lot line ... E w/lot line //Wolfe 3poles, 18 1/2 links ... S//Water St 10poles, 17 1/2 links to Wolfe ... thence along Wolfe to BEGIN.   [Hunter signs self "John **Chapman** Hunter"]
WTT: Wm. Payne, Richd. Ratcliff, Jesse Simms

184 01Apr85
Fm Benjamin Shreeve, TwnALX, FfxCo, StVA
To Thomas Barclay of -do-: lease, £20 annually in silver $ or Half-Joes, as at p.176, part LOT 111, E of Pitt, N of Prince Streets:
BEGIN on Prince 73' 5" E of int Pr-Pitt ... E on Prince 24' 6"... N//?Prince [Pitt] 94'... W//Prince 24' 6"... S to BEGIN. ("it being the Lott...which Samuel Coates Granted unto...[BS]...bearing the date the [blank] day of last Past")
--rent remittable if w/in two years Barclay pays £200 cmv.
WTT: John Reynolds, John Butcher, Robert Whitacre

194 24Mar85
  Anne Ramsay, TwnALX, widow & relict of William Ramsay, **Esquire**, deceased, assigns the £20 rent from William Duvall (for part of LOT 38) to her son, Dennis Ramsay. [See p.42]
WTT: Betty Stewart, Sarah Masterson, Sally Harrison, Sarah Ramsay

197 29Jan85
Fm Baldwin & Catharine Dade, FfxCo
To Samuel Montgomery Brown, TwnALX, FfxCo, StVA: sale @ £175 cmv a 1/2A parcel adjacent & contiguous to ALX:

BEGIN S side Oronoko as extended by BD, and 312' 10" fm W line of Washington St ("A Street lately laid out by him the said BD and others to accommodate the Purchasers of these Lotts laid out by them contiguous to the said Town of ALX")--AND on the W side of another "Street BD engages to lay out to accommodate SMBrown and others who may purchase.." ... W along Oronoko 123' 5"... S//Washingtn/St.Asaph/Pitt 176' 7" ... E//Oronoko 123' 5" "to the Street intended to be laid out by him the said Baldwin Dade"... N w/the street//Wash/St.A/Pitt 176' 7" to Oronoko/BEGIN. --this is part of land bought from Thomas [West].
--BD commits to extending Oronoko "from the termination thereof in the Town of ALX" the same course, direction and breadth--as far west as W line of this new lot;
--AND from the S side of Oronoko 246' 10" W of west line of Washington, another street 66' wide //Washington to the limit of this lot.
--these new streets to be kept by BD forever free of obstructions, etc.
WTT: Elizabeth Dade, Jas. Keith, John Fitzgerald
CMN: James Keith and John Fitzgerald, TwnALX, **Gentlemen,** aptd 29Jan85 to examine Catharine. Rptd back 11Feb85.

208 22Apr85
Fm William & Christiana Hunter, TwnALX, FfxCo, CwlVA
To Godphrey [also **Godfrey**] Miller, **Butcher,** of -do-: lease fm 22April @ 37 1/2 silver $ annually: part LOT [167] S of Wilkes, W of Royal.
BEGIN SE corner of LOT [167] ... W w/lot line 99' 5"... N//Royal 25'... E//Wilkes to Royal ... along Royal to BEGIN.
--and GM w/in 3 years of the "Termination of the late War, Between Great Britain and the United States of America" is to build a "brick, stone or wooden framed house 20' square or to cover 400 sqft, w/ brick or stone chimney/chimneys";
--rent remittable if w/in 20 years GM pays 750 silver $;
--WH will make a 3-foot alley opening on Wilkes and running //Royal to the back of the premises.   WTT: William Hunter, Kitty Hunter, Godfrey Miller

216 25Jun85
Fm Neal Mooney of ALX, **Stonemason**
To William Herbert of ALX, **Merchant**
   Mooney makes a deed of trust to Herbert in favor of NM's unmarried daughter Mary for that part of LOT 110 Mooney bought fm William McKnight, and on which he pays ground rent as per a conveyance dated [blank]Aug80.
WTT: W. Ellzey, G. Deneale, Michael Clarke

222 25Jun85
Fm William Ward, TwnALX, FfxCo, CwlVA
To William Hunter, Jr. AND John Allison of -do-: half of LOT 14, as tenants in common, during Sybil West's lifetime.
(On 21Nov82 Sybil rented LOT 14 to Ward for £80 per annum, during her life. Now, for £90, Ward sells use of half the lot to WHjr & JA):
BEGIN E side Water St 88' fm & N of int Water St & Princess... E//Princess into the Potomac ... From BEGIN, N w/Water St 88' to north lot line of LOT 14 ... thence E into Potomac ... thence S//Water St until intersecting the first line--Hunter & Allison to have waterfront privileges.   WTT: Colin MacIver, William Rea, James Patton

229 16Nov84
Fm Baldwin & Catharine Dade, FfxCo, StVA
To William Howard, TwnALX, FfxCo, StVA: lease fm 12Nov for £6.8.0 per annum in Spanish milled $ at 6/, Half-Johannes weighing 9 pennyweight at 48/

BEGIN on W side of Washington, 35' S of int w/Oronoko (Wash as laid out by, Oro as extended by BD)... S w/Washington 32'... W//Oronoko 100'... N//Washington 32'... E to BEGIN--the rent remittable at any time by paying £128.
--Dade promises a "Street to the Westward of St. Asaph Street of the Breadth of one hundred feet shall be laid out and forever kept open [by BD] extending from Oronoko Street to Queen Street so as to correspond and agree with that part of the said street which was formerly laid out by John Alexander, **Gent.**, and that Oronoko, Princess and Queen Streets shall be extended from their terminations in the said Town in the same Course and Direction which they run in the said Town as far Westerly as the Lotts laid out [by BD]...."
SIGNED [the entire deed]: Baldwin Dade, Caty Dade, Beal [his + mark] Howard
WTT: Robt. Alexander, Jacob Hyneman, William [his + mark] Merchant

239 05Sep84
Fm the Dades [as above]
To Jacob Hynman [w/o the middle "e"], TwnALX, FfxCo, StVA:
lease fm 05Sep for 40 Spanish milled $ per annum, [a LOT in Dade's new area].
BEGIN on W side of Washington 176' 6" N of intersection w/Princess, extended ... N w/Washington 60'... W//Princess 100'... S//Washington 60' ... E to BEGIN.
--rent remittable by paying at any time 800 Spanish milled $.
--Dade promises he will "lay off to the Westward of St. Asaph Street a new Street 100' wide by the name of Washington Street which shall extend from the Northern side of Queen Street in a line parallel to Pitt, Royal and St. Asaph, till it reaches the northern Boundary of the said Addition...."
WTT: Robert Alexander, Willm. [his + mark] Merchant, Beal [his + mark] Howard

251 25Sep84
Fm the Dades [as above]
To William Merchant, TwnALX, FfxCo, StVA, **Blacksmith**: lease fm 25Sept for £10 cmv per annum, payable in Spanish milled dollars and/or, Half-Joes, [as at p. 229], for [another lot in BD's new area].
BEGIN at int Washington-Oronoko,on W side Washington ... S w/Washington 35'... W//Oronoko 100'... N//Royal 35'... E w/Oronoko to BEGIN.
--rent remittable at any time by paying £200 cmv.
SIGNED [entire deed] Baldwin Dade, Caty Dade, William [his + mark] Merchant
WTT: Robt. Alexander, Jacob Hyneman, Beal [his + mark] Howard

End of Book A

ALEXANDRIA HUSTINGS COURT

Deed Book B, 1785-1787

1 21Apr85
Fm William Alexander, PW Co AND William Gibbons Steuart, King George Co AND William Thornton Alexander the younger son of John Alexander: the surviving exxrs of John Alexander of Stafford, deceased. [In the deed abstracts below, these will be the ALXR EXXRS.]
To William Hartshorne, Twn ALX, **Merchant:** lease fm 01Nov @ £41 cmv per yr of-- in this addition to ALX being laid out by the ALXR EXXRS, and surveyed by Robert Boggess--LOT 13:
BEGIN where S side of Wolfe St when extended will int E side of Washington ... S w/Wn 176' 6"... E 123' 5"... N//Wn 176' 6"
... thence to BEGIN; the ALXR EXXRS commit to lay out/extend the following:
--Water St: 762' 4" fm Wilkes
--Ffx, Royal, Pitt & St.Asaph another 595' 9" each
--a Street called Washington St to be 246' 10" West of St. Asaph, 100' wide, fm King to 595' 9" S of Wilkes St
--Gibbons, 66' wide, to be 353' 2" south of south side of Wilkes, from River Potomac west parallel w/Wilkes to a point 123' 5" beyond W side of Washington St.
WTT: Thomas Swann, Francis Digges, Charles Simms

7 21Apr85
Fm the ALXR EXXRS [see p. 1]
To William Hartshorne, TwnAlx, **Merchant:** lease fm 01Nov @ £63 cmv per yr of the Boggess Survey LOT 3:
BEGIN E side of Washington where Prince St extended will intersect with it--the NE corner ... N on Washington 176' 6"... E w/Prince 123' 5"... S//Washington 176' 6"... W to BEGIN.   WTT: as above

14 21Apr85
Fm ALXR EXXRS [see p. 1]
To William Hartshorne, TwnALX, **Merchant:** lease fm 01Nov £75 cmv per yr of the Boggess Survey LOT 35:
BEGIN where W side of Ffx extended will int N side of Gibbons ... W along Gibbons 123' 5"... N on Ffx 176' 6"... E//Gibbons 123' 5"... thence to BEGIN.   WTT: as above

20 21Apr85
Fm William Alexander, PW Co AND William Gibbons Steuart, King George Co AND William Thornton Alexander the younger son of John Alexander: the surviving exxrs of John Alexander of Stafford, deceased. [In the deed abstracts below, these will be the ALXR EXXRS.]
To David Pancoast, TwnALX: lease fm 01Nov @ £12.10.0 cmv per year of part of Boggess Survey LOT 10:
BEGIN W side of Washington, 154' 6" S of int where S side of Duke will intersect ... S w/Washington 22'... W//Duke 123' 5"... N//Washington 176' 6"... E//Duke 30' 10"... S//Washington 154' 6"... E//Duke to BEGIN.
WTT: Thomas Swann, Francis Digges, Charles Simms

27 21Apr85
Fm the ALXR EXXRS [see above]
To James Lownes, TwnALX: lease fm 01Nov @ £12.10.0 cmv per year of part of Boggess Survey LOT 10:
BEGIN where S side Duke will int W side of Washington ... S w/Washington 110' 6"... W ... Duke 30' 11"... N//Washington 110' 6"... E to BEGIN.   WTT: as above

34 21Apr85
Fm the ALXR EXXRS [see above]
To John Casey, PG Co, MD: lease fm 01Nov @ £43 cmv per yr
of Boggess Survey LOT 4:
BEGIN int extended Wn-Prince ... N w/Washington 176' 6"...
W//Prince 123' 5"... S//Wn 176' 6"... E to BEGIN.   WTT: as above

40 21Apr85
Fm the ALXR EXXRS [see above]
To John Graham, TwnALX: lease fm 01Nov @ £33.10.0 cmv of Boggess Survey LOT 28:
BEGIN where W side Pitt extended int S side Gibbons ... W w/Gibbons 123' 5"... S w/Pitt 176' 7"... E//Gibbons 123' 5"... thence to BEGIN.   WTT: as above

47 21Apr85
Fm the ALXR EXXRS [see above]
To John Harper, FfxCo--late of TwnALX, **Merchant**: lease fm 01Nov @ £36.10.0 cmv per year of Boggess Survey LOT 32:
BEGIN where Royal extended will int Gibbon's S side ... W w/Gibbon 123' 5"... S ... Royal 176' 6"... E 123' 5"... thence to BEGIN.   WTT: as above

54 21Apr85
Fm the ALXR EXXRS [see above]
To John Harper, FfxCo--late of TwnALX, **Merchant**: lease fm 01Nov £53cmv per yr of Boggess Survey LOT 9:
BEGIN where S side Duke extended will int E side Washington ... S w/Wn 176' 6"... E w/Duke 123' 5"... N//Wn 176' 6"... thence to BEGIN.
WTT: Thomas Swann, Francis Digges, Charles Simms   [20th century pencilled note: "Rent released. See T4, FfxCo Records"]

60 21Apr85
Fm the ALXR EXXRS [see above]
To Thomas Tobin, TwnALX, **Merchant**: lease fm 01Nov @ £12.10.0 cmv per year of part of Boggess Survey LOT 10:

BEGIN on W side Wn 110' 6" fm where S side of Duke extended will intersect W side of Washington ... S w/Wn 22'... W w/Duke 61' 9"... N//Wn 132' 6"... E w/Duke 30' 10"... S//Wash 110' 6"... E to BEGIN.
WTT: Thomas Swann, Francis Digges, Charles Simms

67 21Apr85
Fm William Alexander, PW Co AND William Gibbons Steuart, King George Co AND William Thornton Alexander the younger son of John Alexander: the surviving exxrs of John Alexander of Stafford, deceased. [In the deed abstracts below, these will be the ALXR EXXRS.]
To Aaron Hewes, TwnALX: lease fm 01Nov @ £12.10.0 cmv per year
of part of Boggess Survey LOT 10:
BEGIN on W side Washington 132' 6" fm where S side Duke extended will int W side of Wn ... S w/Wash 22'... W w/Duke 92' 7"... N//Wn 154' 6"... E w/Duke 32' 10"... S//Wn 132' 6"... E to BEGIN.   WTT: as above

73 21Apr85
Fm the ALXR EXXRS [see above]
To Joseph Caverly, TwnALX, **Ship Carpenter**: lease fm 01Nov @ £40 cmv per yr of Boggess Survey LOT 12:
BEGIN where N side Wolfe extended int W side Washington ... N w/Wn 176' 6"...W w/Wolfe 123' 5"...S//Wn 176' 6"...E to BEGIN.
WTT: Thomas Swann, Frances Digges, Charles Simms

80 21Apr85
Fm the ALXR EXXRS [see above]
To Andrew Wailes, TWN ALX: lease fm 01Nov @ £60 cmv per yr
of Boggess Survey LOT 36:
BEGIN where W side Ffx extended intersects S side of Gibbons ... W w/Gibbons 123' 5"... S w/Ffx 176' 6"... E 123' 5"... thence to BEGIN.
WTT: as above PLUS Lewis Weston "as to Andrew Wailes"

86 21Apr85
Fm the ALXR EXXRS [see above]
To Lewis Weston, TwnALX, **Ship Carpenter**: lease fm 01Nov @ £30.10.0 per year of Boggess Survey LOT 25:
BEGIN where E side St. Asaph extended int N side of Gibbons ... E on Gibbons 123' 5"... N w/St. Asaph 176' 6"... W//Gibbons 123' 5"... thence to BEGIN.
WTT: Thomas Swann, Francis Digges, Charles Simms

92 10Feb85
Fm Baldwin and Catharine Dade, FfxCo, StVA
To Parthenia Dade AND her daughters Catharine, Behethland, Elizabeth & Margaret, all of TwnALX: lease fm 10Feb @ one ear of Indian corn per year of parcel contiguous to TwnALX:
BEGIN E side of new street "lately laid out by...BD" parallel w/Washington, 559' 8" W of Wn, and at dividing line of BD & Reverend David Griffith--176' 7" S of Oronoko ... E w/dividing line //Oro 100'... N//Wn 40'... W//Oro 100' to new street ... S w/new street //Wn 40' to BEGIN.
WTT: Margaret Thompson, Jas. Keith, John Fitzgerald

94 08Aug85
Fm Christian & Mary Devilbiss, Frederick Twn, Frederick Co, MD

To Jacob Pens, Frk Co, MD: lease @ £2.10.0 PLUS each 18June 33 1/3 silver $ to David Arell of TwnALX of part LOT 72:
BEGIN lot's SW corner on Duke ... E w/Duke 20'... N//Water St 76' 7"... W//Duke 20' to line of Harry Beideman ... S//Water St w/Beideman line 76' 7" to BEGIN--the rent remittable if w/in 19 years fm 18Jun Pens pays 666 1/3 silver $ to David Arell.
[Christian & Jacob sign their names; Mary makes a mark]
WTT: Wm. M. Beal, Geo. Murdoch, John Peltz, Elizabeth Short, Val [his-B-mark] Bontz   [Val = Valentine]
CMN: Jacob Young, William Murdoch Beale, George Murdoch of Frederick Co, MD apptd 08Aug85 to examine Mary. Reported back same day.

101   21Apr85
Fm William Alexander, PW Co AND William Gibbons Steuart, King George Co AND William Thornton Alexander the younger son of John Alexander: the surviving exxrs of John Alexander of Stafford, deceased. [In the deed abstracts below, these will be the ALXR EXXRS.]
To James Keith, **Esquire**, TwnAlx: lease fm 01 Nov @ £35 cmv per year of the Boggess Survey LOT 19:
BEGIN NE corner Wasington & Gibbons ... N w/Wn 176' 6"... E //Gibbons 123' 5"... S//Wn 176' 6"... W w/Gibbons to BEGIN.
WTT: Thomas Swann, Francis Digges, Charles Simms

107   21Apr85
Fm the ALXR EXXRS [see above]
To John Harper, FfxCo, **Merchant**: lease fm 01Nov @ £228 cmv per year of [Lot not numbered or named]:
BEGIN at point on E side Water St 176' 6" S of int w/Gibbons, then E//Gibbons into Potomac; from BEGIN, S w/Water St 176' 7" to [blank] Street; E w/[blank] Street 355'; E into the Potomac River; N w/Potomac to intersect the first course.
WTT: as above

113   21Apr85
Fm William Alexander, PW Co AND William Gibbons Steuart, King George Co AND William Thornton Alexander the younger son of John Alexander: the surviving exxrs of John Alexander of Stafford, deceased. [In the deed abstracts below, these will be the ALXR EXXRS.]
To John Reynolds, TwnALX, **Merchant**: lease fm 01Nov @ £26.10.0 cmv per year of Boggess Survey LOT 29:
BEGIN on N side of Gibbon where it int w/E side Pitt-extended ... E w/Gibbons 123' 5"... N w/Pitt 176' 6"... W//Gibbon 123' 5"... thence to BEGIN.
WTT: Thomas Swann, Francis Digges, Charles Simms

120   21Apr85
Fm the ALXR EXXRS [see above]
To John Reynolds, TwnALX, **Merchant**: lease fm 01Nov @ £40.10.0 cmv per year of Boggess Survey LOT 31:
BEGIN where W side Royal will intersect N side of Gibbons ... W w/Gibbons 123' 5"... N w/Royal 176' 6"... E 123' 5"... thence to BEGIN.   WTT: as above PLUS Robert Whitacre

126   21Apr85
Fm the ALXR EXXRS [see above]
To Robert Whitacre, TwnALX: lease fm 01Nov @ £78.10.0 cmv per year of Boggess Survey LOT 37:

BEGIN where E side Ffx when extended will int N side Gbns ... E w/Gibbons 123' 5"... N w/Ffx 176' 6"... W//Gibbons 123' 5"... thence to BEGIN.
WTT: Thomas Swann, Francis Digges, Charles Simms PLUS John Reynolds

133 18Aug85
Fm Thomas Tobin, TwnALX, **Merchant**
To William Reeds AND Merryman Spilman, FfxCo, as Tenants in Common: lease fm 21July @ £13.10.6 current money per year of part of the lot Tobin bought 21Apr85 fm the ALXR EXXRS (William Alexander, PW Co AND William Gibbons Steuart, King George Co AND William Thornton Alexander the younger son of John Alexander of Stafford Co, dec'd):
BEGIN 30' 11" W of S side Duke when extended w/W side Washington ... W w/Duke 30' 10"... S//Wn 68'... E//Duke 30' 10"... N //Washn to BEGIN.
WTT: Aaron Hewes, James Lownes, John Tobin

136 29Jul85
Fm Andrew & Margaret Wailes, TwnALX, FfxCo, StVA
To Robert Lyle -do- : sale @ £100 cmv of part LOTS 28 & 29:
BEGIN on Queen St at line of William Shaw, lately deceased ... N w/that line 86' 8"... E//Queen 22'... S//Ffx 86' 8" to Queen ... thence along Queen to BEGIN. WTT: none

140 11Aug85
Fm Andrew & Margaret Wailes, TwnALX, FfxCo, StVA
To Frederick Weaver -do- : lease, on 26 Oct85 10 1/2 Spanish milled $; fm 26 Oct86 41 2/3 Spanish Milled $ per year of part of new lot [LOT 36] fm ALXR EXXRS on W side Ffx, S side Gibbons [see p.80, above]:
BEGIN on Ffx 101' 7" S of intersection w/Gibbons ... S w/Ffx 25'... W//Gibbons 117' 5"... N//Ffx 25' ... thence to BEGIN. (Wailes has laid out an alley, 6' wide, from Gibbons south w/W line of this lot across the lot. Weaver to have its use.)
WTT: none

145 11Aug85
Fm Andrew & Margaret Wailes, TwnALX, FfxCo, StVA
To Michael Herbert -do-: lease, as Weaver's above, also of part of LOT 36:
BEGIN on Ffx 76' 7" S of intersection w/Gibbons ... S [on Ffx] 25'... W//Gibbons 117' 5"... N//Ffx 25'... thence to BEGIN--w/use of alley as above.
[Michael Herbert signs w/mark]   WTT: none

150 26Jul85
Fm John Graham, FfxCo, StVA
To Andrew Wales, TwnALX, -do-: sale @ £120 cmv of part LOTS 28 & 29:
BEGIN on Queen at line of "William Shaw, lately deceased"
("supposed to be 176' 2" W of intersection of Queen & Ffx") ... N w/Shaw's line 45' 8" to "ground of Andrew Wales"... E w/his line //Queen 44'... S//Ffx 45' 8" to Qn ... thence on Queen to BEGIN. (JG has this through an "Estate of Inheritance.")
WTT: Michael Thorn, William Harper, John B. Fenley, Will. Glass

153 10Jun85
Fm Robert Townshend Hooe, TwnAlx, FfxCo, StateVA AND
  Richard Harrison, City of Cadiz, Kingdom of Spain
To William Hartshorne, TwnALX, FfxCo, CwlVA
WHEREAS on 01Dec80 the Mayor and Commonalty [Mayor = RTH] leased to RTH, RH AND Joseph White Harrison "all that part of Point Lumley as follows"

BEGIN S side Duke 88' E of corner of LOT 77 in seizin of Thomas Fleming--the NE corner; S//Union & Water Sts. 121' to ground leased by Trustees to Thomas Fleming; E w/Fleming's line//Duke to Potomac River; N w/Potomac River to Duke; thence w/Duke to BEGIN, as Tenants in common f/21 years from 16 Oct80...
AND SINCE THEN J.W.Harrison sold his interest to RTH & RH;
NOW RTH & RH lease to Hartshorne this part:
BEGIN on Duke at east end of the scale house built by RTH and RH ... E w/the street 75'... S//Union 22'... W//Duke 75'... N to BEGIN.
Term: to the end of RTH-RH lease and--from 10Sep85, @ 300 Spanish Milled $ per year, paid quarterly.
Commitments by RTH & RH:
--will raise no building on ground between E line of this parcel and the "Extremity of the Wharf towards the River"
--nor "upon that part of the Wharf or Lott which lies within Twenty Feet to the Southward of the said Premises" [thus to keep open a passage].
WTT: Michael Thorne, Elie Nallette, R.W. Ashton

158 22Dec84
Fm John Potts, Jr., TwnALX
To William Herbert   -do- **Merchant**
WHEREAS John Alexander, **Gentleman**, late of Stafford, deceased, on 20Dec74 granted two lots adjoining LOTs 94 & 95, (the Westernmost containing 1/2A, and the other "not so much") to, as tenants in common: Andrew Stewart, William Herbert, John Fitzgerald, and Valentine Peers @ annual rent of £39.10.0 cmv
--w/all water & landing places
--w/"privilege of Digging the Dirt from Wilkes Street until they should come within six feet of the South side of it"
--paying each 20Dec annual rent £39.10.0 current money of VA;
AND Andrew Stewart having since died, his will directing his share be sold:
      --his exxrs (David Stewart; William Herbert; AND John Maxwell Nisbett of City of Philadelphia) selling AS's 1/4 interest on 20Apr84 to John Potts, Jr....
NOW John Potts, Jr. sells for £401 cmv his--Potts'--1/4th interest to William Herbert, and WH will each 20Dec pay £9.17.6 cmv to the heirs of J. Alexander
WTT: Colin MacIver, Wm. Bird, Thos. Maguire, B. Powell

163 19Jan86
Fm Robert Whitacre, TwnALX, FfxCo, StVA
To Robert Fulton   -do- : lease fm 01Nov @ £23.18.0 cmv per year of part of the John Alexander LOT 37 [see Boggess Survey, p.126 above]:
BEGIN on Ffx 112' 7" N of Gibbon ... N w/Ffx 44' to line of lot RW sold to William Harper ... E w/Harper's line 123' 5" to E line of LOT 37 ... S w/ LOT 37 line 44'... thence to BEGIN--PLUS use of RW's alley: fm Ffx at S line of this parcel, E w/line, 10' wide, to E line of LOT 37.
WTT: John Reynolds, Michael Reynolds, William Paton

168 14Jul85
Fm William Ramsay (the late William Ramsay's eldest son)
   TwnALX, FfxCo, StVA
To Dennis Ramsay   -do- : lease fm 01May85 for 10 years, amount to be fixed by Robert McCrea and John Allison of part LOT [blank], N side of King and E side Ffx:
BEGIN on Ffx 10' S of S end of the "Kitchen which stands upon the said Street belonging to...William Ramsay"... E //King 60'... N//Ffx 25'... W//King 22" including a brick Smoke House ... N//Ffx to 4' [wide] alley "lately laid out in the said Lott No.

[blank] by William Ramsay, **Esquire**, deceased"; ... E w/alley line 84'... S to "Ramsay's Alley"... W//King to Ffx ... thence w/Ffx to BEGIN.
WTT: James Craik, Junr; John Ramsay, Robert Allison

172 15Nov85
Fm Richard Clarke, TwnALX, FfxCo, Cwl VA, **Waterman**
To Michael Thorn of same, **Merchant**: sale for 5/ [this transaction is to post bond collateral] of part of LOT [blank]:
30' on W side Water St... bounded on S by Lewis Weston ... on N by Christina Slimmer ... "and runs back the depth of the lot." [MT is security for a bond that Clarke has put up to William Hunter, Sr. for 9000 lbs crop tobacco.]
WTT: Cleon Moore, Jeremiah Williams, John B. Finley

174 15Nov85   Bill of Sale
Richard Clark has sold to Michael Thorn for £200:
--the Sloop Industry "now in Harbour at Alexandria" AND
--the Sloop William PLUS their Rigging and Tackle AND
--3 featherbeds and furniture now in R. Clark's house
--2 black walnut tables, 8 Windsor chairs
WTT: as above

176 22Jun85
Fm Hugh Finley--brother & heir at law of John Finley, late of the Town of ALX, deceased AND Susannah Finley (Hugh's wife) & Robert Daugherty--nephew & heir at law of Windsor Brown, late of ALX, deceased
To David Pancoast of ALX
WHEREAS John Alexander 19Dec74 leased to J. Finley & Windsor Brown as tenants in common a lot on E of St. A, S of Duke--and JF & WB died intestate; NOW to David Pancoast, a part of that lot:
BEGIN on St. Asaph 78' S of int w/Duke ... S w/St A 20' 7"... E//Duke 100'... N//St. Asaph 20' 7"... thence to BEGIN.
--Pancoast to pay the J.ALXR heirs each 19Dec 14/ cmv AND to erect on/before 03Sep next, a dwelling house of Brick, Stone or Frame to enclose at least 400 square feet.   WTT: John Reynolds, John Lomax, James Lawrason, John B. Ford

180 23Feb86
Fm Robert Daugherty [no ID]
To James Lawrason AND Samuel Arell of TwnALX as Tenants in Common: sale [?] for £110 cmv PLUS proportionate part of annual rent due from the late Finley and Brown [see p.176, above] to the heirs of J. Alexander:
BEGIN S side of Duke at int St. Asaph-Duke ... S along St. A 78'... E//Duke 100'... N//St. A 78' to Duke ... thence w/Duke 100' to BEGIN.
--"Rent is denominated in" Deed of Partition between Hugh Finley & Daugherty and deed fm HF & D to "David Pancoast late deceased"
WTT: Wm. Hickman, Junr; John Reynolds, Thomas Barclay, John B. Ford, George Wilson

183 19Aug85
Fm Robert & Ann Allison, ALX, FfxCo, CwlVA, **Merchant**
To Robert McCrea AND Robert Mease of the same place: sale @ £375 lawful money of VA of part of LOT 89:
BEGIN at Ffx and line between LOTS 89 & 81 ... E//Wolfe 123' 5" to corner of LOT 88 ... S w/LOT 88 line, //Ffx 66' to a 10' wide alley ... W//Wolfe 123' 5" to Ffx ... N up

E side Ffx 66' to BEGIN--PLUS opening by the Allisons of a 10' wide alley on the S boundary of this parcel. WTT: Thomas Whiting, James Irvine, John Dundas
CMN: James Kirk, John Fitzgerald, William Herbert, **Gentlemen Justices of ALX**, apptd 21Feb85 to examine Ann Allison. Rptd back 22Feb86.

188 01Jan85
Fm John Tarbuck alias Scott, **Mariner**
To William Patterson, FfxCo, State of VA: sale @ £75 VA Currency of LOT 130 "cornering on Oronoko and Pitt Streets."
WTT: in Beaufort Co, NoCar, by Thos. Alderson, Wm. Brown, John Smaw

190 14Jun85
Fm Michael & Hannah Madden, TwnALX, FfxCo, StVA
To Alexander Smith   -do-: lease fm 08Mar @ 30 5/6 Guineas per year of part LOT 54, being lot conveyed fm William Ramsay to his daughter Hannah 23Feb84: BEGIN on King at E lot line of Mrs. Ann Allison ... E w/King 30' 10"... S//Royal 100' to 20' alley ... W w/alley //King 30' 10"... N to BEGIN--rent remittable on paying £863.6.8 cmv in Spanish Milled $ at 6/ each, half-Johannes weighing 9 penny wt at 40/, each Guinea weighing 5 penny wt 6 grains at 28/ each.
WTT: Thomas Barclay, Joseph Greenway, John Short
CMN: James Kirk & James Keith, **Gentlemen**, apptd to examine Hannah 05Jul85. Rptd back same day.

197 28 Oct85
Fm Robert Townshend Hooe, TwnALX, FfxCo, StateVA AND
  Richard Harrison, City of Cadiz, Spain
To Christian & Mary Slimmer, TwnALX, FfxCo, StVA
WHEREAS RTH & RH have part LOT 64:
BEGIN W side Water St 150' 7" South of Prince Street ...
S w/Water St 26'... W 123' 5";
WHEREAS C. Slimmer has part LOT 72:
BEGIN W side Water St 146' 7" North of Duke ... N w/Duke 30'
W 123' 5";
AND a survey shows about 6' surplus between RTH-RH's south lot line and CS's north lot line;
NOW they will use their 3' strips of the surplus for an alley to be open forever.
[Mary signs self as "**Anne** Mary Slimmer"]
WTT: Jas. Keith, Jacob Harmon, John Saunders

200 29 Oct85
Fm RTH & RH, as above, p.197
To Jacob Harmon, TwnALX, FfxCo, StVA: regarding part LOT 64:
BEGIN at SE corner LOT 64 on Water St ... N w/Water St 26'...
W//Prince 123' 5"... S//Water St 26'... thence to BEGIN--sold by John Mills 25Sep79 to RTH, RH, and Joseph White Harrison--JWH selling his interest to RTH & RH 04Mar82, and RH having sent RTH Power of Attorney;
NOW RTH & RH lease to Harmon fm 01Jan @ 26 Guineas per year:
BEGIN on Water St 150' 7" S of Prince ... S w/Water St 26'... W//Prince 123' 5"... N//Water St 26'... thence to BEGIN--PLUS use of 3' LOT 64 and 3' LOT 72 as an alley 6' wide;
AND JH will pay whatever amount is evaluated by "Indifferent persons chosen by [RTH & RH]" for a house now on the premises occupied by RTH as a kitchen;
AND RTH & RH can remove the "house" now occ. by RTH as a stable--if after careful measuring the house or any part of it is found to be on the property.

(Rent remittable by paying w/in 20 years 520 Guineas)
WTT: Jas. Keith, John Saunders, Christian Slimmer

206 21Nov85
Fm Robert & Ann McCrea AND
  Robert Mease, [all of] TwnALX, FfxCo, StVA
To RTH & RH as at pp.197, 200
WHEREAS 13Jul77 John Dixon conveyed to RMcC & RM & John Boyd of Baltimore part LOT 64, and 17Jul78 Dixon sold his interest to RMcC & RM;
NOW RMcC & RM sell to RTH-RH for £350 cmv part LOT 64:
BEGIN W side Water St 98' 7" South of Prince ... S w/Water St 26'... W//Prince 123' 5"... N//Water St 26'... thence to BEGIN
WTT: John Allison, Robert Allison, Jas. Keith

210 26 Oct85
Fm Robert & Ann McCrea AND
  Robert Mease, [all of] TwnALX, FfxCo, StVA
To RTH & RH as at pp.197, 200
WHEREAS 13Jul77 John Dixon conveyed to RMcC & RM & John Boyd of Baltimore part LOT 64, and 17Jul78 Dixon sold his interest to RMcC & RM;
NOW RMcC & RM sell to RTH-RH as tenants in common part LOT 64:
BEGIN on Prince at NW corner of House wherein RTH lives, belonging to RTH & RH, being 30' 10" west of Water Street ... W/Prince 23' 3"... S//Water St 98' 6" ... E//Prince 23' 3" to the line of RTH & RH ... thence to BEGIN.
WTT: William McWhir, Thomas Whiting, Jas. M. McCrea, Jas. Keith

214 08Nov85
Fm RTH & RH) as above at pp. 206, 210
To RMcC & RM) as pp. 206, 210: for £350, transferring to RMcC & RM Jacob Harmon's annual rent payment of 26 Guineas for part LOT 64 on W side of Water St.   WTT: John Allison, Robert Allison, Jas. Keith

218 24Feb86
Fm Thomas Patterson, FfxCo, StVA
To Mary Burnett & sons George & Charles Burnett, all of ALX:
Sale for £10 cmv of part LOT 130:
BEGIN on Pitt 136' 7" S Oronko ... S w/Pitt 40' to S line LOT 130 ... W w/line //Oro 123' 5" to west lot line ... N w/line //Pitt 40'... thence to BEGIN.
WTT: Henry Lowe, George Hineman, Michael Gretter

221 18Mar85
Fm Thomas & Betty Fleming, TwnALX, FfxCo, StVA
To John Muir   -do-
WHEREAS the Flemings have owed Muir £112.14.8 since 08May73
AND in 1780 they rented @ £30 per year part LOT 96 to Michael Madden;
NOW the Flemings sign over the rents to Muir. Agreement ends when debt satisfied either by pre-payment or accrued rents.
WTT: Jas. Keith, Betty Fleming, D. Arell, Jas. Kirk
CMN: David Arell, Jas. Keith apptd 28Jun85 to examine Betty. Rptd back 19 Oct85.

226 21Feb86
Fm Thomas & Betty Fleming, TwnALX, FfxCo, StVA
To Robert Townshend Hooe, -do- , & Richard Harrison, late of same, now in City of
    L'Orient in the Kingdom of [blank]:

Lease all that part of ground and wharf belonging to Thomas Fleming adj the wharf of RTH & RH.
BEGIN on dividing line between the parties, at intersection of line drawn fm W end of Warehouse & Store lately erected by Wm. Hartshorne ... E w/dividing line as far into the Potomac as RTH-RH choose ... Again from BEGIN: S in an extension of straight line fm W end of Hartshorne's whse until intersecting Jas. Kirk's line ... E w/Kirk's line into Potomac as far as RTH-RH may choose ... thence N to intersect 1st line;
--PLUS all improvements and privilege of extending wharves or making new ones.
Term: same as that between Town of ALX and RTH-RH.
Cost: 150 Spanish Milled $/year
--PLUS TFl will leave open as an alley a piece of ground 15' wide beginning at S end of alley laid out by the Town f/RTH-RH's lease--and extending easterly along dividing line [TFl + RTH-RH] until it reaches the W line of RTH-RH.
--AND RTH-RH may take as much earth as they need (to raise and fill in that part of the wharf made by TFl) from the lot ... "whereon Thomas Fleming now lives."
--AND that at lease end RTH-RH may remove any buildings built on this parcel;
--AND TFl will sign over to RTH-RH any compensation to which he is entitled from Joseph Caverly "for Damages heretofore done to the Wharf...by...JC in Building thereupon and Launching Vessels therefrom." WTT: none

230 25Jan86 Bill of Sale
Fm Alexander Thomas, TwnALX, CwlVA
To Benjamin Hamp, TwnALX, StVA, **Merchant:**
Thomas for £63 cmv sells Negro Man Henry to Hampe.
WTT: Thomas Swann, Thomas Jennings

231 29Jun86
Fm Hiram Chapin, TwnALX, FfxCo, StVA
To Gurden Chapin -do-
WHEREAS Joseph Saunders of Philadelphia on 16 Oct75 sold to Benjamin Chapin, late of ALX, deceased, LOT 65;
--AND BC's will devised the House & LOT to sons HC & GC;
NOW Hiram sells his portion to Gurden for £140 cmv:
BEGIN E side Ffx 98' 5" S from nearest corner on S side Prince
... E//Prince & Duke, joining lines w/Wm & Edw Ramsay, 51' 8" ... S//Water & Ffx Sts (adj 10' alley) 16'... W//Prince & Duke (adj alley running west) 51' 8" to Ffx ... N along E side of Ffx to BEGIN.
WTT: Colin MacIver, Wm. Hickman, Junr; Acquila Browne

234 21Apr86
Fm Charles Jones, FfxCo, StVA
To Daniel McPherson, Junr. AND Isaac McPherson, Twn of ALX
WHEREAS John Alexander's heir William Thornton Alexander is still a minor and WHEREAS Lucy Alexander & Seymour Hooe by Indenture dated [blank] Day of [blank], 17[blank], did grant to Charles Jones a lot of land on E side of Water St and S of a street "which at that time was intended to be called by the name of Abingdon Street but which hath since been altered and is now called by the name of Gibbons Street" called LOT [blank]:
BEGIN at int of Water St & Gibbons/Abingdon... E into the River Potomac ...
BEGIN again, going S w/Water St 167' 7"... E//Gibbons/Abingdon into the River Potomac ... thence at right angles N to intersect w/ 1st line;
AND Jones was to pay annually 1000 lbs Crop Tobacco;

BUT the indenture was witnessed by three, one of whom died before Jones could record it--and therefore had to bring a Chancery suit to fix title;
AND Jones sold a half to Wm. Hunter, Junr for a sum plus the lot's rent payments to the ALXRs;
NOW Jones sells to D & I McPh as tenants in common:
BEGIN on Water St 132' 5 1/4" south of Gibbons/Abingdon... E//Gibbons into River Potomac ... From BEGIN S w/Water St 44' 1 3/4" to south lot line ... E//Gibbons into River ... thence w/right angle to intersect 1st line.
WTT: Jas. Keith, Jonah Thompson, Ichabod Hunter

238 21Jun85
Fm David & Hannah Griffith, FfxCo, StVA
To David Jones, TwnALX: LOT 1 "...in the Addition made by...David Griffith to the said Town of ALX, Described in the plan of the said Addition by the No. (1)"
[LOTS so described will be hereafter designated "Griffith LOT __"]
Lease fm 21Jun88 @ £34.8.7 1/2 Virginia money per year:
BEGIN int E side St. Asaph w/south side of Oronoko ... S w/St. A 75'... E//Oro 43' 5"... N//St. A 75' to Oro ... thence w/Oronoko to BEGIN.
    AND
Griffith LOT 6, E of St. A, S of Oro, and adj S side LOT 1:
BEGIN on St. A at S line LOT 1 ... S w/St. A 21' 7"... E//Oro 83' 5"... N//St. A 21' 7"... thence to BEGIN.
ALSO Jones to erect on one of the parcels by 01Nov87 a "Dwelling House at least 16 ft square w/ brick or stone chimney thereto";
ALSO Jones to pay taxes hereafter due;
ALSO if Jones defaults by 01Nov87 will pay £81.5.10;
ALSO Griffith will extend St. Asaph and Oronoko Streets from their present terminations in the Town of ALX.
WTT: Geo. Richards, John Lomax, Ja. Keith, John Potts, Junr; Burr Powell, Frans. Brooke

243 21Jun85
Fm Griffiths to Jones as above:
Griffith LOT 11 on W side St. A, S side Oronoko:
BEGIN at that intersection ... S w/St. A 75'... W//Oronoko 43' 5"... N//St. A 75' to Oronoko ... thence on Oronoko to BEGIN.
    AND
Griffith LOT 12:
BEGIN on Oro at W line LOT 11 ... W w/Oro 20'... S//St. Asaph 75'... E//Oro 20'... thence to BEGIN.
Lease fm 21Jun88 @ £41.1.7 1/2 per year. Terms as above [see p. 238]: taxes, and by 01Nov87 a 16 sqft dwelling, etc. For non-compliance: £96.19.11
WTT: Geo. Richards, John Lomax, Jas. Keith, John Potts, Junr; Burr Powell, Frans. Brooke.

248 21Jun85
Fm the Griffiths to Jones, as above, Griffith LOT 66:
BEGIN int W side Washington, S side Prince ... S w/Wn 75'... W//Prince 43' 5"... N//Wn 75' to Prince ... thence to BEGIN.
    AND
Griffith LOT 77, adj LOT 66:
BEGIN on Wn St at S line of LOT 66 ... S w/Wn 21' 7"... W//Princess[?] 83' 5"... N//Wn 21' 7"... thence to BEGIN.

Lease fm 21Jun88 @ £46.6.0 VA money. Terms as before: taxes, a 16 sqft dwelling on one parcel by 01Nov87, etc. For non-compliance: £109.6.4 VA money.
WTT: Geo. Richards, John Lomax, Ja. Keith, John Potts, Junr; Burr Powell, Frans. Brooke

253 21Jun85
Fm David & Hannah Griffith, FfxCo, StVA
To David Jones, TwnALX: Griffith LOT 67:
[NOTE: Street names wrong, but as written by clerk.]
BEGIN on Princess 43' 5" W of int Princess-Wn ... W w/Princess 20'... S//Wn 75'... E//Princess 20'... thence to BEGIN.
    AND
Griffith LOT 68, adj LOT 67:
BEGIN on Princess at LOT 67's W line ... W w/Princess 20'... S//Wn 75'... E//Princess 20'... Thence to BEGIN
    AND
Griffith LOT 69, adj LOT 68:
BEGIN on Princess at LOT 68's W line ... W w/Princess 20'... S //Wn 97' 7"... E//Princess 20'... thence to BEGIN.
Lease fm 21Jun88 @ £22.5.0 VA money per year; Jones to erect 1 house on any of the 3 lots. Non-building penalty: loss of the lots + an additional £52.10.7
WTT: as above

260 21Jun85
Fm the Griffiths to Jones as above.
Griffith LOT 81, W side of Wn, N side of Princess:
BEGIN on Wn 75' N of Princess ... N w/Wn 21' 7"... W//Princess 83' 5"... S//Wn 21' 7"... thence to BEGIN.
Terms as above. Annual rent £7.5.0 fm 21Jun88, the non-building penalty an additional £17.2.4   WTT: as above

265 21Jun85
Fm the Griffiths to Jones as above. Griffith LOT 13:
BEGIN on Oronoko 63'5" W of St. A ... W on Oro 20'...
S//St. Asaph 75'... E//Oro 20'... thence to BEGIN.
    AND
Griffith LOT 14, adj LOT 13:
BEGIN W line of LOT 13 on Oro ... W on Oro 20'... S//St. Asaph 96' 7"... E// Oronoko 20'... thence to BEGIN.
    AND
Griffith LOT 15, adj LOT 14:
BEGIN at W line of LOT 14 on Oro ... W on Oro 20'... S//St. Asaph 96' 7"... E//Oro 20'... thence to BEGIN.
Terms as for Griffith LOTS 67-68-69 at p. 253, above: erect 1 house on any lot, etc.
Lease all at £21.5.0 VA money fm 21Jun88. Non-building penalty: £50.3.5
WTT:Geo. Richards, John Lomax, Jas. Keith, John Potts, Junr; Burr Powell, Frans. Brooke

271 21Jun85
Fm David Griffith, FfxCo, StVA, **Clerk**
To Michael Steiver, TwnALX, Ffx, VA:
Griffith LOT 65, W side of Wn, N side of Queen:
BEGIN on Washington 156' 7" N of Queen ... N w/Wn 20'... W//Queen 123' 5"... S//Wn 20'... thence to BEGIN.

Lease fm 21Jun88 at £7.5.0 VA money. All terms as above. Non-building penalty £18.6.0
WTT: Baldwin Dade, Jas. Keith and Philip France to Steiver; John Potts, Junr; Burr Powell, Francis Brooke

277 21Jun85
Fm David & Hannah Griffith, FfxCo, StVA
To Thomas Reed, TwnALX:
Griffith LOT 35, E side St. Asaph, S side of Princess:
BEGIN on St.Asaph 156' 7" S of Princess ... S w/St. A 20'...
E//Princess 123' 5"... N//St.A 20'... thence to BEGIN
Lease fm 21Jun88 at £7.0.0 VA Money per year. Terms as above; penalty fee £16.10.6
Griffith is extending St. Asaph and Princess Streets from Town
WTT: Jas. Keith, William Bryson, Burr Powell, Frans. Brooke; John Potts, Junr.

282 21Jun85
Fm the Griffiths as above
To Bernard Mann of ALX:
Griffith LOT 82, W side Washington, N side Princess:
BEGIN on Wn 96' 7" N of intersection w/Princess ... N w/Wn 20'
W//Princess 123' 5"... S//Wn 20'... thence to BEGIN.
Lease fm 21Jun88 for £6.15.0 VA money. Usual terms [see above] w/penalty fee £15.18.9
WTT: Jas. Keith, John Smith, Hugh Barr, Burr Powell, Frans. Brooke; John Potts, Jr.

288 21Jun85
Fm the Griffiths as above
To Paul Trout [no ID]:
Griffith LOT 78, N side Princess, W side Washington:
BEGIN on Princess 63' 5" W of intersection w/Wn ... W on Princess 20'... N//Wn 75'...E//Princess 20'...thence to BEGIN.
Lease fm 21Jun88 at £8.5.0 Terms as above; penalty: £19.13.2
WTT: Saml. Monty. Brown; Baldwin Dade and Jas. Keith to Trout

293 24Apr86
Fm Sarah Ramsay, TwnALX, FfxCo, StVA
To Hugh Mittchell [sic] -do- : lease fm 01Sep86 at 25 1/4 Guineas per year of part LOT 54:
BEGIN on King at E line of parcel conveyed by Michael & Hannah Madden to Alexander Smith--92' 6" E of Royal ... S w/Alxr Smith's line 100' to alley 20' wide ... E w/alley 25' 3"... N//Royall 100' to King ... thence on King to BEGIN.
WTT: Dennis Ramsay, John Breden, Jno. Ramsay

297 21Jun85
Fm David & Hannah Griffith, FfxCo, StateVA, **Clerk**
To Thomas Wilkinson, TwnALX:
Griffith LOT 24 [see p. 238]: N side Princess, W side St. A: BEGIN on Princess 103' 5" W of St.Asaph ... W w/Princess 20' ... N//St. A 70' to an alley or court 36' wide or deep ... E w/alley or court 20'... thence to BEGIN.
Lease fm 21Jun88 @ £9.5.0 per year on Griffiths' standard [see above] terms. Penalty fee: £21.6.9
WTT: Wm. Hepburn, Francis Hall and Jas. Keith at signing by DG and Wilkinson; To Hannah's signature: Burr Powell, Francs. Brooke, and John Potts, Junr.

302 21Jun85
Fm David & Hannah Griffith, FfxCo, StVA
To Gowen Lamphier, FfxCo, StVA:
Griffith LOT 41, W side St.A, S side of Princess:
BEGIN W side St. Asaph 75' S of intersection w/ Princess ...
S w/St. A 21' 7"... W//Princess 83' 5"... N//St. A 21' 7"... thence to BEGIN.
    AND
Griffith LOT 73, W side of Washington, S side Princess:
BEGIN on Wn 116' 7" S of Prss ... S w/Wn 20'... W//Prss 123' ... 5"... N//Wn 20'... thence to BEGIN. Lease fm 21Jun88 at £15.16.1 per year, usual terms. Non-building penalty: £36.2.6
WTT: Jas. Keith, James McReady, William Price, Burr Powell, Frans. Brooke; John Potts, Junr.

308 21Jun85
Fm the Griffiths as above
To Thomas Moxley of ALX:
Griffith LOT 8, E side St.A, S side of Oronoko:
BEGIN on St. A 116' 7" S of int w/Oro ... S on St. A 20'... E//Oro 123' 5"... N//St. A 20'... thence to BEGIN.
    AND
Griffith LOT 9, E side St A, S side Oro, adj LOT 8:
BEGIN on St. A at S line LOT 8 ... S w/St. A 20'... E//Oro 123' 5"... N//St. A 20'... thence to BEGIN.
    AND
Griffith LOT 10, E side St A, S side Oro, adj LOT 9:
BEGIN on St. A at S line LOT 9 ... S w/St A 20'... E//Oro 123' 5"... N//St. A 20'... thence to BEGIN. Lease fm 21Jun88 at £24.5.0 per year. Usual terms w/penalty fee for not building on any one of the 3 lots: £56.19.9
WTT: Jas. Keith, Joseph Fullmore, David Jones, Burr Powell, Frans. Brooke; John Potts, Junr.

315 21Jun85
Fm the Griffiths as above
To Thomas Moxley, TwnALX:
Griffith LOT 19, W side St. Asaph, S side Oronoko:
BEGIN on St. A 136' 7" S of int w/ Oro ... S w/St A 20'... W//Oro 123' 5"... N//St A 20'... thence to BEGIN.
    AND
Griffith LOT 20, adj LOT 19:
BEGIN at S line LOT 19 on St.A ... S on St A 20'... W//Oro 123' 5"... N//St A 20'... thence to BEGIN. Lease fm 21Jun88 at £17.10.0 per year on usual terms. Penalty fee for not building on one of the 2 lots: £41.6.4
WTT: Jas. Keith, Joseph Fullmore, David Jones, Burr Powell, Francs. Brooke; John Potts, Junr.

321 21Jun85
Fm the Griffiths as above
To John Orpwood of FfxCo:
Griffith LOT 80, N side Princess, W side Washington:
BEGIN on Princess 103' 5" W of Wn ... W on Princess 20'... N//Wn 96' 7"... E//Princess 20'... thence to BEGIN. Lease fm 21Jun88 at £7.5.0, usual terms. Non-building penalty: £17.2.4   [John Orpwood signs w/mark.]
WTT: Burr Powell, Frans. Brooke; John Potts Junr.

327 21Jun85
Fm David & Hannah Griffith, FfxCo, StVA
To Hugh Barr, TwnALX:
Griffith LOT 83, W side Washington, N side Princess:
BEGIN on Wn 116' 7" N of int w/Princess ... N w/Wn 20'... W//Princess 123' 5"... S//Wn 20'... thence to BEGIN. Lease fm 21Jun88 at £6.15.0 per year, usual terms, penalty fee £15.18.9
WTT: Jas. Keith, John Smith, Burr Powell, Francs. Brooke; John Potts, Junr. [A sixth name is illegible. Clerk sketched what is illegible to him, resembling: Ex/njerspf Mellum]

332 11May86
Fm Robert Lyle, senr and Martha his wife
To Robert Lyle, junr. (All of TwnALX, FfxCo, StVA)
For the love and affection of the parents toward their son,
part of LOTS 28 & 29:
BEGIN on Queen Street at Wm Shaw's line ... N w/that line 86' 8"... E//Queen 22'... S//Ffx 86' 8"... thence w/Queen to BEGIN.
WTT: Andw. Jameson, Henry Tait, Ninian Anderson
CMN: Richard Conway & Wm. Herbert aptd 12May86 to examine Martha. Reported back 12Aug86.

336 07Sep86
Fm Patrick & Margaret Murray, TwnALX, CwlVA
To Ann Inglish & William McKinzey, executrix & executor of Samuel Inglish, deceased: mortgage to secure debt of £348 VA currency owed by Patrick Murray & Hugh Neilson since 22Aug75;
Pledged: the LOT whereon Murray now lives at Prince and St. Asaph Streets. [no further particulars]
Terms: this is void if Murray repays the £348 in gold & silver (silver $ @ 6/ each): £150 installments on/before 01May87, 01Jan88, 01Apr88, and balance 07Sep88.
WTT: Tho. Swann, Joseph Lewis, Junr; Elie Vallette, R.T.Hooe

338 24May86 Power of Attorney
Fm Richard Harrison in L'Orient, France
To Robert Townshend Hooe: to sell properties
WTT: Samuel Harper, Richard Harrison, James Cotter

340 11Jul86 Power of Attorney
Fm John Dixon AND Isaac Littledale, Whitehaven, Cumberland Co, **Merchants** in
        Company AND
   Anthony Piper, Harrington, Cumberland Co, **Ship Carpenter**, Brother & Heir at
        Law to Harry Piper, deceased;
To Dennis Ramsay: to settle the affairs of both Dixon & Littledale and of Isaac
   Littledale & Co., AND of Harry Piper [former agent for D&L, and IL & Co.]

346 23Sep86
Fm Thomas Ramsay, TwnALX, FfxCo, CwlVA
To Thomas Hedrick of -do- : lease fm 01 Oct87 @ £8 cmv/annum of part LOT 129 [?] "fronting on the East side of Pitt Street"
BEGIN 136' 7" fm int Pitt-Oronoko ... S w/Pitt 40'... E//Oro 63' 5"... N//Pitt 40'... W 63' 5" to BEGIN--rent remittable on paying £80 any time before 20Sep94. [Hedrick signs w/mark]   WTT: Jno. Oliphant, Thomas Clark

349 25Apr86
Fm Robert & Nancy McCrea AND Robert Mease, TwnALX, FfxCo, StVA
To Michael Thorn -do- : lease fm 01May86 @ 40 silver Spanish Milled $ per year of part of LOT 56:
BEGIN on W side of 10' alley 93' from Union Street, and at "Division line between the ground of John Harper (now occupied by the said Michael Thorn) and McCrea & Mease ... N//Union along the alley 39' to another alley between this ground and that of Andrew Wales ... W//Prince 40' along S side of that other alley ... S//Union 39'... thence by John Harper's line to BEGIN.
--Thorn to erect w/in 3 years brick or framed dwelling at least 16' square;
--McC & M to keep open the 10' alley which binds the property on the east, and the alley on the north;
--rent remittable if w/in 20 years McC & M pay the rent remaining plus 5% interest
WTT: Tobias Zimmerman, James Patton [plus one squiggle--perhaps an exasperated clerk's way of indicating an illegible name on the original deed]

353 30Jan86
Fm George Goodes, TwnALX, FfxCo, StVA
To George Herbert -do-
WHEREAS David Arell on __ __ 17__ [date not filled in] leased to George Goodes for 54 Spanish Milled $/year a part of LOT [blank] on N side of Wilkes and East side of Royal;
NOW for £200 cmv Goodes assigns Herbert the parcel, Herbert now to pay Arell the annual 54 Spanish Milled $/yr.   WTT: Jas. Keith, George Cox, William Brumley

357 20Sep86
Fm John McCrea, Prince William Co, son/heir-at-law of Allan McCrea, PWm Co, **Merchant**, dec'd;
To Alexander Henderson, Robert Adam, Robert McCrea, John Muir, William Hunter, Jr.; John Gibson: all of FfxCo, all devisees & executors of Last Will & Testament of Thomas Kirkpatrick, late of TwnALX, **Merchant**, deceased;
WHEREAS on 04-05May73 William Black of [blank] County, **Merchant**, conveyed to Thos. Kirkpatrick half of LOT 20 [marginal note: LOT 26] bounded on S by Queen, W by LOT 27, N by LOT 21, E by Water Street;
--sold by the late Alan McCrea to Wm Black
--BUT it appears McCrea failed to convey legal title to Black
--THUS leaving legal title in John McCrea
AND WHEREAS Thos. Kirkpatrick's will of 12Jan85 directs his exxrs to divide the estate for the benefit of his sisters Elizabeth Cutler/Colter/Culter; Catharine Cutler/Culter/Colter; and Henrietta Kirkpatrick;
NOW for 5/ John McCrea conveys title to TK's executors.
WTT: David Finlay, Alexr. Buchan; Robert Lyle, Junr.

361 23Feb86
Fm Joseph & Ann Caverly, TwnALX, FfxCo, StVA
To Charles Polk -do- : lease fm 23Jan87 @ 29 1/3 Spanish Milled $/year of part LOT [clerk left lot number blank; unknown person has pencilled in No. 12] "lately added by John Alexander's Executors, W of Washington, N of Wolfe:
BEGIN on Wn at N line of lot conveyed by Caverly to Gerrard Johnstone ... N w/Wn 22'... W//Wolfe 100'... S//Wn 22'... thence to BEGIN--Caverly to leave open for an alley a piece of ground 5' wide, from Washington along N line of this parcel and thence along its W line.

WTT: James Lawrason, John Hickman; William Hickman, Junr; Peter Caverly, Henry Jermingham, Pliercy Davison. [Letters underlined are illegible, and may not be correct.]

364 12Aug86 Deed of Release
Fm John Harper, FfxCo, StVA
WHEREAS on 16Sep82 JH granted to Wm. Lyles, Jr., of ALX part of a lot on N side of Prince, W side of Water Streets;
--Lyles w/in 4 years of end of the war w/Great Britain to erect a 2-story Brick house at least 20' in front;
--Lyles now saying "it will be more convenient...to build with Frame rather than Brick and he can execute the same in a shorter time...and that if he is released...from the Covenant...he...will Immediately erect...a Frame House of larger Size than the Brick House..."
NOW JH releases WL,Jr. w/provison that WL will w/in 12 months erect a larger frame house with a brick or stone chimney and will "finish the same off in a tenantable manner both inside and outside."
WTT: John Murray, John Wheaton, Thomas Rogerson

366 05Nov85
Fm William & Sarah Lyles, Jr., TwnAlx, FfxCo, StVA
To (as Tenants in Common) John Murray AND Obediah Bowen of FfxCo, VA PLUS John Munford of City of New York, **Merchants** and Partners: lease fm 01May86 @ 40 Guineas/annum of part of LOT 57, W of Water St, N side of Prince:
BEGIN at int Water-Prince Sts ... W w/Prince 40'... N//Water St 88'... E//Prince 40' to Water St ... thence 88' to BEGIN;
--conveyed 16Sep82 by John Harper to W. Lyles, Jr.
--these new tenants to pay 80 Spanish Milled $ per year to Harper--the equivalent of 17 1/7 Guineas--and Lyles will discount this fm the partners' 40 Guineas owed him [WL,Jr.]   WTT: Jas. Keith, Edwd. K. Thompson, Joshua Merryman

370 17Aug86
Fm John Murray & John Munford & Obediah Bowen [no IDs]
To Lewis Deblois, Junr, & Edward Kinnicut Thompson [no IDs]
WHEREAS William & Sarah Lyles, Jr. on 05Nov85 granted to JM & JM & OB a parcel on N side Prince and W side Water Street
NOW JM & JM & OB lease to LD & EKT a portion:
BEGIN on Prince 25' W of Wtr St ... W w/Prince 15'... N//Water St 60'... E//Prince 15'... thence to BEGIN.
--from 01May87 for 15 Guineas/annum paid to WLyles,Jr
--JM & JM & OB will lay out a 4' alley beginning on Water St 60' N of Prince, extending W //Prince 40', to be used in common with JM & JM & OB
WTT: O. Winsor, Joseph Jenkes, Joshua Merryman

375 25Jul86 Bill of Sale
Fm Michael Swoope, TwnALX
To sons Adam Simon Swoope & Jacob Swoope
WHEREAS MS owes the following:

Benjamin Hampe	£53.1.6 1/2	Isaac Hoge	£10.16.0
Herbert & Potts	46.14.1	John Hackleroad	10.16.0
John Dunlop	19.14.0	[or Hachleroad]	
Shreeve & Lawrason	7.19.0	James Nicholl	43. 8.0
John Boyce	9.16.0	George Nixon	31.12.7 1/2
Michael Burney	22.19.0	Daniel Ridgway	13.10.0

Jacob Dorsheimer   4. 4.9
John Sutton & Co.   11. 9.9 1/2
Edward K. Thompson
  & Co.   15. 6.7
Jonathan Swift & Co 5. 6.2

Khun & Risberg   118.18.10
[or K<u>ee</u>n & Risberg]
Francis H[?]ickey   8. 4.1
Gurden Chapin & Co.   5.16.0
Jacob Cox   24.8.6

NOW--as my sons are paying these debts--I sell them "all the Stock of Goods as well dry as wet, which I...now have upon hand and also all the Household and Kitchen Furniture and House Linen which I am now possessed of:

8 Mahogany Chairs	75 lbs. Pewter
3 Walnut -do-	1 Copper Kettle1 Iron -do-
6 Windsor -do-	5 Iron Potts
1 Mahogany Dining Table	1 Brass -do-
1 -do- Tea -do-	1 Brass Kettle
2 Wild Cherry Dining Tables	1 baking pan
2 Walnut Dining Tables	1 Dray & Harness
1 -do- Stand	Sundry brass & Copper furniture
1 -do- Tea Table	2 pr And Irons with brass Tops
1 Clock & Case	1 pr -do- -do- -do- Caselings
1 Spennett	1 pr Cast And Irons
1 large Looking Glass	Sundry China and Queen Ware
4 small -do- -do- s	Sundry Iron Furniture
1 Dressing Table	1 Chest & Trunk
1 Desk and Drawers	1 Brass Strainer
1 Writing Desk	6 Table Cloths
2 pair of Drawers	1 Dozen Napkins
11 large Pictures	Sundry Silver Furniture, to wit:
6 small Pictures	2 cream potts
5 beds with all the Furniture and Linen belonging to them and Bedsteads	5 Table Spoons
	6 Tea Spoons
2 Franklyn Stoves	2 Soup Ladles
1 ten plate stove	1 Tankard
1 six plate stove	Negro Woman named Jane and her Chi Jude
2 Cows	
1 riding Chair and Harness	WTT: Jas. Keith, Christian Slimmer

378   14 Oct86
Fm Samuel Montgomery Brown & wife Mary, TwnALX, FfxCo, CwlVA
To William Patterson, Twn Baltimore, StMD: for £150 cmv
1/2 acre LOT contiguous to Alexandria, in FfxCo:
BEGIN on S side Oronoko "when extended by Baldwin Dade from its termination in Twn of ALX," 310' W of W side of Washington St "(a Street lately laid out by...[BD] and others to accommodate the purchasers....)"..."and Immediately upon the Western line of another Street which the said [BD] hath engaged to lay out to accommodate the said [SMB]"... W w/Oro 123' 5"... S//Washington 176' 7"... E//Oro 123' 5" to "the street to be laid out"... N w/that street line, parallel Washington, St. Asaph and Pitt 176' 7" to Oro. WTT: [none]
MEMO: "It is agree to before Signing and Delivery that the House upon the before Described Lott shall be at liberty to be moved of free of rent any time within nine months of this date."
WTT: George Gilpin, Cleon Moore, W. Deneale, Robert B. Jamason
CMN: George Gilpin & William Deneale, **Justices** of FfxCo, aptd to examine Mary 16 Oct86. Rptd back same day.

382 14 Oct86
Fm Samuel Montgomery Brown & wife Mary, TwnALX, FfxCo, StVA
To William Patterson, Twn of Baltimore, StMD
WHEREAS the exxrs of John Alexander 05Aug79 granted to Henry Rozer a 1/2 acre LOT No. [blank not filled in]: E side Ffx, S side Wilkes; S of Ffx 176' 7", E of Wilkes 123' 5"
AND Henry Rozer & wife Eleanor 01Nov84 granted it to SMB
NOW for £160 cmv and rents SMB conveys to Patterson:
BEGIN SE corner int Wilkes-Ffx ... E w/Wilkes 32'... S//Ffx 76' 7"... W//Wilkes 32'... N w/Ffx 76' 7"
Rent: each 05 Aug, figured at 2 shillings per foot of the 32' on Wilkes = £3.4.0
WTT: George Gilpin, Cleon Moore, Robt. Brown Jamison
CMN: Geo. Gilpin & Wm. Deneale, FfxCo Justices aptd 16 Oct86 to examine Mary; rptd same day.

388 29Aug85 Bill of Sale
Fm Thomas Weldon Watson, Loudoun Co
To Jacob Fortner [no ID]: for £71, the Negro Boy Slave Will
[Watson signs w/mark.]
WTT: Richard Clarke, Geo. Deneale

389 18Aug86
Fm Thomas & Elizabeth Reed, TwnALX, FfxCo, StVA
To Michael Gretter -do-
WHEREAS William Hepburn 08Aug82 conveyed To William Anderson part LOT 124 (N side Queen, W side Pitt)
AND Anderson 13Aug86 conveyed it to Thomas Reed
NOW for £50 cmv, the Reeds convey to Gretter:
BEGIN on Queen 40' fm SW corner LOT 124 (which is SE corner of lot granted by William Hepburn to Andrew Judge) ... E w/Queen 24'... N//Pitt 90'... W//Queen 24'... thence to BEGIN--PLUS Gretter must pay Wm Hepburn each 08Aug 12 silver $
[Thomas Reed signs his name; Elizabeth signs w/mark]
WTT: Samuel Whitford, Andrew McMasters, James McReady

392 30Jul86
Fm Nicholas Bryce, brother/heir of John Bryce, late of ALX
To Hannah Bryce, widow, and relict of John Bryce
WHEREAS Nicholas inherited all his brother's real estate
NOW he endows Hannah with 1/3, with a 20' frontage on Prince:
BEGIN on N side Prince adjoining Brick house where Hannah now lives ... W along Prince 20'... N//Ffx & Water Sts 88'... E//Prince 20'... thence to BEGIN--PLUS the alley adj this parcel for use of the "Tenements and LOTT adjoinng on the E side of these premises";
AND another alley 4' wide to be laid off on the N line hereof from the first alley to the lot and tenement adjoining ("communicating there [first alley] and with the LOTT and Tenement adjoining the hereby granted premises")
WTT: Charles Lee, James Hendricks, James Myler, John Wilkinson

394 28Sep86
Fm Mordecai Lewis, City of Philadelphia, **Merchant**, surviving exxr of Jacob Harman, deceased
To Elisha Dick, late of ALX, StVA, **Doctor of Physic**
WHEREAS William & Susanna Hartshorne 22May79 granted property to Jacob Harman AND in accordance w/Harman's will of 18Apr80 registered in Philadelphia

NOW Mordecai Lewis sells to Elisha Dick for £4,375 lawful money of Pennsylvania all of that tract "situate in TwnALX":
BEGIN "at a corner of a Lott marked in the Plan of Lotts now or lately belonging to [Hartshorne] Number 2 and a Survey made by George West, which points to the SE"... thence "running with the range of Lotts nearest to the TwnALX to the Back Line of a Tract of 400 acres"... thence S w/back line to SW corner of the tract ... thence //first line to Potomac ... thence to BEGIN w/meanders of the river.
WTT: Miers Fisher, John Hallowell

398 24Nov86
Fm Oliver Price, TwnALX, FfxCo, StVA
To Samuel Smith -do-: part LOT [178] in ALX:
BEGIN on St. Asaph 77' 6" from int St.A-Prince Sts ... W//Prince 35'... S//St A 7'... W//Prince 25'... N//St A 30'... E//Prince 60'... S 23' to BEGIN.   WTT: Andrew Wales

399 25Sep86
Fm John & Jane Fitzgerald, TwnALX, FfxCo, StVA
To William Anderson -do-: lease fm 01Sep87 @ 18 Guineas per year weighing 5 pennyweight, 6 grains each, part LOT 52, S side King, E side Ffx Streets:
BEGIN on line of LOTS 51-52 ... S w/line 82' 3 1/2" to 12' alley which runs E fm Ffx and //King into Water St ... W w/alley line 18'... N//Ffx St 82' 3 1/2" to King ... thence along King to BEGIN--Rent remittable if WA w/in 20 years pays 360 Guineas weighing 5pwt 6gr each.   WTT: Wm. Hepburn, Jonah Thompson, John B. OKelly

403 21Jul86
Fm James & Elizabeth Myler, TwnALX, CwlVA
To William Sydebotham, Bladensburg, PG Co, MD:
Mortgage to secure Myler's paying 10,000 lbs. tobacco of part LOT 21 [20?], E side Water St--across Union in the River Potomack, and S side Princess:
BEGIN W side Union at line dividing Robert Adam & Richard Conway--118' S of Princess ... W w/line and//Princess 84'... S//Union 23' 6"... E//Princess 84' to Union ... S w/Union to BEGIN--conveyed to Myler by Robert & Ann Adam for annual rent of £23.10.0. If WS gets this land, he will pay the rent to the Adams. If Myler delivers the tobacco to WS, this deed is null and void.
WTT: Ch. Simms, Gilbert Harrow, Thos. Swann

406 08Mar87
Fm Valentine & Catharine Uhler, TwnALX, FfxCo, StVA
To Dederick Schahel/Shahel/Schabelof -do-
WHEREAS David Young 30Jun84 granted to Catharine part of LOT 55, S side King, W side Royal:
BEGIN on King 90 W of int King-Royal ... W on King 33' 6" to W boundary of LOT ... S//Royal 92' 8"... E//King & 1st line 33' 6"... N to King and BEGIN;
AND WHEREAS VU & Cath 22Dec85 conveyed to Jacob Fortnay part of that part:
BEGIN on King at W line LOT 55 (dividing line between VU and James Kirk's land) ... E w/King 15'... S//Royal 92' 8"... W//King 15'... thence to BEGIN--PLUS use of alley adj E line of said piece and extending--with said line fm King S (3' wide) for 40'AND "reserving to [the Uhlers] the Privilege and Liberty of extending the upper Stories of any Building which they...may erect adjoining to the said Alley over the same...."
NOW for £150 cmv V & C Uhler convey to DS the remainder of the ground given Catharine by D. Young and use of the alley--in common w/Jacob Fortnay--and the privilege of building out over the alley.
WTT: Christian Slimmer, William Young, Michl. Gretter

410 27Jun86
Fm David Young, TwnALX, StVA
To Thomas Conn   -do-
WHEREAS David Young the ELDER at the time of his death owned 1/2 acre lot S side King and W side Royal
WHICH, when Young died intestate, descended to this David Young, eldest son and heir at law;
NOW for £160 cmv, DY conveys to TC part LOT 55:
BEGIN on King 50' W of int King-Royal ... W on King 24' to parcel sold to Earp & Wilson ... S//Royal 72' 6"... E//King 24'... thence N to BEGIN.
WTT: Geo. Deneale, Wm. McKnight, Robert Conn

413 21Feb87
Fm James Halladay, TwnALX, FfxCo, StVA, **Shoemaker**
To Joseph Greenway -do-, **Storekeeper**
WHEREAS Robert & Ann Allison 01May84 granted to JH part LOT [lot not numbered here]:
BEGIN on Wolfe 23' fm int Ffx-Wolfe ... E w/Wolfe 20' ... N//Ffx 100' to alley 10' wide called Allison's Alley ... W w/alley //Wolfe 20 perches [sic] ... thence to BEGIN;
NOW for £112 lawful money of the state JH grants it to JG.
WTT: P. Marsteller, John Harper, Robert Hunter

415 18Apr87
Fm John & Elizabeth Longdon, TwmALX, FfxCo, CwlVA
To Samuel Simmonds -do- : for £75 cmv, part LOT 55, W side Royal, S side King Sts:
BEGIN W side Royal 170' 8" S of int King-Royal at N corner of LOT 55 ... S//Royal 15'... W//King 123' 6" to W boundary of LOT 55 ... N//Royal 15'... E//King 123' 6" to BEGIN--this being part of lot conveyed to JL by William Young 13Jan87;
--John Longdon will lay off "sixteen Inches and a half of Ground...adjoining N side of this parcel fm Royal St and extending so far Westwardly as may be necessary and convenient for an Alley to the front Building that may hereafter be erected on Royall Street." Simmonds is to lay off 16 1/2" on the N side of this parcel, to match, so that they both "possess and enjoy in common the full use and advantages, Profits and Emoluments of an Alley Two feet nine Inches in Width from Royal Street under the second Story of their front Building on said Street as far Westwardly as may be Necessary to give each of the parties their Heirs and Assigns free Access of passing and repassing into and out of their adjoining back yards or Lotts without any Hindrance of each other whatsoever."
--"And it is also...agreed...that which ever of the parties...do and shall first Build...a House on the front part of Royall Street: after he raises to the Heights of the first Story...may...extend his Wall above to the Centre of the Alley so that one half the thickness of the Wall or Gavel [sic] end of the same may be on the North side of the Eastwardly or fourth line of the above Described...parcel ...and the other half...on the South side of the same line... and the party who may build afterwards shall have... liberty...to join his House or Building to the one already Built above the first Story... for which he promises to pay ...the party first Building one half the value thereof."
[This finely drawn contract introduces the Federal period streetscape of townhouses with joined facades.]
WTT: Philip Webster, Joseph Gardner, John Keith, John Doyear [or Doye<u>ac</u>]

420 06Nov86
Fm Thomas & Ann West, FfxCo, StVA
To William Hepburn & John Dundas, TwnALX, StVA:
For £250 Virginia Currency, part LOT 8:

BEGIN NW corner of Lot at int Oronoko-Water Sts ... W w/Water St 160' to line of Hunter & Allison ... E along H&A's line paralleling Oro 123' 6"... N//Water St 160' to Oro ... W w/Oro 123' 5" to Water St and BEGIN.
--this property from Hugh West via his will to his daughter Sybil, then from Sybil to Thomas West.
WTT: Thomas Conn, Geo. Deneale, James McKenna, James Scott
CMN: Chas. Little, Wm. Payne aptd 16Apr87 to examine Ann. Rptd back 20Apr87.

425 22Feb87 Bond
Fm George Summers, Cleon Moore, R.T.Hooe and Peter Wagener--all of TwnALX
For £1000, to **Governor** Edmond Randolph **Esquire**, for George Summers--appointed Sergeant of [this ALX] Court of Hustings.

426 26Feb87 Bond
Fm James Mease McCrea and John Allison--both of FfxCo.
For £1000, to **Governor** Edmund Randolph, for JMMcC--appointed Searcher of the District of Alexandria. (Searcher in the Port of ALX. See the Act of the Assembly concerning Naval Officers and the collection of duties.)

[Last page, unnumbered] 04Apr87 Power of Attorney
Fm Stephen Williams, City of London, **Linendraper**
To Thomas Williams & Joseph Cary [no ID]
WTT: Benjamin Everingham, John Williams
[Peter Wagener, the **Clerk** of Court, writes: "At the request of Thomas Williams and Joseph Cary I have recorded the above Instrument of Writing or power of atorney, in L.B. [Liber B] back of the book there not being sufficient proof to admit the same legally to record, done in office this 29th day of April 1789."]

End of Book B

ALEXANDRIA HUSTINGS COURT

Deed Book C, 1787-1789

1 13Nov86
Fm Hugh Mitchell, TwnALX, FfxCo, StVA
To James Hendricks & Francis Peyton -do- as tenants in common;
WHEREAS Sarah Ramsay 24Apr86 leased part LOT 54 to Mitchell at 25 1/4 Guineas each 01Sep;
NOW HM for £285 cmv plus their paying S. Ramsay the rent, conveys to JH & FP a parcel:
BEGIN on King at E line of lot conveyed by Michael & Hannah Madden to Alexander Smith--92' E of Royal ... S w/Smith's line 100' to a 20' alley ... E w/alley 25' 3"... N//Royal 100' to King ... thence on King to BEGIN.
WTT: Robert Allison, Thomas Barclay, James Patton, Edwd. Harper

7 19Mar87
Fm Joseph & Lucy Conway, Northumberland Co, VA
To Richard Conway, TwnALX, FfxCo, StVA:
Part of a lot S of Prince, W Pitt:
BEGIN on Pitt 154' S of Prince ... S w/Pitt 22' 6" to line of Josiah Watson ... W w/Watson's line 123' 5"... N//Pitt 22' 6" ... thence to BEGIN.
(This was Thomas Conway's; fm him via his will to Joseph and others; others conveyed their interest to Joseph 02Apr87)
WTT: Jas. Keith, Colin MacIver, John McIver, George Richards, William Hickman, Junr; John Rogers, John Hull
CMN: John Hull, John Rogers and John Gordon, all of Northumberland Co, aptd 20Mar87 to examine Lucy. Rptd back 02Apr87.

15 [James Mercer's plat for deeds he issued 22May87 to purchasers at public auction by the Vendue Master of the Town of Alexandria. [See p. 16]
WTT: John Murray, Ch. Simms

16 22May87
Account of Sales "for J. Mercer **Esquire** of Seven Lotts of Ground in the Town of Alexandria, late the Estate of Colo. George Mercer deceased."

No.1 William H. Powell for Leven Powell   £260.0
   2 John Murray for Daniel & Isaac McPherson   60.5
   3 [same for same]   60.5
   4 William Lyles   65.0
   5 John Murray for Daniel & Isaac McPherson   71.10
   6 Jonah Thompson   71.10
   7 George Slacum   70.0
                  £658.0.0
  Attested: P. Marsteller, Vend. Mastr.

16   22May87
Fm the **Honorable** James Mercer, Spotsylvania Co
To Daniel & Isaac McPherson, TwnALX, **Merchants**
WHEREAS George Mercer **Esquire**, late of City of London, dec'd
--possessed 1 1/2 acre LOT in ALX, purchased fm ALX Trustees
--"corner Lott Nr [blank]"
--"being one corner of a square" bounded by Duke and Water Streets, in FfxCo Court Deed Books
--and GM died intestate, and w/o wife or child, April 1784
--the lot then vested in James Mercer as oldest brother and heir at law
--James, "unacquainted with the Engagements of the said GM entered into before his death" --and to assure clear title, applied to the late General Assembly at their last session;
--Assembly gave him title, but required him to sell at public auction w/12 months credit, taking bond w/security from purchasers
--and remaining chargeable for the sale amounts to any "Trustee, Mortgagee or Devisee that hereafter might appear and have best title to"
--and at a public sale, this date, advertised in the <u>Alexandria Gazette</u>
    --sold parcels 2,3 & 5 to the McPhersons [note in the Plat, these parcels were purchased for the McPhersons by John Murray] and
    --No. 4 to William Lyles
    --No. 1 to Leven Powell
    --No. 6 to Jonah Thompson
    --No. 7 to George Slacum
    --with both alleys "for the benefit of the said purchasers"
NOW for £192, JM conveys title to Nos. 2, 3 & 5 to the McPhersons
WTT: John Murray, James Lawrason, John Reynolds, George Slacum

22   16Jun86
Fm Baldwin & Catharine Dade, TwnALX, FfxCo, CwlVA
To David Griffith, **Clerk**, FfxCo
[As at ALX Deed Book A, p. 53, this entry recites the Dades' purchase fm Thomas West of a parcel, the description of which seems clearer here:]
BEGIN 123' 5 1/2" fm NW corner of Pitt and Queen, adjoining William Hepburn's LOT 124 ... S80W in line w/N side of Queen 89 poles, crossing the present Georgetown Rd to old Gtwn Rd...
N20W 51 perches along old Gtwn Rd to the line between Alexander and West ...
N80E paralleling first course 80 perches to the old Town Line ... S10E 50 perches along old Town Line to BEGIN--the parcel thus totaling 26 acres + 98 poles;
BUT notes that on 25Aug84, before the Dades' purchase, T.West had sold out of this land certain parcels;
AND that after the Dades had sold certain parcels, they sold what remained of the land to David Griffith, Griffith to pay £100 01Dec86, £200 01Dec87 and £300 01Dec88 and every year thereafter;

FURTHER: on 09Nov84, to secure some £2000 cmv w/interest to Henry Lee, Jr., the Dades signed the rents due from Griffith over to Lee;
NOW as Griffith has undertaken to pay Lee the total Dade note of £2400, the Dades make over all the rents to Griffith.
WTT: John Fitzgerald, Philip Webster, Jas. Keith
CMN: John Fitzgerald & James Keith aptd 24Jun86 to examine Catharine. [Clerk records reporting back 24Jun8<u>7</u>, but probably should be 8<u>6</u>.]

31 22May87
[see page 16, above]
James Mercer conveys to Jonah Thompson title to Mercer LOT 6 within LOT 80.
WTT: Ch. Simms, Thomas Swann, James Hughes, Wm. Herbert

37 22May87
[see pp. 16, 31, above]
James Mercer conveys to George Slacum title to Mercer LOT 7 within LOT 80
WTT: Isaac McPherson, John Reynolds, John Murray, James Lawrason

42 29Mar87
Fm David & Hannah Griffith, **Clerk**, FfxCo, StateVA
To Baldwin Dade "of the same Town County and State" [Clerical inconsistency: either the Griffiths should have been identified as fm Town of Alexandria, or Dade should <u>not</u> have been]
WHEREAS DG by a 15Jan86 note acknowledged himself bound to BD for £900-- £450 to be Virginia Money in specie "or the Value thereof in any paper money which may be emitted by the Assembly of Virginia at the passing Value of such paper money when the same should be renedered in payment"
--and BD signed to forego the interest if the principle of £450 is paid on/before 15Jun90
--and BD has since assigned the promissary note, and is himself now liable for the interest if Griffith fails to pay;
NOW to secure his note, Griffith mortgages to BD:
BEGIN N side of Queen at W corner of land belonging to Butcher and Paton ... W w/Queen to "the said Griffith's Corner at the Old George Town road"... N w/that road to Griffith's corner in Alexander's line ... E w/[ALXR] line to lot formerly Baldwin Dade's ... S w/[Dade] lot line <u>and</u> Griffith's other ground to Princess ... thence w/that line to BEGIN.
(This is the same land BD granted to DG 08Nov84)   WTT: none

47 30Dec86
Fm David Griffith, **Doctor in Divinity**, and wife Hannah, FfxCo, CwlVA
To Henry Roome, City of New York, StateNY, **Merchant**
WHEREAS Elizabeth Colvill late of New Town in Queens Co on Nassau Island, widow, did in her will bequeath to the children of her daughter, Hannah--wife of the Revd. Griffith--1/3 of her estate;
--and as Elizabeth was bound as security for and with David Griffith to Richard Charlton for £100 lawful money of NY w/interest--and if David did not pay, the requisite sum was to be deducted from the grandchildren's bequest;
--and because David was absent from New York when Richard Charlton died, and the exxrs of Elizabeth paid the exxrs of Charlton £137.14--a sum to be drawn from the grandchildren's bequest--leaving the children a balance of £423.16.4, lawful money of New York;
--and at DG's request, Henry Roome has agreed to lend David (at interest) the £423.16.4;

--and as Baldwin & Catharine Dade, **Merchant,** sold David Griffith on 09Nov84 a tract the Dades bought from T. West 25Aug84 [described as at ALX Deed Book A, p.54, and p. 22, above] containing 26 acres and 98 poles--minus what West and the Dade had sold;
--and Dade in 1786 to get £2000 (w/interest) from Henry Lee, Jr., signed over to Lee the rents from Griffith;
--and DG signed £2400 note for BD to give to Lee, thus remitting the Griffith rents;
--and on 21-22June Griffith sold by public vendue certain lots w/in the parcel bought from Dade;
--and Henry Lee, Jr., and Griffith signed an agreement in Philadelphia 05Dec86 that--in return for Griffith assigning to Lee £204 cmv of rents from the property sold 21-22June--that Lee will give Griffith the bond Dade and Lee signed, and give up the mortgage;
BUT--as there may not be enough in rents, Lee may choose an unsold lot(s) and make up the difference at the rate of six shillings per front foot;
NOW to secure Roome's loan of £423.16.4 to Griffith, Griffith mortgages to Roome the land Griffith bought from Dade
    --the loan to be repaid on/before next 30 Dec at 7%
    --or a penal sum of £847.12.8
WTT and signed in New York by: David & Hannah Griffith; John B. Dark [or Dartz]; D. Ritzema Bogert; John Dover, Jr.

67 19Jun87
Fm William & Milly Roach, FfxCo, CwlVA
To John Dowdall   -do-
Lease part of lot N side Princess, W side St. Asaph:
BEGIN SE corner of lot ... on Princess 32'... N//St A 43'... E 32' to St A ... thence w/St. Asaph to BEGIN.
Terms: each 01Jul beginning 1787 £12.10 in Specie, Dollars at 6/ each, 1/2 Johanneses of 9 pennyweight at 48/
[John Dowdall signs; William & Milly Roach each sign w/mark]
WTT: Wm. Allison, Thos. Patterson, Elizabeth Allison

71 13Mar87
Fm David Young [no ID]
To John Weathers Harper, **Taylor,** TwnALX, FfxCo, StVA:
For £200 cmv, "a certain corner Lott" [no ID]:
BEGIN at house of Thomas Conn on King St ... E on King 51' 6" ... S 47' on Royal to the house of David Young ... W 51' 6" ... thence 47' to BEGIN--plus privilege of 3' alley "on the East front on said David Young's Dwelling House"
WTT: J. C. Kempffs, Thomas Ramsay, James Grimes

74 13Aug86
William & Elizabeth Anderson, TwnALX, FfxCo, CwlVA
To Thomas Reed   -do-
WHEREAS 08Aug82 William Hepburn conveyed to WA part LOT 124:
BEGIN SE corner of parcel conveyed by Hepburn to Andrew Judge, and 40' fm SW corner LOT 124 on Qn ... E w/Queen 40'... N// Pitt 90'... W//Queen 40'... thence to BEGIN--for yearly rent each 08Aug of 20 silver $, the rent remittable on paying $400 w/in 20 years;
NOW for £16 paid, the Andersons grant the property to Reed
--Reed now to pay the rent to Hepburn, with the same rent remittal privilege.
WTT: Roger Chew, Michl. Gretter, James Smith

79 05Jun86
Fm Charles Lee, TwnALX, FfxCo, CwlVA
To Dennis Ramsay -do- : lease fm 05Jun87 @ 47 2/9 Silver $
of part LOT 103--N side Wolfe, E side Pitt Sts (LOT 103 and other land fm Thomas Conway to his heirs via his 27Sep84 will, and by the heirs/exxrs to Charles Lee 14Dec84):
BEGIN corner Pitt & Wolfe ... E on Wolfe 32' 3"... N//Pitt 94' 6"... W//Wolfe to Pitt ... thence on Pitt to BEGIN.
--Ramsay w/in 2 yrs to build "one good strong substantial Dwelling house of the dimentions [sic] of twenty feet square at least filled in with Lime and sand and having a brick or Stone Chimney"
WTT: Baldwin Dade, James Smith, Samuel (his+mark) Simmons

86 08Jul85
Fm William & Sarah Herbert, TwnALX, FfxCo, StVA
To Neil Mooney -do- : lease on/from 06Jul91 at 48 Spanish milled $ + taxes due of part LOT 3, N of Oro, E of Water Sts: BEGIN on Oronoko on line between LOTS 3, 4 ... N w/ line one half the line--137' 6"... E//Oro 24'... S//Water St 137' 6"
... thence to BEGIN. (William Herbert "shall and will use his Interest with Robert Adam to lay out an Alley through the said Lotts No. (3 & 4)") [This parcel is to extend to that alley.]   WTT: Jas. Keith, Jacob Cox, John Moss
MEMO: WH will pay taxes on the land. Mooney will pay taxes on improvements, existing and future.   WTT to Memo: Petr. Wagener, G. Deneale

93 20Jul87
Fm McKinsey & Conny [wife] Tallbutt, FfxCo
To Jesse Taylor, TwnALX, FfxCo, **Merchant**: for £100 lawful money of VA, part of a lot on Royal and Queen:
BEGIN S side Queen, 103' 5" from Queen & Royal ... E on Queen 25' to Robert Adam's line ... S w/Adam's line//Royal 88' 3 1/2"... W//Queen 20'... N//Royal to BEGIN. (Part of a larger parcel devised by the will of William Shaw to his daughters, Isabel Elton and Elizabeth Shaw, as tenants in common--and on 20May85 by deed from Isabel to McKinsey Tallbutt)
[Both Tallbutts signed with a mark]   WTT: none

98 06Jul87
Fm John Harper, FfxCo, StVA, **Gentleman**
To William Hickman, Junr., AND John Hickman, TwnALX, StVA:
Lease on/after 01 Oct88 @ 9 2/3 Spanish milled $ or in 9 pennyweight Half Johannes at 48/ each or in 5 pennyweight, 6 grain Guineas at 28/ each, of part LOT 58, on N side Prince:
BEGIN 88' E int Ffx-Prince ... E on Prince 4' 10"... N//Ffx 48' to line between John Harper and Josiah Watson ... W w/line //Prince 4' 10" to line of parcel granted by Harper to James Lownes ... S w/line to BEGIN.
--originally conveyed by Trustees to Geo. Wm. Fairfax
--the Hickmans commit to build w/in 3 years "one Brick house 4' 10" front upon Prince Street and at least 30' deep and 2 Stories high and finish the same in a tenentable manner both inside and out." [4' 10" is spelled out 3 times in the deed.]
--Harper allows that they can "extend one half of the East Gavel [sic] end of the house...upon the Ground of...John Harper adjoining."
--Harper will pay the Hickmans "whatever one half of the said Gavel shall be at that time judged to be worth."
WTT: Geo. Summers, Gurden Chapin, John McIver, Robert Greeves

108 23Jun85
CMN: William McCauley, John Taylor and William Courtney of Orange Co., North Carolina, to examine Susannah Findley about the 16Jun85 sale by her and her husband, Hugh, to John Hickman of a parcel in ALX. [See Deed Book A, p. 79] Rptd back 9Jul85.

110 23Jun85
CMN: William McCauley, John Taylor and William Courtney of Orange Co., North Carolina, to examine Susannah Findley about the 20Jun85 sale by her and her husband, Hugh, to John Hickman of a parcel in ALX. [See Deed Book A, p. 74] Rptd back 9Jul85.

112 29Dec86
Fm James & Sarah Lownes, TwnALX, FfxCo, StateVA
To William Hickman, Junr., AND John Hickman of the same, for £30 a part LOT 58, N side of Prince:
BEGIN 69' E of int Prince-Ffx ... E w/Prince 19'... N//Ffx 48' to line "between him the said John Harper & Josiah Watson" [person drafting this deed has lifted phrasing from the Harper to Hickman deed at p. 98, above, or the Harper to Lownes deed referred to below] ... W w/line//Prince 19' to line of "Lott granted by him the said John Harper unto Aaron Hughes"... S w/lot line to BEGIN--the Hickmans to pay the annual rent due John Harper on/after 01 Oct of 38 silver Spanish Milled $.
By virtue of a 06Nov83 indenture conveying this from Harper to James Lownes, recorded in FfxCo Court Liber O, folio 254:
--instead of Spanish milled $: in Half Johanneses of 9 pennyweight at 48/ each...or Guineas of 5 pennyweight + 6 grains at 28/ ea.
--Lownes was to build one brick house of 19' front on Prince, at least 30' deep and 2 stories [and now the Hickmans must.]
Harper will permit "one half of the East Gable end...to be built on the [Harper] ground" and will pay half the value [see p. 98, above]
WTT: Michl. Swoope, Aaron Hughes, Israel Right

118 28Jun87
Fm John & Rachel Jolly, TwnALX
To Thomas Williams AND Joseph Cary -do- : mortgage to secure £180 owed Williams and Cary, with part of LOT 126, W side Pitt, S side Princess:
BEGIN 93' 3" S of int Pitt-Princess ... S w/Pitt 36' 3 1/2"... W 123' 5"... S//Pitt 36' 3 1/2"... thence E//Princess to BEGIN.
WTT: James Kennedy, Wm. Anderson, John Edw. Ford

121 10Sep87
Fm John Allison, TwnALX, CwlVA
To John Rumney for £400 part LOT 38, W of Ffx, N of Cameron:
BEGIN 117 1/2' on Ffx fm intersection w/Cam ... N w/Ffx 23' to William Herbert's line ... W//Cam 123' 5" to W line of LOT 38 ... S w/lot line//Ffx same as 1st ... thence to BEGIN.
(Sold to John Allison by William Ramsay 20Dec84 and recorded in FfxCo Court)
WTT: Joseph Cary, Thos. Porter, W. Hodgson

125 23Mar87
Fm Michael Swoope, TwnALX, FfxCo, StVA
To Adam Simon Swoope & Jacob Swope [sic] as tenants in common
For £600, part lot on S of Prince, W of Water Streets:

BEGIN on Prince at line between LOTS 64-65 ... S w/line between the lots 98' 6"...
E//Prince 23'... N//Water St 98' 6"... thence W on Prince 23' to BEGIN--conveyed to
Michael Swoope by R. McCrea & R. Mease 20Dec84
[Michael's wife's name is given as Eve]
WTT: Jas. Keith, Christian Slimmer, Jacob Bott

129 22May87
[see pp. 16, 31, 37, above]
James Mercer conveys to William Lyles title to Mercer LOT 4 within LOT 80
WTT: Ch. Simms, Th. Swann, James Hughes, Wm. Herbert

134 22May87
[see pp. 16, 31, 37, 129 above]
James Mercer conveys to Leven Powell title to Mercer LOT 1 within LOT 80
WTT: as above

138 29Sep87
Adam Simon Swoope AND Jacob Swoope, TwnALX, StVA
OWING Benjamin Augustus Hamp £59 cmv AND also Herbert & Potts £46.14.1 1/2
w/ interest from 19Feb86:
CONSTITUTE Hamp their attorney to rent "that Lott of Ground and Brick house
belonging to us upon Prince Street"
--and to apply the rents to the debt, after which the property reverts to the Swoopes
WTT: John Dunlap, Ebenezer Stark

140 09 Oct87
Fm Valentine Peers, Charles Co, MD
To John Rumney, TwnALX, FfxCo, StateVA
For £340 cmv, part of a lot S of King, W of Water:
BEGIN at int King-Water Sts ... W w/King 32'... S//Water St 82' to 10' alley which
divides Peer's land fm John Fitzgerald's ... E w/alley 32' to Water St ... thence on
Water St. to BEGIN--part of LOT 52 sold by Trustees to John Patterson, and by
Patterson's widow to Peers & Fitzgerald--and, upon a land division, this to Peers;
--the alley fm Ffx to Water Sts to be kept open for mutual use
WTT: Jonah Thompson, Thos. Porter, Ichabod Hunter

145 13Jul87   Power of Attorney
Fm Benjamin Bowdon late of Liverpool but at present in ALX
To "my friends" John Hollins of Baltimore; Phillip Marsteller AND Jonah Thompson,
both of ALX to act for "me...the surviving partner of Kirk & Bowdon"
WTT: Ben. A. Hamp, Ebenezer Stark, Michael Shugart

147 16May87
Fm John Steel, TwnALX, StVA
To William Hunter, Jr., **Esquire**, of -do- : a mortgage to secure £19.18.0, of "...a
certain house and Lott of Ground on Queen..." which Steel has on Ground rent of
Eleanor Shaw" at £6 per year. Debt to be repaid on/before 16May88.
WTT: Alexr. Buchan, James Patton

148 23May87   [Deed of Release]
William Sydebotham of Bladensburg remits claim to the negroes Sarah and Jack used
as collateral by James Meyler, late of Berkley Co, VA, to secure a 20Jan85 debt of
10,000 lbs. of inspected crop tobacco.
WTT: Wm. Ward, Wm. Dalton

150 04Dec87
Fm John Wise, TwnALX, FfxCo, CwlVA
To Elizabeth Wise--his wife
--to "enable his said wife Elizabeth to make provision for her children in case the said John Wise should die before her; and in consideration of the love and affection which he beareth towards his said wife"...
--conveys to her "Wise's Lott on Fairfax Street, between King and Prince Streets being 19' in front on Fairfax Street and extending Westwardly...120' with the three storied brick House thereon in which Messers Saunderson & Rumney at present keep Store...." Also: a Negro girl Ramey
WTT: D. Arell, G. Richards, Moses Tandy

152 28 Oct85   Power of Attorney
Fm James Taylor, TwnALX, **Merchant**
To Josiah Watson -do-
WTT: John Brent, Theodorick Lee, John L. [or, more likely, "S."] Pleasants

154 18Jul87
Fm John & Anne Short, TwnALX, FfxCo, StVA
To Thomas Richards -do- : for £37.10.0 cmv PLUS each 01Jan 40 Spanish milled $ to George Gilpin, part of a lot S of Prince:
BEGIN on Prince at NW corner of parcel conveyed by George Gilpin to Washer Blunt ... W w/Prince 20'... S//Water St 44' 4" to parcel of heirs of Jonathan Hall, dec'd... E//Prince 20'
... thence to BEGIN. (Part of half-lot conveyed by George & Jane Gilpin to Andrew Wales, and by Wales to J. Short)
Wtt: Jas. Keith; Jno.Contee Keith; James Keith, Junr; [clerk then sketches names of two people whose signatures he cannot read]: Andrew hay_ _ _ and K. B_bltt_.
CMN: Wm. Brown, Wm. Herbert, Richard Conway aptd 18Dec87 to examine Anne. Rptd same day.

160 09Mar85
Fm Joseph & Rebecca Greenway, TwnALX, FfxCo, StVA
To Robert Lyle -do- : part of LOTS 23-24, W of Ffx, E of Royal, S of Princess:
BEGIN on Ffx at corner of parcel granted by Lyle to Windle Bright, and 31' N of LOT 28 ... N w/Ffx 25'... W// Princess 246' 10" to Royal ... S w/Royal 25'... thence E to BEGIN--(which Lyle on __ __ 17__ granted to Greenway) [Some one has pencilled in the blanks to read Feb 19, 1783]
WTT: Jas. Keith, Edward Harper, Chas. McIver

163 07Jul87
Fm Joseph & Rebecca Greenway, TwnALX, FfxCo, StVA
To William Hunter, Senr. -do- : for £112 cmv, part of the lot N of Wolfe, E of Ffx:
BEGIN on Wolfe 23' E of Ffx St ... E w/Wolfe 20'... N//Ffx 100' to 10' alley--"Allison's Alley"... W w/alley and //Wolfe 20'... thence to BEGIN. (Same parcel conveyed by Robert & Ann Allison to James Holliday, who sold it to Greenway 21Feb87)
WTT: Jas. Keith, S. [or "L."] Hanson of Saml [or "of Taml"]; Robert Allison, Edward Harper

167 11Jul87
Fm Richard & Eleanor Arell, TwnALX, FfxCo, StVA
To William Hunter, Senr. -do-
WHEREAS WH ("by and with the approbation of RA") married Christiana (daughter of RA) "by whom he hath had several children"

--and RA "being desirous of enabling...WH to make a further provision for...Christiana and the Children which he may have"
--"In consideration of the Marriage and £10 cmv"--conveys to WH part of a lot W of Union, N of Duke:
BEGIN on Union at line bewteen Arell and Gilpin ... W w/line 70'... S//Union 29' 6"... E//1st line 70' to Union St ... thence to BEGIN. (This is part of LOTS 69-70 granted by Trustees to Nathaniel Harrison, who sold them to Richard Arell)   WTT: none

172 29Sep87
Fm William & Christiana Hunter, Senr., TwnALX, FfxCo, StVA
To Peter Bohrer -do-: part LOT 163, S of Wilkes, W of Water St BEGIN on Water St 176' 7" S of Wilkes at SE corner LOT 163 ... W w/lot line 123' 5" to lot's west line ... N w/lot line 49' 3"... E//Wilkes 123' 5" to Water St ... thence to BEGIN.
(Conveyed by Robert Adam to William Hunter, Senr.)
WTT: Jas. Keith, Jacob Cox, George Cox

175 29Sep87
Fm William & Christiana Hunter, Senr., TwnALX, FfxCo, StVA
To Peter Bohrer   -do-
WHEREAS the same date indenture [above] conveys ground for which £25 cmv rent is annually due William Thornton Alexander,
AND WHEREAS WH wishes to secure PB from non-payment penalties
NOW the Hunters convey title to that part of lot N of Wilkes, W of Royal:
BEGIN at int Wilkes-Royal, on Wilkes ... W w/Wilkes 123' 5"...
N w/lot line//Royal 88'... E//Wilkes 123' 5" to Royal ... thence to BEGIN--conveyed to WH Senr 15Feb79 by Andrew & Margaret Wales. (Title does not really pass unless the Hunters fail to pay the annual rent to Alexander.)
WTT: Jas. Keith, Jacob Cox, George Cox

180 [undated]   Power of Attorney
Fm George Boden, City of Bristol, Great Britain, **Mariner**
To "my trusty and Loving friend Jesse Taylor of ALX, **Merchant**
WTT: John Edw. Ford, Geo. Clements, Andrew Taylor
(Proven in ALX by Ford and Clements 22Dec87.)

182 24Apr88
Fm James & Ann Thompson, State of Maryland
To John Dowdall, TwnALX, CwlVA
WHEREAS William & Agnes Hepburn of TwnALX on 30Aug85 (and recorded in Court of Fairfax) conveyed 1/4 acre N of Princess, W of St. Asaph to James Thompson, for annual rent of £50 specie beginning 01Jul86:
BEGIN at SE corner of lot ... W w/Princess 63'... N//St. Asaph 176' 6"... E//Princess 63'... thence w/St. Asaph to BEGIN;
AND WHEREAS on ___ __, 178_, [date left blank] (recorded in FfxCo Court), the Thompsons for £25 annual rent conveyed half this parcel to William Roach;
NOW the Thompsons lease to John Dowdall the other half of the parcel for £50 specie each 01Jul payable to Wm. Hepburn. [Ann Thompson signs w/mark]
WTT: William Summers, Joseph Fullmore, Will--- Y[?]--- [name cut off page in rebinding the deed book]

186 18Jan88
Fm William Hunter, Junr., TwnALX, FfxCo, CwlVA, **Merchant**
To Josiah Wattson -do- **Merchant**
WHEREAS Hugh West the Elder died seized of LOT 14

--his will devised it to his widow Sybill West and thence to her daughter--Sybill--the daughter since Hugh's death having died without issue;
--and thereby the lot became vested in Thomas West, heir to Sybill [Hugh's widow];
--and Widow Sybill leased the lot to William Ward for 9 years fm 01Jan83, a lease confirmed by Thomas West;
AND WHEREAS West on 01May84 conveyed to William Hunter, Junr. and John Allison, as tenants in common, part of LOT 14:
BEGIN on Water St 88' N of int Water-Princess ... N w/Wtr St to NE corner LOT 14 ... E//Princess into Potomac River ... down the Potomac to intersect a line paralleling Princess from the BEGIN point ... thence //Princess (on this line) to BEGIN;
--including the ferry and ferry landing,
--PLUS the rights to the ferry and to wharfing out.
AND WHEREAS on 08Dec86 William Hunter, Junr., asked Josiah Wattson to be security for a note signed by WHJr & Robert Townshend Hooe to John Hunter (the security being £2800 for a £1400 note);
NOW to secure Josiah Wattson, WHJr mortgages half the parcel granted Hunter & Allison (final title not passing to Wattson unless Wattson has to make good his security committment.)
WTT: Alex. Buchan, Joseph Darling, David Findlay

192 22Apr88
Fm William Ownbread, TwnALX, FfxCo, StVA
To Jacob Wisemiller -do- : for £120 cmv the corner lot, 20' front on Princess, 88' on St. Asaph.
WTT: C.B.Kempff, James Smith, [clerk sketches a name which he cannot decipher: Migal Rirbre]   [Mary Ownbread signs w/mark]

194 26Jan87
Fm Henry Gardner, TwnALX, FfxCo, CwlVA
To John Reynolds AND Alexander Smith -do-
WHEREAS Gardner is indebted to:

James Hendricks & Co	13.5.1
William Lyles & James Hendricks as admrs of Henry Lyles, dec'd	46.13. 9
Reynolds & Barclay	19.03.10
Alexander Smith	4.19. 3
Lawrence Hoof	10.17. 1 1/2
Samuel Montgomery Brown	7. 0. 0
Hepburn & Dundas	4.15. 2
Jonah Thompson	-. -. 29

"and whereas the said HG having lately sustained considerable losses is at present unable to make payment";
AND WHEREAS Robert Adam **Gentleman** and Ann his wife on 02Apr86 conveyed to HG part Lot S of Princess, E of Water St. and "extending across Union St. into the river Potomack":
BEGIN on W side of "Alley laid out by Robert Adam in the centre between Water and Union Sts"--70' 6" S of intersection of the alley and Princess, the South line of a lot granted by Robert & Ann Adam to Michael & Ann McMahan ... W w/this lot line //Princess 52'... S//Water St 23' 6"... E//Princess 52'... to the Alley ... thence on alley to BEGIN--and to have the benefit of the alley w/Robert Adam;
NOW this property is put in trust to Reynolds & Smith for 12 months but if Gardner
--w/in 6 mos. pays 1/3 of debts
--w/in 9 months another 1/3
--w/in the 12, the remaining 1/3

--then this indenture is void
(If terms are not met after 12 mos. then Reynolds & Smith are to sell and divide the proceeds among the creditors proportionate to sums owed.)
WTT: Cleon Moore, William Warden, Michael Flynn, Henry Gardner, Junr.

199 02 Oct86
"John Tarbuck alias Scott," **Mariner,** hereby confirms receipt of £80 for the sale of part LOT 28 "known by the name of the Long Ordinary" to William Patterson of Beaufort Co., North Carolina, as per an indenture "sometime in the year 1785."
--Signed in Beaufort Co, NoCar:
    John Tarbuck Scott

201 02 Oct86
Fm William & Sarah Herbert, TwnALX, FfxCo, StVA
To Robert Adam "of the County & State aforesaid":
For £250 current money, part of LOT 38:
BEGIN W of Ffx, N of Cameron at int Ffx-Cameron ... N w/Ffx 58' 10 1/3"... W//Cam 41' 1 1/3"... S//Ffx 58' 10 1/3"... E w/Cameron 41' 1 1/3" to BEGIN. (Part of LOT 38, sold by Robert Adam as exxr of James Muir, dec'd, to Wm. Herbert 29Jul83.)
WTT: Saml. Montgomery Brown, Augustus Delarue, Robert B. Jamisson, Ja. Keith

205 22Mar88
Fm William Hunter, Junr., TwnALX, FfxCo, CwlVA, **Merchant**
To Rachel Lomax, widow of John Lomax, deceased, -do- :
For £213 cmv, part of LOT 16:
BEGIN W corner LOT 15, N side Princess ... W w/Princess 24'... N 100' to alley 9' wide ... E w/alley 24' //Princess ... thence 100' to BEGIN.   WTT: none

213 29Feb88
William Willson, late of ALX, now in Glasgow, Scotland
--partner in trade with:
    James Willson the Elder
    James Willson the Younger
    Cumberland Willson
        --all of the Town of Kilmarnock, County of Air [Ayr]
--doing business under the name of James Wilson [sic] & Sons.
NOW the firm is in debt [possibly bankrupt] and surrendering its assets to referees in Antigua, Granada, Dominica, Guadaloupe, Saint Lucia; province of Quebec, Canada; much land in ALX [none identified.]
NOW this is a declaration that WW hereby conveys his titles, as required. [See next entry]

214 01Mar88 [Power of Attorney]
Gilbert Hamilton of Glasgow states that on 02Nov87 the partners of James Wilson & Sons assigned their property to him. He had designated William Willson to act for him in ALX. However, now that WW has returned to Glasgow, he instead designates "James Wilson Lawful Son of...James Wilson the younger now of Kilmarnock but who is soon to sail for the State of Virginia." [This is, in effect, a Power of Attorney for James Wilson.]

219 18Jun88
James Wilson's Power of Attorney [above] is ordered recorded in the ALX Hustings Court.

219 29Feb88 Power of Attorney
Fm (William Paterson of Braehead
   (Bruce Campbell of Mayfield
   (John Gemmill, Town of Irving, **Merchant**
   --all in the County of Ayr, North Britain
To "James Wilson Junior late of Alexandria now residing in Kilmarnock. [See following entry.]

213 18Jun88
This second Power of Attorney, above, for James Wilson is ordered recorded in the ALX Hustings Court.

223 07May88
Fm William Newton, TwnALX
To Thomas Williams AND Joseph Cary -do- :
For £35, part of LOT 126, W of Pitt, S of Princess:
BEGIN 93' S of int Pitt-Princess ... S w/Pitt 36' 3 1/2"... W 123' 5"... N//Pitt 36' 3 1/2"... E w/Princess to BEGIN. WTT: Baldwin Dade, William Summers, Wm. Hodgson

225 20Dec87
Fm Philip & Magdalena Marsteller, TwnALX, FfxCo, StVA, **Storekeeper**
To John Korn -do- **Baker:**
WHEREAS George & Jane Gilpin **Esquire**, FfxCo, 01Jun86 leased to PM part LOT [blank] E of Water St, S of Prince:
BEGIN int Water-Prince Sts ... E w/Prince 45' to line of lot Gilpin conveyed to Samuel Montgomery Brown ... S w/SMB's line //Water St 44' 4" to land of heirs of Jonathan Hall, deceased ... W w/Hall line //Prince 45' to Water St... thence w/Water St to BEGIN--rent each 01Jun 45 Guineas, all this recorded in FfxCo Court;
NOW the Marstellers lease to JK for 23 Guineas each 01June:
BEGIN 22' fm int Prince-Water Sts ... E w/Prince 23' to land granted by Gilpin to SMBrown ... S w/SMB line //Water St 44' 4" to land of Hall's heirs ... W w/Hall line //Prince 23' to the "other part of the same Lott which is in...possession of Philip Marsteller"... N w/ this line and //Water St to BEGIN.
WTT:Christian Slimmer, Philip Marsteller, Junr.; [clerk sketches another name's Germanic script: Iomor Zrillmuller]

232 14Apr88
Fm Thomas & Sarah May, Borough of Wilmington, StDEL, **Esquire**
To John Potts, Junr., Montgomery Co, StPA
WHEREAS on 20Sep49 ALX Trustees conveyed to Gerard Alexander LOTS 31-32, conveyed via GA's will 09Aug60 to wife Mary;
--fm Mary and son Philip and Philip's wife Catharine 10-11Mar67 to John Glassford & Archibald Henderson;
--by JG & AH's attorney Alexander Henderson to John Gibson in 1776, and fm Gibson back to Alexander Henderson 03 Oct76;
--fm Alexander Henderson to William Herbert 01Jan78
--fm WH to Thomas May 18Feb88;
NOW the Mays for £1250 lawful money of PA convey 1/3 of the two lots to John Potts, Junr. [As no description is given this must be 1/3 interest]
WTT: Martha Chapman, Thomas Wilson; Jaco. Broom, Justice of the Peace for the Borough of Wilmington, "Notary and Tabellion Publick"

237 13Jun88
Fm John Rumney, TwnALX, FfxCo, CwlVA

To William Hodgson -do- : for £700, 2 parcels:
No. 1: BEGIN on Ffx 117 1/2' N of Ffx and Cameron ...
N w/Ffx to line of Wm. Herbert ... W//Cam 123' 5" to W line of LOT 38... S w/lot line //Ffx length of 1st line and E to BEGIN. (Conveyed by William Ramsay to John Allison 20Dec84, and recorded in FfxCo Court)
No. 2: on S side King, W of Water Streets:
BEGIN at int King-Water Sts ... W w/King 32'... S//Water St 82' to 10' alley dividing Valentine Peers from John Fitzgerald ... E w/alley 32' to Water St ... thence w/Water St to BEGIN. (No. 1 conveyed to Rumney by John Allison 10Sep87, and No. 2 by Valentine Peers 09 Oct87.)   WTT: Geo. Clementson, Ichd. Hunter, Wm. Bowness

241 13Jun88 Power of Attorney
Fm John Rumney "one of the partners of Robinson, Sanderson & Rumney" on their behalf
To William Hodgson   WTT: as above

243 14Jun88 Power of Attorney
Fm William Mounsher "late of London, having for some time past resided in Alexandria...and there carried on Merchandize ... having shortly an Intention of returning to England."
To "my Friend (living in Alexandria)" Mr [or "W"] Thomas Porter, **Attorney**
WTT: Val. Peers, Gideon Snow, Cleon Moore, Samuel Hanson of Samuel [sic]

244 21Feb88
Fm Arthur Lee, Richmond Co, VA
To Morris Herlihy, TwnALX, FfxCo, CwlVA: lease fm 01Apr89 @ 60 silver $ per year of part, Lot N side Duke, E of St.A, conveyed to Lee 03Jan86, and recorded in FfxCo Court:
BEGIN corner Duke & St. Asaph ... E//Duke 28'... N//St A 100' to alley ... W//Duke 20' w/alley ... S//St A 100' to BEGIN.
[Note difference in E, W lines, but as written by the clerk]
Terms: w/in 14 mos build "one Good strong substantial house ... 20' square at least and filed in with Lime and sand and having a brick or stone chimney." ALSO Lee will lay off 100' fm corner Duke & St. Asaph a 10' alley fm St. A, paralleling Duke, extending 100' back.   WTT: none

251 24 Oct88
Fm Samuel Montgomery Brown & wife Mary, TwnALX, FfxCo, StVA
To Henry Sadler, State of NY:
WHEREAS John Alexander's exxrs on 05Aug79 conveyed a 1/2 acre lot to Henry Rozer, E of Ffx, S of Wilkes:
BEGIN at Ffx and Wilkes ... S w/Ffx 176' 7"... E w/Wilkes 123' 5"[no further metes/-bounds given] ... Rozer to pay each 05Aug £20.10.0 cmv and to build a dwelling at least 400 sq.ft.;
--and Rozer conveyed this 05Nov84 to Saml. M. Brown.
NOW the Browns convey to Sadler for £320 cmv:
BEGIN on Wilkes 32' E of Ffx ... E w/Wilkes 81' 6"... S//Ffx 75'... W//Wilkes 81' 6" ... thence to BEGIN--Rozer to pay each 05Aug to William Thorton Alexander £7.10.0cmv.   WTT: none

258 05Sep87 Power of Attorney
Fm relatives of Thomas Hamilton, dec'd, of Richmond, VA
To Hans Hamilton of Gortree

WHEREAS William Hamilton of Gortree, Taboyne Parish, County Donegal, **Farmer**, married Martha Gillespie (both William and Martha now deceased) and had issue:
--Thomas, dec'd, Richmond, VA;
--Isabella who married William Crawford (both now dec'd) of Drumbarnett and had daughter Mary Crawford, **Spinster**, of Drumbarnett in Rye;
--William, of Gortree, Taboyne Parish, **Farmer**;
--Hans, of Gortree;
--Martha who married John Woods of Dooish, Rye Parish;
--Jennett who married Robert Ralston of Glentown, Taboyne Parish
ALL THIS from depositions by:
--John Crawford, Drumbarnett, Rye Parish, County Donegal, age more than 60 years, **Farmer**, AND George Marshall, City of Londonderry, age more than 55, **Merchant**.
NOW these join to appoint Hans Hamilton of Gortree their attorney: Mary Crawford, William Hamilton of Gortree, Martha Woods, Jennett Ralston. Ordered recorded in ALX 24 Oct Oct88.

263 [undated] Power of Attorney
Fm Duncan Hunter & John MacKenzie, City of London, **Merchants** AND Andrew, James & John Sterling, James Doughlass, and James Hunter--co-partners in trade, residing in Scotland;
To William Hunter the younger:
WHEREAS Samuel Gardner, late of Boston, now of Queen Street, Cheapside, London, is indebted £1235.19.0 sterling of Great Britain, for goods sold and delivered to Gardner, AND as divers goods of his are now in...ALX..., William Hunter is to act to collect to satisfy Gardner's debts.
Ordered recorded in ALX Hustings Court 22Nov88

271 13Mar88
Before the FfxCo Justice of the Peace William Herbert, Richard Conway, **Esquire**, takes the oath as commissioner for the Corporation of Alexandria. Ordered recorded 25 Oct88.

271 22Nov88 Bill of Sale
Fm Peter Steile [also: Steel] of ALX
To John Harper for £37.10.0 cmv rent due: "all the Goods and Chattles...Household furniture, Kitchen Utensils & Store Goods"
WTT: Daniel Roberdeau, Ja. Keith

272 [undated; see above]
Inventory of sundry Furniture and Merchandize taken from Mr. Peter Steel by John Harper on account of House rent:

1 large looking glass £1.16.0	Candlesticks and one
1 Walnut tea table 1.5.0	Copper tea kettle 1.16.0
7 Walnut chairs 2.2.0	Sundry Crockery 12/
1 Mahogany Tea table 1.5.0	1 Iron tea Kettle, 2
1 Dressing Table 1.7.6	Iron Potts 3 pair
6 Pictures 1.4.0	Sad Irons 1 pair hand
1 pair and Irons 0.15.0	Irons 1 pair tongs 1
1 pair Shovel & tongs 5/	Roasting Hook 3 Chimney
1 pair Window curtains 18/	Hooks &c 1.16.0
3 Servers 12/	2 Grid Irons and one
3 Windsor chairs 20/	frying pan 10/
1 Bed,bedstead & beding 3.10.0	Sundry tin ware 15/
1 Brass Kettle 3 Brass	1 table 1 Cloaths horse

Sundry bucketts tubs &c 20/
3 blanketts rugs &c   10/
   Total £22.18.6

Merchandize
38 brushes of Difft kinds 14/
3 doz. bottles of Different
   kinds   7/6
25 yards Oznaburgs   £1.3.0
2 1/2 yards negro Cotten   5/
3 Worsted Caps   3/
4 dozen qt & pt mugs   18/
6 chamber potts   4/6
Sundry Cups and Saucers,
   Bowls, Dishes Porringers
   Plates &c &c including all
   the Crockery not before
   enumerated   £2.10.0
2 Felt Hatts   8/
1 Tinder & 4 pepper boxes   2/6
9 Sticks bttr:ball   2/6
3 bottles Snuff   7/6
8 Nutmed greaters   2/
12 paper Ink stands   3/
26 Gimblets   3/
9 tea Spoons   1/6
1/2 quire rapping paper   2/
1 Silk neck cloth 2 yards
   ribbon and 3 band boxes   12/

Sundry threads Ferretings &c &c   2/
Sundry pamphlets   10/
8 pair brass shoe buckles   4/
1 doz. Stock buckles   4/
6 Razors   5/
Sundry Hat pins Ear rings,
   rings and Sleeve buttons   9/
1 pair scissors and 1 Gauze
   handch'f   2/6
1 dozen pair mens and womens
   gloves   12/
Sundry glass ware   5/
1/2 doz. fans and 1 doz
   wafer boxes   3/
4 yards Callico   5/
2 tin tea Kettles   8/
1 dozen Tin and Copper Sauce
   pans   9/
4 work basketts, 6 speaking
   Trumpets & 4 wood cans   10/1
pair scales & Wts.   20/
2 tin Funnells 2 tin Measures
   & 3 Empty Bbls with Corks
   to each   18/2
Sifters 2 Straw Hatts, 1/2
   doz matts and sundry little
   affairs   4/

   Total £37.8.0

[Harper gave Steel the extra 8/]
Signed: Jacob Bedinger, John B. Dabney, **Appraisers**

275   23Jan89   Bond
Posted by William Summers, Alexander Smith and Lewis Weston.
For £1000, to **Governor** Beverly Randolph, **Esquire,** for William Summers--appointed
Sergeant of [this] Court of Hustings, Alexandria, by the Court.

276   12Jul86   Articles of Agreement
Between William Herbert, TwnALX, AND Daniel Roberdeau [no ID]:
--"it will contribute much to the strength of any buildings which may be erected upon
[their dividing line] if the partition wall...should be of greater thickness than is
provided for by the articles entered into for that purpose by the proprietors of those
Lotts of Ground through which Potomack Street runs..."
--DR "may lay the Foundation wall of the House Which he is now going to erect upon
[their joint] dividing line...eleven inches upon the ground...of WH and carry it up to
the surface of the Earth of that thickness" and continue the wall with 7" width up
from ground level;
--WH "may join any Building he may chuse to erect to the wall...paying...DR half" of
its value
--the value to be ascertained in the manner prescribed in the Articles for laying out
the Potomack Street and Forming Partition Walls...."
WTT: Patrick Hagerty, Frans. Brooke

278 20Dec86
Fm Michael & Hannah Madden, TwnALX, FfxCo, StVA
To William Sydebotham, Town of Bladensburg, StMD
WHEREAS MM owes WS £245.3.6 plus interest fm a 23Nov85 note;
WHEREAS 18Nov83 George & Jane Gilpin conveyed to MM part of a lot on the S side Prince, W of Union:
BEGIN on Prince 51' W of Union ... W w/Prince 40'... S//Water St 44' 4" to land of Jonathan Hall's heirs ... E w/Hall line 40'... thence to BEGIN--MM to pay each 31Dec to Gilpin 80 silver $, all this as recorded in FfxCo Court.
NOW to secure the £245.3.6 debt the Maddens pledge:
BEGIN on Prince at W line of the parcel--91' W of Union ... E w/Prince 18'...
S//Water & Union Sts 44' 4" to land of Hall's heirs ... W w/Hall line 18'... thence to BEGIN--BUT if Madden pays principal and interest on/before 28Sep88, this is void.
WTT: Ja. Keith, Wm. Ramsay, Dennis Ramsay

286 18Jun89   Power of Attorney
Fm David Griffith, FfxCo, StVA, **Clerk**
To Christopher Greenup, **Esquire**, [blank] Co., Kentucky
"WHEREAS I...have had several peices [sic] of Land Surveyd in that part of the western Country known by the name of Kentucky for which I have obtained patents and expect shortly to procure patents for other parts..."
--this is a power of attorney to sell patented and to-be-patented land, except those parts **Colonel** Levin Powell agreed on behalf of DG to give to the people locating & surveying "certain Treasury Warrants of mine"
--Greenup not to sell at lower prices or longer terms of credit than specified in the Letter of Instructions.

288 16Sep89
Fm Dennis & Jane Ramsay, TwnALX, FfxCo, StVA
To Isaac Littledale & Co. of Whitehaven, **Merchants** & Partners
WHEREAS DR owes the company £675.13.6 cmv he now mortgages land E of Union, N of King:
BEGIN on Union 54' 10 1/2" N of King ... N w/ Union 21' 1 1/2" to Fayette ... E w/Fayette //King 70'... S//Union 21' 1 1/2"... thence to BEGIN;
     AND (Also E of Union, N of King):
BEGIN on Union 126' N of King ... N w/Union 46' 6"... E//King 70'... S//Union 46' 6"... thence to BEGIN.
(Void if the £675.13.6 paid w/interest on/before 16Sep95)
WTT: Will Hunter, Junr; James Wilson, John MClanachan, R. Prescott

293 28Feb89
Fm Dennis Ramsay, **Esquire**, & wife Jane, TwnALX
To Uriah Forrest AND Benjamin Stoddart, George Town, StMD
WHEREAS DR owes UF & BS £596.13.3 cmv for which DR 28Feb89 has given 3 bonds;
NOW to secure those bonds the Ramsays mortgage a part lot:
BEGIN at King & Union, W of Union, N of King ... W w/King 75'... N//Union 76' to Fayette ... E w/Fayette 75' to Union ... thence on Union to BEGIN.
(Void if the £596.13.3 plus interest paid on/before 01Jan89)
WTT: John Wise, Ch. Simms, Joseph Cary

297 07May85
Fm Daniel & Jane Roberdeau, TwnALX, FfxCo, StVA

To John Fitzgerald and William Lyles, Junr. of -do- (as tenants in common): lease part of LOTS 93-94-95:
BEGIN S side of Wolfe, W side of Union, at the intersection...
S w/Union 115'... W//Wolfe 62' 6"... N//Union 115' to Wolfe
thence on Wolfe 62' 6" to BEGIN;
--reserving to Roberdeau the right to cut down the bank contained in the lot "to the level of the streets and removing the dirt therefrom to the Wharf which he is now running out and filling in with Earth"
--and if Roberdeau builds first of brick or stone--a Necessary excepted--he may lay 9" of his foundation wall on JF/WL land, carrying it up from ground level 4 1/2" on their land
--DR to pay on 27Aug annual rent £1106.5.6 1/2 VA money in Spanish milled $ at 6/, Half Johannes weighing 9 pennyweight at 48/ each, English Guineas weighing 5 pwt + 6 grains at 28/ each
--and fm 27Aug86 £131.18.0 per year [in the same coin]
--and if JF and WL first build a brick or stone building (a Necessary excepted) on the line [they may build their foundation walls as above]
--and whoever builds second and joins to the wall pays half the value of it
--and the second building's joists should be centered between those of the first
WTT: George Coryell, George Herbert, Ja. Keith
CMN: William Herbert & James Keith, **Gentlemen**, aptd 30May86 to examine Jane. Rptd back same day.

310 23Sep89
Fm Michael Gretter, TwnALX, FfxCo, StVA
To William Hepburn -do-
WHEREAS MG on ___ __, 17__ [blanks left blank, but date was 09Sep74] conveyed to WH a parcel on N side King, part LOT [115]--"upon which the said William Hepburns store house now stands and also joins to that piece of Ground upon which the said WH hath erected two three storied brick Houses..."
--and whereas Elizabeth Gretter [Michael's wife] neither then nor since relinquished the right of dower
--and Hepburn won a Chancery Court suit requiring Michael Gretter to give Hepburn security for £60;
NOW MG mortgages to Hepburn part LOT 115 E of Pitt, N of King:
BEGIN on Pitt 100' N of King ... E//King 72'... N //Pitt including the 10' alley formed by Gretter and Hepburn for their mutual convenience ... W//King 72' to Pitt ... thence 30' on Pitt to BEGIN.
WTT: Henry F. Lowe, James McHenry, Ralph Longden

End of Book C

ALEXANDRIA HUSTINGS COURT

Deed Book D, 1789-1793

1   10Aug89
Fm John Harper, FfxCo, StVA
To Samuel Harper, son of John, TwnALX, FfxCo, StVA: sale for £150, part LOT 89, N of Wolfe, E of Ffx:
BEGIN on Wolfe, 63' E of Ffx ... E w/Wolfe 40'... N//Ffx 100' to 10' alley called Allison's Alley ... W w/alley//Wolfe 40'... thence to BEGIN--conveyed by Robert & Ann Adam to John Harper 07Jun84.
WTT: Ja. Keith, Zachariah Shugart; [clerk does not write, but sketches name of which he is not sure as: Johan Irfmeizer]

[Note: here begins a series of nine deeds between W.T. Alexander and John Harper, all concerning parcels in a single piece of ground, using the same elements fm deed to deed.]

4   23Sep89
Fm William Thornton Alexander, King George Co, StVA
To John Harper, FfxCo, StVA
WHEREAS JH has reconveyed [see p. 63, below] a lot formerly contiguous to ALX, adjacent and below a Water lot on E side Water St and immediately opposite LOT 40 in the plat of lots rented in 1784, reconveyed to WTA so that he may convey again to JH and others in portions, now E of Union, N side Franklin:
BEGIN int Union-Frnkln ... N w/Union 201' 7"... E//Franklin 90'... S//Union 201' 7"... thence to BEGIN.
Terms: from 01Nov89, £12.10.0 per annum.
--In view now decreased rent, if any like water lot property w/in 5 yrs rents for more, this rent will be increased;
--As WTA's wife Lucy is under age and cannot convey her dower rights, WTA covenants she will do so at age if tenants request
Signed: John T. [Taliaferro] Brooke, Attorney in fact f/WTA
Memo: Rent increase shall not exceed £28.10
WTT: Charles R. Scott; Michl. Flannery; Jno. C. Keith; Ja. Keith; Jos. Darling

11   23Sep89 [same to same]

BEGIN W side Union 88' 3 1/2" S of Franklin ... S w/Union 88' 3 1/2"... W//Franklin 62' 6"... N//Union 88' 3 1/2"... thence to BEGIN; terms as above; annual rent £6.5 Virginia currency, not to exceed £12.15. WTT & J.T.Brooke stipulation, as above.

18 23Sep89
Fm William Thornton Alexander, King George Co, StVA
To John Harper, FfxCo, StVA
BEGIN on Madison St. 205' E of E side of Union and 93' 3 1/2" S of S line of Franklin ... S//Union 46' 7 3/4"... E//Franklin into river Potomack and thence returning to the place of beginning, and extending from thence //Franklyn into the river...thence S//Union until intersecting 2nd line [as written; clerk may have twice-copied some of the deed's descriptions.]
Terms: £6.5 per annum, not to exceed £12.15.
--In view now decreased rent, if any like water lot property w/in 5 yrs rents for more, this rent will be increased;
--As WTA's wife Lucy is under age and cannot convey her dower rights, WTA covenants she will do so at age if tenants request
Signed: John T. [Taliaferro] Brooke, Attorney in fact f/WTA
Memo: Rent increase shall not exceed £28.10
WTT: Charles R. Scott; Michl. Flannery; Jno. C. Keith; Ja. Keith; Jos. Darling

24 23Sep89 [same to same]
BEGIN on S side Franklin 90' E of Union ... E w/Franklin 115' to center of Madison St ... S//Union 93' 3 1/2'... W//Franklin 115'... N//Union 93' 3 1/2"; terms as before: £6.5 not to exceed £12.15. WTT & J.T. Brooke stipulation, as above.

31 23Sep89 [same to same] E of Water St, N of Franklin:
BEGIN int Water St-Franklin ... N w/Water St 88' 3 1/2"...
E//Franklin 150' to the center of Poto94mac Street ... S//Water St. 88' 3 1/2"... thence to BEGIN; Terms as before: £12.10, not to exceed £28.10;
--WTA commits to extend Water, Ffx, Royal, Pitt, St.Asaph:
--Water St. to be extended 762' 7" from Wilkes;
--Ffx, Royal, Pitt, and St.A extended 595' 9";
--Washington St. to be 246' 10" to W of St.Asaph, 100' wide, to run from King south 595' 9" to S side of Wilkes;
--King, Prince, Duke, Wolfe, Wilkes to be extended 123' 5" each from W side of Washington;
--Gibbons to be 353' 2" S of S side of Wilkes, running from River Potomack 123' 5" beyond W side of Washington St.
WTT & J.T.Brooke stipulation, as above.

40 23Sep89 [same to same]
BEGIN S side Franklin 62' 6" E of Water St ... E w/Franklin 87' 6" to Center of Potomack St ... S//Water St 88' 3 1/2"... W//Franklin 87' 6" thence to BEGIN.
Terms as above: £6.5, not to exceed £12.15.
TT & J.T.Brooke stipulation, as above.

47 23Sep89
Fm William Thornton Alexander, King George Co, StVA
To John Harper, FfxCo, StVA
BEGIN on Maddison [sic] St 205' E of E line of Union, and 93' 3 1/2" N of N line of Franklin ... N//Union 108' 8"... E// Franklin into River Potomack ... From BEGIN, again, with another line//Franklin, E into river ... thence N//Union until 2nd line is intersected;

Terms as above: £12.10, not to exceed £28.10.
--In view now decreased rent, if any like water lot property w/in 5 yrs rents for more, this rent will be increased;
--As WTA's wife Lucy is under age and cannot convey her dower rights, WTA covenants she will do so at age if tenants request
Signed: John T. [Taliaferro] Brooke, Attorney in fact f/WTA
WTT: Charles R. Scott; Michl. Flannery; Jno. C. Keith; Ja. Keith; Jos. Darling

54 23Sep89
Fm William Thornton Alexander, King George Co, StVA
To John Harper, FfxCo, StVA
BEGIN W side Union 88' 3 1/2" N of Franklin ... N w/Union 88' 3 1/2"... W//Franklin 150' "to the Centre of Potomack Street"... S//Union 88' 3 1/2"... thence to BEGIN. Terms as before: £12.10, not to exceed L28.10. Commitments for street extensions [as at p.31]. WTT & J.T.Brooke stipulation, as above.

63 21Sep89 [same to same]
WHEREAS the exxrs of John Alexander, acting for William Thornton Alexander, on 21Apr85 conveyed to John Harper:
BEGIN on E side Water St, 176' 7" S of Gibbons ... E//Gibbons into River Potomack ... Again fm BEGIN, S w/Water St 176' 7" "to [blank] Street (now demoninated Franklin St"... E w/Franklin 350'... S//Water St 25'... E into River Potomack ... N until 1st line intersected. Terms: each 01Nov £228 cmv.
NOW JH for 5/ conveys parcel back to WTA yielding up "all that peice or LOTT of ground lying to the Eastward of water street and extending into the river Potomack"
--and, JH having paid £400, WTA releases JH from all further £280 per annum rent payments. WTT: as above
"Arranged by John Taliaferro Brooke by Power of Attorney dated 15Sep89 and recorded in Fredericksburg District Court"

68 29Sep89
Fm Samuel Arell, FfxCo, StVA
To William Hunter, Jr., TwnALX, FfxCo, StVA: lease for £200 cmv plus, from 01Sep90, £3.15.0 per year of part of a lot on N side Wilkes, E side of St. Asaph:
BEGIN N side Wilkes 61' 8 1/2" E of St A ... E w/Wilkes 61' 8 1/2" to E lot line ... N w/lot line //St A 176' 7" to N lot line ... W w/lot line //Wilkes 123' 5" to St A ... S w/St A 50'... E//Wilkes 61' 8 1/2"... thence to BEGIN.
[Here begins a section which does not read properly, and is quoted at length except for the abstracted metes and bounds:]
"part of that Lott...granted by John Alexander unto Adam Lynn, who sold and conveyed unto him the said Samuel Arell, and the said SA for himself his Heirs Executors and Administrators doth covenant promise and grant to and with the said William Hunter Junr...that he the said SA and his Heirs [word/words left out] all that part of the premises hereby granted which is contained within the following Boundaries, Vizt."
[begin abstract:]
BEGIN on Wilkes 98' 5" E of St A ... E//St A 176' 7"... W//Wilkes 123' 5" to St A ... S w/St A 25'... E//Wilkes 98' 5";[end abstract] Thence with a straight line to Wilkes St "unto him the said WHJr...against the claim and Demand of him the said SA...."
WTT: Jh.M. Perrin; Lanty Crowe, Robt. McCrea, Charles R. Scott

74 22Jan90
Fm Mayor & Commonalty of TwnALX, FfxCo, StVA

To Jesse Taylor -do- **Merchant**: lease for part of Point West; Bounds: Union St, River Potomack:
BEGIN "at a post on E side Union so fixed as to leave a 15' alley between the Lott, intended to be granted and southwardly of the County Warehouse, thence--"... S w/Union 45'... E// Oronoko into the River ...N//Union 45'...thence //Oro to BEGIN
Terms: 99 years
--fm 22Jan91, 90 Spanish milled $ or other specie per year, each $ to weigh 17 pennyweight, 10 grains;
--standard forfeiture terms for non-payment of rent (60 days after failure to pay specified sums on time, the lessor may enter the premises to seize sufficient goods and chattels, the sale of which will satisfy the amount in arrears; if insufficient goods the lessor may re-enter, eject the lessee, and repossess the property);
--"and if upon survey it should appear there is more than Forty-five feet of Publick Ground southward of the alley" JT may have it for additional, proportionate, rent;
--"provided such survey be made before...JT...hath laid the wharf loggs on the Southernmost line of the Lott";
--and JT to refrain from building steps, stairs or buildings "so as to encumber the alley aforesaid";
--"neither will the Mayor and Commonalty...make any addition to the County Warehouse so as to encumber the Alley";
--the 15' alley to be free and open for public use from Union St to the river Potomack "only allowing the outside stairs as they are now fixed to the County Warehouse to be kept in repair...";
--and that JT at his own cost will "fill in with Earth or Ground and fully compleat the vacancy which will be left between the said County Wharf, and the north line of [this] Lott...being about three feet in width. The front of which three feet...so filled in JT may occupy During the Term...for Vessels to lay at";
--peaceable surrender at end of term of lot and improvements thereon, without compensation.
/s/ Dennis Ramsay [Mayor]
/s/ Jesse Taylor

Philip Marsteller
=
William Duvall   )
Benjamin Shreeve) Members
John Reynolds   ) of
William Paton   ) Council
John Saunders   )
John Longdon   )
=
Oliver Price   )
William Summers) Witnesses
Ralph Longdon   )
[Not clear if Marsteller is a Council Member. The meaning of the clerk's marginal "=" marks is not certain.]

82 01Jul89
Fm William & Magdalena Eichenbrade, TwnALX, FfxCo, StVA
To John Corn AND Jacob Wisemiller   -do-
WHEREAS W.E. by a promissory note is indebted to JC & JW for £140 specie, of which £70 plus interest payable by 01Jul90;
--to secure that payment, the Eichenbrades mortgage to JC & JW as tenants in common part LOT [blank] in Alexandria:

BEGIN corner of "Lott heretofor granted to Jacob Wisemiller ... thence w/St. Asaph and fronting thereon 47'... In depth: 38' 5"... Bounded on the W by St. Asaph ... Bounded on S & E by lands "now or late of Neil Mooney"... Bounded on N by lot of Jacob Wisemiller. (This is void if required payment made on/before 01Jul90.) [Magdalena signs w/mark.]
WTT: George Slacum, Benja. Wade, P. Marsteller

87   30Jul88
Fm Risdon B. Harwood, City of Annapolis
To James Williams -do- : for £400 current money of MD
part of LOT 86 in ALX:
BEGIN 123' 5" E of int Wolfe-Water Sts ... N//Water St 10 poles and 17 1/2 links ... E//Wolfe 3 poles, 18 1/2 links ... S//Water St to Wolfe ... thence along Wolfe to BEGIN.
--RBH certifies except to that which "a certain Michael Madden of TwnALX claims to have..." [but gives no particulars.]
WTT: Jas. Williams, Wm. King; Jona: of Robt. Pinkney
[Note next entry, p. 90]

90   30Jul88
Mayor of Annapolis, James Price, on this date examined Risdon Harwood's wife, Rachel as to her consent. The Risdons are residents of Annapolis. [See above, p. 87.]

92   27 Oct89
Fm Susanna Patterson, FfxCo
To Charles Simms, TwnALX: for £300, 1/2 acre LOT 30--conveyed by ALX Trustees to John & Ann Tarbuck, by the Tarbucks to William Patterson, and by William to Susanna. [Susanna signs w/mark.]   WTT: Wm. McKnight, Ch. Turner, John McCrea

94   21Jun90
Fm John & Sarah Hough, Loudoun Co, StVA
To (as tenants in common) John Butcher & William Paton, TwnALX, FfxCo, StVA: for £160 cmv, part of LOT 178, W of St. Asaph and N of Prince Streets:
BEGIN at int St. A-Prince ... W w/Prince 35'... N//St. Asaph 70' 6"... E//Prince 35' to St A ... thence to BEGIN--conveyed by John Alexander's exxrs 05Aug79 to Oliver Price for £22.3 per year--and by Price to Hough 23 Oct84, Price to continue the rent payments to JA's exxrs.   WTT: Geo. Clements, Philip Wanton, Jonathan Butcher

99   27Aug89
Fm William Hunter, Junr, TwnALX, FfxCo, StVA
To Robert Townshend Hooe -do-
WHEREAS Gov. Thomas Jefferson 19 Oct80 conveyed title to part (1/4 acre) of LOT 33:
--bounded on W by LOT 34, then property of Wm. Ramsay, **Esquire**
--on N by part LOT 33, then property of Robert Adam, **Esquire**
--on S by LOT 38, then property of Carson & Muir, deceased
AND WHEREAS LOT 33 had been property of Colin Dunlap & Son & Co, subjects of Great Britain
--sold by Hector Ross, **Esqr. Gent Escheator** for the commonwealth in FfxCo
--and William Hunter, Junr., in 19Feb85 sold half to William Wilson of ALX, VA
--"so as there now remains only half thereof vested in him...and which he now occupies";

BEGIN at division between Hunter and Wilson ... W w/division line fm Ffx 123' 5"...
N//Ffx 39' 1 3/4" to Robert Adam's lot line ... E w/Adam's line to Ffx ... thence w/Ffx
to BEGIN--containing 1/8 acre;
AND WHEREAS Samuel Arell of FfxCo 01Mar85 conveyed to Hunter:
BEGIN on Wilkes 61' 8 1/2" E of int Wilkes-St. A ... E w/Wilkes 35' 3 1/2"... N//St A
126' 7"... W//Wilkes 36' 8 1/2"... thence South to BEGIN [note disparity between 2nd
and 4th line measurements];
--and the above two lots are now in Hunter's possession;
AND WHEREAS Hooe w/Josiah Watson, at Hunter's request, on 08Dec86 became
security for W. Hunter, Junr.'s bond to John Hunter for the £2800 to guarantee
payment of £1400;
NOW Wm. Hunter Junr. conveys to Robert Townshend Hooe all 3 lots to indemnify
RTH--void if WHJr pays off bond as scheduled
WTT: P. Marsteller, Jos: Lewis, J.[James] H. Hooe

107 19Mar87
Fm Oliver & Jane Price, TwnALX, FfxCo, StVA
To William Paton AND John Butcher -do-: for £24.10 cmv, part of LOT 178, W side
of St Asaph, N side Prince:
BEGIN W side St A, 70' 6" N of int Prince-St A ... N w/St A 7'... W//Prince 35'... S//St
A 7'... E w/John Hough's line //Prince to BEGIN (part of lot leased by OP for £22.3
per year to exxrs of J. Alexander); the Prices will continue to satisfy the rent require-
ment to John Alexander's heir [William Thornton Alexander]   WTT: none

111 03Jul88
Fm Michael Simon & Jane Blondeley, Loudoun Co, StVA
To John Pettit, TwnALX, StVA
WHEREAS James Parsons, late of ALX, dec'd on 08Nov84, conveyed to MSB AND
Pettit part of a lot N of King, W of St Asaph:
BEGIN on King 59' W of St A... W w/King 38 1/2'... N//St A 34'... E//King 38 1/2'...
thence to BEGIN
--PLUS use of 6' alley on back of premises from east to west;
--for annual rent each 25Jun of £19.5.6 cmv in Spanish milled $ at 6/ each; half
Johannes weighing 9 pennyweight at 48/ each, or other specie--all as recorded in
FfxCo Court;
AND WHEREAS 10Aug87 MSB & JP agreed MSB should occupy:
BEGIN on King 59' W of St A ... W w/King 16'... N//St A 34'
... E//King 16'... thence to BEGIN;
--MSB paying James Parson's heirs each 25Jun £8.17.9
--and from King St. a 3 1/2' alley to serve MSB & JP jointly;
NOW MSB and wife Jane lease to Pettit MSB's half-parcel and his half of the alley
for £50 PLUS paying Parson's heirs each 25Jun £8.17.9
WTT: Geo. Richards, Robert Lyle, W. Ellzey
CMN: Jesse Taylor & Robert McCrea, **Gentlemen**, appointed this date to examine
Jane, and reported back 17Sep88.

119 29Sep89
Fm William Thornton Alexander, King George Co, StVA
To Lewis Weston, TwnALX, StVA: WTA's numbered LOT 25:
BEGIN E side St. A where when extended will int N side Gibbon... E w/Gibbons 123'
5"... N w/St A 176' 6"... E//Gibbons 123' 5"... thence to BEGIN.
Terms: fm 01Nov89, £12.10/year;

--but as this rent is appreciably less than when offered in 1784, if a comparably sized and located unimproved lot w/in 5 years should fetch more, Weston agrees to a proportionate rent increase
--as with the Harper lots [pp. 4-54 above], wife Lucy Alexander is not of age so cannot relinquish dower rights. After she turns 21, if Weston requests such will be arranged.
--WTA commits to extend Water, Ffx, Royal, Pitt, St.Asaph:
--Water St. to be extended 762' 7" from Wilkes;
--Ffx, Royal, Pitt, and St.A extended 595' 9";
--Washington St. to be 246' 10" to W of St.Asaph, 100' wide, to run from King south 595' 9" to S side of Wilkes;
--King, Prince, Duke, Wolfe, Wilkes to be extended 123' 5" each from W side of Washington;
--Gibbons to be 353' 2" S of S side of Wilkes, running from River Potomack 123' 5" beyond W side of Washington St.
WTT: Will. Hunter, Junr; Baldwin Dade, John Harper, Joseph Darling

125 22Sep85
Fm William Hunter, TwnALX, FfxCo, CwlVA, **Merchant**
To William Ward -do- **Tavern Keeper**: for £423 cmv, part LOT 16:
BEGIN N side Princess at W corner of a part of this lot conveyed by WH to John Lomax, and 24' W of W corner LOT 15 ... W w/Princess 48'... N 100' to 9' alley ... E 48' w/alley //Princess ... thence 100' to BEGIN.
WTT: Alexander Henderson, John Lomax, John Gibson, Cleon Moore

129 [no date]   Power of Attorney
Fm Christopher Robinson, Robert Sanderson & John Rumney, **Merchants** under the name of Robinson, Saunderson [sic] & Rumney of Whitehaven, Cumberland Co., Great Britain;
To William Hodgson, "now of Alexandria, Commonwealth of Virginia"
WTT: Henry Barns, Miles White, Joseph Rodgers
Notarized by Peter How Younger 01Jul90 in Whitehaven.
Recorded in ALX 25 Oct90

134 04 Oct90
Fm Henry Strowman, TwnALX, FfxCo, StVA
To Dedrick Shakle   -do-
WHEREAS Shakle owes Strowman £70 specie plus interest;
NOW Strowman conveys to Shakle part lot fronting 25' on Royal,
adjoining Strowman's dwelling--"running in depth to the division line and extending to the said HS's other lots...."
BUT if by 04Jul91 Strowman repays Shakle, this is void.
WTT: Jno. C. Kempff, Jno. Harper, Jno. Corn

137 22Sep88
Fm James & Alice Lawrason AND Samuel Arell, TwnALX, FfxCo, StVA
To David Marshall Scott -do- : part lot E of St. A, S of Duke
BEGIN on Duke 60' fm int Duke-St. Asaph ... E//Duke 40'... S//St Asaph 78'... W//Duke 40'... thence to BEGIN--property conveyed to JL & SA 23Feb86 by Robert Daugherty, the dec'd Winsor Brown's heir in law;
--this lease for £75 now and then from 17Dec88 paying 25/ annually;
--and R.M.Scott will leave open on the W side of lot a 4' alley, 25' deep, to serve as an alley in common w/ a 4' alley laid off by Peter Wagener & George Deneale as tenants in common on E side of a parcel sold them by JL & SA 24Apr87

WTT: Jacob Bedinger, Daniel Casey, Joseph Gilpin
CMN: William Brown, John Potts amd George Gilpin, **Gentn**, aptd 16Jun89 to examine Alice. Rptd back 17Jun89.

145 09Jul90
Fm William & Magdalina Eichenbrade, TwnALX, FfxCo, StVA, **Baker**
To John Korn AND Jacob Wisemiller, -do- **Biscuit Bakers**
WHEREAS 19Dec74 John Alexander conveyed to William McKnight, **Cabinet maker**, 1/2 acre LOT 110 [in J ALXR's numbering system], leasing at £9.5 cmv per year;
WHEREAS McKnight leased out several parts of LOT 110 and
WHEREAS McKnight 13 Oct83 conveyed to "William Eichenbrade (under the name of Ownbread)":
BEGIN W corner of House on LOT 110 occupied by Neil Mooney ... W//Prince 38' 5" to St. A ... S 126'... E 38' 5"... N to BEGIN. [Text now concludes that property thus delineated belongs to the "said William Ownbread free of rent forever" with the covenant that if occupants of the other part of the lot default, that Ownbread may take possession of the whole lot--collecting rents conformable to the leases granted by McKnight--"as if the whole lot" was Ownbread's];
NOW the Eichenbrades for £100 cmv from Korn & Wisemiller deed part of the lot sold by McKnight to Eichenbrade:
BEGIN on St. A. 80' S of Prince ... S w/St A 46'... E//Prince 38' 5"... N//St Asaph 46'..."Thence by the other part of the same Lott, whereof this is part now...in the possession of...Eichenbrade, Korn and Weismiller [sic] 38' 6" to BEGIN."
[Signed by William, but by Magdalina Eichenbrade w/ mark]
WTT: Ch. Slimmer, Dedrick Shakle, Benj. Wade, P. Marsteller
CMN: Dennis Ramsay, Olney Winsor, Philip Marsteller "of the Court of Hustings, **Gentlemen**," aptd 19Jul90 to examine Magdalina. Rptd back 22Jul90. [Note the following deed]

154 20Jun90 [same to same]
WHEREAS John Alexander 19Dec74 conveyed to William McKnight LOT 110 [JnALXR lot numbering] (N of Prince, W of St Asaph) for annual rent £9.5, as filed in FfxCo Court;
AND WHEREAS McKnight conveyed parts of LOT 110 to several people--using their rents to satisfy his obligation to JnALXR--and thus holding the residue of LOT 110 rent-clear;
AND WHEREAS McKnight 13 Oct83 conveyed to "William Eichenbrade (party thereto) under the name of William Ownbread" part of LOT 110 reserved as being free of rent payments to JnALXR:
BEGIN W corner of House on Lott occupied by Neil Mooney ... W//Prince 38' 5" to St A ... S 126' then E 38' 5"... thence N to BEGIN "To hold to him the said William Eichenbrade (there named William Ownbread) his Heirs and Assigns, free of rent forever" with the covenant that if others on LOT 110 defaulted, Ownbread/Eichenbrade could take possession of the whole lot, charging them proportionate rent, and proceed as if he had received the entire lot in the first place....
NOW, so that Eichenbrade can secure a £50 debt to Korn & Wisemiller, he conveys that part of the lot not earlier conveyed on 09Jul 90, to wit:
BEGIN 20' fm int Prince-St A ... S//St A 80'... then E 18' 5"... then N 80' to Prince ... thence w/Prince 18' 5" to BEGIN.
BUT void if Eichenbrade pays Korn & Wisemiller the £50 plus interest on/before next 20July.
WTT: Cleon Moore, P. Marsteller, Junr; Robert Brockett, Dedrick Shakle

CMN: Dennis Ramsay, Olney Winsor, Philip Marsteller "of the Court of Hustings, **Gentlemen**," aptd 20Jul90 to examine Magdalina. Reported back 22Jul90.

163 28Apr90
Fm John Dowdall, FfxCo, StVA
To William Hepburn, TwnALX, FfxCo, StVA: for £13 currency of VA, part Lot N of Princess, W of St Asaph:
BEGIN SE corner of lot ... W w/Princess 63'... N//St A 126' 6"... E//Princess 63'... thence to BEGIN--conveyed to JD by James Thompson 24Apr88, earlier conveyed to Thompson by Hepburn 31Aug85, as recorded in FfxCo Court.
WTT: James McKenna, John Dundas, Caleb Earp, Wm. Scot

166 19 Oct90
Fm William & Isabella Summers, TwnALX, FfxCo, CwlVA
To William Frazer, FfxCo, CwlVA
WHEREAS William & Mary Frazer 01Dec88 conveyed to Wm. Summers part of 1/2 acre lot granted Richard Ratcliff by Charles Alexander 22Dec85
--and by Ratcliff 50' was conveyed to Frazier 16May86
--and the Fraziers conveyed 20' of that to Wm. Summers [the 01Dec88 conveyance];
NOW the Summers lease to Frazier part of the same lot:
BEGIN 40' fm SW corner of this 1/2 acre on Washington St, and at N line of John Evans' lot ... N w/Wn 20'... E//Queen 123' 5"... S//Wn 20'... W 123' 5" to BEGIN.
Terms: beginning 25Dec90, Frazer will pay £15 specie/annum in the same currency and rates Ratcliffe will be paying Charles Alexander.
WTT: Dennis Ramsay, William Duvall, James Irvine
CMN: Dennis Ramsay, William Duvall, Jesse Taylor, **Gentlemen** of TwnALX, aptd 25 Oct90 to examine Isabell. Rptd same day

172 20 Oct90
Fm William & Mary Frazer, TwnALX, FfxCo, StVA
To James Irvine   -do-
WHEREAS Richard Ratcliff 16May86 conveyed to Wm. Frazer part of 1/2 acre adjoining TwnALX (conveyed to Ratcliff by Chas. Alexander 22Dec85);
WHEREAS Frazer 01Dec88 conveyed 20' on Washington St's E side to William Summers--which 20' has been reconveyed to Frazer by Summers 19 Oct90;
NOW the Frazers convey/lease to James Irvine part lot on E side of Washington St:
BEGIN 40' fm SW corner of 1/3 acre lot and at intersection of John Evans' line ... N w/Wn 50'... E//Queen 123' 5" ... S//Wn 50'... thence W to BEGIN. Terms: fm 25Dec90 £15 specie (or same currency/rate as Ratcliff pays his rent to Chas ALXR.)
WTT: Dennis Ramsay, William Duvall, William Summers
CMN: Dennis Ramsay, William Duvall, Jesse Taylor, **Gentlemen** of TwnALX, aptd 25 Oct90 to examine Mary. Rptd back same day.

179 13Dec90
Fm Dennis Whalin, TwnALX, FfxCo, StVA
To William Summers -do-: part LOT 126, S of Princess, W of Pitt:
BEGIN int Princess-Pitt ... S w/Pitt 93' 3" to N line of lot sold to Thomas Williams & Joseph Carey by John Jolly's deed [blanks for date not filled in] "which is part of LOT 126"... W w/Williams & Carey lot line 123' 5"... N//Pitt 93' to Princess ... E w/Princess 123' 5" [to BEGIN]--originally fm Trustees to John Carlyle, and fm Carlyle to Jolly "who conveyed all the remaining part by his Deed... 26Jul89 to ... Dennis Whalin...."
WTT: John B. Dabney, Thomas Rogerson, Oliver Price, Andrew Taylor

183 21 Oct90
Fm Valentine Peers, Charles Co, MD
To William Hodgson, TwnALX, StVA: for £600 cmv, part of LOT 52 S of King, W of Water St:
BEGIN on King 42' W of Water St: the W corner of lots earlier granted Hodgson by Peers ... W w/King 79' to line of lot conveyed by John Fitzgerald to William Anderson ... thence w/that line, //Water St 82' to alley 12 1/2 wide fm Ffx to Water St ... thence w/alley 79' to line of lots (earlier mentioned) already conveyed to WH by VP ... thence w/that line to BEGIN.
WTT: George Clementson, I. [Ichabod] Hunter, William Bowness

188 22 Oct90
Fm Valentine Peers, Charles Co, MD
To Thomas Porter, TwnAlx, StVA: for 5/ now, part of a lot E side Union, S of King and upon S side of 30' alley fm Union to the front of the wharf made by Peers & John Fitzgerald:
BEGIN on Union 103' 3 1/2" S of King--the S line of the alley; S w/ Union 73' 3 1/2" to Andrew Wales' line ... thence w/Wales' line //King--East--100'... N//Union 73' 3 1/2" to alley ... W w/alley to BEGIN--"being part of the ground made by...Peers and..Fitzgerald out of the river adjoining to that lott...No. 52." Peers must repay a debt of £298.13.3 + interest on/before22Jul91 owed to William Hodgson [not Thomas Porter; Porter is the trustee in this matter.] If Peers fails to pay, Porter is to advertise the property 4 weeks in the <u>Alexandria Gazette</u> and the <u>Baltimore Gazette</u> and then sell as much as necessary to satisfy the debt.
WTT: Gedion Snow, Samuel Noyes, John B. Dabney

193 29May90
Fm Daniel & Martha McPherson AND Isaac McPherson, TwnALX, FfxCo, StVA
To John Murray -do- : part of LOT 80:
BEGIN on Duke 40' fm NE corner ... W w/ Duke 27' 10"... S// Water St 91' 6" to 10' alley ... E w/alley 27' 10"... N 91' 6" to BEGIN--conveyed to the McPhersons by James Mercer of Spotsylvania 22May87, numbered in Mercer's plat as No. 2.
            AND
Part LOT 80 (Mercer Lot No. 5)
BEGIN on Water St 101' 6" fm LOT 80's NE corner ... S w/Water St 25'... W//Duke 103' 6" to 20' alley ... N w/alley 25'... thence E 103' 6" to BEGIN.
WTT: James Craik, Nath. Ingraham, Thomas Peterkin, Nicholas M. Servat
MEMO: James Craik, Thomas Peterkin and Isaac PcPherson sign 22Feb91 a memorandum that they witnessed Martha's signature after the death of her husband.

197 12Apr91
Fm Adam Blass, TwnALX, StVA
To Jesse Taylor   -do-
WHEREAS Adam Blass owes the exxrs of Robert Adam (for purchases at Adam's estate sale): William Herbert, William Wilson, Roger West and William Hunter, Jr.
--£90 due 21Jun91, the price of the slave, Bristow
--£20.1.0 due 08Jan92, the price of the slave, Bravo
--Jesse Taylor is security for Blass' two bonds for these purchases AND Blass also owes Taylor £60;
NOW to secure all 3 debts/obligations, Blass mortgages to Taylor: Bristow + Bravo + 1 sorrel horse + 1 dray with "all the Geers."   Void if obligations met.
WTT: Charles R. Scott, Peter Murray, Robert Lyle

201 26May90
Fm Samuel & Dolly Arell, FfxCo, CwlVA
To John Murray, TwnALX, FfxCo, CwlVA: for £100 cmv part of LOT 81 on Ffx & Duke Sts:
BEGIN on Ffx 60' fm SW corner LOT 81 ... N on Ffx 20'... E//Duke 101' 5"... S//Ffx 20'... E//Duke 22'... S//Ffx 20'... W//Duke 44'... N//Ffx 20'... thence W to BEGIN.
WTT: Richard Arell, O. Winsor, Geo. M. Murray
CMN: Philip Marsteller, Olney Winsor, Dennis Ramsay, **Gentlemen** Justices of TwnALX, aptd 10Jan91 to examine Dolly. Reported back 22Feb91.

205 18Apr91
Fm Caleb & Phebe Whitacre, Fauquier Co, StVA
To Isaac Nichols, Loudoun Co, **Miller**: part of Wm. T. Alexander LOT 37 drawn in 1784, contig to ALX:
WHEREAS 26Sep89 William Thornton Alexander leased for £4.2.1 each 01Nov part of his LOT 37 to Caleb Whitacre;
NOW for £350 common currency of VA the Whitacres convey it: BEGIN SE corner LOT 37 ... N w/Ffx 66' 7"... E //Gibbons 63' 5"... S//Ffx 66' 7"... thence w/Gibbons to BEGIN--Nichols to pay the £4.2.1 to Alexander;
--Alexander's commitment to street extensions recited [p.31]
WTT: Samuel Spencer, Samuel Nichols, Isaac Hatcher, Ezekiel Smith, William Stallcup
CMN: Francis Peyton, Levin Powell, William Bronaugh, Joseph Lane of Loudoun Co aptd 18Apr91 to examine Phebe. Rptd same day.

215 17Dec90
Fm John & Patty Murray, TwnALX, FfxCo, CwlVA
To John Walter Fletcher -do- : for £100 cmv part LOT 80 S of Duke, W of Water Sts:
BEGIN on Duke 40' fm NE corner ... W on Duke 27' 10"... S// Water St 91' 6" to 10' alley ... E w/alley 27' 10"... N 91' 6" to BEGIN--conveyed to JM by Daniel & Isaac McPherson 29May90.
WTT: George W. Murray, Samuel Packard, Elizabeth Murray
CMN: Philip Marsteller, Olney Winsor, Dennis Ramsay, **Gentlemen** Justices of ALX aptd 01Feb91 to examine Patty. Rptd 22Feb91.

220 10Mar91
Fm Nehemiah Clifford, late of ALX, now of PG Co, MD
To William Hepburn, TwnALX, FfxCo, StVA: for £8 currency of VA "all that Lott or parcel of Ground in the TwnALX made out of Lott numbered 14 in the Original plan of the said town":
BEGIN 106' fm Union & Princess ... W w/Princess 11'... N// Water St 88' to line of Hunter & Allison ... E//Princess 11' ... S//Union 88' 3 3/4 [to BEGIN].
--this parcel "ground rented" to NC by WH by deed dated [blanks not filled in] and recorded in FfxCo Court
WTT: George Darling, James Scot, Wm. Scott, John Dundas

222 21Apr91
Fm William & Agnes Hepburn AND John & Agnes Dundas, TwnALX, FfxCo, StVA
To Robert Going Langphier -do- : lease fm 10May91 @ 24 Spanish milled $ at 6/ or equivalent in specie, per year;
Part Lot: BEGIN on St A 176' 7 1/2" N of Queen ... S w/St Asaph 48'... W//Queen 62'... N//St Asaph 48'... E//Queen 62' to BEGIN.   Terms: the above rent + all future taxes. [Agnes Hepburn signs w/mark]   WTT: Caleb Earp, James Scott

227 05 Oct86
Fm John & Jane Fitzgerald, TwnALX, FfxCo, StVA
To (as tenants in common) John Jenkes, Olney Winsor, Joseph Jenkes, Crawford Jenkes of -do-: lease fm 04Sep87 @ 202 1/2 Spanish milled $ at 6/ or in 9 pennyweight Half Johanesses at 48/ each, of part of a lot S side King, E side Water Sts: BEGIN at King & Water Sts ... E w/King 40' 6"... S//Water St 76' 6"... W//King 40' 6" to Water St ... thence on Water St "...to the BEGINNING the same being a part of the Wharf made by...John Fitzgerald or joining to a part of that Lott of ground, described in the plan of the Town by No. [blank]"
Terms: rent as above; rent remittable by paying 4,050 Spanish milled $ at any time
WTT: Guy Atkinson, William Atkinson

234 29 Oct89
Fm John & Jane Fitzgerald, TwnALX, FfxCo, StVA
To (as tenants in common) John Jenkes, Olney Winsor, Joseph Jenkes [no ID]: lease fm 04Sep90 @ 60 Spanish milled $ [at above rates, p.227] of part lot E side Water, S side King Sts:
BEGIN on Water St 76' 6" S of King--the SW corner of parcel previously granted [above, p. 227] ... S w/Water 40' to alley 20' wide ... E w/alley//King 40' 6"... N//Water St 40' to the parcel aforementioned ... thence w/parcel line W to BEGIN:
--"the same being a part of the Wharf made by...John Fitzgerald and adjoining to a part of that Lott of Ground described in the plan of the ...Town, by No. [blank]"
Terms: rent as above. JF promises to keep open the 20' alley he has laid out E-W fm Water St to Union St.
WTT: Guy Atkinson, William Atkinson

241 28 Oct89 [same to same]
   WHEREAS by 05 Oct86 deed Fitzgerald leased a parcel to the Jenkeses & Winsor for 202 1/2 Spanish milled $;
NOW on receiving £180 cmv, $60 of the rent is remitted forever.
WTT: Guy Atkinson, Willm. Atkinson

244 23Apr91   Power of Attorney
Fm Samuel Merian, City of Philadelphia, **Merchant**
To Lewis D. Hesshuyson "of the City of ALX," **Merchant**
To receive amounts due by:
Alexander Nelson, Richmond, on account of Joseph Darmstat;
David Patterson, Manchester;
Robert Martin, Williamsburg;
[All the following of Fredericksburg:] Richard Kenny, Jacob Kuhn, Steven Lacost, Lewis Therie;
Thomas Vowell AND Messrs Perrin & Brothers of Alexandria;
Moses Jacob, Baltimore, MD;
John Abert, Fredericktown, MD;
William Forbes, Benedict, MD
WTT: John Carson, C. Bagot
Notarized by: "Peter LeBarbier Duplessis, **Esquire**, Notary, and Tabellion public, and Interpreter of Foreign Languages" [Philadelphia]

247 13Apr91
Fm Martha McPherson, exxx, AND Edward Beeson & Isaac McPherson, acting exxrs, all three for Daniel McPherson, TwnALX
To James Wilson, Junr., -do-

WHEREAS 22May 87 James Mercer conveyed to Daniel & Isaac McPherson 3 parcels, one being S of Duke, W of Water Streets:
BEGIN on Duke on W line of parcel sold by Mercer to L. Powell ... S w/Powell line 91' 6" to 10' alley ... then W w/alley 27' 10"... thence //first line 91' 6" to Duke ... thence to BEGIN.
WHEREAS Daniel died before dividing the lot, and in his will directed all to be sold; AND on 11Apr his exxx/exxrs sold at public auction the parcel to Wilson for £70.10; NOW for £35.5 to the Estate and £35.5 to Isaac they convey the parcel to Wilson, w/alley rights.
WTT: Philip Wanton, Jesse Andrew Taylor, Jonas McPherson, William Hewett, Enoch Ward

255 16Jun91
Fm Ninian & Margareth Anderson, TwnALX, FfxCo, StVA
To Robert Lyle AND James McClish -do- : for £166.5 cmv, mortgaging:
--2 Negro men: Isaac & Forester
--2 Negro women: Mary & Grace & the 3 children [does not ID whose] Sampson, Charlotte, Nancy
VOID if Ninian pays £166.5, with interest running from 01Jan91, in quarterly payments of £23.5.
WTT: J.C.Kempff, Josiah Emmit, Roger Chew

258 PLAT w/text
   Text: "Agreeable to the Order of the Worshipful Court of Hustings for the Town of Alexandria we the Subscribers appointed to divide the Estate of James Parsons deceased between John Parsons his son and Elizabeth Parsons his widow do make the Following report, Vizt. We allot to John Parson's as his proportion the lotts in the annexed Plot No. 1 & 4 on King Street, No. 5 on St. Asaph Street, No. 9 on Cameron Street and No. 2 and 3 on Wilkes Street.
            /s/ May 24, 1791 Wm McKnight
                        Peter Wise
                        John Allison"

259 18Apr89
Fm Baldwin & Catharine Dade, TwnALX, FfxCo, CwlVA
To Robert Marshall Scott -do- : for £20, part of a parcel conveyed 29Dec85 by Henry Lee, Junr., to Baldwin Dade--a 1/2 acre lot;
BEGIN NW corner of the 10-acre lot in the indenture ... E w/line of Charles Alexander to parcel sold by B&C Dade to Philip Richard Fendall AND Charles Lee ... S w/Fendall/Lee line to the corner of their land ... W w/another Fendall/Lee line to another corner ... thence N to BEGIN.   WTT: none
CMN: Dennis Ramsay, Wm. Duvall and Jesse Taylor, **Magistrates** of ALX, aptd 18Jun89 to examine Catharine. Rptd back 20Jun89

263 21Jun91
Fm William Hunter, Junr., TwnALX, CwlVA
To George Augustine Washington, FfxCo, CwlVA: for £350 current money, part of LOT 108, sold to John Hawkins by Peter Wise on [date not filled in], recorded in Corporate Court of ALX:
BEGIN corner Pitt & Duke ... thence //Duke 76' 6" to ground sold [no date] by John Hawkins to Gerrard T. Conn ... thence 30' more or less to another [no ID] Conn parcel ... thence 76' 6" w/Conn's line to Pitt St ... thence 30' more or less to BEGIN.
WTT: Bushrod Washington, Dennis Ramsay, W. Hodgson, Jn. McRea, Stes. Thon. Mason

267 27May90
Fm Platt Townshend "formerly of ALX, VA but now of the State of NY, **Physician**
To David Henley "late of ALX & now residing in NY, **Merchant**"
For 2500 Spanish milled $ LOT 73, a 1/2 acre lot bounded on W by Ffx St ... S by
Duke ... E by LOT 72 "now or lately belonging to Richard Earl [?Arell?] ... N by LOT
65.   WTT: Wm. Davies, Aw. Dunscomb, Reuben Brumley

269 22May90
 Platt Townshend swore to the above before Richard Morris, **Chief Justice** of the
"Supreme Court of Judicament for the State of New York";
    On 21 Oct90 **Governor** Geo. Clinton, **Esquire**, of New York certified Morris was
Chief Justice, etc.;
    22Sep91: Ordered recorded by the ALX Court of Hustings

270 09Feb91
Fm Joseph Cary & William Wilson & Philip Marsteller, TwnALX, FfxCo, StVA
To Christian Mayer, Town of Baltimore, MD
WHEREAS 12Dec85 Robert & Nancy McCrea AND Robert Mease sold to Sebastian Schess [also: Schiess] part of LOT 64:
BEGIN on Prince 54' 1" W of Water St (the W line of parcel conveyed by McR & M to Robert Townshend Hooe & Richard Harrison) ... W w/Prince 23' 3" to the line of Baltzer Spangler ... S w/Spangler's line //Water St 98' 6"... E// Prince 23' 3" to H&H's line ... thence w/H&H's line to BEGIN.
AND WHEREAS 27Jan87 Sebastian Schiess conveyed all that parcel (among other assets) to Cary & Wilson & Marsteller;
NOW Cary, Wilson, Marsteller for £700 cmv convey to Christian Mayer that same parcel.   WTT: James Campbell, Jesse Taylor, Junr.; Dun. Nivien

273 20Sep91
Fm Thomas West--"eldest son & Heir at Law of John West Junr who was eldest son and heir at Law of Hugh West, the elder, of the County of Fairfax in the State of Virginia deceased"
To Richard Conway, TwnALX, FfxCo, StVA;
"WHEREAS the said Hugh West was in his lifetime seized in Fee of and in a tract of Land lying upon and binding with the River Potomack a part of which Together with other lands adjoining thereto the Assembly of Virginia condemned and directed to be laid out into a Town by the name of Alexandria and appointed certain persons to lay the same off into Lotts with a sufficient number of convenients [sic] Streets to accommodate them to sell and convey the said Lotts and in every other particular to carry the act respecting the said Town into full effect, who by virtue of the powers vested in them laid out the Lands so appropriated into a number of Lotts some of which were irregular in their shape and different from the others from the irregular surface of the ground which had been appropriated for that use, and the said Trustees from time to time sold and conveyed the Lotts so laid off untill they disposed of the whole of them and WHEREAS among other Lotts so laid off sold and conveyed by the Trustees as aforesaid was one lying upon the East side of Water Street and South side of Princess Street described in the plan of the said Town by the (No. 20) which from the irregular surface of the ground was one of those which were laid off in an irregular shape and different from the Lotts in general at the Southern extremity of which Lott joining upon Water street and extending southwardly with that Street, lay a small slip of ground which was not included in the said Lott (No.20) or in any other Lott of the said Town, nor was the same in any of the sales made by the said Trustees, sold and disposed of by the said Trustees as an appendage to the said Lott (No.20) or any other of the Lotts of the said Town or in any other manner whatsoever

sold or disposed of by them [nor by Hugh West, nor by John West, Jr.,] and thus is become vested in the said Thomas West";
NOW for £250 cmv Thomas West sells to Richard Conway "all that slip of Ground" E of Water St, S side of LOT 20:
BEGIN on Water St at southern extremity of LOT 20 ... E w/lot line into the river ... thence //Water St 117' more or less to Queen ... W w/Queen to Water St ... thence w/Water St to BEGIN.
WTT: Ja. Keith, William Ward, Roger Chew, Benjamin Davis

277 23Dec90
Fm George & Mary Kyger, Hampshire Co., StVA
To Josiah Watson, TwnALX, FfxCo, StVA: for £660 cmv, part of a parcel S of Prince, W of Ffx--part of LOTS 66 & 67:
BEGIN int Prince-Ffx ... S w/Ffx 52' 10 1/2" to ground of Jacob Cox ... W//Prince 90'... S//Ffx 35'... W//Prince 63' to ground of William Hartshorne ... N//Ffx 88' 4 1/2" to Prince ... thence w/Prince to BEGIN--part of LOTS 66 & 67 conveyed to the Kygers 09Aug75 by Christopher Beeler. [Signed by both Kygers, but Mary signs w/mark)]
Wtt: Ja. Keith, Chas. Young, Junr.; Bailey Washington, Jr.; John Kyger
CMN: Edward McCarty, Ignatius Wheeler, Oke Johnson, **Gentlemen** of Hampshire Co., aptd 31Mar91 to examine Mary. Rptd 14Apr91.

282 09Aug91
Fm John Korn & Jacob Wisemiller, TwnALX, FfxCo, CwlVA
To Job Green   -do-
WHEREAS John Alexander, late of Stafford, dec'd, on 19Dec74 conveyed to William McKnight of ALX, **Cabinetmaker**, [Alexander numbered] LOT 110 bounded on N by Prince, W by St Asaph, subject to £9.5.0 cmv yearly rent;
AND WHEREAS McKnight conveyed parts to various people for rents sufficient to satisfy his obligation to JnALXR, and thereby hold the rest rent-free;
AND WHEREAS McKnight 13 Oct83 conveyed to William Eigenbrode "under the name of William Ownbread" part of the rent-free property:
BEGIN at W corner of house on "lott occupied by Neil Mooney ... W//Prince 38' 5" to a "Street now known by the name of Saint Asaph Street" ... S 126' then E 38' 5"... thence N to BEGIN--with a covenant that if those whose rents went to satisfy McKnight's to ALXR should default, Eigenbrode/Ownbread could take those properties and re-rent them in amounts necessary to meet the McKnight-ALXR agreement;
AND WHEREAS WE/WO owed Korn & Wisemiller £50 and therefore with his wife Magdalena on 20Jul90 "made over" [mortgaged] to K&W the unsold part of the parcel:
BEGIN 20' fm St Asaph-Prince ... S//St Asaph 80'... E 18' 5" ... N 80' to Prince ... thence w/Prince 18' 5" to BEGIN:
--and if by 20Jul91 the £50 + interest was not paid, then K&W could make public sale of the 80' x 18' 5" parcel
--and WE/WO having failed to pay
--and K&W having advertised 26Jul91 to sell the parcel 09Aug91 at 4 p.m. for ready money and it "was cried out to the said Job Green at £108.10 cmv"
NOW K&W convey the parcel to Green for the £108.10 cmv.
WTT: Cleon Moore, Aaron Hewes, John Murray, Isaac McPherson

287 10Aug91
Fm Job & Lydia Green, TwnALX, FfxCo, CwlVA, **Marriner** [sic]
To John Korn & Jacob Wisemiller of -do-

[repeats the WHEREAS clauses and conditions of the deed above, but adds that JK & JW = **Biscuit Bakers** in ALX, and partners]
NOW for £120 cmv the Greens sell the same parcel to JK & JW
WTT: Aaron Hews, Alexander Smith, Samuel Harrison, P. Marsteller
CMN: Philip Marsteller, Dennis Ramsay, John Murray, **Gentlemen** of TwnALX, aptd 17Aug91 to examine Lydia. Rptd same day.

294 07Jul91
Fm Andrew & Margaret Wales, TwnALX, FfxCo, StVA
To Jonah Thompson -do-
WHEREAS the Waleses 28Jul74 conveyed to Robert McCrea, Robert Mease AND Matthew Mease part LOTS 56-57-58:
BEGIN E side Ffx at SW corner of that part of LOT 58 Wales then owned--at the dividing line between "Wales and Benjamin Shreve, and since conveyed by him to Josiah Watson" [the "him" who conveyed to Watson is not clear] ... E w/dividing line //Prince across LOTS 58 & 57 to Water St ... N w/Water St 27' ... thence across LOTS 58 & 57 until line intersects Ffx St 36' N of BEGIN ... thence w/Ffx to BEGIN;
--and Wales promised to lay out and keep open a 9' alley on the N side of these parts of LOTS 58 & 57 fm Ffx to Water St
--and 07Aug81 Matthew Mease conveyed his interest to Robert McCrea and Robert Mease
--and Robert & Agness McCrea, and Robert Mease, on 16Nov78 and 22May90 conveyed all the parcel they had gotten from the Waleses to Josiah Watson
--and Josiah Watson on ___ __ 1790 [month & day blanks not filled in] sold a fraction of the parcel to Jonah Thompson:
BEGIN on Ffx at S line of the said alley ... thence w/Ffx 26'... E//Prince [blank number of] feet ... thence //Ffx 26' to the alley ... thence w/alley to BEGIN.
BUT it appears that the parcels from the Waleses to RMcC, Rm AND MM were 9' narrower on Water St than on Ffx St
--and also that the part of LOT 58 conveyed by Watson to Thompson must in the "same degree and proportion lose a part of the breadth intended to be granted to the said Jonah Thompson as it was advanced to the Eastern boundary...which would render the house proposed to be erected thereupon by... Jonah Thompson irregular in the shape and Form...."
--and as Andrew Wales is "willing and desirous" of remedying the problem caused by the "irregular manner in which the said Alley was first laid out"
NOW the Waleses for 5/ from Jonah Thompson convey that part of LOT 58 originally to be laid out as an alley:
BEGIN on Ffx at S line of alley ... E w/alley 41'... N//Ffx 1' 6" and thence to BEGIN;
--and in lieu of [in addition to?] that strip, the Waleses convey: BEGIN on Ffx at N side of alley ... E w/alley 41' and N//Ffx 1' 6"... thence to BEGIN.
WTT: Ja. Keith, Bryan Hampson, George Taylor
[The commission to examine Margaret Wales in this matter is at p. 346, below.]

300 08Jul91
Fm Andrew & Margaret Wales, TwnALX, FfxCo, StVA
To Marcus McCausland, Town of Baltimore, MD
WHEREAS on 03 & 04 Dec 1771 Robert Adam sold Wales 1/2 of LOTS 56-57-58 E of Ffx, S of King, N of Prince:
BEGIN on Ffx on the line which divides the "Lotts now the property of John Fitzgerald & Valentine Peers" fm LOTS 56-57-58 ... S w/Ffx 1/2 the length of LOT 58 ... thence //dividing line, across LOTS 56-57-58 to E side LOT 56 ... thence up the river "the Courses and meanders of the said LOTTS 56 and 57" to the line of Peers and Fitzgerald's lots ... thence w/that line to BEGIN;

WHEREAS [recites conveyance of property fm Wales to McCrea + Mease + Mease 28Jul74 w/9' alley along its N side fm Ffx to Water St. See deed above, p.294]
WHEREAS part LOT 58--fm Wales to McC+M+M is now Jonah Thompson's, and yesterday the Waleses conveyed part of the alley to him, adding and allotting an equal portion of land for the alley on its north side;
NOW the Waleses for £500 convey to McCausland part of LOT 58:
BEGIN on Ffx at N line of alley as laid out in the conveyance to RMcC + RM + MM ... N w/Ffx 43' to Fitzgerald, Peers and others' property ... E 123'... thence //Ffx S 47' 6" to alley ... hence w/original alley line 80'... N//Ffx 1' 6"... thence to BEGIN with the benefit of the alley as now laid off.
WTT: Ja. Keith, Bryan Hampson, George Taylor
[The commission to examine Margaret Wales is at p. 347, below]

306 11Feb91 Mortgage
Fm William Hunter, Junior, TwnALX, FfxCo, StVA
To John Dalrymple, Town of Fredericksburg, StVA: for £1200 cmv, part of LOT 16, E side Ffx, N side Princess:
BEGIN int Ffx-Princess ... with Ffx 100' to 12' alley ... E//Princess 51' 5" to line of William Ward ... S w/Ward's line 100' to Princess ... thence w/Princess to BEGIN;
                    AND
BEGIN on Ffx on N line of the 12' alley ... with Ffx 64' to NW corner LOT 16 [as given, but note S line below is 64' 7"] ... E w/lot line 123' 5"... S w/lot line 64' 7" to alley ... thence w/alley to BEGIN. (These are parts of lot sold Hunter by Ralph Wormley, **Esquire**, 30May85.)
Terms: Hunter to repay £1200 + interest to Dalrymple on/by 11Feb92; if so, this deed void.   WTT: John Donnell, Ja. Keith, Joseph Honeff

311 18Jul91
Fm Michael & Elizabeth Gretter, TwnALX, FfxCo, StVA
To Lawrence Hoof   -do-
For £150 cmv, part LOTS 115 & [blank], N of King, E of Pitt:
BEGIN on King at E line of parcel given by MG to his daughter Elizabeth Simpson, wife of William, "by whom the same was sold...to Lawrence Hoof" and supposed to be [the parcel's E line] 107' 2" E of Pitt ... E w/King 20', 9' W of house now occupied by John Gretter ... //Pitt & Royal, 130' 7" to line of Robert McCrea & Robert Mease ... //King, 127' 2" to Pitt ... S w/Pitt 20' 7" to 10' alley on N line of William Hepburn's lot ... E w/alley its whole 72'length ... S//Pitt 10' to parcel given Elizabeth by Michael as above ... E w/that line 35' 2" to the "end of that line"... N w/another of that parcel's lines 100' to BEGIN.
--and Michael Gretter promises to lay off and keep open a 9' alley on the E line of this parcel, fm King St. to McCrea & Mease's property
--and Lawrence Hoof is also to have use of 10' alley on N side of William Hepburn, with Hepburn. WTT: William Hepburn, Ja. Keith, William Keech

317 21Jul91
Fm Michael Gretter, TwnALX
To Lawrence Hoof   -do-
  MG gives certain clear title to LH for the parcel long ago given to Gretter's daughter, now Mrs. Simpson, and sold by the Simpsons to Hoof. [See above]
WTT: William Hepburn, Ja. Keith

320 01Dec90 Articles of Agreement
Fm John Harper, FfxCo, StVA
To Josiah Watson, TwnALX, FfxCo, StVA

--they, jointly owning the wharf and pier lying on N side of Prince & E side of Union Sts.
--constructed at joint expense
--each entitled to a "communication" w/Prince St
--JH has that part of the pier which "bounds upon Prince Street and the Dock at the head of Prince Street"
--and by building upon or enclosing his ground to the edge of the dock might deprive Watson of communication with Prince St. "which would greatly injure and reduce the value" of Watson's part of the pier
NOW JH grants JW a "passage Road or way of Communication" fm Watson's part of the pier 10' wide "along the out side of [John Harper's] Ground" into Prince St.
WTT: Ja. Keith, Jno. Keith, James Keith Junr

323 24Apr87
Fm James & Alice Lawrason AND Samuel Arell, TwnALX, FfxCo, StVA
To Peter Wagener AND George Deneale, FfxCo, StVA
Lease for £50, plus fm 17Dec87 12/6 annually, part Lot E side St Asaph, S side Duke:
BEGIN on Duke 40' fm Duke-St. A ... E//Duke 20'... S//St Asaph 78' ... W//Duke 20'... thence to BEGIN--conveyed 23Feb86 to Lawrason & Arell by Robert Daugherty, heir of Windsor Brown;
--and L & A will leave open a 4' alley on the lot's E side PLUS the 4' alley left by Wagener & Deneale for the joint use of the Lawrasons and Arell.
WTT: Richd. M. Scott, W. McKnight, Philip [his + mark] Ferno, Henry Walker, Baldwin Stith, Titus Triplett

330 02Apr91
Fm William & Christiana Hunter, Senior, TwnALX, FfxCo, StVA
To Joseph Thomas   -do-
WHEREAS Joseph & Hannah Saunders 04Feb75 conveyed to Edward Ramsay a parcel S side Prince, E of Ffx Sts
--30' 10 1/4" fronting on Prince
--98' 5" deep
--bounded on E by land granted by Joseph Saunders to son John
--on W by land then William Ramsay, **Esquire**'s, but now Joseph Harrison's
--on S by alley 10' wide and 16' deep running S into another alley 10' wide running W into Ffx St and other land of Joseph Saunders
--w/privilege to use both alleys
--Edward Ramsay to pay annual rent of 28 1/3 pieces of eight
AND WHEREAS 21Sep78 Edward Ramsay conveyed the parcel to William Hunter, Hunter then to pay the rent to Saunders
--and Hunter [leased] the parcel to John Jolly for annual rent of 40 Spanish milled $ each 1st May by indenture [date left blank, but recorded as 22May81]
--and Jolly did not pay any rent 1st May 1787-88-89-90
--so that on 02May90 Hunter repossessed the parcel;
NOW the Hunters
--for payment of 51.10.o cmv
--and annual rent each 1stMay of 40 Spanish milled $
--lease the property w/use of both alleys to Joseph Thomas
WTT: Ja. Keith, Richard Weightman, James Fletcher
CMN: Philip Marsteller, Jesse Taylor, Dennis Ramsay aptd 20 Oct91 to examine Christiana. Rptd back same day.
MEMORANDUM of 02Apr91: If John Jolly should evict Joseph Thomas, Hunter is liable only for the £51.10.0 + interest.   WTT: as above

341 22Jul90
Fm Robert Bryce AND William Wilson [No ID]
To James Kennor [also Kenner] [No ID]
WHEREAS Nicholas Bryce is the brother/heir of John Bryce, deceased and
--31Jul86 NB conveyed to RB & WW "sundry Lotts and Houses in the Town of ALX in Trust" to sell for the highest price at public auction
--and RB & WW did put up for sale a lot on Prince, 40' on Prince and 88' back, "whereon the said John Bryce last lived"
--and the lot was subject to dower rights by John's widow (who has since married James Kenner) as well as to £32 annual ground rent to John Harper
--and James Kenner was high bidder for the lot at auction;
NOW for 20/ and for £91 + 9 pence in arrears due John Harper, the trustees (Robert Bryce & William Wilson) convey title to James Kenner--Kenner to continue to pay the £32 cmv annually to **Captain** John Harper.
WTT: James Wilson, Edward Harper, O. Windsor, James Campbell, John Bryan, Thos. Rogerson

346 Commission to examine Margaret Wales on the 07Jul91 deed fm the Waleses to Jonah Thompson [at p. 294, above]: Jesse Taylor, Dennis Ramsay and John Murray "of the Corporation of ALX, **Gentlemen**" aptd 22Sep91 and rptd back same day.

347 Commission to examine Margaret Wales on the 08Jul91 deed fm the Waleses to Marcus McCausland [at p. 300, above]: same men as at p. 346, aptd 20Sep91; rptd back 22Sep91.

350 15 Oct91   Mortgage
Fm John & Sarah Reynolds, TwnALX, FfxCo, StVA
To Nathan Littler, Frederick Co., StVA
--JR owes NL £42.12.6 cmv
--to secure which he pledges parcel E of St Asaph, N of Wolfe:
BEGIN int St Asaph-Wolfe ... N w/St A 106' 5" to 10' alley ... E w/alley //Wolfe 23' 5"... S//St A 106' 5" to Wolfe ... thence to BEGIN--part of LOT [blank] conveyed by John ALXR, **Esquire** to John Garner Hamilton for annual rent
--then by JGH to John Finley
--fm the late John Finley, who died intestate, to his brother Hugh Finley
--fm Hugh Finley 10Jun85 to John Reynolds for annual rent £23.5 cmv.
Terms: void if £42.12.6 + interest paid on/before 15 November next [whether 1 or 13 months from now not clear]
WTT: John Contee Keith, Jesorn Yost [on 20 Oct clerk records this as <u>John</u> Yost]; John Yost, Junr.

355 03Sep90
Fm Uriah Forrest, Montgomery Co., MD
To Peter Casanave [spelled with all **a**'s throughout deed] -do-Part Lot on King St., ALX, "on which the brick house of the said Uriah Forrest standeth":
BEGIN on King at NE "corner of Hepburn & Dundas's ground and near the NW corner of the aforesaid House"... E w/King "the breadth of the said House supposed to be 31 1/2 feet"... S// Pitt 176' 7"... W//King same as first line ... N//Pitt 176' 7" to BEGIN;
                    AND
Part of another lot bounded on S by Pitt, "known as...Lot No. [blank]": BEGIN NW corner of lot, E side of Pitt ... S w/Pitt 20' and E//Prince 100'...N//Pitt 20'...W//Prince 100'to BEGIN.

WTT: Sam. W. Magruder AND Richard Thompson, **Justices of the Peace** for Montgomery Co. who also examined Rebecca Forrest (Mrs. Uriah Forrest). Uriah also swore to all the above, appearing before the **Mayor** of the Corporation of George Town, Montgomery Co., Thomas Beall. Recorded by Montgomery Co. Clerk, Brooke Beall. [pp. 359-361.]

361   02Nov91
Fm John Baptist Petit, TwnALX, FfxCo, StVA
To Margaret Petit "my beloved wife (lawfully married)"
--"for the Natural love and affection...and also for divers other good causes" [John conveys to Margaret]:
"all... my real and personal Estate:" a Brick house & Lot on King St --another small Framed house & Lot adjoining ... another house & Lot on Ffx St ... all my household furniture &c ... all my Merchandize &c ... a Negro girl Mely ... 2 horses ... a Chair and a Dray ... a Cow ... and all Goods and Chattles, outstanding debts whatsover, in token of which [John has delivered] "1 Silver Tea Spoon and a handful of Earth"
WTT: Peter Wise, J.C. Kempff

363   26Sep91
Fm Peter Casanave, Montgomery Co., MD
To William Hodgson, TwnALX, StVA: for £930 "lawfull money of VA" all that part of Lot on King St "on which a Brick house of...Peter Casanave standeth":
BEGIN on King at N corner of Hepburn & Dundas' ground and near NW corner of the house ... E w/King to E end of house (estimated as 31' 6") ... S//Pitt 176' 6"... W//King same as first line ... N//Pitt 176' 6" to BEGIN.
          AND
Part of a lot on Prince:
BEGIN E side of Pitt at NW corner of Lot above ...S w/Pitt 20' ... E//Prince 100'... N//Pitt 20'... W//Prince 100' to BEGIN.
        /s/Peter Casanave [in later years he will sign Casano̱ve]
WTT: Thomas Williams, Joseph Hodgson, John Wren

367   13May91
Fm Joseph & Rachel Thomas, TwnALX, FfxCo, StVA
To Richard Weightman -do-
WHEREAS William & Christiana Hunter, Senior, 02Apr91 conveyed to Joseph Thomas a parcel:
--on S side Prince, E of Ffx
--fronting 30' 10 1/4" on Prince and 98' 5" deep
--bounded E by John Saunder's parcel
--on W by Joseph Harrison's
--on S by alley 10' wide & 16' deep running S into another 10' wide alley which runs W into Ffx St "and other ground the property of Gurden Chapin"
--paying [JT paying Hunter] each 01 May 40 Spanish milled $;
NOW for £300 cmv the Thomases convey to Weightman the parcel and use of the 2 alleys
--Weightman must pay Hunter the 40 Spanish milled $ each 01May
--if John Jolly (fm whom Hunter repossessed this parcel) ejects Weightman, Joseph Thomas will refund £150 + interest to Weightman
WTT: John Brander, William Duvall, Thomas Daniell

374   14Jan92   Non-Importation Compliance
  Before Jesse Taylor, one John Edward Ford swears on the occasion of his move into Virginia that he is in compliance with Virginia's act re: non-importation of slaves.

375 [no month/day] 1791 Power of Attorney
Robert McCrea of McCrea & Mease, partners in trade, is about to move away and appoints Robert Mease his attorney to conclude their business matters. [Signed [blank] Day of [blank] 1791, and ordered recorded 19Jan92. [N.B.: p. 395, below, gives missing date as 10 Oct91].
WTT: Jesse Taylor, Jr.; Charles Bryan, Jana. Mandeville [spelled out on p. 379 as Jonathan]

380 05Jan92
Fm William & Kitty Hunter, Senior, TwnALX, FfxCo, StVA
To George Slacum -do- : part LOT 59, N of Prince, W of Ffx BEGIN int Prince-Ffx ... W w/ Prince 60'... N//Ffx 20'... E//Prince 60' to Ffx ... thence to BEGIN;
--conveyed 07Jun83 to Hunter by David Arell & James Lawrason
--by Hunter to Joseph Greenway 08Mar85
--by Greenway back to Hunter "by several indentures of record in the County Court of Fairfax" [Mrs. Hunter signs herself "Kitty Hunter"]
WTT: John Longdon, George Goode
CMN: Philip Marsteller, Jesse Taylor, Thomas Porter "of the TwnALX, Gentlemen," aptd 26Jan92 to examine Kitty. Rptd 27Jan92.

386 24Jan92
Fm Henry & Elizabeth Stroman, TwnALX, FfxCo, StVA
To Diederick Scheckel -do- : For £96 cmv, part LOT 39:
BEGIN NW corner on Royal, 27' 6" on Royal ... E 123' //Henry Stroman's ground to dividing line "surveyed and conveyed...by Cyrus Copper to...Stroman"... S 27' 6" //Stroman's parcel ... W 123' from the dividing line parallel w/Stroman's lot to Royal to BEGIN (It would seem that "parallel to Stroman's parcel means "binding with" the lot line, and that the BEGINNING is the parcel's NW corner]
WTT: J.C. Kempff, Caleb Earp, John Harper

389 10Jan92   Mortgage
Fm John & Sarah Reynolds, TwnALX, StVA
To Andrew Wagener AND Colbert Anderson, Berkley Co., StVA
--JR owes £40 cmv to AW & CA
--JR thus pledges part Lot E of St. A, N of Wolfe, LOT [blank] BEGIN int St. Asaph-Wolfe ... N w/St A 106' 5" to 10' alley ... E w/alley//Wolfe 23' 5"... S//St Asaph 106' 5" to Wolfe ... thence to BEGIN--conveyed to Reynolds by Hugh Finley 10Jun85 for annual rent £23.5 each 16Jul.
Terms: void if Reynolds pays £40 + interest on/before 10Jan93
WTT: Jonah Thompson, James McCormick, John Kleinhoof

393 09Apr92
Fm Robert & Nancy McCrea, & Robert Mease, late of TwnALX, StVA, **Merchants**
To Robert Peter, Town of George-Town, MD
WHEREAS as "McCrea & Mease, **Merchants**, of the TwnALX"
23Jun89 conveyed to RP part LOTS 45 & 50 on W side of Royal:
BEGIN on Royal 20 1/4' S of N boundary of LOT 50 ... N along W side Royal 44 1/4'... W//King 123' 5"... S//Royal 44 1/4' ... E//King 123' 5" to BEGIN. This [mortgage] was meant to secure payment by M&M of £1200 cmv to James & Robert Dunlap of City of London--thereafter assigned by the Dunlaps to Innes Beveridge & Co. (w/Robert Peter acting for IB & Co), the debt payable on/before 23Jun90.
AND WHEREAS Robert McCrea has left Virginia, but on 10 Oct91 gave P/Atty to Robert Mease--and the debt not having been paid;

NOW title hereby passes to Robert Peter.   WTT: John Clark, George Chapman, William Hall

398 28Sep91   Power of Attorney
Fm Elizabeth Kirkpatrick Cutlar, widow of Roger Cutlar of Orraland, deceased AND Catharine Kirkpatrick Coltart, widow of William Coltart of Bluehill, deceased AND Henrietta Kirkpatrick, daughter of Thomas Kirkpatrick of Raeberry, deceased
--"all Sisters german and heirs at Law of the now also deceased Thomas Kirkpatrick of Alexandria in the State of Virginia in America **Merchant**"
To Mr. William Wilson AND Mr. Roger Coltart of ALX, **Merchants**
WTT: (in Kirckcudbright, Kirkcudbright County, Scotland) George Craig, Daniel McLellan

399 [blank]Sep90
Fm William & Susanna Hartshorne, FfxCo, CwlVA
To Samuel Arell -do- : lease @ £20 now; on/after 01Nov90, @ £10 cmv per year of part of lot E of Washington, N of Prince:
BEGIN SW corner of lot at int of Wn-Prince ... N w/Wn 100' to 10' alley to be laid out for benefit [of all contiguous property holders] ... E//Prince w/alley 40'... S//Wn 100' to Prince ... along Prince 40' to BEGIN.
--the Hartshornes remain responsible for annual rent owed Wm. Thornton Alexander of King Geo. Co.
--they will lay out an alley along N side this lot beginning on Washington 100' fm Wn. & Prince, 10' wide, for 100'
--if Arell rents any of this, and exceeds the original amount, then his rent will be increased--just as Hartshorne's rent will be increased to W.T. ALXR in the same circumstances, as per the original Alexander-Hartshorne lease
WTT: Charles Lee, Jao. Lear, Gurden Chapin

407 12Jun92   Power of Attorney
Fm William Semple, City of Philadelphia, **Merchant**
To George Deneale of ALX, StVA
For: "amounts due me by or through heirs, executors or assigns of Cuthbert Bullitt, **Esquire**, deceased, late of Prince William County"
WTT: Benjn. Tate, Abraham Singer
Attested by Matthew Clarkson, **Mayor** of Philadelphia, 12Jun92

409 15Sep91
Fm William Miller, TwnALX, FfxCo, StVA
To Thomas White, **Shop-keeper**, -do- : for £18 cmv, a House and part of Lot 111, E of Pitt, N of Prince:
BEGIN E side Pitt 119' N of int Pitt-Prince ... N w/Pitt 12' 8"... E//Prince 99'... S//Pitt 12' 8"... W to BEGIN.
--and paying each 01Jun 25 1/3 silver $ rent to John Saunders
Chain of title: John & Mary Saunders to Susanna Hamilton 20May85 "recorded in the Court of Fairfax 18Jul85 in No.4 Ledg. R.L.Q. folio 10";
--Susanna Hamilton to William Miller 06Aug90
--now Miller to White. [William Miller signs, but Jane Miller signs w/mark.]
WTT: Lanty Crowe, Edmond Edmonds, Thos. Coller

413 03Mar91
Fm Bridget Kirk, widow & relict of James Kirk, late of TwnALX, dec'd, and guardian of Robert Kirk, son and heir at law
To Andrew Jamieson, TwnALX, FfxCo, StVA:

Lease of part of LOT 85, E of Union, N of Wolfe:
BEGIN at dividing line between LOT 85 and "land of which Thomas Fleming died seized"... E w/line to 21' alley laid out by Bridget Kirk through LOT 85, fm the dividing line into Wolfe ... S w/alley 60'... W line//dividing line, to Union ... thence w/Union to BEGIN
Terms: fm last 01Jan [1791], for 11 years and 7 1/2 months, quarterly payments of the annual £50 rent;
--"and repairing the Bake house and Ovens and building an half Story over the Ovens, and finishing the Tenement contiguous to the said Bake-house, and building thereto a Shed Kitchen" [at the back of the tenement];
--to keep all in good repair, and at term's end to give up possession of the "Ground... buildings and woodyard"
--Jamieson's costs of new construction--labor and materials--to be deducted from the rent, and he gets use of the alley;
--he can build whatever else he and she agree to, using sand and dirt from contiguous Kirk property;
--when the lease is up she and he will each choose an evaluator to appraise the additional buildings. Either Bridget reimburses him the declared value w/in 5 weeks, or w/in 3 weeks there after he may remove the buildings.
WTT: Ja. Keith, Geo. Coryell, Jos. Caverly, Robt. Brockett, John Hill

418   26Mar92
Fm Bridget Kirk [ID as above]
To John Hill, TwnALX
Lease part LOT [blank] E of Water St, N of Wolfe:
BEGIN on Water St at S corner of "Mr. John Gill's Ground now fenced in...for a Garden"... E//Wolfe 120' then S//Water 30'... W//Wolfe 120' to Water St ... thence to BEGIN;
Terms: fm today for 10 yrs + 5 mos.; 1st 5 yrs: £5 cmv per annum; remainder: £35 per year, in quarterly payments.
WTT: Ja. Keith, Geo. Coryell, Andw. Jamieson

421   21Apr92   Deed of Release
Fm William Ownbread, Port Tobacco, MD
To John Korn & Jacob Wisemiller, ALX, StVA: part LOT [blank]
--mortgaged by WO to JK & JW
--sold by them to Job Green via P/Atty given for that purpose
--sold by Job Green back to JK & JW
WTT: Ja. Keith, John Stewart, P. Marsteller, P.G. Marsteller

423   09May92
FM Betty Stewart [also Steuart] TwnALX, StVA, **widow**
To James Montgomery Stewart, of the same place, son of Betty
WHEREAS the late William Ramsay, father of Betty, on 15Feb77 "soon after the marriage of...Betty with James Steuart" gave them 3 parcels--and the 3 were devised by James' will as follows: half to Betty; half to son William Ramsay Steuart AND to the child then carried by the pregnant Betty, the child who is now James Montgomery Stewart;
AND WHEREAS after James Steuart's death some doubts arose as to the validity of the deed, William Ramsay, **Esquire**, on 15Jan85 reconveyed the parcels to his daughter Betty and his grandsons William R. Stewart & James M. Stewart as follows:
--half the land to Betty and the other half to William and James as tenants in common, 2 of the 3 parcels being bounded: BEGIN E side Water St, N side of "what was formerly called Ramsays Alley, but which is now called Fayette Street" ... W w/Fa-

yette 30'... N to 4' alley "between the ground of William Ramsay and the Lott of Ground late the property of **Col.** John Carlyle"... W to Water St ... S to BEGIN
AND
BEGIN also on E side Water St, at int Water St-King ... thence w/Water St. 75'7" to Ramsay's Alley, now Fayette St ... E w/Fayette 30' then S to King ... thence w/King to BEGIN [and the relevant documents are in FfxCo Court records];
AND WHEREAS William Ramsay Stewart "hath departed this life at a tender age..."
NOW Betty "for the love and affection which she doth bear unto the said James" conveys all the parts of the 2 above parcels which once belonged to her;
BUT if JMS should die before his 21st birthday, this is void.
[Signed by Betty: "Betty Steuart".]
WTT: Ja. Keith, Dennis Ramsay, Robert Allison, Thos. Porter

427   01May92
Fm William Thornton Alexander & wife Lucy [no ID]
To John Cassey of the State of MD [Cassey signs name Casey]:
Lease fm/on 01Nov92 for £15 VA currency per year of a lot "contiguous to TwnALX upon the Patowmack and laid off according to a plot of Lotts demised in the year 1784":
BEGIN W side Washington where Prince St. "when extended will intersect the W side of Washington" ... N w/Wn 176' 6"... W// Prince 123' 5"... S//Washington 176' 6"... E to BEGIN.
Terms: "whereas Lucy...is now under age" and can't convey her dower rights, WTA-- when she turns 21 and at JC's request-- will have the conveyance done.
[Signed by John Casey and for WTA, by his attorney Jno.T. Brooke]
WTT: Jesse Simms, Robert B. Jamesson, Dan. Casey

431   11Nov91
Fm James Kidd, TwnALX, StVA, **Sadler**
To John Bryan   -do-   **Sadler**
WHEREAS John Muir, late of ALX, dec'd, leased on 28 Oct90 to James Kidd "all that lott... upon Ffx St...granted by the Proprietor of the Northern Neck of Virginia unto Robert Muir... and which by the [Robert's] death Intestate without Issue descended unto the said John Muir..." and
WHEREAS James Kidd leased a part of the lot "and the Tenement thereupon erected during the said [lease] to Bartholemew Duffey"
NOW Kidd leases the remainder of the lot to John Bryan, reserving at the end of the lot--adjoining Kirk's lott "now in the occupation of [blank] Gordon a passage or foot way for the use of...Duffey...large enough to take a Cow or horse through...[the] way most convenient to them the said Duffy and Bryan"
Term: from 20Nov91 for 5 yrs, 10 mos.--except that part of the tenement which is now in possession of John Mason, **Silversmith**, until 01Jun92 (Mason paying the rent to Bryan);
Rent: [Bryan to Kidd] £40 cmv per year, paid quarterly;
Proviso: [Bryan is to] "finish the said Tenements as well as that occupied by the said James Kidd, as that part in the possession of John Mason the partitions to be made with plank, and the upper Floors to be laid in a proper manner with plank, the several partitions to be run where most convenient to...John Bryan"
--"and also to Glaze the Several windows with Glass, and paint the Gavel end and front of the house"
--[in a later repeat of this proviso] "and also that he will finish the house or tenement upon the said premises by running plank partitions in such places as he shall find most suitable for himself, lathing and plaistering such parts as require it if he shall think it Convenient,"

--"and that he will lay the upper Floors with plank in a proper manner if he shall think it convenient and Glaze all the windows of the said house, and paint the Gavel end and front of the house...."]
AND: if he erects any other buildings or make any improvements he will leave them intact and turn them over at the end of the lease;
AND: each--Kidd & Bryan--will put up a £100 bond to the other to show good faith
WTT: Ja. Keith, William McKnight, Chas. McKnight
MEMO: if Kidd and Duffy fail to pay the John Muir estate £18 when due, then Bryan can pay and deduct same from his obligation.

436 13Mar92   Non-Importation Compliance
   Before Dennis Ramsay, Richard Croke swears the slaves he brought from Maryland--Negroes James, Silvia, Amelia, Stace--are for his own use and not for sale.

436 03Feb92   Mortgage
Fm William & Mary Bushby, TwnALX, CwlVA
To George Suckley [no ID]: for £79.6.2, part lot on W side Ffx
BEGIN 24' fm NE corner of Presbyterian Church Yard ... N w/Ffx 22'... W//Duke 70' 6"... S//Ffx 22'... thence to BEGIN.
--void if the Bushbys repay £79.6.2 + interest on/before 01Jan93
--[in case of Bushby default] Suckley will be attorney to advertise 3 weeks in advance in the Alexandria Gazette of public sale, to then sell and apply proceeds against the debt
WTT: Jacob H. Manning, Joseph Bushby, William Allison

440 19Jun92   Mortgage
Fm William & Mary Bushby, TwnALX, CwlVA
To Anna Bell, Frederick Co., StVA for £82.5.0 cmv part lot: BEGIN NE corner of Presbyterian Church Yard on Ffx St ... N w/Ffx 24' then W//Duke 80'... S//Ffx 24' then E//Duke, in N line of Presb.Ch.Yard to BEGIN--void if the Bushbys repay £82.5.0 + interest on/before 19Jun94.   WTT: none

443 25May92
Fm James & Hannah Kenner, Botetourt Co., StVA
To Thomas Vowell, TwnALX, FfxCo, StVA
WHEREAS John Harper granted John Bryce land on N side Prince and W of Union--40' fronting on Prince and 88' 3 1/2" back--for annual rent of £32 cmv;
WHEREAS by John Bryce's death w/o issue the property descended to his brother Nicholas;
WHEREAS Nicholas 31Jul86 conveyed this and other property in trust to Robert Bryce & William Wilson;
WHEREAS RB & WW 22Jul90 conveyed the Prince St property to James Kenner, recorded both in ALX Hustings & Ffx Co. Courts; NOW the Kenners for £250 cmv from Thomas Vowell convey the property to Vowell (Vowell now to pay the annual £32 rent to John Harper)
WTT: Ja. Keith, P. Marsteller, George Slacum; Thomas Vowell, Jr.; Ebenezer Vowell
CMN: George Skillern, John Bealle and John Castmill, **Gentlemen** of Botetourt Co., aptd 28May92 to examine Hannah. Rptd 03Jul92

449 08May92
Fm Stephen & Catherine Cook [no ID]
To John Rawlins, TwnALX: lease from 01Jun93 @ £6/annum of part of a lot "contiguous to the TwnALX upon the Potowmack" [the town, apparently, not the lot] "which

was laid off and known by No.2 according to a plot of Lotts demised in the year 1784":
BEGIN SW corner LOT 2 ... N w/Washington St 20'... E//King 123'...S//Wn 20'... thence to BEGIN.
WTT: William Smith, Samuel Craig, Samuel Vowell
MEMO [p.452]: rent remittable upon paying 12 years rent w/in 12 years of 08May92.

453 08May92
Fm the Cooks, as above [no ID]
To William Smith, TwnALX: another part LOT 2, as above:
BEGIN on E line of Washington, 20' N of SW corner of LOT 2 ... N w/Wn 20' ... E//King 123'... S//Wn 20'... thence to BEGIN.
Terms: as above, including rent remittal option
WTT: Saml Craig, Samuel Vowell, John Rawlins

456 18Apr92 Collateral
Fm Dennis Ramsay to Jesse Taylor, Taylor having co-signed a note for £445.19.0 WHEREAS they jointly purchased from William Lowry "goods, wares and merchandize"
--giving Lowry 3 notes, due 13 June, 13 Sept, and 13 Oct87
--Ramsay's portion, for merchandise received = £445.19.0, plus interest thereon, still due and payable
NOW Ramsay makes over the following slaves, household furniture and articles:

Ismael, Ellis, Daniel, Sall
"my...part" of Mulattos
   William and Dennis
the future increase of Sall
3 featherbeds, bolsters, and pillows
6 pairs of sheets
6 blanketts
6 Coverlids
2 setts of bed Curtains
2 -do- window -do-
12 large silver spoons
12 silver tea spoons
1 large silver Soup Spoon

1 silver punch ladle
1 mahogany Tea Table
2 mahogany dining Tables
1 walnut Table
1 maple Table
1 walnut Desk
1 small mahogany dining Table
1 Looking-glass
18 Windsor Chairs
7 mahogany Chairs
1 riding chair with a top and harness
1 large Scow

WTT: John Dundas, Achd. J. Taylor, Daniel Lightfoot

459 7Sep92
Fm Peter & Susanah Tartzback [also: Tertzback and Susannah]
   TwnALX, FfxCo, CwlVA
To Mordechai Miller -do- : part of LOT 81:
BEGIN on Ffx 20' fm SW corner of LOT 81 ... N w/Ffx 20'... E//Duke and Wolfe 123' 5"... S//Ffx 20'... thence to BEGIN--subject to annual ground rent £10 in silver $ to Samuel Arell each 01Jun--as per lease 24Sep83 to be found "upon Record Lg. R.L.O. folio 164" WTT: J.C. Kempff, Jane Wilkinson, Job Green

461 12Nov92
Fm William Herbert & John Dundas as "Commissioners under decree of High Court
   of Chancery of State of Virginia"
To Benjamin Dulany, FfxCo, StVA

WHEREAS Robert Lyle the Elder, late of ALX, dec'd--by indenture of [blank] [blank] 178[blank] to secure payment of £500 cmv, plus interest fm 01May88 until paid, to Robinson Sanderson & Rumney mortgaged land W of Ffx, S of Princess: BEGIN on Ffx on S side alley running through LOTS 23-24 (at intersection of Ffx and the alley) ... S w/Ffx 29'... W//Princess 84' to include the Dwelling of Robert Lyle the Elder ... N//Ffx 29' to alley ... thence w/alley to BEGIN;
AND WHEREAS soon after the mortgage was signed Lyle died w/o paying the note; --his heirs also did not pay it, and Robinson Sanderson & Rumney brought suit in the High Court of Chancery against:
William Hunter, Jr.)
Andrew Wales   ) Exxrs of Robert Lyle the Elder
Thomas Hewett)
Robert Lyle   )
Martha Lyle - Lyle's widow and
    William, Jane, Robert Lyle --Lyle's children
--on 01Nov91 the Court in Richmond ruled the defendants to pay prior 01Aug92 OR
--William Herbert, John Dundas, Richard Harris (any two, as commissioners for the court) to give 3 weeks notice in the <u>Virginia Gazette</u> for public auction of the property;
AND WHEREAS neither the exxrs nor the heirs paid the note, and a notice was run on 10 Oct92 for a sale 10Nov92 at which
--Robert Lyle bid £350, but could not pay the money agreeable to the decree
--Benjamin Dulany bid £300, payable immediately
NOW Herbert and Dundas for the £300 from Dulany convey him title to the property. WTT: Geo. Clementson, Wm. Wilson, Jas. Wilson, Joseph Hodgson
[N.B.: see below, p. 467]

467   15Nov92
Fm Martha Lyle [no ID]
To Benjamin Dulany of ALX: for £80, Martha sells her dower rights to the above parcel. [The deed notes Robert Lyle, dec'd, as a **Merchant** of ALX; Robinson, Sanderson & Rumney as **Merchants** in Whitehaven.]
WTT: George Clementson, George Sweeny, William Hodgson

468   20Dec92
    Catharine Brown, widow of William Brown, late of ALX, deceased states "whereas... William did...devise unto me certain Legacies, and make certain provisions for my support, which provisions appearing to me inadequate," and she now renounces the legacies and provisions, and claims "that Interest...which by the Laws of the County I am entitled to." [She signs: Cath. Browne] WTT: Jas. Keith, Samuel Lowe

469   11Dec92
Fm Joseph Caverly   [no ID]
To Andrew Jamieson [no ID]
WHEREAS Bridget Kirk (widow of James Kirk and guardian of son and heir Robert) conveyed to JC part of Kirk's lot and wharf
NOW JC leases to AJ:
BEGIN on W side of alley running into Wolfe St, through Kirk's and Thomas Fleming's lots, 2' N of SE corner of Jamieson's dwelling ... S w/alley to NE corner of warehouse built by James Kirk ... W//Wolfe into Union St ... N w/Union 2' beyond SW corner of Jamieson's woodyard "as it is now enclosed"... thence to BEGIN.
PROVISO: if a line fm NE corner of warehouse to Union St should include any part of the whse or its chimney, Jamieson will not hinder access to it nor pull down the

chimney, etc., AND both parties will leave the alley free and clear.   WTT: Wm. McKensie, Robt. Anderson, William Shaw
MEMO [p. 473]: Jamieson may remove the old house now on the premises being used now as a stable, and any buildings he may erect on the premises.

474   13Dec92
Fm William & Ann Wright, TwnALX, StVA
To Charles Lee   -do-
For £250 lawful money of VA, part of LOT 129:
BEGIN on Oronoko at line dividing LOT 129 fm adj lot (123' 5" fm Pitt & Oronoko) ... W w/Oro 60'... S//Pitt 176' 7"... E// Oro 60'... thence to BEGIN--parcel conveyed to William Wright by Thomas Ramsay, heir of John Ramsay.
WTT: Vincent Gray, William Wilson, Edmund Lee
CMN: Jesse Taylor, Robert Mease, William Wilson, **Gentlemen**, aptd 13Ded92 to examine Anne. Rptd same day. [Note her name as Ann in the deed, Ann<u>e</u> in the record of the commission to examine her.]

479   23May92   Mortgage
Fm Robert & Ann Allison, Fauquier Co., StVA
To James & William Miller, City of Philadelphia, **Merchants**
WHEREAS Allison is indebted to John Mease of Ireland for £255, for the Millers advancing same to Mease, the Allisons convey to the Millers a part of LOT 47, N of King, E of Ffx:
BEGIN on King at E line of parcel granted by William Ramsay to James Steuart ... N w/lot line 77' to Ramsays Alley ... E w/alley 34' 4"... S//first line to King ... thence 34' 4" to BEGIN--this parcel granted the Allisons by William Ramsay 16Jul77 and numbered in the Ramsay plot No. 32. [No terms for repayment, foreiture, etc., given]
WTT: W. MacRea, Jas. Wilson, Hiram Chapin, Robert Mease
CMN: John Thomas Chunn, Laurence Ashton, John P. Harrison of Fauquier Co., **Gentlemen**, aptd to examine Ann. Rptd 19Nov92.

486   10 Oct92   Non-Importation Compliance
    Before P. Marsteller, George Slacum swears his move to Virginia was not to evade the Slave Non-importation Act, and that he is abiding by its provisions.

486   31 Oct92   Non-Importation Compliance
As above, by Walter Lyon before Jesse Taylor, **Mayor** of ALX

487   16 Oct92
Fm Baldwin & Catharine Dade, FfxCo, StVA
To Thomas Patten, TwnALX, FfxCo, StVA
[N.B.: in 1785 David Griffith purchased and subdivided a large parcel, numbering the lots within it by his own system. The lot numbers below are these Griffith lot numbers. See Deed Book B, beginning p. 238]
WHEREAS David Griffith, late Clerk of FfxCo, dec'd, conveyed 21Jun85 to Michael Gretter LOT 75 on W of Washn, S of Princess
BEGIN on Washington 156' 7" S of Princess ... S w/Wn 20'... W//Princess 123' 5"... W//Wn 20'... thence to BEGIN--Gretter to pay each 21Jun £8 Virginia money;
AND WHEREAS Griffith 21Jun85 sold to David Jones LOT 66, W of Washington and S of Princess:
BEGIN int Wn-Princess ... S w/Wn 75'... W//Princess 43' 5"... N//Wn 75' to Princess ... thence to BEGIN--Jones to pay for that AND the adj LOT 71 each 21Jun £46.6.0 Virginia money;
AND WHEREAS Griffith also sold 21Jun85 to Jones LOT 67:

BEGIN on Princess 43' 5" W of Wn ... W w/Princess 20'... S//Washington 75'... E//Princess 20'... thence to BEGIN
               AND
LOT 68: BEGIN on Princess 63' 5" W of Wn ... W w/Princess 20'... S//Wn 75'... E//Princess 20'... thence to BEGIN
               AND
LOT 69: BEGIN on Princess 83' 5" W of Wn ... W w/Princess 20'... S//Wn 96' 7"... E//Princess 20'... thence to BEGIN
--Jones to pay each 21 Jun for these latter 3 parcels £22.5.0 Virginia money;
AND WHEREAS Griffith sold to Gowing Lamphier LOT 41:
BEGIN on St A. 75' S of Princess ... S w/St A 21' 7"... W// Princess 83' 5"... N//St A 21' 7"... thence to BEGIN
--Lankphier [sic] each 21Jun to pay for LOT 41 and for another Griffith--LOT 73-- £15.16.1;
AND WHEREAS Griffith on [blank] [blank] 178[blank] assigned all these rents to Henry Lee, as well as selling Lee Griffith LOT 70: BEGIN 123' 5" W of Wn ... W w/Princess 20'... S//Washington 96' 7"... E//Princess 20'... thence to BEGIN;
AND WHEREAS Henry Lee 30Mar90 conveyed to Baldwin Dade all the rent assignments and deed for LOT 70;
AND WHEREAS David Jones has failed to pay rent on LOTS 66-71-67-68-69
--and Dade is unable to find anything on the lots to sell
--he, Dade, has repossessed LOTS 66-71-67-68-69
--and, for the same reasons, repossessed Going Lankphier's LOTS 41 and 73;
NOW the Dades for £150 cmv fm Thomas Patten convey to him the Griffith LOTS 41-66-67-68; and also LOTS 69-70:
BEGIN on Princess 83' 5" W of Wn ... W w/Princess 40'... S// Wn 75'... E//Princess 40'... thence to BEGIN.
--PLUS rents from Gretter for LOT 75 AND the rents for the other LOTS, LOTS 41-66-67-68-69. WTT: Jesse Taylor, Charles Turner, Dennis Ramsay
CMN: Jesse Taylor, Dennis Ramsay, Robert Mease of TwnALX, **Gentlemen**, aptd 26 Oct92 to examine Catharine. Rptd same day.

505 20Dec92
Fm Thomas & Casina Conn, TwnALX, FfxCo, CwlVA
To Peter Wise -do-
WHEREAS 27Jun88 [clerical error; Deed Book B, p. 410 shows the year as 178<u>6</u>] David Young conveyed to Thomas Conn part LOT 55:
BEGIN on King 50' W of King & Royal, S side of King ... W w/King 24' to parcel sold by Young to Earp and Wilson ... S// Royal 72' 6"... E//King 24' and thence to BEGIN.
NOW the Conns, for £706 cmv fm Wise, convey him the property. WTT: none

508 02Mar92
Fm Michael & Hannah Madden, TwnALX, FfxCo, StVA
To Alexander Smith -do-
WHEREAS 14Jun85 the Maddens conveyed to Smith part of LOT 54, S of King and E of Royal:
BEGIN on King at E line of Mrs. Ann Allison's land ... E w/King 30' 10"... S//Royal 100' to 20' alley ... W w/alley //King 30' 10"... thence to BEGIN--for annual rent each 08Mar of 30 5/6 Guineas.
NOW for £400cmv the Maddens remit the rent and release the property to Alexander Smith.
WTT: Elisha C. Dick, Jh. Mr. Perrin [Joseph M.],Matzurin Perrin [also Mathurien]

511 07Jan93
Fm Thomas West, FfxCo, CwlVA
To Henry McCue, TwnALX, FfxCo, CwlVA: for £300 cmv, part of the LOT [blank] S of Princess, and which "contains the houses in which...Henry McCue lives"--part of property sold by John Lomax to John Wise, and by Wise to Thomas West. [No description of the property other than this.]
Wtt: Cleon Moore, Andrew Fleming, Ralph Longdon, Thomas Redman [Redman signs w/mark]

End of Deed Book D

ALEXANDRIA HUSTINGS COURT

Deed Book E, 1793-1794

1 21Feb93   Power of Attorney
Fm William Hartshorne, TwnALX, StVA
To William Gibb, **Esquire**, Accomack Co., VA: to secure debts to WH owed by [first name left blank] Sharlock, who mortgaged land in Accomack Co. Now dead, Sharlock's will directs sale of property to satisfy debts; Gibb to manage all this.

2 29Jul93
Fm Robert Adam as exxr of James Muir, late of TwnALX, FfxCo, StVA, **Merchant**, deceased
To William Herbert -do- **Merchant**
WHEREAS Thomas Carson & James Muir, late of TwnALX, **Merchants** and Partners, bought fm Henry Salkeld part LOT 38, on credit
--and both TC & JM died, owing this and other debts
--and Robert Adam, as directed by Muir's will offered at auction in 1780 the parcel divided into four pieces
--and William Herbert bought the first of the four for £250:
BEGIN W side Ffx at Ffx-Cameron ... N w/Ffx 58' 10 1/3"... W//Cam 41' 1 1/3"... S//Ffx 58' 10 1/3"... thence to BEGIN;
AND William Herbert has offered £320 for the 4th of the 4: BEGIN W side Ffx 141' 1" N of Cam ... N w/Ffx 35' 6" to corner of LOT [blank], which is now possessed by Wm. Hunter, Jr.... thence w/lot line //Cam 123' 5" to back lot line ... S w/lot line//Ffx 35' 6"... thence to BEGIN;
NOW for £570 fm Herbert, RA conveys him the two titles.
WTT: Samuel Montgomery Brown, Augustus Delarue, Robert B. Jamesson, Jas. Keith

7 28Jun91   Bill of Sale
Fm James Taylor, TwnALX, StVA
To William Halley   -do- [Amount not given]:
For slaves, to serve the term indicated, and then be freed:
Negroes: Charity - 6 years; Bob - 20 years; Jacob - 23 years.
[On p. 8, same date]: William Haley acknowledged the above.
WTT:[for both bill of sale and acknowledgement] J. Gilpin, James Watson

8 30 Oct92
Fm Henry Lee, Westmoreland Co.
To Arthur Lee, Middlesex Co.
WHEREAS David Griffith, dec'd, & wife Hannah 22Nov 87 conveyed several lots in ALX to H. Lee;
NOW Henry for £500 conveys to Arthur Lee the following six:
No. 1: BEGIN on Washington 96' 7" N of Princess ... N w/Wn 20'... W//Princess 123' 5"... S//Wn 20'... thence to BEGIN--Griffith LOT 82 leased by Griffith to Bernard Mann for £6.15.0 per year from 21Jun88;

No. 2: BEGIN on St Asaph 156' 7" S of Princess ... S w/St A 20'... E//Princess 123' 5"... N//St A 20', thence to BEGIN;
--Griffith LOT 35, leased by Griffith to Thomas Reed for £7 per year from 21Jun88

No. 3: BEGIN on Princess 123' 5" W of St A ... W w/Princess 20'... N//St A to an "Alley or Court 36' deep"... thence w/Alley line 20'... thence to BEGIN--Griffith LOT 24 leased by Griffith to Thomas Wilkinson for £9.5 beginning 21Jun88;

No. 4: BEGIN on Wn 156' 7" N of Queen... N w/Wn 20'... W// Queen 123' 5"... S//Wn 20'... thence to BEGIN--Griffith LOT 65 leased by him to Michael Stieber for £7.15.0/year fm 21Jun88;

No. 5: BEGIN on St A 96' 7" S of St Asaph [sic] [must be <u>Oronoko</u>] ... S w/St A 20'... W//Oro 123' 5"... N//St A 20'... thence to BEGIN--Griffith LOT 17 leased by Griffith to Joseph Fullmore for £10 per year beginning 21Jun88;

No. 6: BEGIN on Princess 123' 5" W of Wn ... W w/Princess 23' 5"... N//Wn 96' 7"... E//Princess 23' 5"... thence to BEGIN;
--Griffith LOT 100 leased by Griffith to John Smith for £8.4.0 per year from 29Mar87
--all above w/provisos that each lot be improved w/house at least 16' square by 01Nov87 OR pay rent as from 21Jun85 to 01Nov 87 OR the lots would be repossessed
--and neither improvements nor penalty rents transpired
--and the 22Nov87 deed conveyed these properties to Henry Lee who <u>did</u> repossess and now conveys them to Arthur Lee.
WTT: Vincent Gray, J. Mason, Phil. Rd. Fendall, John Potts, Junr.

17 26Jan93
Fm William & Nancy Duvall, TwnALX, StVA
To President, Directors and Company of the Bank of ALX: for £100 cmv, a part of LOT 38, N of Cameron, W of Ffx:
BEGIN on Cameron at SE corner of Brick House now occupied by William Duvall ... W w/front of House and Cameron 41' 1 2/3" ... N//Ffx 62' 8"... E//Cameron 41' 1 2/3"... thence to BEGIN;
--"saving unto the said William Duvall his heirs and Assigns all and every part of the necessary except that one apartment the Door of which opens into the yard and premises hereby granted"
WTT: Ja. Keith, Jno. Abert, Lanty Crowe, William Reardon
CMN: Jesse Taylor, Robert Mease of TwnALX, **Gentlemen**, aptd 26Jan93 to examine Nancy. Rptd back 31Jan93.

22 14Dec89
Fm John & Rebecca Allison, TwnALX, FfxCo, StVA

To William Hunter, Jr. -do-
WHEREAS Thomas West 01May84 conveyed to WH Jr & J. Allison
as tenants in common 1/2 LOT 14 "together with the Ferry and Ferry-Landing
appertaining... and all the water and the right...of extending a Wharf therefrom into
the River Potomack" [as recorded in the FfxCo Court];
--and "which parcel...[they] have at their common expence extended and filled in a
Wharf into the River and Erected thereupon a Warehouse which stands upon the
west side of Union Street..."
NOW the Allisons for £900 cmv:
--convey the Allison part of the parcel, ferry and ferry landing [N.B.: ferry landing
apparently still distinct, not incorporated nor swallowed up by later improvements]
--and the Allison half of the warehouse they built "upon the wharf which they have
extended into the river Potowmack from the said piece of ground"
--and Hunter may w/in 12 months remove the Warehouse "from off the ground where
it now stands"   WTT: Robert McCrea, James Wilson, Thomas Rather

26 11Dec92
Fm John Stone Webster & wife Mary, PG Co., MD
To William Irvin, TwnALX, FfxCo, CwlVA
WHEREAS the Websters now own part of a lot bounded on: N by King; W on St
Asaph; S by Patrick Murray's lot; E by LOT 114
--this lot bought by Adam Lynn from Charles Jones and wife
--this parcel lying on St Asaph and bequeathed to Adam Lynn's daughter Mary Lynn
[Webster];
NOW John & Mary for £80 cmv sell the parcel to Irvin:
BEGIN W side of lot on St Asaph 136' S of King ... S w/St Asaph 20'... E at right
angles to St A 92'... N//St A 20'... thence 92' to BEGIN.
WTT: Philip Webster, Jesse Taylor, Jr., Charles Love, Jr., John Longdon, Mungo
Dykes
CMN:Jesse Taylor and Robert Mease, TwnALX, **Gentlemen**, aptd
11Dec92 to examine Mary. Rptd back same day.

30 10Nov91   Manumission
    Eleanor Hawkins manumits her slave Celia, Celia paying Hawkins £45 cmv to do
so.   WTT: John Hawkins, Ja. Keith, James Lawrason, John Taylor

32 08Aug91
"To all to whom these presents shall come
WHEREAS the Mayor & Commonalty of the Town of Alexandria did on motion of
Peter Wagener **Esquire** in council the Twelfth day of February 1791 Resolve that the
said Peter Wagener should have Liberty to occupy the Town school house as an office
for the County and town records on the county court of Fairfax assenting thereunto,
and passing an order securing to the town their right to the said house notwithstanding such an occupancy--
AND WHEREAS the county court of Fairfax at February court 1791 reciting that
WHEREAS Peter Wagener clerk of the County of Fairfax is desirous of removing the
County court records to the town of Alexandria and having obtained an order of the
common council to occupy the Town School house as an office for the county and
town records,
PROVIDED the county court of Fairfax give their consent and pass an order securing
to the Town their right in the said house notwithstanding such an occupancy and also
that the common Council for the said Town may occupy the old court house for
public purposes Upon consideration the court do agree to the said order for the
common council and give their consent thereto accordingly

NOW Know Ye that we the Mayor and Commonalty of this said Town of Alexandria for & in consideration of the said Peter Wagener having given up to us his title to the bricks of the old Court house and indemnified us for pulling down and using the same for and in consideration of the sum of Five shillings to us in hand paid by the said Peter Wagener at or before the sealing and delivery of these Presents--
HAVE given granted Bargained and by these presents Do give grant bargain and sell to the said Peter Wagener and his representatives the aforesaid Town school house with the appurtenances to have and to hold the said Town School house with the Appurtenances unto the said Peter Wagener and his representatives so long as he may or any person for him may want the same for the purpose of keeping the County and corporation Office therein. In Testimony where of the said Mayor recorder and aldermen & common council men for the time being have hereunto set their hands & Seals this Eighth day of August Anno Dom: 1791.

Philip Marsteller, Mayor (seal)
Jesse Taylor   Recd. (seal)
Dennis Ramsay   Ald   (seal)
William Hunter   Ald   (seal)
Thos. Porter   Ald   (seal)
William Paton   (seal)
Peter Wise   (seal)
William Hunter   (seal)
Robert Mease   (seal)
Sealed and Delivered
Done in Council the 26th Day of Augt. 1791 in the Presence:
Oliver Price
Wm. Summors
John Longdon
At a Court of Hustings...18Apr93 this Deed was proved...which is ordered to be recorded.
　　/s/ Test P. Wagener

34 18Jun93
Fm Isaac McPherson, TwnALX, StVA
To Jane & Elizabeth McPherson, daughters of Isaac [no ID]:
WHEREAS Isaac has received several sums of money from the estate of his late wife [name left blank], mother of Jane & Elizabeth, and feels the money should go to the daughters;
NOW to secure payment of the accrued £610.7.3 to them, Isaac deeds in trust to them part of a lot S of Prince, W of Union:
BEGIN on Prince 171' W of Union ... W w/[Prince] 40'... S// Union 44' to line of Jonathan Hall's heirs' lot ... E//Prince 40'... thence to BEGIN--subject each 01Jan to rent of 80 Spanish milled $ to George Gilpin. (This parcel conveyed to Isaac 05Apr93 by Elisha Jenny [sic] [should be Janney; see following].) Deed is void if Isaac pays £610.7.3 in his lifetime or makes effective provision for same in his will.
WTT: none

37 05Apr93
Fm Elisha Janney, TwnALX, FfxCo, StVA
To Isaac McPherson -do-
WHEREAS George Gilpin & [blank] his wife 20Mar86 conveyed to Daniel & Isaac McPherson part lot S of Prince, W of Union:
BEGIN on Prince 171' W of Union ... W w/Prince 40'... S//Union 44' to line of Jonathan Hall's heirs' lot ... E w/lot line //Prince 40'... thence to BEGIN--the two McPhersons paying the Gilpins 80 Spanish milled $ each 01Jan;

AND WHEREAS the exxrs of Daniel together w/Isaac 01Apr93 for £350 cmv sold the parcel to Elisha Janney (who was then to pay the Gilpins the rent);
NOW Elisha for £350 cmv sells the parcel to Isaac, Isaac to pay the rent to the Gilpins.
WTT: Abraham Hewitt [Hewitt lined out, and Hewes written over], Guy Atkinson
WTT: to Janney's receipt of £350: Scudamore Nicholls, Abraham Hewes

41 20May93
Fm William Ramsay) Exxrs of Wm
   Dennis Ramsay) Ramsay, late
   Robert Allison) of ALX, FfxCo
   Michael Madden) StVA, dec'd, **Gentleman**
To Lemuel Brent & John Bass Dabney, of the same place
[Dabney's name, each of several times, is written by the clerk: John Bass ~ ~ ~ Dabney]
--Ramsay's will directed sale of property to pay debts
--exxrs advertised in Alexandria Gazette and got a £130 bid from Brent & Dabney for part LOT 61, N of Prince, W of Royal:
BEGIN on Prince on W line LOT 61 ... E w/Prince 40', N//Royal 157' 6"... W//Prince 40'... thence to BEGIN--Part LOT 61, once property of William Sewall, deceased, and sold by Thomas Pollard, FfxCo Sheriff, to satisfy creditors, at auction, to William Ramsay as highest bidder 20May82.
WTT: Frank Elliott, John Horner, Bernard Bryan

46 11Jun93   Non-Importation Compliance
      Before William Herbert, Horatio Ross swears his move to Virginia is in accord w/Virginia Non-Importation Act.

47 19Jun92
Fm John & Sarah Reynolds, TwnALX AND Nathan Littler, Frederick Co
To Andrew Wagoner & Colbert Anderson, Berkley Co.: for £44 the Reynolds convey to Wagoner & Anderson part of a lot, E of St Asaph, N of Wolfe:
BEGIN int St A-Wolfe ... N w/St A 106' 5" to 10' alley ... E w/alley //Wolfe 23' 5"... S//St A 106' 5" to Wolfe ... thence to BEGIN--conveyed 20Jun85 by Hugh & Susannah Finley to the Reynolds, and mortgaged 15 Oct91 by the Reynolds to Littler to secure payment of £42.12.6. Littler now for 5/ quits claim to the property.   WTT: none
MEMO: parcel is subject to annual rent of 23/5, now to be paid by Wagoner & Anderson [terms and to whom not stated]
WTT: James Kennidy, Jonah Thompson, John Kleinhoff [also: Keimhoff]

50 21May93
Fm Lemuel & Betsey Bent AND John Bass Dabney & wife Roxa, TwnALX, StVA
To John Horner -do- : for £140 cmv, part of LOT 61 N of Prince, W of Royal:
BEGIN on Prince at W line of LOT 61 ... E w/Prince 40'... N//Royal 157' 6"... W//- Prince 40'... thence to BEGIN;
--conveyed to Bent & Dabney 20May93 by exxrs of Wm. Ramsay
WTT: Job Green, John Lockwood, Jacob Wisemiller, George Deneale, James Wallace
CMN: Robert Mease and Philip Marsteller aptd 23May93 to examine Betsey & Roxa. Rptd back same day.

55 17 Oct92
Fm Robert & Ann Allison, Fauquier Co., StVA

To (as tenants in common) James Patton & David Finley, TwnALX, FfxCo, StVA:
for £240 cmv, part of LOT 47 on N side King, E side Water St:
BEGIN on King at E line of parcel granted by William Ramsay **Esquire** to James
Steuart ... (30' E of Water St) ... E w/King 30'... N//Water St 77' to "Fayette St
(formerly Ramsay's Alley)"... W w/Fayette 30'... thence to BEGIN--given by Wm.
Ramsay to Robert Allison 16Jul77.
WTT: Thomas Porter, Joseph Riddle, Robert Donaldson, James Porter
CMN: John Thomas Chunn, Lawrence Ashton, John P. Harrison, **Gentlemen** of
Fauquier Co., aptd to examine Ann. Rptd 19Nov92.

61 17Apr93
Fm Thomas & Sarah Porter of ALX, StVA
To Valentine Peers, Loudon Co, StVA
WHEREAS 02 Oct90 Peers (for £290.19.3 from William Hodgson) conveyed to
Porter in trust, as security for the £290.19.3,
Part lot E side Union, S side King and S side of 30' alley from Union to Front of
Wharf made by Peers & John Fitzgerald:
BEGIN on Union 103' 3 1/2" S of King, at S line of the alley ... S w/Union 73' 3 1/2" to
line of Andrew Wales ... E w/ Wales' line //King 100'... N//Union 73' 3 1/2" to 30' alley
... W w/alley to BEGIN.
NOW in view of the annexed certification by Hodgson that the debt is paid, the
Porters relinquish title to the parcel.
WTT: George Crabb, James Porter
MEMO: 17Apr93: William Hodgson acknowledges receipt of £298.19.3

63 24Apr93
Fm William & Catharine Bird, TwnALX, FfxCo, StVA
To (as tenants in common) Jonah Thompson & David Finley - do-
WHEREAS Trustees of ALX conveyed to John Dalton LOTS 36 & 37 bound by
Cameron on S, Ffx on W, and "extending into the River Potowmack upon the east
according to the survey and Platt thereof made by John West"
WHEREAS Dalton in his will devised "unto his Eldest daughter Jane, since inter-
married with Thomas Herbert":
BEGIN from int Ffx-Cameron, w/Cameron into the Potowmack ... and w/Ffx from 3'
north "of the brick House which he...was then building (the whole upon Fairfax street
being sixty feet according to the Terms of the said Devise)"... from thence parallel
"Cameron into the River Potowmack";
AND the remainder he devised "unto his daughter Catharine (who hath intermarried
with the said William Bird)";
AND WHEREAS the Birds conveyed [no date given] to Thomas West part of
Catharine's parcel:
BEGIN on Ffx at S end of the "dwelling House built by the said John Dalton"... N
w/Ffx 60'... E//Cam 246' 10" to Water St ... S w/Water St 60'... thence to BEGIN--and
Thomas West [blank]Sep90 leased it to William Bird @ £16.4.0 each 12Jun;
NOW the Birds for £1500 cmv from Thompson & Finley convey a parcel E of Ffx, N
of Cameron:
BEGIN on Ffx, 60' N of Cameron, being the N boundary of parcel John Dalton gave
[left] to Jane ... N w/Ffx 119' 3" to line of Herbert Potts and Wilson ... E//Cameron
"crossing Water and Union Streets into the River Potowmack"... S//Ffx 119' 3" thence
to BEGIN--Thompson & Finley to pay West the £16.4.0 each 12Jun. and reserving to
William Bird the "use and occupation of the Dwelling House now occupied by the
said William Bird and Kitchen and Garden untill the first day of October next and
also reserving unto Lanty Crowe the House demised unto him to the end of his Term
he paying the annual rent thereof unto... Jonah Thompson & David Finley.."

[David signs his name Finlay]
WTT: Jesse Taylor, Philip Marsteller, John Fitzgerald, James Keith
CMN: Jesse Taylor, Philip Marsteller, Robert Mease "of the Court of Hustings, **Gentlemen**," aptd 30Apr93 to examine Catharine. Rptd back same day.

70 17Feb93 Power of Attorney
Fm Priscilla Hicks of Whitehaven, Cumberland Co., widow & administratrix of William Hicks, late of Whitehaven, deceased
--who [William, that is] was Heir at law of George Hicks, late of St. Mary's Co., MD, **Gentleman**, deceased
To Elizabeth Wilson, St. Mary's Co., MD
WTT: Philip Magruder, William Renwick, Anthony Adamson
Proven in TwnALX 25Jun93 by the oaths of Magruder and Renwick

73 08Feb93
Fm Josiah & Jane Watson, FfxCo, StVA
To Jonah Thompson   -do-
WHEREAS 28Jul74 Andrew & Margaret Wales conveyed to Robert McCrea, Robert Mease and Mathew Mease parts of LOTS 57-58 E of Ffx and W of Water Sts.--and agreed to lay off on the N side of those parts a 9' alley fm Ffx to Water St;
AND WHEREAS 16Nov78 and 22May90 McCrea & Mease conveyed to Josiah Watson the use of the alley [and the land];
NOW the Watsons for £250 cmv convey to Thompson that part of LOT 57 conveyed by M & M:
BEGIN W side Water St, S side alley: 115' 3 1/2" N of Prince ... S w/Water St 27'... W//Prince 123' 5" to W line of LOT 57 ... N//Water St 31' 6" to S side of alley which runs from Ffx-Water St ... thence w/alley to BEGIN--PLUS the use of the alley, with Wales.
WTT: Ja. Keith, John Taylor, James Watson. To Mrs. Watson:
Dennis Ramsay, Robert Mease
CMN: Dennis Ramsay, Robert Mease, Philip Marsteller 09May93 aptd to examine Jane. Rptd back 10May93

79 08Feb93
Fm Jonah & Margaret Thompson, TwnALX, StVA
To Josiah Watson, FfxCo, StVA
WHEREAS 29May90 Watson conveyed to Thompson a parcel E side Ffx and N of Prince:
BEGIN E side Ffx, S side of alley running from Ffx to Water St (124' 3 1/2" N of Ffx-Prince) ... E w/alley 114'... S//Ffx 26'... W//Prince 114' to Ffx ... thence to BEGIN;
NOW the Thompsons for £5 convey to Watson part of above:
BEGIN on 2nd line of ground which extends fm S side of alley 114' to the E of Ffx, and at a distance of 26' 8" S of alley ... run thence S//Ffx 4' 4"... W//alley 114' to Ffx ... thence to BEGIN.
WTT: Ja. Keith, John Taylor, James Watson. To Margaret Thompson: Dennis Ramsay, Robert Mease
CMN: Dennis Ramsay, Robert Mease, Philip Marsteller, **Gentlemen**, aptd 09May93 to examine Margaret. Rptd 10May93.

83 08Jun93
CMN: Dennis Ramsay, Jesse Taylor and Philip Marsteller aptd to examine Hannah Madden on 02Mar92 conveyance to Alexander Smith of part of LOT 54. [Deed Book D, p. 508] Rptd back 08Jun93.

85 17Jun93
Fm John Parsons, King George Co., StVA
To William Summers, TwnALX, FfxCo, StVA
WHEREAS John Alexander's exxrs sold 05Aug79 to James Parsons at auction 1/2
acre LOT 180 N of King, W of St Asaph:
BEGIN int King-St A ... N w/St A 176' 7"... W//King 123' 5"... S// St A 176' 7"... thence
to BEGIN--Parsons to pay ALXR's exxrs £10 cmv rent each 05Aug;
AND WHEREAS James Parsons willed his son John 1/3 of his estate, and by
Hustings Court order Commissioners William McKnight, Peter Wise and John Allison
divided the estate into thirds, John Parsons getting of LOT 180:
BEGIN int King-St A ... On King 24'... On St Asaph 166' 6" to 10' alley--a parcel
designated on the commissioners' plat as No. 1, AND ALSO

BEGIN at W line of ground conveyed by James Parsons in his lifetime to John Petit
& Simon Michael Blondelet ... W w/King 26' 7" to W line of LOT 180 ... N w/line 166'
6" to 10' alley which extends from thence w/lot's N line into King St in accordance
with the Division ... thence w/alley the length of 2nd line ... thence to BEGIN--Parcel
No. 4 in the Commissioners' plat. The indentures and will are filed in FfxCo Court;
the plan of division is filed in the Hustings Court.
NOW John Parsons for £75 cmv conveys to William Summers parcel No. 4 plus use
of the alley--(and Parsons will see to the annual rent.)
WTT: John Mason, Ephraim Weylie, William Allison

91 17Jun93
[As above in all aspects. Here John Parsons is mortgaging to Summers Parcel No. 1
as security against Summers never having to pay the ground rent due from Parsons to
Alexander's exxrs.]

97 18Feb93   Non-Importation Compliance
    Before Jesse Taylor, John Watts swears he is abiding by Virginia's Non-Importation Act, and that the negro woman Janey brought from Maryland is for his own use
[not for resale].

98 11Mar93
Fm Dennis Whalen, FfxCo, StVA
To William Summers, ALX, FfxCo, StVA
WHEREAS John Jolly 26Jul89 conveyed to Dennis Whalen one 1/2 acre LOT 126 on
the S side Princess, W side Pitt--subject to the reservation of a Conveyance to Messrs.
Williams & Cary for a House plus the benefit of a 4' alley;
WHEREAS Whalen 13Dec90 conveyed all ground N of the 4' alley to William
Summers:
BEGIN int Princess-Pitt ... S w/Pitt 93' 3" to N line of alley in common use w/Williams
& Cary ... W w/Williams-Cary line 123' 5"... thence //first line 93' 3" to Princess ...
thence to BEGIN;
NOW Dennis Whalin [sic] for £3.10 sells to Summers the rest of LOT 126:
BEGIN on Pitt 129' 6" S of int Pitt-Princess (at S corner of lot conveyed by John Jolly
to Williams & Cary) ... S w/Pitt 47' to 1/2 acre lot line ... W w/lot line 123' 5"... N//Pitt
47' to Williams-Cary's line ... thence w/W-C line to BEGIN.
WTT: John Dalton, William Allison; Francis Summers, Junr.

101 15 Oct92
Fm David Young, TwnALX, FfxCo, StVA
To Nancy Hineman, widow of George Hineman, dec'd, of same

"...for the Love, good will and affection which I have and do bear towards my loving friend Ann Hineman" [conveys] "half that house and LOTT 51":
BEGIN on Royal at the end of John Longdon's lot ... thence 25' towards King ... thence "in a straight line parallel with King...51' 10"... thence //Royal 25'... thence to BEGIN--with a two story House on said Lott 25' x 18' and likewise a privilege of the 3' alley from "said house joining David Young and the Alley to run the Depth of the said Lott" which is 51' 10"... "to have and to hold the said half of House and Lott joining John Longdin"
WTT: Frederick Wm. Rice, John Coryll, Daniel Lintch
WTT of 12/ paid by Ann Hineman: Frederick Wm. Rice, Titus Triplett, Giles Fitzhugh

102 20May93
Fm William Ramsay) Exxrs of Wm.
   Dennis Ramsay) Ramsay, late
   Robert Allison)   of ALX,
   Michael Madden) deceased
To Samuel Simmonds, TwnALX, FfxCo, StVA
--in accordance with Wm. Ramsay's will, to sell property to pay debts, having first advertised in "one of the <u>Alexandria Gazettes</u>," and thus sold for £81--the high bid of Simmonds:
Part of LOT 61, W of Royal and N of Prince:
BEGIN at N line LOT 61 ... S w/Royal 19'... W//Prince 123' 5" N//Royal 19'... thence to BEGIN--formerly William Sewell's LOT 61, sold by County Sheriff Thomas Pollard (to satisfy Sewell's debts) to Wm. Ramsay
WTT: Lemuel Brent, John Horner, Bernard Bryan

107 18Jul93
Fm Samuel & Jane Simmonds, TwnALX, FfxCo, CwlVA
To Ann Hineman   -do-
WHEREAS Samuel Simmonds has part of LOT 55, S side King, W side Royal--conveyed by David Young to Simmonds and recorded in FfxCo Court records; NOW the Simmonds for £75 cmv convey to Ann:
BEGIN E side of Lot, on Royal (NE corner of Lot now in possession of John Longdon) ... N w/Royal 12 1/2'... W//King 51' 10" to part of lot belonging to Peter Wise ... S w/Wise's line //Royal 12' 6" to John Longden [sic] ... E//King and Longden's line 51' 10" to BEGIN. [The Simmons sign w/marks:]
/s/ Samuel his + mark Simmons ... /s/ Jane her x mark Simmons
WTT: Thomas Jacobs, Philip Webster, Elizabeth Webster

110 24Aug87
Fm John Harper, FfxCo, StVA
To William Harper, son of John, TwnALX, FfxCo, StVA
For "natural love and affection for my son William" [John conveys] part of LOT 89, E of Ffx, N of Wolfe:
BEGIN on Wolfe 43' E of Ffx ... E w/Wolfe 20'... N//Ffx 100' to Allison's Alley ... W w/alley 20'... thence to BEGIN.
WTT: John Fitzgerald, William Hartshorne, James Keith

111 10Apr93
Fm John Harper, FfxCo, StVA
To Edward Harper   )
   Charles Harper   ) of the
   William Hartshorne) same

James Keith   )
WHEREAS John Harper conveyed to Aaron Hewes a parcel on N side of Prince, E side Ffx (recorded in the Hustings Court) for annual rent of £11.8.0 in Spanish milled $ at 6/ each;
NOW John for the love he bears his daughter Peggy and to "secure unto her a suitable Support and establishment in life" ASSIGNS to the group in trust for Peggy the annual rents from Hewes PLUS a parcel on N of Prince and adjoining Hewes' E line on which is a brick house "now in the occupation of John Gill and used as a Store house":
BEGIN on Prince at Hewes' E line (69' E of Ffx) ... E w/Prince 23' 10" to E corner of the house ... N//Ffx and w/house wall 48' to line of Dr. Kennedy's ground ... W w/Kennedy's line 23' 10" to Hewes' line ... thence w/Hewes' line to BEGIN;
AND ALSO another parcel E of Water St and N of Prince:
BEGIN on Water St 22' S of McCrea & Mease's line ... S w/Water St 22'... E//Prince 40' to 10' alley laid off by John Harper 40' from Water St and running N from Prince to McCrea & Mease's line ... N w/alley //Water St 22'... thence to BEGIN
--plus use of alley with others adjoining it AND "possession and use of the Negro Girl Kitt" [and all her increase]
--effective after John Harper dies. If Peggy dies w/children, then to them. If she dies w/o children, these bequests to be divided among his other heirs.
WTT: Edward Harper, Charles Harper, William Hartshorne, James Keith

119 10Apr93
Fm John Harper, FfxCo, StVA
To Edward Harper   )
   Charles Harper   ) of the
   William Hartshorne) same
   James Keith   )
WHEREAS John Harper, as recorded in FfxCo Court, granted to John Bryce part of a lot N of Prince, W of Union, for rent due each 01Jul of 106 2/3 Spanish milled $;
NOW John for the love and affection he bears toward his daughter Mary "to secure unto her a suitable support and Establishment" ASSIGNS to the trustees that annual rent, noting that the property itself has been conveyed to Thomas Vowell--AND makes over to the trustees, for Mary, part of a lot N of Prince, E side of Union:
BEGIN int Prince-Union ... W w/Prince 30' to the "West corner of the Brick House now built upon the said piece of Ground"...
N w/"the Wall of the said Brickhouse" //Union 46' 3 1/2"... to the line of the lot conveyed by John Harper to Christian Slimmer & John Boyer ... E w/Slimmer-Boyer line 30' to Union ... thence to BEGIN;
AND ALSO part of a lot N side Prince, E side Water St:
BEGIN int Prince-Water Sts ... N w/Water St 22' 3 1/2" to line of lot granted by John Harper to the same trustees for daughter Francis Rush Harper ... E w/lot line 40' to 10' alley laid off by Harper from Water St and running fm Prince N to line between Harper's and McCrea & Mease's lots ... S w/alley 22' 3 1/2" to Prince ... thence to BEGIN--PLUS use of alley w/the others adjoining it AND ALSO use of Negro girl Mary and her increase --as w/deed of trust above: all rights and rents are reserved to John while he lives, thereafter as laid out here to Mary. If Mary predeceases John, then to her children;
--if she predeceases him and is childless, then all to be divided among John's other heirs.   WTT: the trustees

128 10Apr93 [From same to same]
[For daughter Elizabeth Harper, for the same reasons]:

Part lot N side Prince and W of Water Sts "upon which is erected a three Story Brick Dwelling House which is now in the occupation of Doctor Craik":
BEGIN on Prince at SW corner of parcel sold by John Harper to William Hodgson "whereon is erected a three Story Brick House now in the Tenure of said Wm.Hodgson" 104' W of Water St ...
W w/Prince to SW "corner of the said Brick House"... N//Water St 88' to Jonah Thompson's line ... W w/line the length of the 1st ... thence to BEGIN.
AND ALSO a parcel on E side Water St and N of Prince:
BEGIN on Water St at line dividing McCrea & Mease from John Harper (88' 3 1/2" N of Prince) ... E w/line 40' to 10' alley laid out by Harper 40' from Water St, running from Prince to the dividing line ... S w/alley//Water St 22'... thence //Prince 40' to Water St ... N w/Water St to BEGIN;
PLUS use of 3' alley "adjoining to the West end of the Brick House erected upon the said piece of Ground lying upon Prince Street in common with the Persons who may occupy the House ... which John Harper is now building upon the West Side of the said Alley" ;
AND ALSO Negro Girl Slave Esther and all her future increase--with the same reservations as above for Peggy and Mary
WTT: Edward Harper, Charles Harper, William Hartshorne, James Keith

135 10Apr93
Fm John Harper, FfxCo, StVA
To Edward Harper   )
   Charles Harper   ) of the
   William Hartshorne) same
   James Keith   )
[For daughter Francis Rush Harper, for the same reasons as above]:
Parcel N of Prince, W of Union:
BEGIN on Prince at the "West Corner of the Brick House built at the Intersection of the said Streets supposed to be thirty feet to the Westward of Union"... N w/"the Wall of the said House" //Union 46' 3 1/2" to the lot conveyed by John Harper to Christian Slimmer & John Boyer ... W w/lot line 53' to 10' alley ... S w/alley 46' 3 1/2" to Prince ... thence to BEGIN;
AND parcel E side of Water St, N side of Prince:
BEGIN on Water St 44' S of line dividing McCrea & Mease from John Harper ... S w/Water St 22'... E//Prince 40' to 10' alley ... N w/alley 22'... thence to BEGIN--plus use of the alleys with others adjoining them, AND ALSO a Negro Girl Lucy and her future increase--with the same reservations as above, for Peggy, Mary and Elizabeth
WTT: the trustees

141 07May88
Fm Thomas Williams & Joseph Cary, TwnALX
To William Newton   -do-
WHEREAS 26Jun87 [Deed Book C states 28Jun87] John & Rachel Jolly conveyed to TW & JC a part LOT 126, W side of Pitt, S side of Princess:
BEGIN 93' 3" S of Pitt-Princess ... S w/Pitt 36' 3 1/2"... W 123' 5"... N//Pitt 36' 3 1/2"... thence to BEGIN--to secure Jolly's debt to TW & JC of £180, which Jolly did not repay;
--TW & JC advertised in the <u>Alexandria Gazette</u> a public auction at which "Philip Marsteller **Esquire, Vendue Master,** struck off to the said William Newton" for the sum of £35 cmv the parcel.
NOW TW & JC convey title to WN.   WTT: none

144 18Jul93 Non-Importation Compliance
Before Jesse Taylor, John Heard swears he is complying with the Slave Non-Importation Act, and that Negro Boy Orwell brought from Maryland is for Heard's own use.
(Marginal note by Clerk: "forwarded to Lucas Vanersdel Herredsburg Kentucky"]

145 08 Oct93
Fm David Young, TwnALX, FfxCo, StVA
To Diederich Scheckel -do- : for £120 cmv, part of house and lot adjoining the "part of the house and Lott of Nancy Hineman ...on Royal Street":
BEGIN a 12' 6" front on Royal from the part of the house and Lott...of said Nancy Heineman ... Extend: 12' 6" to the lot of John Weathers Harper on Royal ... Run back 51' 6" to division line with Thomas Conn.
WTT: John Christopher Kempff, Philip Conn, John Harper

147 22Jul93 Mortgage
Fm Michael Gretter, TwnALX, FfxCo, StVA
To George Deneale -do-
WHEREAS Gretter owes James Craik [also, and probably correct: Craig] of Augusta Co., VA £72.14.1 1/2 + interest, NOW to secure payment he mortgages to George Deneale part LOT 50, N side of King and E side of Pitt:
BEGIN on King on E line of 9' alley laid out by MG, running//Pitt and Royal, N to McCrea & Mease's line (E line of alley = 136' 3" E of Pitt) ... thence w/alley line 130' 7" to McCrea & Mease's line ... thence w/that line //King 16'... S//Pitt & Royal 130' 7" to King ... thence to BEGIN--plus use of alley with MG.
Void if Craig is paid on/before 22Jul94.
WTT: Titus Triplett, Giles Fitzhugh, James Collins, James Wallace

151 06Aug93
Fm Samuel Harrison, Charles Co., MD and wife Barbara "late Barbara Hess relict of Jacob Hess late of TwnALX, dec'd"
To Philip Marsteller, TwnALX, StVA
WHEREAS Jacob Hess owned parcels in different parts of town
--and by his will disposed of them: "As to my two brick Houses in the Town of Alexandria the one being and situate in Fairfax Street adjoining the possession of Mr. John Wise and Samuel Simmons respectively and the other being Situate on King Street adjoining the House of Mr. [clerk sketches name he cannot make out, resembling J-i-b-o] being the same wherein I now live..."; [see also p. 255, below]
--wife Barbara to get properties and benefits while she lives;
--thereafter, the house and lot on Ffx to Jacob Butt, son of brother-in-law Adam Butt (Jacob then = "an infant about six months old,") and Jacob to pay the exxrs £25;
--the house and lot "in King Street wherein I now live" to his sister's son, Jacob Adam of Maryland, Jacob to pay the exxrs £15; the lot is subject to ground rent of 86 Spanish milled $ to be paid to Abraham Faw;
AND WHEREAS Jacob Adam has sold to Philip Marsteller his rights to the King St property to which he would succeed on Barbara's death;
NOW for £18 cmv, the Harrisons convey the lot to Marsteller
WTT: Thomas Lefewick, Vilinda Harrison, Ferdinand Marsteller
CMN: George Dent and Andrew Baillice, **Justices of the Peace** of Charles Co. examined Barbara 05Sep93. Jno. B. Turner, **Clerk** of Charles Co., attested the two men as being JPs.

156 23Nov93 Mortgage
Fm John Babtist Petit, TwnALX, FfxCo, CwlVA

To Henry Dedier, Twn of Baltimore, MD
WHEREAS James Parsons, late of ALX, dec'd, 08Nov84 conveyed to JPB & Michael Simon Blandely a parcel on N of King, W of St A:
BEGIN on King, 59' W of St Asaph ... W w/King 38 1/2', N//St A 34'... E//King 38 1/2'... thence to BEGIN:
--plus use of 6' alley on back of premises from E to W limits
--JBP & MSB to pay each 25Jun £19.5.6 cmv in Spanish milled $ at 6/ each or half Johanes weighing 9 pennyweight at 48/ each.
Void if JPB pays Dedier £230 cmv + interest on/before 23Nov95.
WTT: Cleon Moore, John James Neblon, Jh. M. Perrin, Bernard Ghequiere

161 27May93
Fm George & Sarah Headley, Mason Co., Kentucky
To Henry Headley, Richmond Co., StVA
For £5, LOT 4: In front 41' 1 2/3"... On "south by Camon [sic] Street on the West by Lott No. 5. On the East by the Bankers Lott No. 3" WTT: none [On p. 162 Sarah is identified as "Sarah Gordon Heiress to David Gordon deceased." But see also p. 292, below.]

163 18Dec93
Fm Josiah & Jane Watson, FfxCo, CwlVA
To Jacob Cox, TwnALX, FfxCo, CwlVA
WHEREAS George & Mary Kyger 03 Oct75 granted to Cox a part of LOT 66, W side Ffx, S of Prince:
BEGIN W side Ffx 73' 6" fm NE corner of lot and at NE corner of parcel granted by the Kygers to William Hunter ... W w/Hunter's line //Duke & Prince 90'... N//Ffx 10'... E//Prince 25'... N//Ffx 10'... E//Prince 65' to Ffx ... thence to BEGIN;
--Cox to pay annual rent [date left blank] of £6.6.8 cmv to the Kygers;
AND WHEREAS the Kygers 05Apr91 assigned the Cox rent to Watson
NOW for £65.17.3 from Cox, the Watsons sell their rights to the rent to Cox.
WTT: Titus Triplett, George Deneale

165 05Apr91
Fm George & Mary Kyger, Hampshire Co., StVA
To Josiah Watson, TwnALX   [Deed above is referred to].
The Kygers, for £60 cmv, assign Jacob Cox's annual rent of £6.6.8 to Watson
WTT: John Kyger, John Yost, James Keith, Joseph Coleman.
ALSO, the payment of £60 by Josiah Watson is WTT by the above and by Charles Young, Junr.
CMN: Edward McCarty, Ignatius Wheeler, Oke Johnston, **Gentlemen** of Hampshire Co., aptd 06Apr91 to examine Mary Kyger. Rptd back 14Apr91.

170 11Jun93   Mortgage
Fm Edward Mitchell Ramsay & wife Mary, **Merchant**, TwnALX, CwlVA
To James Smith the younger, of Philadelphia, **Merchant**
WHEREAS EMR signed a note for £2029 lawful money of Penna. to secure a loan of £1010.10, on 11Dec93:
NOW, to secure payment of the note, EMR mortgages the parcel conveyed to EMR 09Jun80 by Richard & Eleanor Arell of TwnALX on S side King and W of Prince [sic; probably should be W of Ffx] (and further conveyed 13Nov89 by EMR to Augustus Hamp of TwnALX for a term of six years [metes and bounds not given].
Void if EMR pays JS L1010.10 + interest by 11Dec93.
WTT: Jos. Thomas, Daniel Shepard

ALSO: EMR appeared before Matthew Clarkson, Mayor of Philadelphia, in Philadelphia 11Jun93 and attested to this transaction

173 16Jan94
CMN: Dennis Ramsay, Jesse Taylor, Philip Marsteller of TwnALX, **Gentlemen**, aptd to examine Jane Watson re: Watson to Cox conveyance above. [See p. 163] Rptd back 17Jan94. [N.B.:In this entry her name is given as Jane once, as Jean 4 times.]

174 11Jan94
Fm Michael Thorn, TwnALX, FfxCo, StVA
To Michael O'Mara, FfxCo, StVA
WHEREAS John Harper conveyed [no date] to Michael Thorn parcel N of Prince, W of Union:
BEGIN on Prince 88' W of Union ... N//Union 88' to North/back line of Harper ... W w/Harper's line 40'... S//Union 80 [not 88] to Prince ... thence to BEGIN--for annual rent 100 Spanish milled $ each 01Jul;
WHEREAS Michael Thorn conveyed to Thomas Vowell:
BEGIN on Prince 109' W of Union ... W w/Prince 19' to parcel W line ... N/line 36' 6" to 5' alley ... E w/alley//Prince 19'... thence to BEGIN--Vowell to pay 47 1/2 $ of the rent to Harper;
AND WHEREAS Thorn and Harper in their conveyance agreed to lay off from their respective ground a 10' alley from Prince to their Northern or back line
--and Thorn and Vowell's conveyance included Thorn laying out a 5' alley to run (from the 10' alley) W along the N property line to the W line of the parcel Thorn got from Harper;
NOW Michael Thorn for £700 cmv conveys to Michael O'Mara all that parcel Thorn got from Harper which has not already been conveyed to Vowell--O'Mara to pay Harper 52 1/2 Spanish milled $ annually each 01Jul
WTT: Patk. Byrne, Jas. Keith, Washer Blunte

179 09 Oct93   Non-Importation Compliance
Before Jesse Taylor, John Watts swears he is abiding by the Slave Non-Importation Act as he moves into Virginia.

180 07Aug93   Non-Importation Compliance
Before George Gilpin, Captain Joseph Clark [also: Clerke] swears that Negro Maria whom he brought into Virginia in July was for family use, and that he is abiding by the Slave Non-Importation Act.

180 08Jan94
Fm James Irvine, guardian of John Adam, Robert Adam, Jane Adam--orphans of Robert Adam of FfxCo, StVA, deceased
To Robert Brockett, TwnALX, StVA
JI leases parcel on E side of 24' alley from Prince through LOT 20, equally distant from Water and Union Sts:
BEGIN on the alley 94' 6" S of Prince St ... S w/alley 23' 6" to Richard Conway's line ... E w/line//Prince 52'... N//alley 23' 6" thence to BEGIN--part of the land Robert Adam devised by his will to his children and in his division of LOT 20 given the number 17.
Terms: fm last 25Dec for 12 yrs, @ £4.16.0 per year;
--Brockett may remove any buildings he may build, when the lease ends
--if removal is inconvenient Brockett may have 9 more months at a rent to be fixed by representatives of both parties

--if the orphans wish to buy the buildings and if Brockett is inclined to sell, both parties may nominate assessors who will price the buildings; their sale will be at that price.
WTT: James McHenry, Thomas Broad

184 08Jun94
Fm James Irvin [as above]
To James McHenry, TwnALX, StVA
Lease as above, but for Adam parcel No. 20 of Town LOT 20:
BEGIN W side of alley 48' S of Princess St ... S w/alley //Water-Union 23' 6"... W//Princess 52'... N//alley 23' 6"... thence to BEGIN. Terms: as above at £4.16.0 cmv
WTT: Robert Brockett, Thomas Broad

187 10Aug93   Tripartite Deed
I-Charles Alexander & Cleon Moore, FfxCo, StVA
II-Charles & Sarah Jones -do-
III-William Hepburn & John Dundas, **Merchants** & Partners, TwnALX, StVA
WHEREAS Peggy Bowling & Samuel Shreve 07May91 conveyed to Alexander & Moore slaves in trust for Sarah Jones: Mary, Anne, Elizabeth, Daphne, John;
WHEREAS Charles & Sarah Jones for £68 cmv sold Mary and John to Hepburn & Dundas [no date];
NOW the trustees, Alexander & Moore, convey title to John and Mary to Hepburn & Dundas.
WTT: James Keith and George Darling to the Joneses; Archd. J. Taylor to Cleon Moore; William Stuart, Junr., to Moore & Alexander
CMN: Jesse Taylor and Robert Mease of FfxCo, **Gentlemen**, aptd 12Aug93 to examine Sarah Jones. Rptd back 10Aug93 [dates as written.]

193 11Mar93
Fm Dennis Whalen, FfxCo, StVA
To William Summers, TwnALX, FfxCo, StVA
WHEREAS John Jolly 26Jul89 conveyed to Dennis Whalen all of LOT 126 (except a conveyance of a house to Messrs. Williams & Cary) plus the use of a 4' alley;
AND WHEREAS 13Dec90 Whalen conveyed to Summers all ground N of the 4' alley:
BEGIN int Princess-Pitt ... S w/Pitt 93' 3" to N line of the 4' alley used in common w/ W & C ... W w/William & Cary line 123' 5"... thence //first line 93' 3"... thence to BEGIN.
NOW DW conveys to WS for £3.12.0 all the rest of LOT 126:
BEGIN on Pitt 129' 6" S of intersection w/Princess and at corner of lot conveyed by Jolly to Williams & Cary ... S w/Pitt 47' to the edge of the 1/2 acre lot ... W w/lot line 123' 5"... N//Pitt 47' to W & C's line ... thence to BEGIN.
WTT: William Allison, Francis Summers, Junr.; John Dalton

196 21Nov95
Fm Patrick & Mary Allison, Twn of Baltimore, MD
To Jacob Furtney, TwnALX, StVA:
Part LOT 39, E side Royal, N side of Cameron:
Begin int Cameron-Royal ... E w/Cameron 41' 1 2/3"... N//Royal 117' 8 2/3"... W//Cameron 41' 1 2/3" ... thence to BEGIN--sold by Henry Salkeld to William Spencer, and by Spencer to William Smith, James Christie, Junr., and Thomas Ewing;
--then by Smith, Christie and Ewing 28Apr74 to Patrick Allison
WTT: James Calhoun, George Salmon, James Calhoun, Junr., all of Baltimore Co.
Attested by William Gibson, Clerk of Baltimore Co.

200 12Jan92   Bill of Sale
Fm Robert Brockett & James McLish, exxrs of Ninian Anderson, TwnALX
To Thomas Richards for £37 cmv
WHEREAS Anderson possessed
--Negro Woman Grace, to serve a term of years and be free
--Negro Girl Nancy, age 3, daughter of Grace, to serve until 28 years old
--Negro Girl Ellsey, 9 months, [presumably Grace's] to serve until 28 years old;
AND WHEREAS Anderson, at death, was in debt, we had to sell his interest in these slaves;
NOW we convey to TR titles:
--to Grace for 11 years from 01Jan92
--Nancy and Ellsy to serve until 28, and any of their children to serve until 28;
--then each to be emancipated at term end
WTT: James Kidd, Thomas Stewart

204 25Sep93   Mortgage
Fm Adam Bence, late of TwnALX, StVA
To Jonah Thompson, TwnALX, StVA
WHEREAS AB owes JT £25.9.8 cmv, to secure payment of same Bence mortgages parcel N side Gibbons, E of Ffx:
BEGIN on Gibbons 123' E of Ffx ... W w/Gibbons 60'... N//Ffx 102' 7" to 10' alley ... E w/alley 60'... thence to BEGIN--the same as conveyed by Wm. T. Alexander to Bence [blank]Sep89. Void if debt paid w/interest on or before 25Mar94.
WTT: John Dunlap, Robert Young, John Kleinhoof

207 20Jun93   Mortgage
Fm Thomas & Jane Herbert, FfxCo, StVA
To John Casey, Prince George's Co., MD
WHEREAS TH is indebted to JC:
£115 cmv payable 01Jan94
£110 cmv   01Jan95
£105 cmv   01Jan96
£100 cmv   01Jan97--and to secure these payments he mortgages a part LOT 37, E side Ffx, N side Cameron:
BEGIN int Ffx-Cameron ... N w/Ffx 60'... E//Cam 46' 4"
S//Ffx 60'... thence to BEGIN. Void is sums repaid on schedule.
WTT: James Keith, Jonah Thompson, Philip Marsteller
CMN: Dennis Ramsay, Philip Marsteller, Jonah Thompson, of TwnALX, **Gentlemen**, aptd 06Jan90 to examine Jane. Rptd same day

212 06Jan90   Non-Importation Compliance
   Before William Hunter, Jr., **Magistrate** for ALX, Rev. James Muir swears he is abiding by the Slave Non-Importation Act; the Negro Wench Kate is the only one to accompany his move.

213 26 Oct92
Fm John Harper, FfxCo, StVA
To William Harper, TwnALX, FfxCo, StVA: for £180 cmv, a part of LOT 96 on S side Wolfe, W of Water Sts:
BEGIN S side Wolfe 92' W of Water St and W side of 12' alley running //Water St through LOT 96 and 80' from Water St ...
W w/Water St 31' 5" to line between LOTS 96-97 ... S w/line 150' to ground lately Samuel Montgomery Brown's ... E w/line //Wolfe 31' 5" to alley ... thence to BEGIN--

sold to John Harper 17Sep84 by Thomas & Betty Fleming w/use of alley w/others in LOT 96.
WTT: George Coryell, William Bushby, James Keith

217 01Nov93
Fm Samuel & Mary Hanson, TwnALX, StVA
To Isaac McPherson -do-
WHEREAS exxrs of John Alexander conveyed to David Arell 1/2 acre lot N of Duke, W of St A, extending on St Asaph 176' 7" and 123' 5" on Duke for annual rent £14.10 to Wm. Thornton Alexander;
AND Arell conveyed half of it to Adam Lynn, from its NE corner 88' 3 1/2" on St A and from thence //Duke to the W lot line, Lynn to pay half the annual rent;
AND Lynn 21 Oct84 conveyed to Alexander Smith 1/2 the parcel:
BEGIN NE corner of lot, on St A ... W w/lot line 123' 5" to lot's West line ... S w/line//St A 44'... E//Duke to St A ... then to BEGIN--AND Lynn conveyed [date left blank] a parcel to Richard Ratcliff:
BEGIN on St A 44' S of lot's NE corner ... S w/St A 44' 3 1/2"... W//Duke 123' 5" to W lot line ... N w/line 44' 3 1/2"
... thence to BEGIN--AND Ratcliff 16 Oct87 conveyed that parcel to Samuel Hanson, Hanson to pay Alexander the £7.5 annual rent;
AND 21Feb91 Samuel Hanson released Alexander Smith from paying the 44 silver $ rent--Smith conveying to Hanson the land he had had from Lynn;
NOW the Hansons for £381 cmv from Isaac McPherson conveys to McPherson the parcel once conveyed by Arell to Lynn, now in Hanson's hands:
BEGIN at NE corner of the lot Arell got from ALXR's exxrs ... thence w/lot line to lot's W line ... S w/line 88' 3 1/2"... E//first line and //Duke to St Asaph ... thence to BEGIN--McPherson to pay £7.5 per year to Wm. Thornton Alexander.
WTT: James Keith, John Dundas, Robert Mease
CMN: Dennis Ramsay, John Dundas, Robert Mease of TwnALX, **Gentlemen**, aptd 06Nov93 to examine Mary Hanson. Rptd 08Nov93

224 25Jun93
Fm Robert & Nancy McCrea, late of TwnALX, StVA, but now of State of Georgia
AND Robert & Betty Mease, TwnALX, StVA
To Thomas Crandle, TwnALX, StVA:
WHEREAS Andrew & Margaret Wales conveyed to Robert McCrea, Robert Mease and Matthew Mease part LOT 56--and agreed to lay off a 12' alley on N side of the parcel from Water St to Union
WHEREAS Matthew Mease conveyed his interest to RMcC & RM;
WHEREAS McCrea by Letter of Attorney 10 Oct91 made Robert Mease his attorney;
NOW the McCreas and the Meases lease to Thomas Crandle a parcel on W side Union, N of Prince:
BEGIN on Union at line dividing McC & M from John Harper--8' 3 1/2" N of Prince ... N w/street 38' to the 12' alley ... W w/alley 83' to 10' alley dividing McC & M land from that of Michael Thorn ... S w/alley 38' to the former John Harper line, now John Boyer's, and thence to BEGIN--plus joint use of the alleys w/others adjoining.
Terms: from 01May94 $114 in half yearly payments, the 1st due 01Nov94. [Currency is in U.S. dollars];--rent remittable at any time on payment of $1900
WTT: Robert Young, Lawrence Hoof, Bernard Ghequier

229 02Aug93
Fm Philip Richard Fendall, TwnALX
To Andrew Wales -do-

WHEREAS the two have adjoining property E of Union on the Potomac, and see a mutual advantage to an alley from Union to the river:
NOW each donates 6', from Union to the river//King to make a 12' alley.
WTT: John Lockwood, P.A. Chernin [?Chewin?], Robert Young, John Burke

231 28Jun93 Tripartite Deed
I-Aaron & Mary Hewes
II-William Cunningham
III-Thomas Rogerson & John Bass Dabney--all of TwnALX, StVA:
WHEREAS 21Apr85 the exxrs of John Alexander conveyed to Aaron Hewes parcel W of Wn, S of Duke, No. 10 in the exxrs' plan:
BEGIN on Washington 132' 6" S of Duke ... S 22'... thence W//Duke 92' 7"... N//Wn 154' 6"... E//Duke 30' 10"... S//Washington 132' 6"... E to BEGIN--paying each 01Nov £12.10.0 to William Thornton Alexander;
AND WHEREAS the Hewes conveyed [no date] to George Hale part of their parcel, Hale then to pay the £12.10.0 to Alexander;
AND WHEREAS Aaron Hewes later for £100 conveyed to David Henly the rest of the parcel:
BEGIN on W side Wn 132' 6" S of Duke ... S w/Wn 22'... W//Duke 92' 7"... N//Wn 54'... E//Duke 30' 10"... S//Wn 32'... E//Duke 61' 9" to BEGIN--which Henley conveyed to William Cunningham who "erected a Dwelling House" and made "other Improvements thereupon";
BUT as no deeds were recorded conveying the improved property from Hewes to Henley to Cunningham, the title remained with Hewes--yet Cunningham has sold the improved parcel to Rogerson & Dabney;
THEREFORE, for £100 from Henley and a token 5/ from Rogerson & Dabney, the Heweses convey title to Rogerson & Dabney,
--and for £180 from Rogerson & Dabney, Cunningham conveys them his interest.
WTT: Lemuel Bent, John Lockwood; John Korn and George Heale to Cunningham
CMN: Dennis Ramsay, Jesse Taylor, Philip Marsteller, TwnALX, **Gentlemen**, aptd 22Jan94 to examine Mary. Rptd same day.

238 24Sep93
Fm William & Ann Duvall, TwnALX, StVA
To William Downman, Prince William Co., StVA
For £400 cmv, part of LOT 38 W side Ffx, N of Cameron:
BEGIN on Ffx at line dividing the "two Brick Houses belonging to and built by him the said William Duvall on Fairfax Street"--87' 10 1/3" N of Cameron St ... N w/Ffx 29' to N line of ground conveyed to WD by William Ramsay, **Gentleman** ... W w/line //Cameron 82' to ground lately David Gordon's, now Lawrence Hoof's ...S//Ffx same as 1st line ...thence to BEGIN --"parts of those two pieces of Ground, Sold and Conveyed unto [Duvall] by...William Ramsay and Adam Lynn..."
WTT: John Abert, Lanty Crowe, James Keith
WTT to receipt of the £400: the above plus Edmond Edmonds.
CMN: Richard Conway, William Herbert, Benjamin Dulany of TwnALX, **Gentlemen**, aptd 24Sep93 to examine Ann. Rptd 25Sep93

242 17May93
Fm Benjamin Augustus Hamp, TwnALX, FfxCo, StVA
To James Patton & James Kennedy of the same:
For £220 cmv parcel N side King and E of Water St:
BEGIN on King at SE corner of lot conveyed by Robert Allison to James Patton & David Finley ... N w/line //Water St 81' to alley ... E w/alley 30' to lot line of Hannah

Madden, wife of Michael ... S w/lot line //Water St 81' to King ... thence to BEGIN--
sold 04Jan93 to BAH by William Ramsay
WTT: Ebenezer Stark, John Foster, Jonah Thompson

245 11Feb94
Fm Gerrard Trammell Conn & wife Amelia Thame Conn, Washington Co., StVA
To James Kennedy, TwnALX, FfxCo, StVA:
For £300, a parcel W side of Pitt, N of Duke:
BEGIN on Pitt at S line of parcel sold by G. T. Conn to Charles Simms and now
occupied by Simms ... W w/Simms' line //Duke 84' 4"... S//Pitt 31' 2 1/4" to property
formerly John Hawkins'... E w/lot line//Duke 77' 2" to Pitt ... thence to BEGIN--
w/privilege of "building to the Wall of the Brick house Standing upon the piece of
Ground" sold by Conn to Simms
WTT: John Dundas, Bryan Hampson, William Summers
MEMO from Charles Simms: "I do agree to give Gerrard Trammell Conn or his
Assigns leave to adjoin my Wall in building and to make use of the same to build
upon provided it is done [in] such a manner as not to Injure my wall or House or
expose in any manner any Room in my House to the Weather while the Building is
carrying on"
/s/ Charles Simms, February 14th 1794. Test: Bernard Ghequiere
MEMO of G.T.Conn: "I do assign all my Interest of the within Agreement to James
Kennedy for value received...this 18th February 1794" /s/ Gerrard T. Conn
WTT: John Dundas, Bryan Hampson, William Summers

249 10Feb94
Fm Josiah Watson, TwnALX, FfxCo, StVA
To Gerrard Trammell Conn of [blank] County, StVA
WHEREAS GTC 17Mar88 conveyed to JW "a piece or parcel of Ground, Messuage
and Tenement":
BEGIN S side of lot where Charles Simms lives on Pitt St ...
thence along Pitt to lot & house of John Hawkins ... W//Duke to lot of J. Minchin ...
N//Pitt to Charles Simms' lot ... thence w/that lot to BEGIN;
--the conveyance to secure payment of £79.1.5 which is the amount of "an Execution
Issued by Joseph Janney and Company" against GTC which JW engaged to pay;
--and if GTC paid the sum + interest on/before 17Jul88 then the deed was void.
NOW GTC having paid, Watson conveys full title back to GTC
WTT: James Watson, Jonah Thompson, John Kleinhoof

251 04Nov93
Fm James & Mary Ann Patton & David Finley, TwnALX, FfxCo, StVA
To James Kennedy   -do-
WHEREAS Robert & Ann Allison 17 Oct92 conveyed to JP & DF a parcel on N
side King, E of Water Sts:
BEGIN on King at E line of parcel granted James Stuart by William Ramsay,
Gentleman--30' E of Water St ... E w/King 30'... N//Water St 77' to "Fayette Street
formerly called Ramsay's Alley"... W w/Fayette //King 30'... thence to BEGIN;
NOW for £500 cmv the Pattons and David Finley convey the parcel to James Kennedy.   WTT: Charles R. Scott, Robert Patton, Jr., Guy Atkinson

255 19Jul93
Fm Jacob Adams, Town of Baltimore, MD
To Philip Marsteller, TwnALX, StVA
WHEREAS [quotes the will of the late Jacob Hess. See p. 151, above. House where
Hess lived is here said to be next to that of "Mr. Jeboe"]

NOW for £120 cmv Jacob Adams conveys to Marsteller the property he--Adams--expected to inherit on the death of Barbara Hess: the King Street property.
--Marsteller is to pay the rent the property earns to those entitled to receive it, and the £15 Adams would have paid (on receipt of the property) to Hess' executors.
WTT: Robert Townshend Hooe, James Keith, Philip G. Marsteller

258 19Apr94 Quadripartite Deed
I-George Deneale, TwnALX, FfxCo, StVA
II-Michael Gretter, of the same
III-John Gretter, son of Michael G. & wife Margaret, -do-
IV-Michael Gretter Junior, Mary Goulding Gretter, Ann Hoof Gretter: John & Margaret's children
WHEREAS Michael Gretter has a parcel on N side King, E of Pitt
BEGIN on King on E side of 9' alley laid of by MG //Pitt-Royal north to the property lately owned by McCrea & Mease--the alley's E line being 136' 3" E of Pitt ... N w/alley 130' 7" to former McCrea & Mease property ... E w/that line //King 16' ... S//Pitt 130' 7" to King ... thence to BEGIN;
AND ALSO owing one James Craig £72.14. 1 1/2 cmv, in order to secure payment of that sum + interest for the period 22Jul93-22Jun94, conveyed the parcel in trust to George Deneale (to sell at auction if MG fails to pay on time);
AND WHEREAS MG owns a parcel on N side King, E of Pitt:
BEGIN on King 16 E of 9' alley mentioned above--the E side of the above parcel ... N w/the line 130' 7" to line of ground lately McCrea & Mease's ... E w/their line //King 18'... S// Pitt 130' 7" to King ... thence to BEGIN
--and by deed 25Feb82 this parcel after the death of MG's wife, Elizabeth, to John & Margaret's children;
--and doubts having arisen about this deed:
NOW MG gives George Deneale £75.5.9 cmv--the full amount due James Craig--and thereby returning title back to MG of the parcel mortgaged;
AND MG for £81.5.9 conveys to John & Margaret both parcels, (part of LOT 50), with the use of the alley
BUT reserves to Michael & Elizabeth Gretter the "Use, Occupation and possession of that peice of Ground where she now lives...being the second piece of Ground...."
WTT: Peter Wise, James Irvine, Lawrence Hoof [Wise & Irvine witness MG paying Deneale £75.5.9; John & Margaret paying MG L81.5.9 1/2; the children paying MG $1] [N.B.: Elizabeth Gretter does not sign, witness, nor is she examined. Possibly she and Michael are living apart.]

264 10Nov93
Fm Valentine & Eleanor Peers, Loudon Co., StVA
To Thomas Irvine, ALX, FfxCo, StVA
For £270 cmv, a parcel W of Union:
BEGIN at S side of Thomas Parton's lot, 40' S of King and Union intersection ... S w/Union 30' to Alexander McConnell's lot ... W w/that lot 70' to 10' alley ... N w/alley 30' to Thomas Patton's line ... thence E to BEGIN--w/use of the alley.
WTT: Josiah Faxon, Thomas Vowell Junior, Thomas Meazowy [?] [Not clear to clerk, either, who also copied it: Mezewey]
CMN: John Brown and John Love, **Gentlemen** of Prince William Co., aptd 28Nov 93 to examine Eleanor. Rptd back 22Feb94.

267 01Apr94
Fm Richard Parker, City of Philadelphia, PA
To Thomas Richards, TwnALX, StVA
For £1500 cmv, LOT 116, N side King, W of Pitt:

--granted by Trustees Harry Piper & John Muir to Robert Rutherford [no date]; by RR to James Hendricks [no date];
--by James & Kitty Hendricks 25+26Jan89 to Richard Parker.
WTT: William Coates, Thomas Stewardson
MEMO: Richard Parker swore to this 16Apr94 before William Coates and Jacob Sowess, Justices of the Peace, Philadelphia Co., PA.
MEMO: 17Apr94 Charles Biddle, Protonotary of Court of Common Pleas, Philadelphia Co., certified Coates & Sowess as being JPs.

270 08Feb88
Fm Baldwin & Catharine Dade, TwnALX, FfxCo, StVA
To James Lawrason   -do-
For £300 cmv, a parcel E side Ffx, S of Duke Sts:
BEGIN on Ffx at SW corner LOT [blank], 176' 7" S of Duke ... E w/lot line 123' 5"... N//Ffx 20'... W//1st line 123' 5" to Ffx ... thence to BEGIN--conveyed by Samuel Arell to Thomas West, then by West to Dade.
WTT: Edward Sanford, Washer Blunt, Daniel Casey
CMN: William Brown and George Gilpin, FfxCo **Gentlemen**, aptd 17Jun89 to examine Catharine. Rptd back 20Jun89.

274 16Apr94
Fm Dennis & Jane Ramsay, TwnALX, FfxCo, StVA
To Thomas Richards   -do-
For £274 cmv, part of LOT 46, N side King, E of Union:
BEGIN int King-Union ... N w/Union 54' 10 1/2"... E//King 30'
... S//Union 54' 10 1/2"... thence to BEGIN--"part of that Lott of Ground and Wharf described in the Plan of the said Town by the Number (46)"--and part of that conveyed to Dennis by William Ramsay, **Gentleman.**
WTT: Jonah Thompson, Robert Mease, Charles Turner, Bernard Ghequiere
CMN: Robert Mease, Jonah Thompson, Francis Peyton, **Gentlemen** of TwnALX, aptd 10May94 to examine Jane. Rptd back same day.

279 19Jul94
Fm Daniel Roberdeau, TwnALX, StVA
To Abraham Morehouse and Company of the same place: lease for 10 years of a parcel on E side Water St, S side Wolfe:
BEGIN int Water-Wolfe Sts ... E w/Wolfe 50' to NE corner of stone warehouse on the parcel ... S//Water St, w/warehouse line, 176' 7" to ground of John Fitzgerald ... W w/his line //Wolfe 50' to Water St ... thence to BEGIN--this lease including the stone warehouse.
Terms: quarterly payments of annual rent of £120 cmv, 1st payment due 30Sep94;
--buyer commits to build another warehouse, of stone or brick
--further building permitted, but to be "with sound substantial Materials";
--buyer may alter the present stone warehouse if he wishes;
--Morehouse & Co., within the 10-year lease period, may buy the property for $6000.
WTT: James Keith, Washer Blunt, Archd. McLean, Andrew Jamieson

283 21Feb94   Mortgage
Fm William Downman, Prince William Co., StVA
To John White, TwnALX, FfxCo, StVA
For £305 cmv, a parcel W side Ffx, N of Cameron Sts:
BEGIN on Ffx at line dividing the 2 brick houses built by William Duvall, 87' 10 1/3" N of Cameron ... N w/Ffx 29' to N line of parcel sold Duvall by William Ramsay, **Gentleman** ... W w/that line //Cameron 82' to parcel lately owned by David Gordon

but recently purchased by Lawrence Hoof ... S//Ffx the length of 1st line ... E//2nd line to Cameron, 82' to BEGIN.
WTT: George Deneale, Edmond Edmonds, Lanty Crowe, Charles McKnight

287 09Jul94
Fm William & Ann Duvall, Prince William Co., StVA
To John White, TwnALX, FfxCo, StVA
Part of LOT 38, W side Ffx, N of Cameron:
BEGIN on S line of parcel sold by Duvall to Downman [above]--87' 10 1/3" N of Cameron ... W w/line 82' to line of property lately David Gordon's, now Lawrence Hoof's ... S w/line 29' to the "Ground belonging to the Bank of Alexandria"... E w/line 82' to Ffx ... thence to BEGIN--this being the southern half of ground sold Duvall by William Ramsay, **Gentleman**. Void if Duvall pays White £52.10.0 by 09Jul95.
WTT: Jonah Thompson, Robert Mease, Jas. Keith, John Kleinhoof

291 09Jul94
CMN: Robert Mease, Jonah Thompson, Francis Peyton, **Gentlemen** of TwnALX, aptd to examine Jane Ramsay. Rptd back same day. [Possible clerical error, citing Jane Ramsay instead of Ann Duvall for examination required by the transaction above.]

292 06Sep93
Fm Henry Headly, Richmond Co., StVA
To Lawrence Hoof, TwnALX, StVA
WHEREAS David Gordon, late of ALX, dec'd, owned part LOT 38, N of Cameron, W of Ffx (LOTS 38 and 39 having been owned by Henry Salkeld who subdivided, numbered, and sold the parcels, Gordon buying Salkeld's No. 4):
BEGIN on Cameron at W line of Salkeld's No. 3--the parcel "presently the property of the Bank of Alexandria"... W w/Cameron 41' 1 2/3" to line of Salkeld No. 5 ... N w/line //Ffx 117' 8 2/3"... E//Cameron 41' 1 2/3" to Salkeld parcel No. 3 ... S w/No. 3 //Ffx 117' 8 2/3" to BEGIN;
WHEREAS David Gordon was survived only by his daughter Sarah, who inherited the parcel; Sarah married George Headly, and later they conveyed the parcel 07May93 to Henry Headly.
NOW Henry for £135 cmv conveys the parcel to Hoof.
WTT: James Keith, George Taylor, James Keith, Junr., Baldwin Stith

296 26May94
Fm Andrew & Margaret Wales, TwnALX, FfxCo, StVA
To Jonah Thompson -do-
WHEREAS Robert Adam on 03 + 04DEC71 conveyed to Andrew Wales one half of LOTS 56-57-58, they "being the Northern moiety and adjoining upon those other Lotts ...known at that time by the name of Pattersons Lotts at this time by the name of Fitzgeralds and Peers Lotts";
AND WHEREAS the Waleses 28Jul74 conveyed part of their half to Robert Mc-Crea, Robert Mease and Matthew Mease--Wales laying off on his ground a 9' alley on LOTS 57 + 58 for their mutual advantage to run from Ffx to Water Sts:
BEGIN on Ffx 36' N of S line of those parts of LOTS 57 + 58 Wales bought from Robert Adam ... thence across those lots so that the "Southern Line of the said Alley should strike Water Street...27 feet from the Southern Line [of the parcel]";
NOW the Waleses for £375 cmv sell to Thompson part of LOT 57:
BEGIN on Water St at N line of the Alley ... W w/alley 123' 5" to dividing line of LOTS 57 + 58 ... N w/line 47' 6" to line of lots once Patterson's, now Peer's and Fitzgerald's ... E w/those lots' lines 123' 2" to Water St ... S w/Water St 52' to BEGIN.

WTT: Robert Mease, James Lawrason, Josiah Faxon
CMN: James Lawrason, Robert Mease, **Gentlemen** of TwnALX, aptd 06Jun94 to examine Margaret. Rptd back same day.

301 20Mar94
Fm George & Jane Gilpin, TwnALX, FfxCo, StVA
To Robert Hamilton -do- :
For $1, a parcel S side Prince, E of Water Sts:
BEGIN on Prince 45' E of Water St on E line of parcel conveyed [no date] to Philip Marsteller by the Gilpins ... S w/line //Water St 44' 4" to ground of the heirs of Jonathan Hall, deceased ... E w/that line //Prince 4' to W line of parcel conveyed by the Gilpins to Robert Hamilton ... thence to BEGIN.
WTT: James Keith, Francis Peyton, James Lawrason
CMN: Robert Mease, Francis Peyton, James Lawrason, TwnALX **Gentlemen**, aptd 11Apr94 to examine Jane. Rptd back 14Apr94.

305 22Jan94   [Same to same]:
Lease of a parcel S side Prince, E of Water Sts:
BEGIN on Prince 49' E of Water St ... E w/Prince 36'... S// Water St 44' 4" to ground of heirs of Jonathan Hall, dec'd ... W w/line//Princess 36'... hence to BEGIN.
Terms: 72 silver $ each 31Dec;
--and Hamilton will lay off on the parcel's E side a 4' alley from Prince to the parcel's S line for him and the Gilpins
--and the Gilpins will lay off a 4' strip between this parcel's E line and the W line of the parcel they conveyed to Daniel & Isaac McPherson, from Prince to the parcel's S line, the two strips making an 8' alley.
WTT: James Keith, Francis Peyton, James Lawrason
CMN: Robert Mease, Francis Peyton, James Lawrason, **Gentlemen** of ALX, aptd 11Apr84 to examine Jane. Rptd back 14Apr94.

311 25Jan94   Quinquepartite Deed
I-Samuel Arell, exxr of David Arell, late of ALX, StVA, dec'd
II-Richard Arell Junr, son & devisee of David
III-Christiana Arell, daughter & devisee of David
IV-Phoebe Arell, widow of David
V-Absalom Wroe [later: Roe] of ALX, VA
--David's will is quoted; he appoints Samuel (his brother) exxr and guardian of the children until they reach their majority or marry, whichever happens first;
--to Christiana: Backlick Run tract "whereon my Brother now lives"; ALSO the "House in the TwnALX wherein I lately lived, taking in the Garden extending on Wilkes Street to the Ground rented to Shakespear and extending with Shakespears Line North to the Ground of William Hartshorne and thence with his Line to Royal Street, so as to include the Tenement formerly occupied by Doyle";
--to Richard: all the rest of the real estate;
--if one heir dies before receiving the property, the estate goes to the survivor;
--if both die, then to brother Samuel "except the property in Town Devised to my Daughter in which case I give to William Ramsay natural Son of Doctor William Ramsay of Alexandria.."
--will is recorded in FfxCo Court records.
NOW Samuel Arell leases to Absalom Roe a parcel W side Water, N of Duke Sts:
BEGIN on Water St at SE corner of parcel granted by David Arell to Lewis Weston "upon which there is erected a two story Brick house"... W w/Weston's line 63' 5"... S//Water St 21'... E//Duke 63' 5" to Water St ... thence to BEGIN.

Terms: beginning 01Jan95 and each 01 Jan, £10.10.0 to Samuel Arell until the heirs reach their majority, etc.   [Absalom signs his name W̲roe]
WTT: John Rhodes, Robert Walker, Adam Shum

318   20Dec92
Fm John & Rosannah Korn, TwnALX, StVA
To Robert Hamilton -do-
WHEREAS Philip & Magdelena Marsteller 20Dec87 conveyed to Korn a parcel S side Prince, E of Water Sts:
BEGIN on Prince 22' E of Water ... E w/Prince 23' to line of parcel once granted by George Gilpin to Samuel Montgomery Brown but now Gilpin's, again ... S w/Gilpin's line 44' 4" to ground of heirs of Jonathan Hall, deceased ... W w/Hall's line 23' to ground reserved by Marsteller ... N w/Marsteller's line //Water St to BEGIN--Korn to pay each 01Jun 23 Guineas.
--this parcel is part of that conveyed to Marsteller 01Jun86 by George Gilpin, part of LOT No. [blank].
NOW the Korns for £150 cmv convey to Hamilton the entire parcel granted Korn by Marsteller
--PLUS Hamilton to pay Korn each 01Jun 23 Guineas
--PLUS Korn to procure from Gilpin a grant for a 3 1/2' alley along the E edge of this parcel, from Prince St. [Both Korns sign, but she signs her first name: Rosina]
WTT: Jacob Wisemiller, Jesse Taylor, Philip Marsteller
CMN: Jesse Taylor, Philip Marsteller, Dennis Ramsay, **Gentlemen** of TwnALX, aptd 22Dec92 to examine Rosina. Rptd back same day

323   19Mar94
Fm George & Jane Gilpin, TwnALX, FfxCo, StVA
To Philip Marsteller -do-
WHEREAS the Gilpins 01Jun86 conveyed to PM a parcel E of Water St, S of Prince:
BEGIN int Prince-Water Sts ... E w/Prince 45'... S//Water St 44' 4" to ground of heirs of Jonathan Hall, deceased ...thence w/Hall's line //Prince 45' to Water St ... thence to BEGIN--on terms: each 01Jun, 45 Guineas.
NOW for 230 Guineas from PM to GG, GG remits 23 of the 45 Guineas forever;
AND PM is to pay 22 Guineas each 01Jun for a parcel:
BEGIN on Prince 22' E of Water St ... E w/Prince 23'... S// Water St 44' 4" to ground of heirs of Jonathan Hall, deceased ... W w/Hall's line//Prince 23'... thence to BEGIN. [In other words, the other part of the parcel is now rent free by virtue of the 230 Guineas just paid]
WTT: James Keith, Francis Peyton, James Lawrason
CMN: Robert Mease, Francis Peyton, James Lawrason aptd 11Apr94 to examine Jane. Rptd back 14Apr94

328   20Mar94
Fm Philip & Magdalena Marsteller, TwnALX, FfxCo, StVA
To Robert Hamilton -do-
WHEREAS the Marstellers 12Dec87 conveyed to John Korn a parcel S side Prince, E of Water St:
BEGIN on Prince 22' E of Water St ... E w/Prince 23'... S// Water St 44' 4" to ground of heirs of Jonathan Hall, deceased ... W w/Hall's line//Prince 23' ... thence to BEGIN--part of parcel conveyed to Philip Marsteller by the Gilpins 01Jun86;
--Korn to pay Marsteller each 01Jun 23 Guineas;
--Korn having since sold to Robert Hamilton.
NOW for 230 Guineas from Hamilton to Marsteller, the Marstellers remit any further 23 Guinea rent from Hamilton.

WTT: James Keith, Francis Peyton, James Lawrason
CMN: Robert Mease, James Lawrason, Francis Peyton, **Gentlemen** of TwnALX, aptd 11Apr94 to examine Magdalina. Rptd 14Apr94.

332 13Mar94
Fm John & Ann McClanachan, Prince William Co., StVA
To Thomas Patton AND Joseph May, Twn of Boston, MASS
WHEREAS 05Jun85 Charles Lee conveyed to McClanachan part of LOT 110, S side Prince, W of Pitt:
BEGIN on Prince 51' 5" W of Pitt ... W w/Prince 24'... S//Pitt 100' to 9' alley running //Prince through LOT 110 ... E w/alley //Prince 24'... N//Pitt to BEGIN
--conveyed to Charles Lee 04Dec84 by Robert & Susannah Conway, John & Mary Conway, Cuthbert & Mary Elliston, and Hannah Webb--McClanachan to pay Lee each 05Jun 56 silver $.
NOW the McClanachans for £604 cmv from Patton & May convey them the parcel
--Patton & May to pay Lee the 56 silver $ each 05Jun
--Patton & May to have use of the 9' alley w/others adjoining.
WTT: James Keith, John R. Wheaton, Lemuel Bent
CMN: Charles Broadwater, Richard Chichester, Daniel McCarty, Thompson Mason, **Gentlemen** of FfxCo, aptd 20Mar94 to examine Ann. Rptd back same day.

337 06Jan94
Fm George Hunter, surviving exxr of Thomas Fleming, late of TwnALX, deceased
To George Slacum, TwnALX
WHEREAS Fleming died owning LOT 77, S of Duke and "East and West sides of Union Street";
AND Fleming's will aptd Hunter exxr and Fleming's wife Betty exxx, but Betty having since died;
AND Hunter advertising in 3 <u>Alexandria Gazettes</u> a public auction on "which day being unfavorable the said [GH] did on the twelfth day of December being the next good day" put parts of LOT 77 up for auction:
BEGIN E side Union at int w/Duke ... E w/Duke 56' 1"... S//Union 56'... W//Duke 56' 1" to Union ... thence to BEGIN
        AND
BEGIN E side Union, S of Duke and at S line of plot above ...
E w/line 56' 1"... S//Union 24'... W//Duke 56' 1" to Union ...
thence to BEGIN--and George Slacum being high bidder at £250 cmv, Hunter now conveys both parcels to him.
WTT: James Keith, Francis Peyton, Lemuel Bent

341 10Nov93
Fm Valentine & Eleanor Peers, Loudon Co., StVA
To Thomas Meazarvey, TwnALX, StVA [also Mea<u>s</u>ervey]
For £180, a parcel W side Union:
BEGIN on line where Peer's land adjoins Andrew Wales' on Union ... N fronting on Union 20' to Boyer's lot ... W w/Boyer's line 83' to 10' alley established by Peers "in his Deed to Boyer"... S w/alley 20' to Wales' line ... E w/line 83' to BEGIN.
WTT: Robert Young, John Boyer, Andrew Wales
CMN: John Brown, John Love, **Gentlemen** of PWm Co., aptd 28Nov93 to examine Eleanor. Rptd back 22Feb94.

344 08 Oct93
Fm Valentine & Eleanor Peers, Loudoun Co., StVA
To Alexander McConnel, TwnALX, StVA

For £234 cmv, a parcel W side Union St:
BEGIN N corner of Rutter's lot, 20' N of N side of 20' alley running fm Water to Union as established by John Fitzgerald and Valentine Peers ... N 26' fronting on Union ... W//King 70' to 10' alley established by Peers between King and the 20' alley above ... S w/10' alley 26' to Rutter ... E w/Rutter's line 70' to BEGIN--w/free use of the alleys.
WTT: John Orr, Charles Eskridge, James Henry, John Abert, Robert B. Jamieson
CMN: John Orr, Charles Eskridge, **Gentlemen** of Loudon Co, aptd 12 Oct93 to examine Eleanor. Rptd back 19 Oct93.

347 20Jul93
Fm Charles & Frances Alexander, FfxCo, StVA
To Mayor & Commonalty of the Town of Alexandria, StVA
Lease of a parcel in FfxCo near the Town of Alexandria:
BEGIN "on a Knowl upon the South side of Queen extended from its present termination in the said Town of Alexandria and the West side of the fifth Street to Westward of Washington Street and runing [sic] parallel thereto, the said Streets to be laid off at a distance of [246' 10"] from each other according to the directions of the Act of Assembly"... W w/"Queen extended" 123' 5"... S//Washington 176' 7"... E//Queen 123' 5" ... thence to BEGIN.
Terms: from 01Jan93, for 20 years; each 31 Dec 1 ear of Indian corn if demanded;
--and if the house built on it, by the Mayor & Commonalty, as a powder house, if found to be on Queen or upon the new street running//with Washington, the trespassing part will be torn down and rebuilt on a "legal" part of the lot;
--and if entirely in the street, it will all be pulled down and re-erected on the lot.
/s/ Charles Alexander
Dennis Ramsay   Mayor
John Dundas   Recorder
Robert Mease   Alderman
Jesse Taylor   Alderman
Philip Marsteller Alderman
William Paton, Thomas Porter, Benjamin Shreve, Peter Wise, Lawrence Hoof, William Hickman
WTT: William Summers, Titus Triplett, Oliver Price

351 [no day]Jun91
    PLAT for the deed above, with the following text: "At Request of the Trustees of the Corporation of Alexandria laid off half an Acre of Ground which they have purchased of Mr. Charles Alexander agreeable to and of the same dimensions of the Lots in the said Town of Alexandria situate on a Nole and laying on the South side of Queen Street Extended and on the West side of the fifth Street Westward of Washington per platt above."   /s/ W. Payne S.Fx.C
N.B. I Dennis Ramsay Mayor of Alexandria in behalf of the Town of Alexandria do hereby certify that the above Lot is only Leased and not absolutely sold. /s/Dennis Ramsay Mayor
            January 3rd 1793
Test: William Summers, Oliver Price, Titus Triplett

251 24Jul94
Fm John & Jane Fitzgerald [no ID]
To Henry Lee [no ID]: For £500 [written out as: five hundred and   pounds] cmv, several "lotts" [parcels]:
BEGIN on Prince 30' E of dividing line of Lotts [blank] ... E w/Prince 18 1/2'... S//Royal 80'... W//Prince 18 1/2'... thence to BEGIN--part of LOT [blank] conveyed by

the Fitzgeralds 05 Oct86 to Thomas Redman for annual rent 55 Spanish milled $ each 16Jul;
                             AND
BEGIN at dividing line between LOT [blank] and LOT [blank] ... thence w/Prince 30'... S//Royal 80'... W//Prince 30'... thence N//Royal 80' to Prince [BEGIN]--conveyed by the Fitzgeralds 15Mar84 to Andrew Hayes for annual rent of £15 cmv each 15Jul; see FfxCo Court records. [This deed for only 2 parcels, not "several Lotts," is casually drawn; abstracted as written.]

354 25Jul94
Fm John Walter Fletcher & wife Mary, TwnALX, FfxCo, CwlVA
To Samuel Arell, FfxCo, CwlVA: for £82.16.8 cmv, part of LOT 80 S of Duke, W of Water Sts:
BEGIN 40' fm NE corner LOT 80 ... W w/Duke 27' 10"... S//Duke 91' 6" to 10' alley ... E w/alley 27' 10"... thence to BEGIN--conveyed to John Walter Fletcher 07Dec90 by John & Patty (John's wife) Murray of ALX.
WTT: James Camock, James Graham, Gerrard Briscoe

356 30Jul94
Fm Joseph & Elizabeth Massey AND Abraham & Sarah Falconar, all of Twn of Baltimore, MD
To John Walter Fletcher, TwnALX, StVA:
For £625 cmv, a parcel W of Union:
BEGIN on Union 67' fm int Prince-Union, on S side Prince--"The Extreem part of a Lot sold by Abraham Falconar to Francis Peyton"... S w/Union 22' 2"... W//Prince 150"... N//Union 22' 2"... thence E//Prince and Peyton's line 150' to BEGIN:
--part lot conveyed by George Johnston's heirs to Jonathan Hall and George Gilpin; when Hall died intestate, the land descended to his daughters Sarah and Elizabeth
WTT: Robert Taylor, Archibald Taylor, and sworn before George Salmon and James Calhoun, Justices of the Peace of Balt.Co., and attested by Wm. Gibson, Clerk, Balt.Co.

361 05Sep94
Fm William Thornton & Lucy Alexander, King Geo. Co., StVA
To Isaac McPherson, TwnALX, StVA
WHEREAS exxrs of John Alexander conveyed to David Arell 1/2 acre lot W of St Asaph, N of Duke:
BEGIN int St A-Duke ... N w/St A 176' 7"... W//Duke 123' 5" ... S//St A 176' 7"... thence w/Duke to BEGIN--David Arell to pay each 05Aug £14.10.0;
AND WHEREAS David Arell 30Jun81 conveyed half the lot to Adam Lynn, Lynn to pay half the ground rent to W.T.Alexander:
BEGIN on St A at NE lot corner ... W w/lot line to lot's NW corner...S//St A 88' 3 1/2"...E//Duke to St A..thence to BEGIN AND WHEREAS by several indentures Lynn's portion has now passed to McPherson:
NOW for £145 cmv fm him WTA & Lucy remit the £7.5.0 rent arrangement by Arell with Lynn.
WTT: Jesse Simms, William Hartshorne, Benjamin Marshall, Junr., Edmund J. Lee, John Walter Fletcher
MEMO: 18Sep94. This transaction done by WTA's attorney, John Taliaferro

364 05Sep94
Fm William Thornton Alexander & wife Lucy, King Geo. Co, StVA
To William Hartshorne, FfxCo, StVA

WHEREAS exxrs of John Alexander conveyed on [blank] day of [blank] 178[blank] a 1/2acre lot to Hartshorne, E of Washington and N of Prince Sts:
BEGIN int Wn-Prince ... N w/Wn 176' 6"... E//Prince 123' 5" ... S//Wn 176' 6"... thence to BEGIN--for annual rent ea 01Nov of £61 cmv, granted a 2nd time 08Jan90 for £30.10.0 by WTA attorney John Taliaferro Brooke;
AND WHEREAS [on similarly blank date] the exxrs conveyed to WH another 1/2 acre lot, E of Wn and S of Wolf:
BEGIN int Wn-Wolfe ... S w/Wn 176' 6"... E//Wolfe 123' 5"... N//Wn 176' 6"... thence to BEGIN--for annual rent ea 01Nov of £41 cmv, granted 2nd time 08Jan90 for £20.10.0 by WTA atty JTB
AND WHEREAS [on similarly blank date] the exxrs conveyed to WH a third 1/2 acre lot W of Ffx, N of Gibbons:
BEGIN int Ffx-Gibbons... W w/Gibbons 123' 5" ... N//Ffx 176' 6" ... E//Gibbons 123' 5" ... thence to BEGIN--for annual rent each 01Nov £75 cmv, regranted 08Nov90 by WTA's attorney JTB.
NOW for £258.10.3 WTA remits: for Wn-Prince parcel all but £22.3.0; for Wn-Wolfe all but 12.3.0; for Ffx-Gibbons all but 17.1.0 [all amounts = cmv];
AND Hartshorne agrees to--w/in 3 years--erect and finish on Wn-Prince parcel "one dwelling house to contain at least [400 sqft] and a kitchen for the same"; likewise on the Ffx-Gibbons parcel
WTT: Jesse Simms, Benjamin Marshall Junr., Edmund J. Lee, John W. Fletcher
[on p. 364 clerk notes in margin "N.B. An acknowledgement to this deed is recorded in Liber F, folio 273." Same for deed below]

369 05Sep93
Fm William Thornton & Lucy Alexander, King Geo. Co., StVA
To William Hartshorne, FfxCo, StVALease 1/2 acre W of Pitt, S of Wilkes Sts
BEGIN int Pitt-Wilkes ... S w/Pitt 176' 6"... W//Wilkes 123' 5" ... N//Pitt 176' 6"... thence to BEGIN--this same 1/2 acre exxrs of J.ALXR leased 05Aug79 to David Arell at £10 per year; then Arell to Hartshorne 05Aug79;
--the exxr-to-Arell conveyance not admitted to record because a witness died, and this WTA-WH conveyance is to remedy that.
NOW for £10 cmv each 05Aug WTA conveys the lot to William Hartshorne.
WTT: as above.   Acknowledgement as above.

373   04Jan94
Fm **Doctor** William Ramsay, TwnALX
To Benjamin Augustus Hamp -do-: for £180 cmv parcel in ALX:
BEGIN N side King, SE corner of David Finlay & James Patton lot ... N//Water St 81 to alley ... E w/alley 30' to corner of lot of Hannah Madden (wife of Michael) ... S//Water St 81' to King ... thence to BEGIN.
WTT: Elisha C. Dick, John Foster, John Janney

375   20Mar94
Fm Charles Cartlish, TwnALX, FfxCo, StVA
To John Baptist Bading -do- : lease parcel S of Prince, E of St A "adjoining to the Brick house belonging to Korn and Wisemiller"--the same parcel conveyed by Thomas West [blank date] to Charles Cartlish; [no metes and bounds given]
Terms: 10 years at £15 cmv in quarterly payments beginning 20 Jul
--Cartlish keeps any structures Bading builds.
WTT: John Beall, John Korn, Joseph Fullmer

377 20Aug93
Fm Richard & Mary Condon, TwnALX, FfxCo, StVA
To James Young -do- : lease parcel on W side of 20' alley running fm S side Conway's wharf N across wharf <u>and</u> across wharf "late the property of Robert Adam," into Princess St:
BEGIN W side alley at dividing line of Conway and Adam [which is] "also the SE Corner of an House built upon the wharf of the said [RA] by Robert Evans"... W w/line 70'... S//alley 40'... E//1st line 70' to alley ... thence w/alley to BEGIN.
Terms: each 20Aug, $40 specie;
--Conway to extend alley fm Conway-Adam dividing line across Conway wharf to the wharf's southern line
--Young to share alley w/Conway
--rent remittable f/$800 specie [no time limit stated].
WTT: Jas. Keith, Jas. Kerr, Jas. Kenney, Jonah Thompson, Robert Mease
CMN: Robert Mease and Jonah Thompson, **Gentlemen** of ALX, aptd 18Sep93 to examine Mary. Rptd back 17Sep94.

382 30May94
Fm William Thornton Alexander & wife Lucy, King Geo. Co., VA
To Stephen Cook, TwnALX: lease of 12 acres near TwnALX:
BEGIN on Hunting Creek at high water mark where line dividing lots between Ffx & Royal Sts, when extended, intersects creek
... thence up creek to int of creek and lines [as above] of Royal-Pitt ... N w/line //Royal until a right angled line across the Royal-Ffx line will contain 12 acres ... thence at rt angles until int Royal-Ffx line ... thence to BEGIN.
Terms: each 01Jun beginning 1795, $60 silver. [N.B.: WTA does not commit to lay out streets, etc., as was once his custom.]
WTT: Charles Simms, Joshua Riddle, Robert Townshend Hooe, G. Swoope

386 30May94 [Same to same]
WHEREAS 02May92 WTA conveyed to Stephen Cooke a lot contiguous to ALX, known as LOT 2 in the 1784 Alexander plat:
BEGIN int S side of King, W side of Washington Sts ... S w/Wn 176' 6"... W//King 123' 5"... N//Wn 176' 6"... thence to BEGIN
Terms: £11.5.0 annually.
AND on the same date conveyed a 2nd lot contig to ALX: LOT 1:
BEGIN int S side King w/E side Washington Sts ... S w/Wn 176' 6"... E//King 123' 5"... N//Wn 176' 6"... thence to BEGIN.
Terms: £11.5.0 annually
AND on same date, a 3rd lot contig to ALX [no number]:
BEGIN int N side King w/E side of Washington Sts ... N w/Wn 176' 6"... E to W side of the lot conveyed to Mr. Pearsons in 1779 ... S w/Pearson's line 176' 6"... thence to BEGIN [the usual 123' 5" measure not used.]   Terms: same
AND -do- a 4th lot contig to ALX [no number]:
BEGIN int N side King, W of Wn ... N w/Wn 176' 6"... W//King 123' 5"... S//Wn 176' 6"... thence to BEGIN.   Terms: same
NOW for £350 VA money WTA remits all the above rents.
WTT: Chs. Simms, Joshua Riddle, Robert Townshend Hooe, G. Swope [sic]
[Alexander atty John Taliaferro executes this for them.]

390 01Sep94
Fm Stephen & Catharine Cooke, TwnALX, FfxCo
To Robert Townshend Hooe -do-
Lease of a parcel "between Hunting Creek and the [TwnALX]":

BEGIN where N boundary line of 12 acre parcel sold to Cook by W. T. Alexander 30May94 will, when continued, intersect the middle of Pitt St ... thence, in the middle of Pitt, parallelling Gibbons, to intersect center line between Pitt-St A...
S//St Asaph to Hunting Creek ... E w/the meanders of Hunting Creek to center of Pitt ... N up center of Pitt to BEGIN [N.B.: this private property appears to includes include public street space.]
Terms: for 21 years from this date, for 15 Spanish milled $ each 01Sep. Within 3 months after lease ends RTH may remove any improvements he makes.]
WTT: none

393 30May94
Fm William Thornton Alexander & wife Lucy, King Geo. County
To Stephen Cooke, TwnALX: for £100 current money a 1/2 acre lot in ALX S of Prince, W of Washington Sts:
BEGIN int Wn-Prince ... S w/W line Wn St 176' 7"... W//Prince 123' 5"... N//Wn 176' 7" to S line of Prince, thence to BEGIN.
[Alexander atty John Taliaferro executes this for them.]
WTT: Charles Simms, Joshua Riddle, Robert T. Hooe, G. Swope

395 23Jun94 [Same to same]
For £274 cmv, a parcel S of and adjoining Town of Alexandria:
BEGIN at SE corner of 12 acre lot conveyed by WTA to SC 30May94 ... N along E line of 12 acre lot for the same length
... E to intersect at rt angles W line of Ffx St ... S w/Ffx "untill it Strikes or Intersects at Right Angles the North edge or Line of the Marsh or low Grounds"... E w/meanders of the Marsh "into the River Potowmack"... thence--from the BEGIN point--E at right angles into the river Potowmack, and "Northerly with the River untill it Intersects [the line across the edge of the marsh]"
[Alexander atty John Taliaferro Junr executes this for them.]
WTT: Joseph Riddle, Joshua Riddle, G. Swope

398 01Sep94 [Same to same]
Lease of a parcel between Hunting Creek and TwnALX:
BEGIN NW corner of the 30May 12 acre lot [see above] ... W//Abingdon or Gibbons St 312' 10" until intersecting center line between Pitt-St Asaph ... S//St A to Hunting Creek ... E w/meanders of Hunting Creek to SE corner of 12 acre lot ...
from SW [sic; should be SE] corner, N along 12 acre lot's W line to BEGIN.
Terms: from today, 21 years, at 30 Spanish milled $ each 01Sep; within 3 months after lease-end Cooke may remove any improvements he makes.
[Alexander atty John Taliaferro Junr executes this for them.]
WTT: Samuel Arell, William Neil [also Neel], John Longdon, Joseph M. Perrin

401 20Aug94
Fm Thomas & Sarah Porter, TwnALX, FfxCo, StVA
To Francis Peyton   -do-
For £40 cmv, part of LOT 54 S of King, E of Royal Sts:
BEGIN on King at E line of parcel conveyed by Sarah "while sole by the name of Sarah Ramsay" to Hugh Mitchell, now vested in Francis Peyton--92' 6 3/4" E of Royal ... E w/King 5' 7 1/4" to line of Richard Arell ... W/Arell's line //Royal-Ffx 100' to 20' alley ... W w/alley //King 5' 7 1/4" to line of Francis Peyton ... thence to BEGIN--granted by William Ramsay **Gentleman** to his daughter Sarah [date left blank]
--Peyton to share alley use w/ others adjoining it;
WTT: Robert Mease, Jonah Thompson, Jesse Wherry

404 30Jul94
Fm Thomas & Anne Richards, TwnALX, FfxCo, StVA
To (as tenants in common) John Thomas Ricketts & William Newton of same place
For £600 cmv, part of LOT 65 S of Prince, E of Ffx:
Begin int Ffx-Prince ... S w/Ffx 98' 7"... E//Prnce 30' 10" ... N//Ffx 98' 7"... thence to BEGIN--granted by Joseph White Harrison to Thomas Richards 15Apr 94
WTT: George Darling, Charles McKnight, Caleb Earp
CMN: James Lawrason, Jonah Thompson, Francis Peyton, **Gentlemen** of TwnALX, aptd 05Aug94 to examine Ann. Rptd back 06Aug94.

409 19Sep94
Fm Andrew & Margaret Andrew Wales, TwnALX, FfxCo, StVA
To Thomas White   -do-
WHEREAS 23 + 23Jul72 Chistopher Beelor & Henrietta Wilhemina his wife sold to Wales part LOTS 28-29 W of Ffx, N of Queen:
BEGIN on Ffx at N line of parcel sold by Beelor to John Graham ... N w/Ffx to S line of parcel sold by Beelor to Joel Cooper ... W w/Cooper line 167' 2"... S//Ffx to the Graham line ... thence to BEGIN;
AND WHEREAS Wales 10Mar85 conveyed to Hugh McCaughen:
BEGIN on Ffx at S line of Joel Cooper's parcel ... S w/Ffx 25'--4' from a "House which...Wales owned"... W//Queen 167' 2"... N//Ffx 25'... thence to BEGIN:
--and leaving open the 4' space between the S line and the house, extending it 100' W to serve as an alley for the Waleses and Hugh McCaughen
--for which McC promised to pay £300 in 3 installments, but failed to make 2 of them
--so that Wales sued successfully in ALX Hustings Court, but McCaughen "enjoined in Chancery"
--which in Aug94 decreed "William Summers Sergeant of the said Town" should auction the property, w/proceeds to Wales for the debt, surplus if any to McCaughen; Summers advertised 3 times in the <u>Alexandria Gazette</u> and sold on 17Sep to Thomas White for £200.5.0;
NOW for that sum the Waleses convey the former McCaughen property to Thomas White, Wales as before to keep open the 4' alley extended another 100'
WTT: James Lawrason, Robert Mease, <u>William Summers</u>
CMN: Robert Mease, James Lawrason, **Gentlemen** of TwnALX, aptd 22Sep94 to examine Margaret. Rptd back same day.

416 30Apr94
Fm William & Mary Bushby, TwnALX, FfxCo, StVA
To William Reynolds -do-
WHEREAS the Bushbys own 2 "Lotts or half Acres of Land being half a square" bounded on the S by the Presbyterian Churchyard and Parsonage House, on W by Royal, N by Duke, E by Ffx Sts--and now for £85 cmv, convey a parcel:
BEGIN on E side of the half square or 2 half acre lots on Ffx St and 47' 6" N of churchyard's NE corner ... S w/Ffx 15'... W at right angle w/Duke 70' 6"... N at rt angle w/Ffx 15'... E at rt angle w/Duke 70' 6" to Ffx and BEGIN:
--w/privilege of 3' alley on Ffx on N side of lot, running along N line of lot to "Chappel Alley and originally Granted for the Accommodation of the Methodist Church";
--Bushby "retains the privilege of running a building over, so as to Join the Lott or building of the said William Reynolds"
WTT: <u>William Summers</u>, John Adams, Josiah Emmit

419 01Jan94
Fm George Hunter, surviving exxr of Thomas Fleming
To Robert Townshend Hooe, TwnALX

WHEREAS Fleming owned LOT 77 on S side of Duke, and E and W sides of Union Sts;
--when his widow, Betty, died GH advertised 3 times in the Alexandria Gazette that on 04Dec he would sell parts of the estate, and on 11Dec ("the said fourth and successive days being foul weather and unfit for doing business") sold parcel: BEGIN S line LOT 77, 136' 1" E of Union "at the intersection of a Line drawn Southerly from the West line of the said Hooes Warehouse"... E w/that line into the river ... from BEGIN, again: N//Union 25' to the line of the ground belonging to the TwnALX ... E//1st line into the river ... thence//Union until it intersects the 1st line--all this is part of LOT 77 "and the made ground adjoining thereto";
--LOT 77 conveyed by George Chapman to Fleming 19Sep70
--RTH was auction high bidder at £300, to whom Hunter now conveys the property
WTT: John Muncaster, Thomas Lewis, James Keith

422 30Jun94
Fm Mordecai & Hannah Lewis, City of Philadelphia, **Merchant**
To Josiah Watson, TwnALX, FfxCo, StVA, **Merchant**
For £1000 "all that Messuage or Tenement and four adjoining Lotts," parts of LOT 67
No. 1: "one of which Lotts with the Messuage thereon:"
BEGIN on Prince 31' 1" from NW corner of lot--int Royal-Prince
... E w/Prince 31' 1"... S//Ffx 59'... W//Prince 31' 1"... then to BEGIN;
No. 2: BEGIN on Prince 62' 2" from NW corner LOT 67 ... E w/Prince 31' 1"... S//Ffx 59'... W//Prince 31' 1"... N 59' to BEGIN;
No. 3: BEGIN on NW lot corner, int Royal-Prince ... E w/Prince 31' 1"... S//Ffx 59'... W//Prince 31' 1" to Royal ... thence to BEGIN;
No. 4: BEGIN E side Royal 59' from int Prince-Royal ... S w/Royal 29' 4 1/2"... E//Prince 93' 4"... N//Royal 29' 4 1/2'... thence to BEGIN
--which messuage and parcels William & Susanna Hartshorne, **Merchant** of TwnALX conveyed to M. Lewis 18Dec92, as recorded in FfxCo Court, Lib. W, folio 27.
WTT: Samuel Coates, Henry L. Waddell, Thomas Mifflin Junr.
(Above sworn to 30Jun94 before Matthew Clarkson, **Esquire, Mayor** of Philadelphia

426 12Apr94
Fm Michael & Hannah Madden, FfxCo, StVA
To James Kennedy, TwnALX, FfxCo, StVA: for £120 cmv, to Kennedy "as a tenant in common", part of LOT 46 N of King, E of Water Sts:
BEGIN on King 120' E of Water St ... E w/King 15'... N//Water St 80' to Fayette St ... W w/Fayette 15 ... thence to BEGIN
--conveyed to Hannah by William Ramsay, **Gentleman,** 20Dec84.
WTT: Dennis Ramsay, James McCrea, Robert Mease
CMN: John Dundas and Robert Mease, **Gentlemen** of TwnALX, aptd 26May94 to examine Hannah. Rptd back same day.

431 23 Oct94
Fm Eleanor Shaw & William Shaw her son, TwnALX, FfxCo, CwlVA
To Jacob Furtney -do- : for £141 cmv, part of LOT 29
BEGIN on Queen at SW corner of part LOT 29 sold by Christopher & Henrietta Wilhemina Beeler 17 + 18Jan72 to John Graham ... W w/Queen 42'... N//Ffx length of LOT 29 to intersect w/line dividing LOT 29 fm LOT 24 "formerly belonging to Carlyle & Dalton"... E w/line //Queen 42'... thence to BEGIN--this parcel sold 24Jul72 by the Beelers to William Shaw, husband of Eleanor & father of William, as recorded in FfxCo Court 18Aug72.
WTT: Philip Webster, Thomas Stewart, James Jobson, John Duff

434 08Sep94
Fm Benjamin & Susannah Shreve, TwnALX, FfxCo, StVA
To George Clementson   -do-
Lease of a parcel E of St Asaph, N of Wolfe Sts:
Begin on St A at center of square former by Wolfe & Duke, 176' 7" N of Wolfe ... S w/St A 20' to ground sold by John Finley to John Hickman ... E//Wolfe 113' 5"... N//St A the length of 1st line ... thence to BEGIN--part of 1/2 acre lot sold by John Alexander to Finley; and by Finley 02 Oct84 to Shreve;
--annual payment by GC to Shreves @ 20 Spanish milled $ on 15Aug
WTT: Philip Wanton, John Hunter, Henley Boggess

438 11Sep94
Fm Benjamin & Susannah Shreve, TwnALX, FfxCo, StVA
To Francis Peyton   -do-
WHEREAS [the conveyance above is repeated]
NOW for £50 cmv the Shreves assign the annual rent to FP
WTT: same

441 22Aug94   Manumission
       John Hunter, TwnALX, StVA, recites that--to satisfy indebtedness of Joseph Caverly, late of ALX--Caverly's Negro slave Peter was publicly auctioned by William Summers, Sergeant of the Town. Hunter bought Peter, and hereby emancipates him.
WTT: J. Gilpin [and] John Gilpin

442 20 Oct94
Fm Michael & Hannah Madden, FfxCo, StVA
To James Wilson Junior, TwnALX, FfxCo, StVA
For £240 cmv, part of LOT 46 N of King, E of Water Sts:
BEGIN on King 90' E of Water St ... E w/King 30'... N//Water 81' to Fayette ... W w/Fayette 30'... thence to BEGIN
--conveyed to Hannah by Wm. Ramsay, **Gentleman,** 20Dec84.
WTT: John Dunlap, Bryan Hampson, James Kennedy--all to Hannah's signature
CMN: Jonah Thompson, John Dundas, Robert Mease, **Gentlemen** of TwnALX, aptd to examine Hannah. Rptd back same day.

446 01Nov94
Fm James & Letitia Kennedy, TwnALX, FfxCo, StVA
To James Wilson, Junr. -do-
For £135 cmv, a parcel N of King, E of Water Sts:
BEGIN on King 120' E of Water St at E line of parcel conveyed by the Maddens [above] to John Wilson, Jr. ... N w/line //Water St 81' to Fayette ... E w/Fayette//King 15'... S//Water St 81' to King ... thence to BEGIN--part of parcel conveyed by the late Wm. Ramsay to his daughter Hannah, and by Hannah and husband Michael Madden to James Kennedy.
WTT: Robert Hamilton, John Foster, Bryan Hampson
CMN: Robert Mease, James Lawrason, Jonah Thompson, **Gentlemen** of TwnALX, aptd to examine Letitia. Rptd same day.

451 03Nov94
Fm Thomas & Sarah Porter, TwnALX, FfxCo, StVA
To James Wilson Junr. -do-
For £135 cmv, a parcel N of King, E of Water Sts:
Begin on King 135' E of Water St ... E w/King 15'... N//Water St 81' to Fayette St ... W w/Fayette //King to line of parcel sold by James Kennedy to James Wilson, Jr...

W/line//Water St 81' to BEGIN--part of parcel granted by the late Wm. Ramsay, **Gentleman**, to his daughter, then Sarah Ramsay.
WTT: John Foster, Robert Hamilton, Bryan Hampson
CMN: Robert Mease, James Lawrason, Jonah Thompson, **Gentlemen** of TwnALX, aptd 16Nov94 to examine Sarah. Rptd back same day.

455 10Apr94
Fm Diedrick Scheckel, TwnALX, FfxCo, StVA, **Backer** [sic]
To Joseph Thornton, **Backer** -do- : for £350 cmv part of LOT 55 "as it appears by Indenture" dated 08Mar87 granted by Valentine & Catharine Uhler, S of King, W of Royal Sts:
BEGIN on King 90' W of int King-Royal ... W w/King 33' 6" to W boundary of lot ... S//Royal 92' 8"... E//King 33' 6"... thence to BEGIN;
AND WHEREAS Valentine & Catharine Uhler 22Dec85 conveyed to Joseph Fortney a parcel:
BEGIN on King at W line of LOT 55--the line dividing Uhler fm James Kirk ... E w/King 15'... S//Royal 92' 8"... W//King 15' ... thence to BEGIN
--w/use of alley along the E line, fm King S for 40', 3'wide;
--reserving to Thornton the right to extend the upper stories of any building he might build over the alley;
NOW Scheckel sells the "rest and residue of the said ground" to Joseph Thornton--including the use of the alley and the right to build upper stories over it.
WTT: Jno. C. Kempff, George Darling, Daniel McClain

459 10Apr94   Mortgage
Fm Joseph Thornton, TwnALX, FfxCo, StVA, **Backer** [sic]
To Diedrick Scheckel **Backer** -do-
For £150 cmv, part of LOT 55 as per 08Mar87 indenture fm Valentine & Catharine Uhler to Scheckel, and Scheckel to Thornton 10Apr94 [above];
--void if JT pays £150 + interest on /before 10Apr95.
WTT: Jno. C. Kempff, George Darling, Daniel McClain

462 29Mar91
Fm George & Mary Kyger, Hampshire Co., StVA
To Jacob Cox, TwnALX, FfxCo, StVA: for £5, part of LOT 66:
BEGIN at end of N line of parcel conveyed by the Kygers to Cox 23 Oct75--65' W of Ffx ... S w/"another line of the same piece of ground" for 10'... W w/"another line" 25'... N//Ffx 10'... thence to BEGIN.   [Mary Kyger signs w/mark]
WTT: James Keith, Charles Young, R. Marshall, James Watson
CMN: Abraham Johnston, Edward McCarty, **Gentlemen** of Hampshire Co., aptd 31Mar91 to examine Mary. Rptd back 26Jul94.

465 22Jul94
Fm Alexander & Mary McConnell, TwnALX
To John Dunlap, TwnALX, **Merchant**
For £312 current money, a parcel W side of Union:
BEGIN NW corner of Rutter's lot--20' N of N side of 20' alley fm Water St into Union St, made by John Fitzgerald & Valentine Peers ... N 26' "in front of...Union St"... W//King 70' to 10' alley made by Peers, linking King to 20' alley ... S w/10' alley 26' to Rutter's line ... and thence to BEGIN.
WTT: Peter Murray, Matthew Robinson, John White
CMN: Robert Mease, Francis Peyton, James Lawrason, **Gentlemen** of TwnALX, aptd 18Dec94 to examine Mary. Rptd back same day.

469 14Nov94
Fm William Hodgson, TwnALX, FfxCo, StVA
To John Crips Vowell AND Thomas Vowell Junr.,   -do-
WHEREAS Peter Casanave 26Nov91 conveyed to Hodgson a parcel S of King, E of Pitt Streets:
BEGIN on King at NE corner of John Dundas' ground near NW corner of Brick house thereon ... E w/King to E end of the house, 31' 6"... S//Pitt 176' 6" to back line of LOT [blank] ... W w/line, same as 1st line ... N 176' 6" to BEGIN;

AND ALSO E of Pitt, N of Prince:
BEGIN E side Pitt at NW corner LOT [blank] ... S w/Pitt 20'... E//Prince 100'... N//Pitt 20'... thence to BEGIN;
AND WHEREAS W. Hodgson 17Jul92 conveyed to John Dundas part of 1st lot:
BEGIN on King at NW corner of the ground--the NE corner of John Dundas' ground ... E w/King only 6 1/2"... S//Pitt 34'... W//King 6 1/2"... thence to BEGIN--w/privilege of joining the wall (which he [Dundas] was building) to wall of Hodgson's house and to "raise upon the Gavel end of said house which Wall was to serve as a common partition Wall";
NOW Hodgson for £960 cmv conveys to Vowell & Vowell both parcels sold him by Casanave, (but not that part of the first one sold by Hodgson to Dundas,)--and half the partition wall
WTT: William Bowness, B. Rawlings, George Clementson

474 17Jul93   Manumission
William Johnston of FfxCo manumits mulatto woman slave Milly, age about 21, for the £50 received from William Halley "the late Master of her husband Negro Nace"   WTT: Peter Wise, French Simpson, Esther Halley, William Halley

474 20Jun93
Fm John Casey, PG Co, MD
To Thomas Herbert, FfxCo, StVA
For £460 cmv, part of LOT 37 N of Cameron, E of Ffx Sts:
BEGIN on Cameron 46' 4" E of Ffx ... E w/Cameron 28'... N//Ffx 60' to property late that of William & Catharine Bird ... W w/line //Cameron 28'... thence to BEGIN
--conveyed by Thomas & Jenny Herbert to John Casey 24Sep84
WTT: James Keith, John Dunlap

End of Deed Book E

ALEXANDRIA HUSTINGS COURT

Deed Book F, 1793-1796

1 27Apr93   Power of Attorney
Fm Joseph Hadfield, City of London, **Merchant**
To James Barry, Baltimore, MD, **Merchant**
--done before Robert Robson, **Notary Public**
WTT: Jonathan Swift, ALX, VA and Leonard William Johnson of the Royal Exchange, London
Attest: James Sanderson, **Mayor** of London; Joshua Johnson, **U.S. Consul**, Port of London

5 12Dec94
Fm Charles & wife Frances Alexander, FfxCo, StVA, **Gentleman**
To James Irvine, TwnALX, FfxCo, StVA
Lease of a 1/2 acre E of Washington, S of Queen Sts:
BEGIN int Wn-Queen ... S w/Wn 176' 7"... E//Queen 123' 5"...
N//Wn 176' 7"... thence to BEGIN--each 25Dec $83 1/3 silver;
--JI to pay taxes & assessments;
--JI w/in 4 years to build at the intersection a brick dwelling at least 34' square and at least 2 stories;
--CA will issue a deed for the house and the ground Irvine wishes to include with it for half the rent: $41 2/3 silver, "exonerating all the rest of the said Lott from the payment of the said $41 2/3 silver;
--if w/in 5 years JI builds another brick house, at least 20' square/2 stories, on any other part of the lot except the intersection "and that part where the two story frame house now stands" CA will issue a lease for $26 5/6 silver for the house and as much land as Irvine chooses--exempting the rest of the lot.
WTT: Robert Mease, Jonah Thompson, Ja. Keith
CMN: Robert Mease, Jonah Thompson, John Dundas, **Gentlemen** of TwnALX, aptd 12Dec94 to examine Frances. Rptd back same day.

12 12Apr89
Fm Jacob Mattart, Frederick Twn, Frederick Co., MD, **Butcher**
To Thomas Price of the same place [vocation not stated]
For £340 current money of MD: 2 parcels in LOT 111, TwnALX, conveyed by John Hendricks 20Aug82 [not further described, but see below, p. 16]

WTT: George Scott, Wm. Luckett, **Justices of the Peace**, Frk Co.
Attest: Wm. Ritchie, Frk Co. **Clerk**. [N.B.: Jacob's wife, Magdalena, was privately examined. Jacob signed his name "Medtart," and the Clerk, ALX Hustings Court recorded the conveyance as "Mettart."]

16   31 Oct94
Fm Thomas & Mary Price, Frederick Co., MD
To Samuel Craig, TwnALX, FfxCo, StVA:
For £250 current money of MD: a parcel N of Prince, E of Pitt:
BEGIN on Prince at SE corner of LOT 111 ... W w/Prince 24' 6" ... N//Pitt 94'... E//Prince 24' 6"... then to BEGIN;

AND a parcel E of Pitt, N of Prince:
BEGIN on Pitt, 94 ' N of Prince ... N w/[Pitt] 25'... E// Prince 97'... N//Pitt 58'... E//Prince 24' 6"... S//Pitt 113' ... W//Prince 123' 6" to BEGIN--both parcels in LOT 111 conveyed by John Hendricks 20Aug82 to Jacob Mattart, and by Mattart to Price 12Apr89.
WTT: Wm. Craik, **Chief Justice**, 5th District of MD, W.M. Beall
Attest: Wm. Craik, Wm. Ritchie, **Clerk**, Frk Co Court

20   22Apr94
Fm John Fitzgerald, TwnALX, FfxCo, StVA
To Abraham Morehouse [no ID]:
Lease part LOT 93, W of Union, S of Wolfe:
BEGIN int Union-Wolfe ... S w/Union 115'... W//Wolfe 62' 2"
... N//Union 115' to Wolfe ... thence to BEGIN--conveyed by Daniel Roberdeau to JF and William Lyles, Lyles since selling his interest to JF;
--and also on this ground the "Distillery and all the Houses and Buildings...and the several Stills, worms, tubbs, Cesterns, casks, pumps, and every piece of machinery and other articles and things now in and about the said Distillery"
--"and also the woodyard at the end of the Wharf below the said piece of Ground as the same is now inclosed"
--"and also the use and labour of the two men slaves called Jack and Matt" for 2 years
--the rest for 10 years, at $1000 each 31May
--feeding, clothing, paying taxes on/for the 2 slaves
--Morehouse may build anew or alter present structures, provided he does not destroy the present structures
--and can remove distillery equipment he introduces, but must leave his buildings
--the whole may be purchased at any time for $10,000
--Morehouse may convert all/part to a brewery, but must leave any conversion intact
WTT: Baldwin Stith, Jas. Douglass, Mattw. F. Bowne

27   29Jul94
Fm Daniel & Jane Roberdeau, TwnALX, FfxCo, StVA
To Abraham Morehouse   -do-
WHEREAS 18Mar74 John Hughs conveyed to Roberdeau LOTS 93-94-95 S of Wolfe, E of Water St;
WHEREAS the Roberdeaus 17May85 conveyed part of these to John Fitzgerald & William Lyles, Junr., for annual rent each 27Aug of £131.18.0 cmv;
AND conveyed 04Jul94 to Archibald McClean yet another part, and 19Jul94 to Abraham Morehouse yet another part for 10 years fm 01Jul paying £120 annually in quarterly payments w/proviso: Abraham Morehouse & Co. could remit rent by paying £1800;

NOW the Roberdeaus will for $1 (and the rents below) convey or assign to Abraham Morehouse a lease to the following:
--all of LOTS 93-94-95 not conveyed to Fitzgerald & Lyles, A. McClain, or Morehouse & Co;
--and the wharf Roberdeau made, adjacent to LOT 93;
--and the £131.18 rent from Fitzgerald & Lyles, and the £120 rent from Morehouse & Co;
FOR rent from 01Jul9--for 10 years--at £430 annually, in quarterly payments (£430 cmv in Spanish milled $ at 6/ each and "all other silver and gold coins according to the value now fixed upon them by act of Congress") beginning 01Sep
AND A. Morehouse can have all rent remitted (except the £120 fm A. Morehouse & Co) by paying at any time £4650 cmv plus the Fitzgerald & Lyles' and the A.McClain rents due.
WTT: John Harper, Ja. Keith, Alexander Smith, Archd. McClean

37 23Sep94
Fm Nathaniel Chapman Hunter & wife Sarah Ann, Twn Dumfries, PW Co, StVA
To Aaron Hewes, TwnALX, FfxCo, StVA
For £156.5.0 cmv, part of LOT 74, W of Ffx, N of Duke Sts:
BEGIN on Ffx "at Centre of the square formed by Prince Street and Duke Street" on dividing line between ground "late the property of Christopher Beeler now Jesse Hollingsworth" and that of N.C.Hunter--176' 7" "from each of the said Streets of Prince and Duke"... W w/dividing line 118' to 10' alley laid out by NCH in the center of his ground, fm Ffx to Royal ... S w/alley parallelling Ffx & Royal 30'... E//Duke 118' to Ffx ... thence to BEGIN;
--NCH will lay off for his and Hewes' common use a 10' alley 118' W of Ffx fm Jesse Hollingsworth's line //Ffx, to Duke St.
WTT: Ja. Keith, Mordecai Miller, Elisha Janney
CMN: Alexander Lethgow, John Lawson, John McCrea, **Gentlemen** of PW Co, aptd 08 Oct94 to examine Sarah Ann. Rptd 07Nov94

44 13 Oct94
Fm William & Ann Duvall, PWmCo, StVA
To (as tenants in common) John White & Matthew Robinson, TwnALX, FfxCo, StVA: part of LOT 38, W of Ffx, N of Cameron
BEGIN at S line of parcel conveyed by William Duvall to William Downman, and by Downman to John White [no dates]--87' 10 1/3" N of Cameron ... W w/"that piece" [line?] 82' to line of parcel lately David Gordon's, now Lawrence Hoof's ... S w/line 29' to parcel of Bank of Alexandria ... E w/line and line of ground of Robert Adam, deceased, 82' to Ffx ... thence to BEGIN--this is half the parcel sold by William Ramsay, **Gentleman**, to William Duvall, part LOT 38.
WTT: Ja. Keith, Robert Mease, John Dundas
CMN: Robert Mease, Jonah Thompson, John Dundas, **Gentlemen** of TwnAlx, aptd 13 Oct94 to examine Ann. Rptd back same day.

51 16Jan93
Fm Abraham & Sarah Falconer, Twn of Baltimore, MD AND
  Joseph & Elizabeth Massey, Queen Ann Co., MD
To George Gilpin, TwnALX, StVA: parcel E of Water St in TwnALX
BEGIN on Water St 44' 8" fm int Prince-Water Sts and on S side of Prince "being the extreme part of a lott rented by the said George Gilpin to Philip Marsteller"... S w/Water St 22' 2"... E//Prince 150'... N//Water 22' 2"... thence to BEGIN--part of lot conveyed by George Johnston's heirs to Jonathan Hall and George Gilpin;
--J. Hall dying intestate, property descended to his daughters Sarah & Elizabeth

WTT: Geo. Gouldth. Presbury [Gouldsmith], Geo. Salmon, and sworn before Presbury & Salmon, **Justices of the Peace** of Baltimore Co., MD. Attested by Wm. Gibson, **Clerk**, Balt. Co.

56 10 Oct94
Fm Valentine & Eleanor Peers, PWm Co, Cwl VA
To (as tenants in common) Joseph Riddle, TwnALX, FfxCo, CwlVA AND James Dall, Twn of Baltimore, Balt.Co., MD - part of LOT No. [blank]:
BEGIN S of 12' alley "called Swifts alley at that part which Jonathan Swifts line touches"... E w/alley //King & Prince 23' to line of John Fitzgerald ... S w/JF's line //Ffx & Water Sts 82' to line of Andrew Wales ... W w/Wales' line //King & Prince 23' to the "back line of Joseph Janney"... N//Ffx & Water Sts. "along Janney's line to end thereof"... W//King & Prince to another parcel owned by Riddle & Dall ... N w/their line to Jonathan Swift's line ... thence w/Swift's line to BEGIN--part of land purchased as tenants in common by Valentine Peers & John Fitzgerald fm the widow and devisees of John Patterson, and part of Peers' part, after a division with JF;
--clear of encumbrances except: when Peers conveyed property to Janney, Peers promised Janney the right to a "water passage by which the water falling upon the back yard of the premises ... might conveniently pass off to the bank or else where so as not to remain or stand thereupon" (and Riddle & Dall agree to honor this.)
WTT: Bryan Hampson, Jno. Watts, John Neill
CMN: John Brown, John Love, Charles Tyler, **Gentlemen** of PWm Co, aptd 10Dec94 to examine Eleanor. Rptd back 16Dec94.

63 27Dec94
Fm William Thornton Alexander & wife Lucy, King Geo. Co, CwlVA
To Stephen Cooke, TwnALX, CwlVA: lease of parcel southward of TwnALX "commonly called Jones's point containing about six acres more or less"... bounded on N by parcel conveyed by WTA to Cooke 23Jun94, and by the River Potomac ... on E by River Potomac, on W by Hunting Creek: for £19 cmv annually, beginning 01Jan96.
WTT: Ch. Simms, Charles Lee, R. West, Thos. Patten

67 [Memo]
ALX December 27, 1794
Received of Stephen Cooke the sum of Two hundred Dollars as a farther consideration for the within mentioned Jones's Point over and above the yearly ground rent of Nineteen pounds, and I do hereby acknowledge that I have relinquished and Assigned to the said Stephen Cooke his heirs and Assigns for ever all my claims on the United States for the Consideration money they may allow for the use of the ground on which they are now building a Fort.
/s/William Thornton Alexander by John Taliaferro Junr.
Atty in Fact for [WTA]
WTT: R. West, Ch. Simms, Thos. Patten, Charles Lee

68 25Dec94
Fm William Thornton Alexander & wife Lucy, King Geo. Co, CwlVA
To Stephen Cooke, TwnALX, CwlVA
Lease of a parcel contiguous to ALX:
BEGIN intersection N side King-E side Columbus Sts ... E w/King 123' 5" to SW corner of 1/2 acre granted by Cooke and "now occupied by John Heisler"... N//Washington "to the fence inclosing the Church burying ground"... W//King to E side of Columbus ... S w/Columbus to BEGIN
--paying annual rent £8 VA currency beginning 01Jul95
[Alexander atty John Taliaferro Junr executes this for them.]

[On p.72, next to WTA/JTjr. signatures:] "If Mr. Charles Alexanders land extends to the Southward of the Church fence, Stephen Cooke claims no farther than to his line, & at any rate to no land Northerly of the fence on the South side of the Church burying ground."
WTT: John Gill, Ch. Simms, Leml. [Lemuel] Bent, Ja. Keith

72 25Dec94
Fm William Thornton Alexander & wife Lucy, King Geo. Co, CwlVA
To Stephen Cooke, TwnALX, CwlVA - lease land contiguous to Twn ALX:
BEGIN NW corner LOT No. 2 in the 1784 Plot [WTA's land sale plat] S of King, W of Washington Sts ... W w/King 123' 5" to Columbus ... S w/Columbus 176' 7"... E//King 123' 5" to SW corner LOT No. 2, and thence to BEGIN
--paying annual rent £8 VA currency beginning 01Jul95
[Alexander atty John Taliaferro Junr executes this for them.]
WTT: as above

77 25Dec94 [Same to same]
Lease parcel contiguous to ALX:
BEGIN on W side Ffx 176' 7" S of NE corner of LOT 36 formed by intersection S side Gibbons and W side Ffx Sts ... W//Gibbons 436' 3" to middle line between Royal & Pitt ... S w/middle line //Royal to NW corner of 12 acre lot lately conveyed by WTA to Cooke ... E//Gibbons to W side Ffx ... thence to BEGIN;
--paying annual rent £20 VA money beginning 01Jul95
--executed by John Taliaferro [no "Junr."] as atty f/ALXRs
WTT: Josiah Watson, Ch. Simms, Elisha C. Dick, Geo. Sweeney

82 17Jan95
Fm Stephen & Catharine Cooke, TwnALX, StVA
To Joseph Riddle   -do- : One acre contiguous to TwnALX:
BEGIN SE corner LOT 36 "now in possession of Andrew Wales" on S side Gibbons, W side Ffx Sts ... W//Gibbons 436' 3" to middle line between Royal & Pitt ... S w/middle line //Royal 100'... E//Gibbons 436' 3" to W side of Ffx St ... N w/W side Ffx 100' to BEGIN--paying annually L17.10.0 VA currency beginning 17Jan96.
WTT: none   MEMO: if after 5 years Riddle wishes to return the property, Cooke will release him from any further rents thereafter.

86 30Dec94
Fm William Thornton Alexander & wife Lucy, King Geo Co., StVA
To Robert Townshend Hooe, FfxCo, StVA: lease for 21 years fm 01Jun94 of a parcel: 21 acres in FfxCo adjacent to TwnALX:
BEGIN at point on E side Washington 583' 2" fm SE corner int Gibbon-Wn ... E//Gibbon 436' 3"... S//Wn into Hunting Creek... W w/meanders of Hunting Creek to E side of Wn "directly produced"... thence to BEGIN--paying annually £15 "good and lawfull money of VA" beginning 01Jun95.
WTT: Ludwell Albers, Washington John Washington, Zachariah Muncaster

90 26Sep94   Power of Attorney
Fm Amelia Finlay of Queen St, Soho, Middlesex Co., widow; natural and lawful
     Mother of the late David Finlay, ALX, VA, **Merchant**, deceased
To James Patton, ALX, **Merchant**
--to settle debts and collect accounts and to convey to Mr. James Kennedy, **Merchant**, ALX, half of a parcel lately sold to JK but not yet conveyed;
--sworn before **Notary** Robert Robson of London

WTT: Henry Lunt, **Master** of the Ship Peggy; W. Shackley of Royal Exchange, London, **Gentleman**
Attested by: Paul LeMesurier, **Mayor** of London; Joshua Johnson, **Esquire, Consul** of the U.S. for the Port of London

96 [see above, p. 90] John Knight, **Minister** of Nightengale Lane Chapel, Middlesex Co., certifies that "David son of David and Amelia Finlay was baptized" July 21, 1767.

98 27Aug94 Tripartite Deed
I-John Harper, FfxCo, StVA
II-John Boyer, TwnALX, FfxCo, StVA
III-Christian Slimmer, -do-
WHEREAS JH 06Dec83 conveyed to JB & CS a parcel W of Union, N of Prince:
BEGIN on Union at dividing line between Messrs. McCrea & Mease property (now belonging to Thomas Crandel) and John Harper ... S w/Union 42'... W//Prince 83' to 10' alley ... N w/alley 42' to M & M's line ... thence to BEGIN--paying each 01Jan 126 Spanish milled dollars;
WHEREAS Slimmer & Boyer made a partition, Boyer to have:
BEGIN at the M&M-JH line ... S w/Union 21'... W//Prince to alley ... N w/alley to division line ... thence to BEGIN--Boyer to pay Harper half of the rent;
NOW for £208 cmv Harper remits the half-rent due fm Boyer and certfies Slimmer to be free and clear of it, as well (owing only 63 Spanish Milled $) for his own parcel.
WTT: Ja. Keith, Geo. Coryell, Robert Allison

104 30Dec94
Fm William Thornton Alexander & wife Lucy, King George Co.
To Josiah Watson AND William Hartshorne, TwnALX
WHEREAS 05Aug79 heirs of John Alexander conveyed to JW & WH a parcel "containing about three quarters of an acre laid off in two lotts in the plan of the Lotts adjoining the Town...numbered 161 and 162," S of Wilkes and E of Water Sts, "opposite to the South side of the two Lotts numbered 94 and 95 in the plan" of TwnALX:
BEGIN E side Water St, S side Wilkes at termination of line extended fm SW corner of LOT 95 //west side of LOT 95 and w/Water St south of Wilkes ... S continuing the parallel course 176' 7"... E//Wilkes to Potomack River ... N up Potomack w/meanders thereof to Wilkes ... W w/Wilkes to BEGIN;
--"to have and to hold the said two lotts or piece of land numbered 161 and 162" [in other words, they leased all of 161-162, which totalled approx. 3/4 of an acre]
--paying annual rent £78.5.0 cmv from 05Aug80, rent to be paid to the then-minor William Thornton Alexander
--recorded in FfxCo Court;
NOW for £800 cmv WTA & Lucy remit further rent payments.
WTT: Chs. Young, Junr., Jesse Simms, Jh. [Joseph] M. Perrin, W. Nell, Mathrin. Perrin

109 20Jan94
Fm Job Green, TwnALX
To Stephen Cooke -do-
WHEREAS Green rented to Lemuel Bent a parcel "with a warehouse thereupon erected" for 5 years, from 20Jan94, for £75 annually paid in half-yearly payments
NOW for $775, Green assigns the rent to Cooke; if the warehouse [the basis for the rent] should be destroyed, Green will pay Cooke the £75 annually.
WTT: Joseph Riddle, James Russell, G. Swope

111 24Dec94
Fm George & Jane Gilpin, TwnALX, FfxCo, StVA
To Benjamin Shreve AND James Lawrason of the same place
WHEREAS the Gilpins 11Aug84 leased to BS & JL parcel S of Prince, W of Union:
BEGIN intersection Prince-Union ... W w/Prince 51'... S//Union 44' 4" to line of
property lately of Jonathan Hall, deceased ... E w/Hall line//Prince 51' to Union ...
thence to BEGIN--for an annual rent of 51 Guineas each 01Jun;
WHEREAS the Gilpins on [blank date], 17[blank] remitted £20.8.0 of the 51 Guineas
NOW for £510 cmv they remit the remainder of the rent.
WTT: Robert Mease, Francis Peyton, Jas. Keith, Junr.
CMN: Robert Mease, John Dundas, Francis Peyton, **Gentlemen** of TwnALX, aptd
01Jan95 to examine Jane. Rptd back 22Jan95

116 21Aug92   Non-Importation Compliance
[Following the heading "Corporation of Alexandria Sct"]
Dennis Ramsay and Thomas Porter, styling themselves "Magistrates for said Borough" and hear David Easton swear that the "Negro Boy Named Prince, Tom Lee imported in the Brig Cornwallis from Curacoa" is for his own use, and not for resale.
--Easton recorded this 1792 affadavit in court only on 24Apr95.

117 10Jan95   Non-Importation Compliance
    Before John Dundas, James Graham swears he is complying with the Slave Non-Importation Act with regard to Negroes Sam and Linder.

117 20Feb95   Non-Importation Compliance
    As above, before Richard Conway, Lanty Crowe swears for his slaves Mima, William and Eleanor.

118 14Jul94
Fm John Robert Wheaton & wife Elizabeth, TwnALX, FfxCo, StVA
To Bernard Ghequire -do-
Part LOT 52 S of King, W of Water Sts:
BEGIN on King 92' W of Water St ... W w/King 25'... S//Water St 82'to 12 1/2' alley ...
E w/alley//King 25'... thence to BEGIN--conveyed by Valentine Peers to William
Hodgson, and by Hodgson 13Mar94 to J.R. Wheaton; w/use of the alley.
WTT: Thomas Rogerson, John Dundas, Francis Peyton, Lemuel Bent
WTT to receipt of money: Lemuel Bent, Thomas Rogerson, George Ubrich
CMN: John Dundas, Jonah Thompson, Francis Peyton, **Gentlemen** of TwnALX, aptd
02Feb95 to examine Eleanor. Rptd back 04Apr95.

122 02Apr95
Fm Thomas & Ann Barclay, Twn of Georgetown, MD
To Samuel Craig, TwnALX, FfxCo, StVA
WHEREAS Benjamin Shreve 01Apr85 conveyed to T.Barclay a part of LOT 111, N of Prince, E of Pitt:
BEGIN on Prince 73' 5" E of Pitt ... E w/Prince 24' 6"... N//Pitt 94'... W//Prince 24' 6",
then to BEGIN--paying annually £20 cmv 01Apr;
--which rent Shreve has [no date] assigned to Isaac Nickolls;
NOW the Barclays for £120 cmv convey the property to S. Craig
--Craig to pay Nicholls [sic] each 01Apr £20 cmv in Spanish milled $ at 6/each, or Half Johannes weighing 9 pennyweight at 48/ each, or other gold and silver.
WTT: to Craig: Jas. Keith, Bryan Hampson, John C. Vowell; to the Barclays: Thos. Turner [Turner is **Mayor** of Georgetown].

120

127 09May94
Fm Nathaniel Chapman Hunter & wife Sarah Anne, PWmCo, CwlVA
To Ephraim Evans, TwnALX, StVA
WHEREAS now NCH owns LOT [blank] in TwnALX at int Duke & Royal
NOW for £190 lawfull money of VA, the Hunters convey:
BEGIN on Duke 60' E Duke-Royal ... W w/Duke 60'... N w/Royal 100'... E at right angles w/Duke 60'... S//Royal 100' to BEGIN.
WTT: Jesse Simms, Samuel Boling, Chs. Turner
CMN: Alexander Lethgow, John Lawson, William Grant, **Gentlemen** of PWm Co, aptd 28Feb95 to examine Sarah Anne. Rptd 02Mar95.

132 06Jun94
Fm William & Sarah Lyles, PG Co., MD
To George Coryell, TwnALX, StVA
WHEREAS the Trustees sold George Mercer LOT 80, W of Water and S of Duke Sts--George dying intestate, it went to brother James Mercer;
--James obtained an act of the assembly and "laid of the said half Acre of ground into small divisions agreeable to a platt wherein the said divisions were numbered, which Platt he proposed to have recorded in the Court" of FfxCo;
--one of the divisions, No. 4, he sold 22May87 to William Lyles
   --bounded by Duke 27' 10" upon the North
   --extends S 91' 6" to a 10' alley and
   --joins the 91' 6" line with Lot No. 3
NOW the Lyles for £80 cmv convey No. 4 to Coryell.
WTT: James Taylor, Thomas Irwin, Benjn. Shreve

136 26Aug94 Bill of Sale
Charles Turner, Deputy Sheriff of FfxCo under Sheriff James Wren, has sold at auction to Joseph Saul one Negro boy slave Andrew for £24.10.0, formerly owned by William Ward, in order to satisfy a county court judgement against Ward by the admrs of Robert Adam, dec'd.

137 20Mar95
Fm James & Laetitia Kennedy TwnALX, FfxCo, StVA
To Robert Brockett -do-
For £270 cmv, parcels N of Fayette, E of Water Sts:
BEGIN on Fayette 30' E of Wtr St ... E w/Fayette 30'...N//Water St 65' 7" to line of the late Col. John Carlyle ... W// Fayette w/JC's line 30'... thence to BEGIN
--conveyed to Kennedy 12Feb95 by Robert & Ann Allison;
                    AND
Parcel also N of Fayette, E of Water Streets:
BEGIN on Fayette 60' E of Wtr St ... E w/Fayette 30'... N// Water St 65' 6" to JC's line ... W w/JC line 30'... then to BEGIN--conveyed to Kennedy 18Mar95 by Dennis Ramsay, and Robert & Betty Mease;
                    AND
Parcel also N of Fayette, E of Water Streets:
BEGIN N side Fyt, 90' E of Wtr ... E w/Fayette 30'... N//Water St 65' 6" to Carlyle line ... W w/JC line 30'... then to BEGIN
--conveyed to Kennedy 06Feb95 by Dennis Ramsay, and Robert & Ann Allison;
WTT: Bryan Hampson, John Dundas, Jonah Thompson
CMN: John Dundas, Jonah Thompson, **Gentlemen** of TwnALX, aptd 21Apr95 to examine Lettitia [sic] and rptd back same day

142   12Jan95
Fm William & Ann Wright, TwnALX
To William Hoye   -do-: lease parcel in TwnALX:
BEGIN on Prince 280' 1 1/4" W of Union at the "Western corner of the framed house built by John Harper"... W w/Prince 17' 2 1/4"... N//Union 88' 3 1/2" to the dividing line between Harper and McCrea & Mease ... E w/line 17 2 1/4" ... then to BEGIN--paying from 12Jan96 each 12Jan £18 current money.
[Ann Wright signs w/mark]
WTT: George Slacum, Washer Blunt, Zacharius Liles

146   19Dec92
Fm Jacob Cox, TwnALX, FfxCo, CwlVA
To William Wright -do-: lease parcel W of Water, N of Wilkes: BEGIN int Water-Wilkes Streets ... N w/Water St 50' 2"... W// Wilkes 74'... S//Wtr St 50' 2"... thence to BEGIN--part of lot conveyed 19Dec74 by John Alexander to Cox--paying annually from 20Jun93 41 1/2 silver $.
WTT: James Keith, Thomas Taylor, John Cohagen

150   13Sep94
Fm Thomas West, FfxCo, CwlVA
To Henry McCue, TwnALX, FfxCo, CwlVA
Part LOT 22 which John & Rachel Lomax conveyed 27Jun85 to John Wise, and John & Elizabeth Wise 12Sep94 to Thomas West
--this part conveyed 07Jan93 by West to McCue but w/o stating metes and bounds and before West had clear title, so NOW:
BEGIN NE corner LOT 22 and NW corner LOT 21 ... W//Princess along line 26 1/2'... S//Ffx into LOT 22 124'... E//Princess 26 1/2' to line between LOTS 21 + 25 ... thence to BEGIN.
WTT: Cleon Moore, Maurice Herlihy, James McHenry, John Brownell

152   13Sep94
Fm Thomas West, FfxCo, CwlVA
To Henry McCue, TwnALX, FfxCo, CwlVA
WHEREAS Richard & Mary Conway 01Jul82 conveyed to John Lomax "late of ALX" part LOT 21:
BEGIN NW corner LOT 21 on Princess St ... E w/Princess 71'... S//Water & Ffx Sts 72' 2"... W//Princess, Queen Sts 71'... N w/E line LOT 22//Ffx & Water Sts to BEGIN--for annual rent £17.15.0 w/option w/in 20 years: remit rent by paying £350 cmv AND WHEREAS John & Rachel Lomax [blank] June 1785 conveyed the same on the same terms to John Wise, and Wise 12Sep94 to West; NOW for £110 cmv West conveys the above parcel to McCue, on the same terms.   WTT: as above

155   09Jul94
Fm John Harper, FfxCo, StVA
To Alexander Smith, TwnALX, StVA: for £600 cmv part LOT 52 [51] S side King, W side Water Sts:
BEGIN int King-Water Sts ... W w/King 42'... S//Water St 82' to 10' alley dividing this fm John Fitzgerald ... E w/alley to Water St 42'... thence to BEGIN
--conveyed by Valentine Peers to William Hodgson by 2 indentures [not identified], and by Hodgson 01Jun90 to Harper.
WTT: Jonathan Swift, Archd. McClean, Jas. Keith

158   12Feb95
Fm Robert & Ann Allison, TwnALX, FfxCo, StVA

To James Kennedy -do-
Parcel N side Fayette, E side Water Sts:
BEGIN on Fayette 30' E of Water St--the E line of parcel conveyed by William Ramsay, **Gentleman,** to James Stewart ... E w/Fayette 30'... N//Water St 65' 7" to property line of the late Col. John Carlyle, deceased ... W w/JC line to Stewart line ... thence w/Stewart line to BEGIN--parcel being one of those conveyed to Robert Allison by William Ramsay 16Jul77.
WTT: Jno. Thos. Ricketts, John Harper, John Winterberry, Junr., William Ash
CMN: Jonah Thompson, James Laurason, Francis Peyton, **Gentlemen** of TwnALX, aptd 07Mar95 to examine Ann. Rptd back same day.

162 06Feb95   Tripartite Deed
I-Dennis Ramsay, TwnALX, FfxCo, StVA
II-Robert & Ann Allison -do-
III-James Kennedy -do-
WHEREAS William Ramsay, **Gentlemen,** late of ALX, dec'd, on 12Dec84 out of the affection he bore his wife Ann and his daughter [Ann Ramsay Allison] deeded to Dennis Ramsay parcel--on N side of Fayette St "a street laid out by [WR] through certain Grounds belonging unto him" E of Water St
--"part of the Ground which...[WR] was at that time Banking out from the River adjoining to...LOTT...46" and "in the plan and division made by [WR] of his Lotts adjoining the Water by the number (10)"
BEGIN N side of Fayette, 90' E of Water St ... E w/Fayette 30'... N//Water St 65' 6"... W w/"the said alley" ["Fayette"] 30' ... thence to BEGIN--conveyed thus in trust to Dennis, 1/3 of its rent to Ann Ramsay, 2/3 to Ann Ramsay Allison until her mother died--thereafter all to ARA;
--however, both [parents] William & Ann soon after died and Dennis found no renters;
--the others to whom WR conveyed adjoining parcels on Fayette "considered it conducive to their several Interests to contract [Fayette] from 50' in Breadth to 30' and accordingly" did so;
--"Representatives of the said John Carlyle failing to lay off any part of that Ground to form a part of the alley intended by [WR],...the several persons holding Ground under [WR] joining upon the said Alley have concluded to stop up the same and to extend their respective Lines to the Ground of...John Carlyle" [and continues with the following]
--"AND WHEREAS the piece of Ground...has never been properly banked out from the river and finished in such manner as to enable any person to improve it which has put it out of the power of the said Dennis Ramsay to procure any rent from it"
--[and the Allisons wishing to dispose of it]
NOW for the £60 cmv Dennis Ramsay conveys to James Kennedy the parcel granted him in trust for his mother and sister
--"and which by the contracting of Fayette Street and Stopping up the Alley adjoining the Ground lately belonging to John Carlyle begins:
BEGIN N side of Fayette, 90' E of Water St ... E w/Fayette 30'... N//Water St 65' 6" to line of ground belonging "to the Devisees of John Carlyle"... W w/JC line 30', thence to BEGIN.
WTT: Jno. Thos. Ricketts, John Harper, John Winterberry Junr., William Ash
CMN: Jonah Thompson, Francis Peyton, **Gentlemen** of TwnALX, aptd 25Feb95 to examine Ann Allison. Rptd back 07[sic]Feb95.

169 04Apr95
Fm Thomas & Cassina Conn, TwnALX, FfxCo, StVA
To William Hepburn & John Dundas of the same place

WHEREAS the Conns 17Feb95 conveyed to Charles Bryan parcel N of King, W of Royal:
BEGIN on King at W corner of William McKnight's parcel ... thence w/King N78W 19' 3 1/2"... N into the Lott//Royal 50' to McKnight's line ... S78E 19' 3 1/2" to another McKnight line ... S12W w/line 50' to BEGIN--paying each 20Dec $22 1/2;
--subsequently conveyed [no date] by Charles Bryan to Charles [William?] McKnight
NOW for £67.10.0 cmv the Conns assign the $22 1/2 rent to Hepburn & Dundas.
WTT: George Darling, William Noble, James Camock, Caleb Earp

173 22Apr95
Fm Samuel & Elizabeth Johnston, Twn of Baltimore, MD
To Robert Townshend Hooe, TwnALX, StVA
WHEREAS RTH & Richard Harrison 29 Oct85 conveyed to Jacob Harman part LOT 64 on W side Water Street:
BEGIN on Water St at line dividing LOTS 64-72 ... W w/line //Prince 123' 5"... N//Water St 26'... E//Prince 123' 5"... then to BEGIN--Harman paying 26 Guineas per year, half each 01Jan and 01Jul;
AND 08Nov85 RTH & RH assigned the rent to Robert McCrea and Robert Mease, who on 22Dec90 assigned it to Samuel Johnston;
NOW for £156 cmv the Johnstons assign the 26 Guinea rent back to RTH.
WTT: James Keith, George Slacum, John Muncaster, Zachariah Muncaster

179 18Mar95 Tripartite Deed
I-Dennis Ramsay, TwnALX, FfxCo, StVA
II-Robert Mease & wife Betty, "late Betty Steuart" -do-
III-James Kennedy -do-
Parcel N side Fayette St "laid out by William Ramsay through certain Ground belonging to him" and E of Water St:
BEGIN on Fayette 60' E of Wtr E w/Fayette 30'... N//Water St 46' 6" to alley between Wm. Ramsay's Ground and the late Col. John Carlyle's ... W w/alley 30'... thence to BEGIN.
[From this point the text is almost identical to that beginning p. 162, above:
--property conveyed in trust to Dennis by William for William's wife Ann and daughter Betty Ramsay Steuart;
--to be rented with money 1/3 to Ann, 2/3 to Betty until Ann's death, thence all to Betty;
--property not rented and "has never been properly banked out from the River and finished in such a manner as to enable any person to improve it";
--the street contracted, and the alley stopped up.]
NOW for £72.10.0 cmv the Meases convey to Kennedy
BEGIN N side Fayette 60' E of Water St ... E w/Fayette 30'...
N//Water St 65' 6" to Carlyle's devisees' line ... W w/line 30'... thence to BEGIN.
WTT: none

185 17Dec94
Fm John Harper, FfxCo, StVA
To William Wright, TwnALX, FfxCo, StVA
Two parcels N side Prince, W of Union Sts:
No. 1: BEGIN on Prince 188' W of Union ... W w/Prince 9 3/4 <u>inches</u> ... N//Union 88' 3 1/2" to line of McCrea & Mease [line is between Harper, and M & M] ... E w/ line 9 3/4 inches ... thence "to the Beginning of the other piece of Ground...."
No. 2: BEGIN on Prince 208' 1 1/4" W of Union--at "Western Corner of the Frame house built by Jn. Harper"... W w/Prince 17' 2 1/4"... N//Union 88' 3 1/2" to line between Harper and M & M ... E w/line 17' 2 1/4"... thence to BEGIN.

AND-for Harper or Wright-whoever first builds ["erects a house"] upon or adjoining these premises may "lay one half of the Gavel Wall next to the dividing Line upon the Ground of the other"--the wall to be considered a common wall;
--the second builder, joining to the wall, paying half the value of the wall "before he or they shall begin to lay his or their Foundations";
--the value as "ascertained by workmen indifferently chosen for that purpose...."
WTT: James Keith, Job Greene, Thomas Rogerson, John Reynolds

189 16Apr95
Fm Jacob Heineman, TwnALX, FfxCo, StVA
To Henry Zimmerman -do-
For £25 cmv "a Certain House and Lot with all the Buildings thereunto belonging" BEGIN W side Washington St 176' 7" N of Princess ... N w/Wn 60'... W//Princess 100'... S//Wn 60'... thence to BEGIN--and paying each 05Sep to Baldwin Dade 40 Spanish milled $ as per deed of 25Jun85, Book A, folio 239 in ALX Hustings Court.
[Heineman and Zimmerman sign; Maria Heineman signs w/mark]
WTT: J. C. Kempff, Alexander McConnell, Samuel Arell

193 08 Oct94
Fm Bernhard & Johanna Mann, TwnALX, FfxCo, StVA
To Thomas Patten -do-
WHEREAS George Chapman 21Sep84 conveyed to Bernhard Mann parcel S of Duke, E of Water St:
BEGIN of Water St 90' from Duke ... S w/Water St 28'... E// Duke 90' to 6' alley ... thence w/alley//Water St 28' to 8' alley ... W w/alley//Duke 90' to Water St and BEGIN--paying each 01May £17.14 in gold or silver;
NOW for £136 cmv the Manns convey the parcel to Patten,
Patten paying Chapman the rent. [Johanna signs w/mark]
WTT: James Keith, Robert Mease, Francis Peyton, Philip G. Marstiller [sic]
CMN: Robert Mease, Jonah Thompson, Francis Peyton,
Gentlemen of TwnALX, aptd to examine Johanna. Rptd same day.

199 26Dec94
Fm William Thornton Alexander & wife Lucy, King Geo Co., StVA
To George Coryell, FfxCo, StVA: Lease of 1 acre in FfxCo, adjacent to TwnALX:
BEGIN intersection Columbus & Duke, N of Duke, W of Columbus ... N w/Columbus 176' 5" "or a half Square"... W w/"Prince Street extended" 246' 10" to Alfred St ... thence at right angles and //Alfred "till it Intersect at Right angles Duke St extended"... thence N w/Duke to BEGIN "so as to contain one Acre or a regular half of a Square as genneraly laid of in the said TwnALX"--paying £12 good and lawfull money of VA per year beginning 01Jul95.
[Signed by John Taliaferro as agent for WTA]
WTT: Ra. [Richard] Hewitt, Thos. Conn, John Horner
CMN: Michael Wallace, John Pollard, William Hooe, **Gentlemen** of King Geo. Co., aptd 06Feb95 to examine Lucy. Rptd 26Feb95

205 26Dec94
Fm William Thornton Alexander & wife Lucy, King Geo Co., StVA
To George Coryell, FfxCo, StVA - lease of 2 acres in FfxCo, adjacent to TwnALX: BEGIN int Alfred-Prince, S side Prnc, W side Alf ... W and //Prince until intersecting at right angles w/Patrick ... S and//Patrick until int at right angles w/Duke ... E and//Duke until int at right angles w/W line of Alfred ... N and//Alfred to BEGIN-- paying each 01Jul from 01Jul95 £18 good and lawful money of VA
WTT:as above, Hewitt swearing to Taliaferro's having acted as WTa's agent.

CMN: same as above but aptd 26Feb95, rptd back that same day.

210 24Dec94
Fm William Thornton Alexander & wife Lucy, King Geo Co., StVA
To Ezra Kinzey, FfxCo, StVA - lease 1/2 acre in FfxCo, adjoining TwnALX
BEGIN int Wolf-Alfred, S of Wolfe, W of Alfred Sts: S w/Alfred 176' 7"... W//Wolfe 123' 5"... N//Alfred 176' 7" then to BEGIN--paying fm 04May95, annually, £7 good and lawful money of VA.
WTT: Francis Peyton, Geo. Gilpin, John Gill
[As above, Taliaferro acts and signs for WTA]
CMN: same men/dates as above

216 06Jan95 Same to Elisha C. Dick, TwnALX, StVA
Lease 2 acres in FfxCo, adjacent to TwnALX:
BEGIN int King-Columbus, S of King, W of Col ... W w/King to Alfred ... S w/Alfred to Prince ... E w/Prince to Columbus ... thence to BEGIN--paying fm 01Jul95, annually, £24 good & lawful money of VA
WTT: George Gilpin, Francis Peyton, Jesse Simms
[As above, Taliaferro acts and signs for WTA]
CMN: same men/dates as above

226 24Jan95
Fm Philip Godhelp Marsteller & wife Christiana, TwnALX, FfxCo, StVA
To Jacob Resler [no ID]: Part LOT 59 N of Prnce, W of Ffx:
BEGIN on Prince 80' W of Ffx ... W w/Prince 20'... N//Ffx 100'
... E//Prince 20'... thence to BEGIN--conveyed to PGM December 1794 by Thomas Whiting.
WTT: James Taylor, Washington John Washington, Ludl. Albers, P. Marsteller

231 06Feb95
Fm Nathaniel Chapman Hunter & wife Sarah Ann, Twn of Dumfries, PWm Co
To Stephen Cook, TwnALX, FfxCo: Parcel in ALX:
BEGIN W side Ffx 104' N of int Ffx-Duke ... S w/Ffx 20'... W// Duke 118' 6" to 10' alley ... N//Ffx 20'... thence to BEGIN.
WTT: Jh. [Joseph] M. Perrin, Mathvin. Perrin, Edward Ramsay, Charles Simms
MEMO: Cook is to have use of the alley w/others adjacent to it
CMN: Alexander Lithgow, John Lawson, James Smith, **Gentlemen** of PWmCo., aptd 01May95 to examine Sarah Ann. Rptd 21May95

235 12Dec94
Fm Thomas & Mary Whiting, Gloucester Co., StVA
To Philip G. Marsteller, TwnALX, FfxCo, StVA: for £190 cmv part LOT 59 N side Prince, W of Ffx Sts:
BEGIN on Prince 80' W of Ffx ... W w/Prince 20'... N//Ffx 100'... E//Prince 20'... thence to BEGIN--conveyed 15May86 by Benjamin & Susanna Shreve to Thomas Whitinge [sic, but Whiting signs his name w/o the "e"]
WTT: James Keith, Archibald Dobbin, Jacob Cox, P. Marsteller
CMN: On 15Dec94 a commission was ordered to examine Mary Whiting. Although the commissioners are not identified, Thomas Lewis and J. Whiting, **Justices of the Peace** for Gloucester Co. report back [no date]--presumably from having conducted the examination of Mary Whiting.

240 23Jun95
Fm Thomas & Ann Richards, TwnALX, FfxCo, StVA

To John Turpin Brooks -do-
For £100 cmv parcel E of Royal, S of Queen Sts:
BEGIN on Royal 34' N of parcel conveyed by the late William Ramsay the elder to
Henry Stroman ... N w/Royal 24' 3" to 10' alley ... E w/alley//Queen 123' 5"... S//Royal
24' 3", then to BEGIN--part of one of the parcels Wm. Ramsay's will directed be sold
for debt payment, and sold by his exxrs (William & Dennis Ramsay, Robert Allison,
Michael Madden) 20Mar95 to Thomas Richards.
[Ann Richards signs herself **Nancy** Richards]
WTT: Jesse Taylor, James McGuier, Daniel Bishop
CMN: John Dundas and [blank] **Gentlemen** of TwnALX, apted [blank date] to
examine Ann. Rptd back 25Jun95.

244 21Apr94
Fm John & Jane Fitzgerald, TwnALX, FfxCo, StVA
To George McMunn   -do-
Lease of part of LOT 61 W of Royal, N of Prince Sts:
BEGIN int Royal-Prince ... N w/Royal 88', W//Prince 24' 6"...
S//Royal 88' to Prince ... thence to BEGIN
--paying fm 01 Oct94, annually, £16.10.0 cmv.   WTT: none

247 15May95
Fm John & Jane Fitzgerald, TwnALX, FfxCo, StVA
To George McMunn   -do-
Lease parcel S of Prince, W of Royal Sts:
BEGIN on Prince on E line of parcel granted by the Fitzgeralds to George Spangler
this same date ... E w/Prince 43' to intersection w/Royal St ... S w/Royal 75'... W
//Prince 43' to Spangler's line ... thence to BEGIN.
WTT: James Keith, Vincent Gray, Charles Page, George Spangler

250 09Feb95
Fm Francis & Sarah Peyton, TwnALX
To Charles Simms -do- : parcel W side Water St, N side of "an Alley 20' wide laid out
by William Ramsay **Gent.** dec'd":
BEGIN at int Water St & alley ... N on Water St 28'... W// alley 123' 4"... S//Ffx to
alley ... thence to BEGIN.
WTT: James Watson, Washington John Washington
CMN: John Dundas, Jonah Thompson, James Irvin, **Gentlemen** of TwnALX, aptd
24Jul95 to examine Jane. Rptd back same day.

253 27May95
Fm John & Jane Fitzgerald, TwnALX, FfxCo, CwlVA
To Joseph Riddle of same AND James Dall, Baltimore, MD
For $100, part of LOT [blank]:
BEGIN S side of 12' alley--Swifts Alley--at Fitzgerald's line ... E w/alley //King and
Prince 5'... S//Fitzgerald's line 82' to line of Andrew Wales ... W w/Wales' line to
Fitzgerald's ... N to BEGIN--this is to be half of a 10' alley for these two parties,
Fitzgerald supplying the other 5' to the East.
MEMO: the parties reserve the right to build stables to the center of the alley, not to
exceed 25' fm alley's S end
CMN: a cmn to examine Jane was aptd 27May95, but the names not given. On
[blank]May95 the return is recorded, but again w/o the commissioners' names.

257 23Feb95
Fm Stephen & Catharine Cook [no ID given]

To Samuel Riddle, Chambersburgh, PA: lease parcel contiguous to TwnALX, on the
Potowmack, W of Ffx, S of Franklin Sts:
BEGIN W side Ffx 533 S of int of S side Gibbons w/W side Ffx ... S w/Ffx 100'...
W//Gbbns 436' 3"... N//Ffx 100'... thence to BEGIN--paying each 23Feb, beginning
23Feb96, £15 cmv. (Rent remittable if Riddle pays $625 on/before 23Feb1800)
WTT: Joseph Riddle, Thomas B. Dyer, Charles Turner

259 18Jul95
Fm Dennis & Jane Allen Ramsay [no ID]
To Mathew Sexsmith, TwnALX, FfxCo, StVA
For £165 cmv, part of LOT 47, E of Ffx, N of King Sts:
BEGIN on Ffx, 70' 7 1/2" N of King St ... N w/King 17' 8" to Ramsay's Alley ... E
w/alley 59' 1 1/2"... S//Ffx length of 1st line ... thence to BEGIN--conveyed by William
Ramsay, **Gentleman**, dec'd to Dennis 15Jan85;
--Dennis and Mathew agree each will give 18 inches for an alley adjoining the East
line which divides them, from Ramsay's Alley the whole length of the line
[Jane signs: Jane A. Ramsay]
WTT: James Keith, Bernard Bryan, William Smith

262 18Jul95   Mortgage
Fm Mathew & Elizabeth Sexsmith, TwnALX, FfxCo, StVA
To Dennis Ramsay   -do-
The Sexsmiths mortgage the above parcel to Ramsay, as they owe him £100. Deed
void if £100 paid on/before 25Dec95.   WTT: as above

265 11Feb95
Fm John D. & Lucinda Orr, TwnALX, FfxCo, StVA
To James Keating   -do-
BEGIN S corner of Thomas Fitzpatrick's lot on St. Asaph ... S on St A 22' 2"...
E//Duke 100'... N//St A 22' 2"... thence to BEGIN--leasing, paying from 28Sep95,
annually, £9 cmv;
--Keating agrees "that their [sic] shall always be kept upon the premises in proper
repair a good Substantial Dwelling house...of 20' square at least filled with brick and
morter, or lime and sand and having a brick or stone chimney..."
WTT: Elisha Thom. Bayly, George Wm. Bayly, Thomas Evans

267 21Jul95
Fm John Harper, FfxCo, StVA
To Cavan Boa [no ID]: lease parcel W of Union, N of Prince:
BEGIN on Union 30' N of Prince--the NE corner of Harper's brick warehouse ... W
w/gavel end of whse 30' "and the same course continued with the Gavel end of the
Frame Shed adjoining the said Warehouse 7' further"...N//Union 16' 3 1/2" to Christian Slimmer's line ... E w/line 37' to Union ... S w/Union to BEGIN--lease begins
01Jun96, running for John Harper's lifetime; 31Dec each year Boa to pay £15 cmv.
WTT: James Keith, William Hoye, Patrick Byrnes

270 15May95
Fm John & Jane Fitzgerald, TwnALX, FfxCo, StVA
To George Spangler -do-
Lease parcel S of Prince, W of Royal Sts:
BEGIN on Prince at East line of parcel conveyed by the Fitzgeralds to Lodowick
Trissler today ... S w/line 78'... E// Prince 20'... N//Royal to Prince ... thence to BEGIN
--paying 25May96, and annually, £14.10.0 cmv in silver $ at 6/ each, half Johanes
weighing 9 pennyweight at 48/ each, or some other gold or silver.

WTT: James Keith, Vincent Gray, George McMunn, Charles Page

273   02Jun95
MEMO by William Thornton Alexander, for a deed to William Hartshorne at Book E, p. 369: "...doth in his own proper person, ratify and Confirm all and every grant, release, remnant and clause in the Within Indenture"
WTT: Wm. Hartshorne, Jr.; Jno. Taylor, Sr.; G. Swope, John Taylor, Junr., Steph. Cooke

273 [same] for Book E, p. 364

274 [same] for Book E, p. 104

275   15May95
Fm John & Jane Fitzgerald, TwnALX, FfxCo, StVA
To Lodowick Tressler -do-
Lease of a parcel S of Prince, W of Royal:
BEGIN on Prince at E line of parcel conveyed by the Fitzgeralds to Thomas Redmon ... E w/Prince 20'... S//Royal 78'... W//Prince 20'... thence to BEGIN
--paying each 25May, beginning 1796, £14.10.0 cmv in silver $ at 6/ each [and so on, as at p. 270 above.]
WTT: James Keith, Vincent Gray, Charles Page, George McMunn

278   16Apr94   Manumission
   Charles Noland of FfxCo manumits Negro Dennis, Dennis paying £54.
[Noland signs w/mark]
WTT: Wm. Summers, Peter Wise, Junr., Charles Young, Robert Young

279   16Jun95
Fm Jacob Butt, TwnALX, FfxCo, StVA
To Jacob Leap -do-: parcel on Duck [sic] St, part of LOT 72:
BEGIN SW corner LOT 72 ... N along W line LOT 72 //Water St 96' 7"... E//Duck St 20'... S//Water St 20'... E//Duck St 20' S//Water St 76' 7" to Duck ... W on Duck 40' to BEGIN--Leap to pay David Arell each 18Jun 36 2/3 silver $, as per the deed to Jacob Butt from Henry & Charlotte Beideman 07Jul84, Book P "folio 39 No. 41" [in some other, unnamed jurisdiction's deed book.]
WTT: Samuel Arell, J.C. Kemp, Michael Steiber

281   23Jul95   Non-Importation Compliance
   Before Francis Peyton, **Justice of the Peace** of ALX, Philip Poyer swears that the Negro boy brought from the Bay of Honduras was for Poyer's own use, not resale.

281   12Aug95   Non-Importation Compliance
   Before John Dundas, **Justice of the Peace** of ALX, William Oden swears that he is abiding by the Slave Non-Importation Act of 1778 regarding slaves Mint and Mary. [no details]

282   15Aug95   Non-Importation Compliance
   As above, before John Dundas Charles Page swears he is abiding by the 1778 Act regarding the Negro girl Arianna given him by Adam Craig of Bladensburgh. Craig is Page's father-in-law.

85   26Apr95   Deed of Re-entry
WHEREAS the now deceased David Arell 21Dec84 rented for 40 silver $/annum to George Tumbler, due each 24Feb, part LOT 72:
BEGIN on Water St 30' 6" fm SE corner LOT 72 ... N w/Water St 20' to Bentz' line ... W w/line//Duke 63' 5" to Devilby's line ... S//Water St 20' to Beideman's line ... E w/line to BEGIN;
--after waiting the prescribed 60 days (24Feb + 60 days) Samuel Arell--guardian of David's children--went with 3 witnesses "good and lawful Freeholders of the Town to the house" and "three times aloud demanded payment of the said Rent" but no one came forward, and the house was empty of goods to be seized and sold
--[this procedure allowed Arell to reclaim the property, and void the David Arell-Geo. Tumbler deed.]   WTT: Jacob Shuck, Jacob Bott, Philip G. Marsteller

286   18Mar84   Manumission
For £40 received, John Gist of Loudoun Co. frees his slave, George [Not clear who paid.]   WTT: Mordecai Miller, Edward Stabler

286   29Sep94
Fm John & Elizabeth Wise, TwnALX, FfxCo, CwlVA
To Thomas West, FfxCo, CwlVA: for £500 cmv, part of LOT 22 conveyed 27Jun85 by John & Rachel Lomax to John Wise:
BEGIN NE corner LOT 21 ... W//Princess along lot line 26 1/2' ... S//Ffx into LOT 22 124'... E//Princess 26 1/2' to line between LOTS 21-22 ... thence to BEGIN.
WTT: Lemuel Bent, Cleon Moore, Jesse Moore
CMN: Commission to examine Elizabeth ordered 24Apr95 w/names blank. John Dundas and James Irvin rptd back 24Sep95.

290   29Sep94
Fm John & Elizabeth Wise, TwnALX, FfxCo, CwlVA
To Thomas West, FfxCo, CwlVA
WHEREAS Richard & Mary Conway 01Jul82 conveyed to John Lomax part LOT 21:
BEGIN NW corner LOT 21 on Princess ... E w/Princess 71'... S// Water & Ffx Sts 72' 2"... W//Princess & Queen Sts 71'... N w/E line LOT 22 72' 2" to BEGIN--paying annually £17.15.0, remittable w/in 20 year period on paying £355 cmv;
AND [blank] Jun85 John & Rachel Lomax conveyed all to J. Wise, same terms;
NOW for £100 cmv the Wises convey this to West, West to pay the annual rent.
WTT: Lemuel Bent to JW; Cleon Moore to JW & TW; Jesse Moore for JW; Maurice Herlihy, James McHenry and John Brownell to TW
CMN: on 24Apr95 a blank commission order directs examination of Elizabeth Wise. On 24Sep95 John Dundas and James Irvin rptd back.

294   17Jan94   Tripartite Deed
I-Mayor & Commonalty of ALX
II-George Hunter, surviving exxr of Thomas Fleming
III-Robert Townshend Hooe, TwnALX
WHEREAS the Act of Assembly establishing ALX appointed Trustees to make rules and regulations "for the benefit and Convenience of the proprietors of the Ground...-and other Inhabitants thereof" and "to have the Charge, Management and Disposition of the ground appropriated to the use of the Town";
WHEREAS 29Mar74 the Trustees agreed to rent to Thomas Fleming for 63 years part of Point Lumley adjoining Fleming's LOT 77
--"and to extend from his Ground Northwardly 25' in Front, and from thence East-4wardly of that Breadth into the River Potomack"
--paying each 01Jan the first 21 years 6d. per front foot

--paying each 01Jan the 2nd 21 years 7/ per front foot
--paying each 01Jan the last 21 years 14/ per front foot
--all beginning 01Jan76
--but Fleming never procured a lease for all this
--although the Act of Incorporation confirmed all the acts of the trustees and vested the same powers in the Mayor and Commonalty;
WHEREAS Thomas Fleming's will directed as much land be sold as needed to settle his debts
--by his wife Betty the exxx and George Hunter the exxr, Betty since then having died and Hunter surviving;
--Hunter advertised 3 times in the <u>Alexandria Gazette</u> that he would auction Fleming land 11Dec, including the parcel demised by the Trustees to Fleming:
BEGIN on N line LOT 77 136' 1" east of Union ... N//Union 25' ..."Eastwardly of the Breadth of 25' into the River Potomack"; River--Robert Townshend Hooe being high bidder;
NOW the Mayor and Commonalty
--complying with the Fleming-Trustees contract
--and the Hunter-Hooe sale
--for rents, lease to RTH:
BEGIN N line LOT 77 136' 1" E of Union St "at the Intersection of the Line drawn Southerly from the West line of the said Hooes warehouse"... thence w/line E into River Potomack ... from BEGIN, again, N//Union 25'... thence E//1st line into Potomack ... thence S//Union until intersecting 1st line;
TERMS: from 01Jan for 44 years:
--1st 2 years, 6d. per front foot
--next 21 years, 7/ per front ft
--last 21 years, 14/ per front ft
--and George Hunter, for £160 cmv from Hooe quits claim to the property
WTT: W<u>illiam Summer</u>s, James Keith, Oliver Price; to Col. Hooe: James Keith, John Muncaster, Thomas Lewis; James Hamilton
SIGNED BY: Dennis Ramsay, Mayor
John Dundas, Recorder
Aldermen: Robert Mease, Jesse Taylor, P. Marsteller, Jonah Thompson; Common Councilmen: William Paton, Thos. Porter, Benja. Shreve, Peter Wise, Lawrence Hoof, William Hickman
Also signed by the principals: George Hunter, Robert Townshend Hooe
ACKNOWLEDGED IN COURT by Ramsay, Dundas, Marsteller, Thompson, Patton, Porter, Shreve, and Hoof on 24Jul94; by Taylor and Wise, 18Sep94; by Mease 24Jul95; by Hickman, 25Sep95; and ordered recorded by P. Wagener

303 21Sep95
Fm Charles & Frances Alexander, FfxCo, StVA
To James Irvin, TwnALX
Lease 1 acre parcel N of Cameron, E of Washington, W of St A:
BEGIN int Cameron-Washington... N w/Wn 176' 7"... E//Cameron 246' 10" to St. Asaph ... S w/St A 176' 7" to Cameron ... thence to BEGIN--paying on 25Dec96 66 2/3 silver $, and--from 25Dec97, and annually, 133 1/3 silver $.
[Stock clauses f/non-payment, re-entry, etc. not abstracted.]
MEMO: Irvin to pay land taxes   WTT: none
CMN: John Dundas and Jonah Thompson, **Gentlemen** of [blank] aptd 21Sep95 to examine Frances. Rptd back 25Sep95.

309 08Sep95
Fm Robert Hamilton, TwnALX, StVA
To Robert Henderson -do-
Lease parcel N of Wolfe, E of Union, W side of alley "running through a piece of made Ground known [as] Kirks Wharf":
BEGIN int "of the said Street and Alley" and "SE Corner of that two Story framed dwelling house lately built by Joseph Caverly upon the said Wharf"... W w/Wolfe to another alley-"Jamieson's Alley"... N w/alley to extend 4' to the Northward of the house ... E//Wolfe and "passing 4' to the Northward of the said Dwelling house" to the first alley ... S w/alley to BEGIN--for 7 years "from hence next ensuing" at £36 cmv yearly, paid quarterly.
WTT: James Keith, Baldwin Dade, J. Gilpin

311 06Mar95
Fm James Irvin as guardian of John, Robert and Jane Adam, orphans of Robert Adam, late of FfxCo, StVA, deceased
To William Hodgson, TwnALX, FfxCo, StVA
Lease "all that Pier lying upon the South side of Princess St...which was framed and finished by the said RA in his lifetime and commonly known by the name of Adam's Pier"
AND "also the Warehouse thereupon erected and the vacant Ground adjoining the said Pier and Warehouse"
AND "also that piece of Ground adjoining Capt. Conways Warehouse now fenced in by the said William Hodgson"
--from this 03Mar for 7 years
--at £60 cmv per year, paid quarterly, beginning 02Jun95
--Hodgson may, at lease end, remove any of his improvements
--Hodgson to maintain and repair as necessary the pier, and the warehouse.
WTT: James Keith, Geo. Clementson, John Ritchie

313 22Jun95
Fm James Cavens AND John Muir, TwnALX, FfxCo, StVA
To William Hartshorne -do-
WHEREAS 09Jun80 Richard and Eleanor Arell conveyed to Edward Mitchell Ramsay part LOT 53, S of King and W of Ffx Sts:
BEGIN on King 40' W of Ffx--the W line of a parcel conveyed by the Arells to Benjamin Shreve ... W w/King 20'... S//Ffx 90'
... E//King 20'... thence to BEGIN--for annual payment of 1000 lbs. (net) of merchantable tobacco, in cask, inspected, in ALX, free of charges & taxes OR of 100 bu. "good sound merchantable Indian Corn", by EMR's choice;
AND on 15Dec94 Ramsay & wife Mary conveyed it to--as tenants in common--William Hartshorne, James Cavens and John Muir
--[the trio] to pay the Ramsays' rent to the Arells PLUS paying a financial obligation owed by the Ramsays to Benjamin Augustus Hamp;
NOW for £1209.6.0 cmv paid by Hartshorne to Cavens and Muir AND for Hartshorne paying the annual rent to the Arells, C & M convey to Hartshorne "two equal undivided [third] parts of the above parcel subject: to the Remainder of the Term for which [Ramsay] demised the same [to Hamp] and to the payment [to the Arells]"
WTT: Charles Love, Titus Triplett, James McKenna, Gurdin Chapin

316 01Jul95
Fm Amelia Finlay, Middlesex Co., Great Britain, Mother & heir of David Finlay, late of TwnALX, FfxCo, StVA, deceased
To Jonah Thompson, TwnALX, FfxCo, StVA

WHEREAS William & Catharine Bird 04Apr93 conveyed to Jonah Thompson and David Finlay as tenants in common part of LOTS 36-37 E of Ffx, N of Cameron: BEGIN on Ffx 60' N of Cameron--the N boundary "of the Ground devised by John Dalton to his Daughter Jane who hath since intermarried with Thomas Herbert"... N w/Ffx 119' 3" to the "line of Herbert, Potts and Wilson"... E//Cameron "and crossing Water and Union Street into the River Potowmack"...
S//Ffx 119' 3"... thence to BEGIN;
AND WHEREAS David Finlay died intestate and the property passed to his mother, Amelia:
--Amelia gave power of attorney to James Patton of ALX 26Sep94
--Patton advertised he would publicly auction Finlay's half of the parcel on 10Jun95;
--Charles Robert Scott was high bidder at £1500.12.0 cmv "and the Vendue Master struck it off to him";
--for "certain considerations" Scott is letting Jonah Thompson pay the £1500.12.0;
NOW for that sum Thompson buys Finlay's half of their joint holding.
WTT: James Kennedy, Charles R. Scott, Richard Veitch

320 01Jul95
Fm Jonah Thompson, TwnALX, FfxCo, StVA
To Charles Robert Scott, TwnALX, FfxCo, StVA
WHEREAS Robert & Ann Allison 17 Oct92 conveyed to James Patton and David Finlay as tenants in common half the parcel N of King, E of Water Sts:
BEGIN on King at E line of parcel granted by William Ramsay, **Gentleman**, to James Stuart-30' E of Water St ... E w/King 30'... N//Water St 77' to "Fayette Street (formerly called Ramsay's Alley") ... W w/Fayette//King 30'... thence to BEGIN
--and Patton & Finlay conveyed it to James Kennedy;
BUT Finlay died before his portion was conveyed, and it passed to his mother, Amelia;
AND Patton, as atty in fact for Amelia, had the parcel publicly advertised and auctioned 10Jun95--that is, Finlay's portion, 1/4 of the parcel;
AND Scott being high bidder at £370 cmv:
NOW for that sum Scott receives 1/4 of that original Stuart- Allison property, that is: half of the half Patton and Finlay bought together.
WTT: Walter Lyon, Jonah Thompson, James Kennedy

324 24Jun95
Fm same to James Kennedy, TwnALX, FfxCo, StVA
Re: the same large parcel as described above
WHEREAS 04Nov93 David Finlay and James & Mary Ann Patton sold James Kennedy half of their part for £500;
BUT Finlay died and the property passed to Amelia;
NOW the Kennedy £500 payment goes to Amelia, and another of Finlay's parts of the parcel passes to Kennedy.
WTT: Walter Lyon, Charles R. Scott, Jonah Thompson

327 27Aug95
Fm Charles & Frances Alexander, **Gentleman**, FfxCo
To John Dundas, TwnALX, FfxCo, **Merchant**
Lease of a 2 acre parcel W of Washington, N of Oronoko Sts:
BEGIN int Wn-Oro ... N w/Wn 353' 2"... W//Oro 246' 10"... S// Wn 353' 2" to Oro ... thence to BEGIN
--01Jan97 paying 66 2/3 silver$; 01Jan98, and annually, 133 1/3 silver $

--ALXR agrees to lay out streets all around the perimter and keep them open for John Dundas and the adjoining ALX inhabitants "except Oronoko Street which is already laid off by an Act of Assembly"
WTT: Caleb Earp, William [?S.] Noble, Diederk Shekle
MEMO: Dundas to pay land taxes
CMN: Jonah Thompson, Francis Peyton, James Irvin, William Hickman, **Gentlemen** of [blank], aptd 07Sep95 to examine Frances. Rptd back 17Sep95

331 06Jul95
Fm William Ramsay, TwnALX, FfxCo, CwlVA
To Guy Atkinson -do-
WHEREAS 10Mar95 GA conveyed to WR a part of a parcel whose boundaries:
BEGIN at southernmost line of parcel sold 28 Oct94 on Ffx St (by a decree of FfxCo Court) to Bernard Bryan, deed of 29 Oct94 ... E w/his line 60'... S//Ffx 25'... W//King 60' to Ffx ... then to BEGIN--which had by the same decree, and a deed also of 29 Oct, been granted to Guy Atkinson;
AND WHEREAS 11Mar95 WR conveyed to GA a parcel:
BEGIN on Ffx on N line of 20' alley parallelling King from Ffx to Water St ... N w/Ffx 25'... E//King 60'... S//Ffx 25' to the alley ... W w/alley to BEGIN--and within this parcel is a piece of the first parcel;
AND WHEREAS since the above transaction Ramsay has contracted with one Daniel Moxley for the remainder of the first parcel, has received part of the price but not conveyed title as yet;
AND WHEREAS the Ramsay-Atkinson deed for the first parcel (now about to pass to Moxley) has been lost or mislaid:
NOW Ramsay, for £100 cmv paid by Atkinson, releases Atkinson from any and all responsibility for the property.
WTT: Cleon Moore, Bernard Bryan, Thomas Gill

333 06Jul95
Fm Daniel Moxley, TwnALX, FfxCo, CwlVA
To Guy Atkinson -do-
WHEREAS 10Mar95 Atkinson conveyed to William Ramsay:
BEGIN at southernmost line of a parcel on Ffx St sold last 28 Oct to Bernard Bryan by virtue of a FfxCo Court decree, and by a 29 Oct deed conveyed to Atkinson ... E w/line 60'... S//Ffx 25'... W//King 60' to Ffx ... thence to BEGIN;
WHEREAS 11Mar95 William Ramsay conveyed to Guy Atkinson:
BEGIN on Ffx on N line of 20' alley parallelling King fm Ffx to Water Sts ... N w/Ffx 25'... E//King 60'... S//Ffx 25' to the alley ... W w/alley to BEGIN--part of this parcel includes a strip of the parcel above;
WHEREAS since 11Mar95 Ramsay conveyed to Daniel & Ann Moxley the rest of the first parcel, and the Atkinson-to-Ramsay deed being lost or mislaid:
NOW for £100 cmv paid by Atkinson to Moxley, Atkinson is freed of any claim to or responsibility for 1st parcel.
WTT: Cleon Moore, Bernard Bryan, Thomas Gill, James Reedston Cuttar

335 28Jul95
Fm Dennis & Jane Allen Ramsay, TwnALX, FfxCo, StVA
To Bernard Bryan -do-: part of LOT 47 E of Ffx, N of King:
BEGIN on Ffx 46' 9" N of King ... N w/Ffx 24' 1" to line of parcel sold by Ramsay to Matthew Sexsmith ... E w/line //King 59' 1 1/2"... S//Ffx 24' 1"... thence to BEGIN--part of parcel conveyed to Dennis 15Jan85 by Wm. Ramsay, **Gentleman**, late of ALX, dec'd;

--both Dennis and Bernard--each--will allot 18 inches to an alley along the E line, fm N to S;
--and Dennis will lay off a 4' alley along the S line from Ffx St to be used--like the 36" alley--in common with Bernard.
WTT: Charles Slade, Junr., Matthew Sexsmith, John Morris
CMN: John Dundas, Francis Peyton, James Irvin, **Gentlemen** of TwnALX, aptd 06Sep95 to examine Jane. Rptd back 03Nov95.

339 29Jul95 Mortgage
Fm Bernard & Mary Ann Bryan, TwnALX, FfxCo, StVA
To Dennis Ramsay -do-: a mortgage of the above property, Bryan owing £189 cmv.
Void if Bryan pays £120 on/before 07Nov next, plus £69 on/before 01Jul96.
WTT: as above

342 16Sep95
Fm William Thornton Alexander & wife Lucy, King Geo. Co, StVA
To George Hunter, FfxCo, StVA
Lease parcel E of Water St, S of Gibbons:
BEGIN on Water St 88' 3 1/2" S of Gibbons ... S w/Water St 44' 1 3/4"... E//Gibbons into River Potomack ... N//Water St 44' 1 3/4" ... thence to BEGIN--paying each 01Nov, beginning this year, £6.5.0 cmv
[Executed by John Taliaferro, Junr., atty for the ALXRS]
WTT: John Wise, Charles Simms, James Keith

345 13Apr94 Tripartite Deed
I-William Lowrey & Company, late of TwnALX but now of Baltimore [hereafter, throughout deed spelled: Lowery]
II-John Jolly, TwnALX, StVA
III-Baldwin Dade -do-
WHEREAS 13Aug87 John & Rachel Jolly conveyed to Wm. Lowery & Co. part of LOT 126 W of Pitt, S of Princess Sts:
BEGIN on Pitt 46' 3" S of Princess ... S w/Pitt 44'... W// Princess 70'... N//Pitt 44'... thence to BEGIN--a mortgage to secure £91.16.9 cmv + interest fm 13Aug87, payable on/before 13Feb88, and Jolly designated the Lowery Co. as agent to sell the property at public auction should the repayment terms not be met;
WHEREAS Jolly failed to pay, Lowery advertised the auction in the <u>Alexandria Gazette</u>, and Baldwin Dade was high bidder at the auction at £15 cmv:
NOW for that sum Wm. Lowery & Co conveys the property to Dade.
WTT: John Gill, Richard Walker, John Bumill [possibly: Burnill]

349 16Apr 95
Fm Richard Marshall Scott & wife Mary, PWmCo., StVA
To (as tenants in common) Matthew Franklin Bowne AND
    Theodore James Hamilton, TwnALX, FfxCo, StVA
Lease of a parcel S of King, W of Union:
BEGIN on King on W line of 10' alley 80' W of Union ... W w/King 40'... S//Union 66'... E//King 40' to the alley ... thence to BEGIN--conveyed by Valentine Peers to John Dalrymple Orr, and by Orr to Scott;
--MFB-TJH to pay 01Jun96, annually thereafter, 126 silver $
--rent remittable if w/in 5 years MFB & TJH pay £400 cmv.
WTT: James Keith to all; Robert Mease and John Gill to Hamilton; Dennis Ramsay to Scott and to Hamilton; Hugh West and Mordica C. Fitzhugh to Bowne

352 02Jul95
Fm Charles Robert Scott, TwnALX, FfxCo, StVA
To James Patton -do-
WHEREAS Robert & Ann Allison 07 Oct92 conveyed to James Patton & David Finlay as tenants in common a parcel N of King, E of Water Sts:
BEGIN on King at E line of parcel conveyed by Wm. Ramsay, **Gentleman**, to James Stuart--30' E of Water St ... E w/King 30'
N//Water St 77' to Fayette St. "(formerly... Ramsay's Alley)"
... W w/Fayette//King 30'... thence to BEGIN;
--Finlay died intestate, and his estate went to his mother, Amelia, who 01Jul95 conveyed 1/4th of the parcel to Scott;
NOW for £370 cmv Scott conveys that 1/4th to Patton.
WTT: Jonah Thompson, James Kennedy, Richard Veitch

355 25Sep95 Manumission
"...considering the Blessings of freedom as invaluable to the human race" William Rhodes certifies that--provided she has children--he will free his Negro girl Rachel, now "about twelve years of age" when she is 30. Her issue will likewise be free: males at 30, females at 28.

355 14Apr94
Fm Baldwin & Catharine Dade, FfxCo, StVA
To William Lowry and Company, Twn of Baltimore, MD
For £15 cmv, the parcel on p. 345, above. WTT: none

357 06Feb95
Fm Nathaniel Chapman Hunter & wife Sarah Ann, Twn of Dumfries, PWmCo., StVA
To Stephen Cooke, TwnALX, FfxCo, StVA:
BEGIN W side Ffx 104' N of int w/Duke, at SE corner of house built by Dr. William Baker ... N w/Ffx 45' to corner of "Aaron Hewes's Lott"... W//Duke 118' 6" to 10' alley ... S w/alley [45'] ... thence to BEGIN--leased, from 06Feb96, @ £45 current money per annum.
WTT: Charles Simms, George Deneale, James Kennedy, Alexander Smith
CMN: Alexander Lithgow, John Lawson, James Smith, **Gentlemen** of PWmCo., aptd 01May95 to examine Sarah Ann. Rptd 21May95

362 15Apr94
Fm William Lowry and Company & William's wife, Olivia, Baltimore, MD
To William Summers, TwnALX, FfxCo, StVA
For £10 cmv, part of LOT 126, W of Pitt, S of Princess Sts:
BEGIN on Pitt 46' 3" S of Princess ... S w/Pitt 44'... W// Princess 70'... N//Pitt 44'... thence to BEGIN--conveyed to WL & Co 14Apr94 by Baldwin Dade.
WTT: Robert Hamilton, John Casson, John Gill, Dennis Ramsay (to W.L.), Charles Simms

365 14Sep95
Fm William Thornton Alexander & wife Lucy, King Geo. Co, StVA
To Phoebe Arell, TwnALX, FfxCo, StVA: lease of "Lott or Half-acre of Ground" W of Washington, N of Wolfe in that addition made by John ALXR's exxrs, and in that addition numbered 12:
BEGIN int Wn-Wolfe ... N w/Wn 176' 7"... W//Wolfe 123'5"...
S//Wn 176' 7" to Wolfe ... thence to BEGIN--granted by J. ALXR's exxrs 21Apr85 to Joseph Caverly for annual rent payable to William Thornton Alexander;

--rent not paid; lease lapsed and property reverted to WTA.
--Phoebe to pay from 01Nov96, annually, £12 cmv.
[Alexander atty John Taliaferro Junr executes this for them.]
WTT: Samuel Arell, Alexander McConnell, Henry Boyer
[Clerk's marginal note: "Acknowledgement to this deed is in Liber H page 283"]

368 08Jul93
Fm Michael & Hannah Madden, FfxCo, StVA
To Patrick Burnes, TwnALX, FfxCo, StVA
WHEREAS George & Jane Gilpin 08Nov83 conveyed to Michael Madden a parcel S of Prince, W of Union:
BEGIN on Prince 51' from int Prince-Union ... W w/Prince 40' ... S//Water St 44' to ground of heirs of Jonathan Hall ...
E//Prince w/Hall land 40' to BEGIN--Madden paying Gilpin each 31Dec 80 silver $;
AND WHEREAS MM on the one part, and Benjamin Shreve & James Lawrason on the other, own land adjoining this property's E line--and they have agreed that whoever built first could lay 7" of foundation on the other's land;
--and the second builder could have use of the common wall by paying half its value;
NOW the Maddens lease to Burnes:
BEGIN on Prince 51' W of Union ... W w/Prince 22'... S//Union 44' 4" to Ground once Jn. Hall's, now Francis Peyton's ... E w/Peyton's line //Prince 22'... thence to BEGIN;
--Burnes gets same building rights w/Shreve & Lawrason;
--Burnes to pay from 31Dec93, annually, 44 silver $ to George Gilpin and assume Madden's obligations to Shreve & Lawrason. [Patrick signs his last name: **Byrne**]
WTT: Washer Blount, William Hoye, James McCready
CMN: John Dundas, Jonah Thompson, Francis Peyton aptd 13Nov95 to examine Hannah. Rptd back same day.

373 02May95
CMN: CMN: John Dundas, Jonah Thompson, Francis Peyton aptd to examine Mary Scott [see p. 349]. Rptd back 04May95.

375 28Mar95
Fm John & Mary Hickman, Frederick Co., StVA
To William Hickman, TwnALX, FfxCo, StVA: parcel E of St Asaph, N of Wolfe--in the John Alexander addition, John Alexander's deed to John Garner Hamilton stating:
BEGIN SW corner LOT 104 ... thence w/lot line to its NW corner ... thence at right angles 123' 5"... S//1st course for same distance ... thence E to BEGIN;

AND this parcel:
BEGIN on St A 136' 5" N of int St A-Wolfe ... N w/St A 20'... E//Wolfe 113' 5"... S//St A 20'... thence to BEGIN:
--conveyed by John Garner Hamilton to John Finley
--Finley dying intestate, it passed to Hugh Finley
--Hugh Finley 20Jun85 conveyed it to John Hickman
--now Jn. Hickman to Wm. Hickman
--John will pay the ground rent to the John ALXR estate.
WTT: Peter Wise Junr., Richd. Parrott, Robert Patton Junr., John Winterbury Junr.

379 18Sep95   Tripartite Deed
I-James Irvin, guardian of John, Robert & Jane Adam, orphans & devisees of Robert Adam, FfxCo, deceased

II-Daniel & Mary Barry, Mary = another devisee of Robert Adam
III-Robert Brockett, TwnALX, FfxCo, StVA
Lease to Robert Brockett of part LOT 20, S of Princess, W of Union Sts devised by Robert Adam to his four children: John, Robert, Jane, Mary Adam:
BEGIN on Princess 46' W of Union ... W w/Princess 92' to line of 24' alley laid out by RA across his part of LOT 20, equidistant between Union & Water Sts, fm Princess to the line of Richard Conway ... S w/alley //Union 48'... E//Princess 92'... thence to BEGIN--described in the plan of LOT 20 Adam made during his lifetime as [Robert Adam] parcels 11-12-13-14

AND a parcel on E of alley, S of Princess:
BEGIN on alley 48' S of Princess ... E//Princess 52'... S// Union and the alley 23'... W//Princess 52'... thence to BEGIN--Adam parcel No. 15 in TwnALX LOT 20

AND a parcel W of Union, S of Princess:
BEGIN on Union 48' S of Princess ... S w/Union 70' 6"... W// Princess 84'... N//Union 70' 6"... thence to BEGIN--Adam parcels Nos. 6-7-8 in TwnALX LOT 20
Terms: 10 years starting 25Dec95
--Brockett to pay £24.7.6, annually, beginning 25Dec96
--Brockett may remove buildings and improvements he makes within [blank] months after lease ends
--if any of the children want to purchase Brockett additions they and he will buy/sell at prices fixed by two or more mutually nominated persons.
WTT: Wm. Glasscock, Thoms. Barry

384 18Dec95
Fm James Irvin, TwnALX, FfxCo, StVA
To John Bogue -do-: lease parcel E of Washington, N of Cameron
BEGIN int Wn-Cam Sts ... E w/Cam 122'... N//Wn 120'... E//Cam 2'... N//Wn 56' 7"... W//Cam 24'... S//Wn 56' 7"... W//Cam 100' to Wn ... thence S w/Wn 120' to BEGIN;
--part of ground conveyed by Charles Alexander to James Irvin [blank] day of [blank] 1795 for annual rent [not spelled out]
--Bogue to pay 01Jan97 £15.16.0 cmv; 01Jan98 and annually thereafter £31.12.0 cmv.
WTT: James Keith, John Dunlap, Samuel Craig

389 24Dec95
Fm Dennis Ramsay, TwnALX, FfxCo, StVA
To Matthew Sexsmith -do-
WHEREAS 18Jul95 Sexsmith conveyed [mortgaged] property he had just purchased from Dennis N of King, E of Ffx [see p. 259, above] against £100 to be paid on/before 25Dec95;
NOW the sum having been paid, Dennis gives Matthew full title.
WTT: none. [Marginal note: "Acknowledgement on p. 423 of this book" is accurate but not in the Clerk's hand.]

391 24Dec95
Same to Bernard Bryan, TwnALX, FfxCo, StVA
The mortgage of property N of King, E of Ffx (bought by Bryan 28Jul95 from Ramsay) having been satisfied, Ramsay now gives Bryan unencumbered title.
WTT: none

393 08Aug95
Fm William Summers "Sergeant of the Town of Alexandria in the State of Virginia"
To Benjamin Shreve [same place]
WHEREAS 20Dec86 Michael Madden conveyed [mortgaged] to William Sydebotham parcel S of Prince, W of Union:

BEGIN on Prince 91' W of Union ... E w/Prince 18'... S//Union-Water Sts 44' 4" to line of ground of Jonathan Hall's heirs ... W w/Hall line 18'... then to BEGIN--for annual rent $36 to George Gilpin each 31Dec, remittable if Madden paid Sydebotham £245.3.5 + interest from 23Nov85 on/before 28Sep88;
AND WHEREAS Madden having paid nothing, WS brought suit in ALX Hustings Court:
--WS won judgement for a sale of the ground, payment of the money, and cost of the suit
--but WS died before the decree could be executed and
--WS's executors, Richard Cramphin & David Ross, revived the suit, got a judgement for £245.3.5 + 5% annual interest from 01Nov85, to be paid on/before 01Jul95
--if Madden again defaulted, the decree directed the Sgt. of the Town to advertise in the <u>Alexandria Gazette</u> 4 weeks and sell the property at auction
--Madden defaulted; the Sgt advertised the sale for 08Aug: the buyer to pay the sale price, annual rent of $36 to George Gilpin to the Dower of Hannah Madden, and £25.11.11 back rent;
NOW Benjamin Shreve being high bidder at £390, the various sums paid in full, <u>William Summers</u> conveys title to Shreve.
WTT: Chs. Turner, Titus Triplett, G. Deneale

397 06Jun95
Fm Thomas & Ann Richards, TwnALX, FfxCo, StVA
To William Mitchell -do-
For £100 cmv, part of LOT 80 S of Duke, W of Water Sts:
BEGIN on Duke 40' W of Water St ... W w/Duke 27' 10"... S// Water St 91' 6" to 10' alley ... E//Duke 27' 10"... then to BEGIN--conveyed 18Sep94 to Richards by Samuel Arell. WTT: Jesse Taylor, Henry S. Earl, Benjn. Lanston
CMN: John Dundas, Francis Peyton, James Irvin, **Gentlemen** "of the Corporation" aptd 23 Oct95 to examine Ann. Rptd back 23Aug95. [Dates are as written, but wrong- -probably reversed.]

402 06 Oct95
Fm Richard & Eleanor Arell, TwnALX, FfxCo, StVA
To Henry Walker -do-
Lease part of LOT 70 E of Royal, N of Prince Sts:
BEGIN on Royal 106' 7" N of Prince ... N w/Royal 1' 6"... E// Prince 123' 5"... S//Royal 18' 1" to line of parcel conveyed by the Arells to [blank] Hague ... W w/Hague line //Prince 20'... S w/another Hague line //Royal 5' 5"... W w/Prince 33' 5" ... N//Royal 22'... thence to BEGIN--paying, starting 05 Oct96, £9.2.6 cmv in specie per annum.
WTT: Michael Steeber, Philip G. Marsteller, Jas. Keith

405 07Nov95
Fm William & Mary Paton AND John & Ann Butcher, TwnALX, StVA
To Smith Keith -do-
For £90 cmv, a parcel N of Prince, W of St Asaph Sts:
BEGIN on Prince 60' W of St A ... W w/Prince 21'... N//St A 100' 7"... E//Prince 21'... thence to BEGIN--part of piece conveyed 21Jul83 by Oliver Price to John Stewart, and by Stewart 21Sep95 to W. Paton & J. Butcher.
WTT: none; all four sign.

409 15Apr95
Fm Samuel & Mary Davis, TwnALX, FfxCo, CwlVA
To John Boling -do-

WHEREAS William Thornton Alexander & wife Lucy 06Jan95 leased to Samuel Davis 1 acre in FfxCo adjacent to TwnALX:
BEGIN int Prince-Columbus Sts, S of Prince, W of Columbus ... W w/Prince to Alfred ... S w/Alfred 176' 7"... E//Prince-Duke to Columbus ... N w/Columbus to BEGIN;
NOW the Davises lease to Boling:
BEGIN W of Columbus adjoining the land of George Coryell--176' 7" S from int Columbus-Prince ... W w/Coryell's line //Prince and Duke 100'... N//Columbus-Alfred Sts 21'... E//Prince-Duke-Coryell 100' to Columbus ... thence to BEGIN;
--Boling to pay from 15Apr95, annually, £2.12.6 good and lawful money of VA
--Boling will build w/in a year a framed or brick house, w/brick chimney, at least 15x12 1/2'
--for not building, or for non-payment of rent, seller may enter property and force a distress sale.
["Boling" signs w/mark, but someone has spelled his name: John Bowling]
[William Harper represented the Davises in court as their attorney in fact]
WTT: Charles Harper, Francis Peyton, Cleon Moore

413 22Dec95
Fm Samuel & Mary Davis, TwnALX, FfxCo, CwlVA
To Philip Furneau, TwnALX, FfxCo, CwlVA
WHEREAS William Thornton Alexander & wife Lucy 06Jan95 conveyed [leased] to Samuel Davis [the same acre as above]:
NOW the Davises lease to Furneau 2 parcels (within that acre) which they number 10 +11:
BEGIN S of Prince 82' 9" E of Prince and Alfred Sts ... S// Alfred-Columbus 100' to an "established alley 13' 7" wide through the said acre"... E w/alley //Duke-Prince 41' 8"... N//Alfred-Columbus 100' to Prince ... thence w/Prince 41' 8" to BEGIN--Furneau to pay--beginning 15Apr96, annually--£5.4.2 good and lawful money of VA
--Furneau to build w/in year framed or brick house at least 15x12 1/2' w/ brick chimney
--unlike Bowling, above, no penalties for no-build or no-rent.   WTT: none
[Wm. Harper acts for the Davises as their attorney]

418 25Jun94
Fm Stephen & Catharine Cooke, TwnALX
To Abel Blakely   -do-
Lease of a parcel contiguous to TwnALX, on the Potomack, S of King, E of Washington Sts:
BEGIN NW corner of house now occupied by James B. Nickolls ...
W w/King 21' 6"... S//Wn 100'... E//King 21' 6"... thence to BEGIN--Blakely beginning 01Jul95, annually, paying $43 or that value in gold or silver;
--Blakely not to destroy or remove any structures erected or to be erected
WTT: G. Swoope, Wm. Newton, Josa. Riddle, Joseph Riddle
MEMO: If w/in 10 years Blakely pays "twelve Years purchase of the within granted part of a lot, and all arrears of rent... due at the time of said purchase" Cooke will give a deed for that part;
--also, if Blakely will leave 18" of ground on the west part of his lot, Cooke will leave 18" adjoining "so as to make a three foot alley to be in common between us."
WTT: G. Swoope, Wm. Newton, Josa. Riddle, Joseph Riddle

422 22May95
CMN: John Dundas, Francis Peyton, James Lawrason, **Gentlemen** of TwnALX, aptd to examine Christiana Marsteller [Philip's wife] for deed of 24Jan to Jacob Rester, for a parcel N of Prince and W of Ffx Sts. Rptd back 23May95.

423 [no date given]
CMN: William Hickman, Jonah Thompson, **Gentlemen** of TwnALX, aptd to examine Jane Allen Ramsay re: 18Jul deed to M. Sexsmith of parcel in ALX. Rptd 22Dec95.

425 09Jul94
Fm James & Elizabeth Keith, TwnALX [no county, no state]
To Thomas Williams "of the same Town, County and State"
WHEREAS William Thornton Alexander 23Sep89 leased to Adam Bence parcel E of Ffx, N of Gibbons Sts:
BEGIN on Ffx 66' 7" N of Gibbons ... N w/Ffx 36' to 10' alley ... E w/alley //Gibbons 63' 5"... S//Ffx 36'... thence to BEGIN--paying £5 cmv each 01Nov;
WHEREAS Adam Bence 27May94 conveyed the parcel to James Keith, Keith to pay WTA the £5 annual rent;
NOW the Keiths for £40 cmv convey the parcel to Williams, Williams to pay WTA the £5 each year.
WTT: Robert Mease, James Lawrason, Wm. Hall, Leroy Ewell, Joseph Cary
CMN: Robert Mease, Jonah Thompson, James Lawrason, **Gentlemen** of TwnALX, aptd 20Sep94 to examine Elizabeth. Rptd back 22Sep94.

432 27May94
Fm Adam Bence, TwnALX, FfxCo, StVA
To James Keith -do-
For £40 Bence conveys the parcel to Keith [see p. 425 above], Keith to pay £5 cmv each 01Nov to W. T. Alexander.
WTT: John Yost, Samuel Keech [spelled: Keatch, p. 436, by the Clerk], James Keith, Junr.

436 12Nov95
Fm John Harper, FfxCo, StVA
To Philip Conn, TwnALX, FfxCo, StVA
For £90 cmv, a parcel S of Duke, E of Washington Sts:
BEGIN int Duke-Wn Sts ... E w/Duke 28'... S//Wn 100' to 10' alley ... W w/alley //Duke 28'... thence to BEGIN--part of lot conveyed to Harper by exxrs of John Alexander;
--Harper commits to laying off a 10' alley from Washington, parallel Duke, beginning 100' S of Duke, eastward 100' to the line of Benjamin Shreve.
WTT: Ja. Keith, Jacob Cox, Wm. Wright

441 22Dec95
Fm John Harper, FfxCo, StVA, in trust
To Dennis Foley, TwnALX, FfxCo, StVA:
Parcel adjoining TwnALX, S of Duke, E of Washington Sts, "in the Addition made to the said Town...by the Executors of John Alexander...described in the Plan of the said addition by the Number [blank]":
BEGIN on Duke 76' E of Wn St ... E w/Duke 24'... S//Wn 100' to 10' alley ... W w/alley //Duke 24'... thence to BEGIN.
Terms of the trust: property for the use of Matty Dunn, daughter of Foley's wife Elizabeth by her first marriage to William Dunn;
--Foley to convey the property on Matty's death to her issue

--if no issue, to Matty's heirs
--Harper will lay off a 10' alley 100' S of and parallel to Duke, running E from Wn for 100' WTT: Jesse Simms, Charles Young, Junr., Jas. Keith, John Wise

445 24Aug95
Fm George Deblois, Boston, Suffolk Co., CwlMASS, **Merchant**
To William James Hall, TwnALX, FfxCo, CwlVA, **Merchant**
For £150 lawful money of MASS "all [his] right, title, and interest" in lot on Prince St:
BEGIN at W corner of John Murray & Company's land ... W 15' on Prince... N 60'... E 15'... S 60' on land of J. Murray & Co
--the same lot conveyed to Lewis Deblois Junior & Edward Kinnicutt Thompson by the John Murray & Co., "with the Buildings now thereon standing";
--Lydia Deblois, George's wife, surrenders her dower rights.
WTT: James S. Deblois
Attested by Suffolk Co. Justices of the Peace George Richards Minot and Saml. Cooper.
Validated by Ezekl. Price, **Clerk** of Court, Suffolk Co

450 31Aug95
Fm Gurden & Margaret Chapin, TwnALX, FfxCo, StVA
To Samuel Harper -do-
WHEREAS Joseph Saunders 16 Oct75 conveyed to Benjamin Chapin a part of LOT 65 E of Ffx, S of Prince Sts:
BEGIN E side Ffx 98' 5" S of Prince ... E//Prince-Duke "upon the lines of William and Edward Ramsay (now belonging to Ricketts and Newton and to Richard Weightmen)" 51' 8"... S// Ffx-Wtr Sts 16' to 10' alley ... W w/alley //Duke-Prince 51' 8"... thence to BEGIN--Benjamin Chapin paying Saunders each 16 Oct £4 current money;
--the parcel conveyed by Chapin's will to sons Hieram [sic] and Gurden Chapin, Hieram conveying his part 29Jun86 to Gurden
--and Joseph Saunders' exxrs 17Jan93 sold the ground rent proviso to Mordecai Lewis, and Lewis sold it to Gurden Chapen;
NOW the Chapins for £640 cmv convey the parcel to Harper.
WTT: Michl. Flannery, Wm. Hartshorne, James McKenna, John R. Wheaton
CMN: Jonah Thompson, Francis Peyton, Wm. Hickman, **Gentlemen** of ALX, aptd 01 Oct95 to examine Margaret. Rptd back 20Jan96.

458 17Nov95
Fm Richard & Eleanor Arell, TwnALX, FfxCo, StVA
To Michael Steiber -do-
Lease of part of LOT 60 E of Royal, N of Prince Sts:
BEGIN on Royal 48' 7" N of Prince ... N w/Royal 36'... E// Prince 103' 5" to line of parcel conveyed by the Arells "to Hague"... S w/Hague line //Royal 22'... W//Prince 33' 5"... S//Royal 14'... W//Prince 70' to BEGIN--paying from 01Jul96, annually, 90 silver $ "according to the present weight and fineness of the Dollar"
WTT: Jas. Keith, Philip G. Marsteller, Thomas Preston

462 05 Oct95
Fm John & Mary Harper, FfxCo, StVA
To James Kennedy, TwnALX
For £50 cmv, a parcel E of Ffx, N of Prince:
BEGIN of Ffx at S line of ground conveyed by Josiah Watson to James Kennedy "being the division line between...John Harper and James Kennedy"... E w/line //Prince 50' 10" to line of parcel conveyed by Harper to Aaron Hewes ... S w/Hewes' line //Ffx 5'... W//Prince 50' 10" to Ffx ... thence to BEGIN.

WTT: Jas. Keith, James Cavan, Jno. C. Vowell, Charles McKenna

466 05 Oct 95
Fm James & Latitia Kennedy, TwnALX, FfxCo, StVA
To John Harper, FfxCo, StVA
For £50, a parcel E of Ffx, N of Prince:
BEGIN on S line of ground conveyed by Josiah Watson to James Kennedy, where the line strikes the line of ground conveyed by Harper to Aaron Hughes--50' 10" E of Ffx ... N//Ffx 1' 9"... E//Prince 42' 4 1/2" to the W line of "ground belonging to the Brick house now occupied by David Easton"... N//Ffx 16' 3"
... E//Prince 30' 2 1/2" to the "western Line of the ground belonging to the Brick house now occupied by Doctor James Craik, the said Western Lines being produced and extended from the said Brick house in the same direction Northwardly with the Western Walls of the said Houses"... S w/line of that ground//Ffx 18'... thence w/- straight line to BEGIN
--plus the benefit of "that nine-foot Alley...layed off by Josiah Watson from the Wales Alley, now Thompson's, to the Ground...conveyed by...Watson to...Kennedy, of which the permises hereby granted are a part, in common with...Kennedy..., for him the said John Harper...holding, occupying and possessing the Brick House now in the Tenure of David Easton, but not for the use of any other person but the Occupant from time to time of that Brick house."
--Kennedy will extend the 9' Watson alley from its present termination (at the N line of ground granted Kennedy by Watson) to the N line of the "premises hereby granted."
--"and that he the said John Harper his Heirs and Assigns occupying the Brick house now in the Tenure of David Easton" shall have joint use of the alley. ["Latitia" signs: Letitia]
WTT: Jas. Keith, James Cavan, John C. Vowell, Charles McKenna

471 14Nov95
Fm William & Isabel Summers, TwnALX, FfxCo, CwlVA
To William Jackson, Baltimore, MD
WHEREAS John Parsons 17Jun93 conveyed a parcel to Summers:
BEGIN on King at W line of ground conveyed by James Parsons to John Petit & Simon Michael Blondelet ... W w/King 26' 7" to W line of 1/2 acre conveyed by exxrs of John Alexander to James Parsons ... N w/line 166' 6" to 10' alley ... E w/alley 26' 6"... then to BEGIN;
WHEREAS William Summers erected a brick house on the parcel "next to and adjoining the lott of the said...Petit and Blondelet extending in front upon King Street about 22' 6" more or less to a framed House erected by Joseph Jackson which said house, by a mistake of a former Survey of the Town Lotts, stands four feet more or less upon the lott conveyed by John Parsons to the said William Summers"--and this deed is to remedy that;
NOW the Summerses for £20 from William Jackson convey:
BEGIN on King at the W line of the Summers' brick house ... W w/street 4' to the "centre of the Squares between St. Asaph and Washington Streets"... N w/center line 120'... E//King 4' ... thence to BEGIN.   WTT: none
CMN: Jonah Thompson, James Irvin, William Hickman, **Gentlemen** of TwnALX, aptd 14Nov95 to examine Isabel. Rptd back 09Jan96.

478 10Jun95
Fm Robert & Nancy McCrea, late of ALX, now of State of Georgia
    AND Robert & Betty Mease, TwnALX, StVA
To John Harper, FfxCo, StVA

WHEREAS Andrew & Margaret Wales conveyed to McCrea & Mease & Matthew Mease part LOT 56 and in the deed agreed to lay off a 12' alley on the N side of the parcel, from Water to Union Sts AND WHEREAS Matthew has since sold his interest to McC & M;
WHEREAS Robert McCrea by Letter of Attorney 10 Oct91 appointed Robert Mease his atty:
NOW the McCreas and the Meases for £105 cmv convey to Harper:
BEGIN on S side of the alley--where the W line of some Harper land (now occupied by Joseph Faxon) on Prince Street when extended //Water-Union "will strike the same supposed to be 91' 11 1/4" E of Water St"... E w/alley line 30'... S//Water & Union 39' 7 3/4" to William Wright's line ... W w/Wright's line (and Harper's) 30'... thence to BEGIN.
WTT: James Patton, Bernard Ghequiere, Jas. Keith

483 07Nov95
Fm John & Margaret McIver, TwnALX, FfxCo, StVA
To William Crammond, City of Philadelphia
For £450 cmv, part LOT 61 N of Prince, W of Royal:
BEGIN on Prince 24' 6" W of Royal ... N//Royal 88' to 6' alley ... W w/alley 24' 6"... S//Royal 88'... thence to BEGIN
--conveyed by William Ramsay to Colin McIver 26Jan85 and passing to John McIver on Colin's death;
--leased by John to James Kennedy for 5 years fm 01May96;
--if w/in next 30 days McIver can get more than £450 for the property, Crammond will either pay the difference or collect the greater amount and convey the property.
[Charles Taylor signs for William Crammond]
WTT: Jas. Keith, John Dundas, Alxr. MacKenzie [also, same page: McKenzie], John McKenzie

488 26Dec95
John McIver signs a release from the 30-day "higher price" covenant in the deed above.

490 10Nov95
CMN: a commission whose names are left blank is aptd to examine Margaret McIver on the deed above. However, John Dundas and Francis Peyton are shown to have reported back the same day.

492 07Nov95
Fm John & Margaret McIver, TwnALX, FfxCo, StVA
To William Crammond, City of Philadelphia
WHEREAS William Thornton Alexander 10Jan90 leased to John McIver a parcel S of Prince, E of Washington:
BEGIN int Prince-Wn ... E w/Prince 123' 5"... S//Wn 100'...
W//Prince 123' 5"... then to BEGIN--paying annually each 01Jan £9 cmv;
NOW the McIvers for £750 cmv from Crammond lease him all that parcel, on the following terms:
--the part 25' 8" in front "including the part on which the house stands" and running 100' S to the back lot line, McIver has leased for 10 years to Charles Love, from 01Mar96 for £40 per annum, paid quarterly
--Crammond is to pay WTA the £9 cmv each 01Jan
--if w/in 30 days McIver can find a larger price, Crammond will either pay the difference or collect that price and convey the property.
[Charles Taylor signs for William Crammond]

WTT: Jas. Keith, John Dundas, Alexr. McKenzie

498 26Dec95
　　McIver releases Crammond from the 30-day covenant in the deed above.

499 10Nov95
CMN: John Dundas and Francis Peyton, **Gentlemen** of TwnALX, aptd to examine Margaret McIver in the deed above. Rptd same day.

501 15Feb96
Fm William & Agnes Hepburn, TwnALX, FfxCo, StVA
To William Mosely -do- : lease of a parcel in TwnALX:
BEGIN on St Asaph 176' 7 1/2" N of Prince ... S w/St A on W side 36'... W//Princess 63'... N//St A 36'... E//Princess 63' to BEGIN--Mosely to pay from 15 Oct95, annually, 40 Spanish milled $ at 6/ each or equivalent in specie coin
--Mosely to pay all taxes due, and to leave all buildings now built or later built.
[Agnes signs w/mark]   Wtt: none

506 10Nov95
Fm James Irvin, FfxCo, StVA
To Leven Powell -do-: lease of a parcel in TwnALX:
BEGIN int St Asaph-Cameron, W of St A, N of Cameron ... N w/St A 120'... W//Cameron 100'... S//St A 120'... thence to BEGIN
--"being part of one acre of Ground leased from Charles Alexander to said James Irvin"
--Powell to pay from [blank] day Jan97, annually, £21 cmv
Wtt: G. Deneale, Michl. Flannery, J. H. Oneil

510 01Sep95
Fm Dederick Sheckle, TwnALX, FfxCo, StVA
To William Smith -do-
For £100 cmv, part of LOT 39 E of Royal, N of Cameron:
BEGIN at center of Square formed by Cameron and Queen, on the N line of LOT 39 ... E w/line //Cameron-Queen 123' 5" to E line of the lot ... S//Royal 27' 6" to Henry Stroman's line ... W w/Stroman //Queen-Cameron 123' 5" to Royal ... N w/Royal 27' 6" to BEGIN--sold by Stroman to Sheckle.
[DS signs self: Diedrik Shekle]
WTT: Jas. Keith, John Hubball, Thos. Locke

514 25Sep95   Manumission
　　William Summers of ALX manumits his Negro slave boy Henry, now 8, when Henry is 28--20 years from this date.

515 18Dec95
Fm Francis & Sarah Peyton, TwnALX, FfxCo, StVA
To William Smith -do- : for £72 cmv a parcel contiguous to TwnALX W of Columbus, N of Prince St extended:
BEGIN on Columbus 100' 7" N of Prince and on N line of alley 11' 7" wide ... W w/alley //Prince 113' to another alley 20' 10" wide ... N//Columbus 22'... E//Prince 113'... thence to BEGIN--part of 2-acre square conveyed by William Thornton Alexander [no date] to Elisha Dick for rent of £24 cmv;
--since conveyed to Francis Peyton (subject to the rent) [date not given; inference is that Peyton got all of the 2 acres, but there is room for doubt].
--Peyton confirms he will pay the rent to WTA.

--Peyton will lay off an 11' 7" wide alley //Prince-King, from Columbus to Alfred, beginning 89' N of Prince.
--Peyton will also lay off another, 20' 10" wide, from the N line of the alley above//Columbus-Alfred, N 66' to yet another alley;
--that third alley is to be 20' wide, beginning on the N line of the 1st alley, 113' W of Columbus.
WTT: Lewis Beckwith, Wm. Doerhy, Robert Darne
[Clerk's note: "The acknowledgement of this will be found on page 82 of Liber H."]

521   15Sep84   Bond
Fm Richard Arell, TwnALX, FfxCo, CwlVA
To Robert McLeod [no ID] : for £600 cmv, a bond
WHEREAS McCleod has sold, this date, 1/2 acre LOT 109 to Arell but earlier had conveyed the lot to James Kirk "now of ALX"
--if Kirk finally proves he has title, this bond is void
--if Arell gets clear title, he will pay McLeod £100, 12 months later another £100, and 12 months later a final £100, this settling the entire conveyance.
WTT: Peter Tartsback [see p. 524, below]; John Harper, James Grimes

523   17Jan86
    Robert McLeod [see above], Frederick Co., MD, assigns his rights in this bond to Samuel S. Thomas [no ID for Thomas]
WTT: Joshua Caton

524   20Jan91
    Bond [above, p. 521] proved by oath of Peter Tartzpaugh, and on 19Feb91 further proved by oath of Harper & Grimes

524   16Nov95
Fm William & Sarah Herbert, TwnALX, StVA
To Leven Powell -do-: for £500 current money, half of a parecl in TwnALX, part of LOT 32:
BEGIN SE corner Ffx-Queen Sts ... E w/Queen 84'... S//Ffx 55' 6"... W//Queen 84'... thence to BEGIN. [One reference to Powell in the body of the deed refers to him as Leven Powell Junr.]   WTT: Jonah Thompson, Francis Peyton
CMN: Jonah Thompson, John Dundas, Francis Peyton, **Gentlemen** of TwnALX, aptd 16Feb96 to examine Sarah. Rptd back same day.

528   17Nov95
Fm William & Rebecca Hickman, TwnALX, StVA
To Israel Wheeler & Joseph Miller, **Merchants** of the City of Philadelphia
For £500 VA currency, a parcel E of St. Asaph, N of Wolf [sic] BEGIN 136' 5" N of Wolf ... N w/St A 20'... E//Wolf 113' 5"...
S//St A 20'... thence to BEGIN.
WTT: Jacob Leap, Francis Peyton, Isaac Gibson

End of Deed Book F

ALEXANDRIA HUSTINGS COURT

Deed Book G, 1795-1796

1 30Jan96
Fm Samuel & Elizabeth Cooper, TwnALX, FfxCo, StVA
To John Limrick, FfxCo, StVA: for £93 cmv, "all that undivided fourth of land"...
BEGINNING N corner LOT 28 on Ffx St ... S w/Fffx 63'... W//Queen 164'... N//Ffx 63'... thence to BEGIN.
--"part of three LOTTS known [as] the Long Ordinary Lotts."
[Elizabeth signs herself **Betsy**]
WTT: Henry F. Lowe, Thomas Mezarvey, Titus Triplett, Donald Campbell

2 28Sep95
Fm Andrew & Margaret Wales, TwnALX, FfxCo, StVA
To Andrew Fleming: for £120 cmv, parcel N of Queen and W of Ffx Sts, part of LOTS 28 & 29.
BEGIN on Queen at E line of ground conveyed by Wales to Robert Lyle (145' 2" W of Ffx) ... E w/Queen 22'... N//Ffx 45' 8"... E//Queen 23' 2" "or such a distance as to terminate 100' W of Ffx" ... N//Ffx 41'... W//Queen 45' 2" to the line of Robert Lyle ... S w/Lyle's line//Ffx to Queen and BEGIN.
WTT: Ja. Keith, Robt. Lyle, Thos. Stewart

[Clerk's marginal note for the following entry: "Acknowledgement will be found in Liber L page 64."]
4 12 Oct95
Fm Francis & Sarah Peyton, TwnALX, FfxCo, StVA
To Josias Milburne Speake, State of MD, **Mariner**: for £452 cmv, parcel S of Prince, W of Union:
BEGIN on Prince 131' W of Union ... W w/Prince 20'... S//Union 44' 8"... E//Prince 1'... S//Union 22' 4"... E//Prince 20'... N//Union 22' 4"... W//Prince 1'... N//Union 44' 8" to BEGIN--this is the entire piece of ground conveyed to Peyton by Thomas Richards plus the W end of the parcel conveyed to Peyton by Abraham Faulkener and wife.
WTT: Ja. Keith, George Slacum, James Keating

7 25 Oct94
Fm Jonah Thompson, TwnALX, FfxCo, StVA

To George Irish of -do-:
WHEREAS Adam Bence 25Sep93 conveyed to Thompson a parcel N of Gibbons, E of Ffx:
BEGIN on Gibbons 123' E of Ffx ... W w/Gibbons 60'... N//Ffx 102' 7" to 10' alley ... E w/alley //Gibbons 60'... thence to BEGIN, on these terms: if Adam Bence paid Thompson £25.9.8 cmv + interest from 25Sep93 on/before 25Mar94, deed was void.
--however, Thompson advanced still more money to Bence, totaling £30.13.6 cmv (interest to date included), today.
WHEREAS Adam Bence 08Apr94 conveyed the parcel to James Keith, and Keith this same day (25 Oct94) conveyed it to George Irish.
NOW Thompson, for the £30.13.6 just received from Irish, hereby conveys clear title to the parcel to Irish.
WTT: Robert Young, Jas. Keith, Bryan Hampson

9 18Mar95
Fm James Irvin as guardian of John, Robert & Jane Adam--orphans of Robert Adam late of FfxCo, StVA, deceased
To Andrew Jamieson & Robert Anderson, TwnALX, FfxCo, StVA: a lease of parcel N of Oronoko, E of Water Sts:
BEGIN at int Oronoko & Water Sts ... N w/Water St to River Potowmack ... E "with the River" to the line of Neil Mooney ... S w/Mooney to Water St ... thence to BEGIN--"and the Bakehouse and all the other Buildings and Improvements & the use and Benefit of the River Joining thereupon"
TERMS: from 18Jun95 for 10 years ... for £25 cmv per annum in quarterly payments ... tenants to keep the Bakehouse "in good order and tenantable Repair" ... w/in 40 days after lease-end, tenants may remove buildings or improvements they have made.
WTT: George Coryell
MEMO: a 25' square of the above is excepted:
BEGIN on Oronoko at W corner of Neil Mooney's ground ... W w/Oro 25'... N//Water St 20' [sic]... E//Oro 25' to Mooney's line ... thence with line to BEGIN--"on which Ground stands an old frame house..." [No clues as to its identity, nor why it and its ground are excepted.]

12 10 Oct94
Fm Dennis & Jane Ramsay, TwnALX, FfxCo, StVA
To Thomas Richards of   -do- : for £126 cmv, parcel E of Union, N of King Sts.
BEGIN on Union 54' 10 1/2" N of King, at N line of parcel conveyed by the Ramsays to Thomas Richards ... E w/line 30'... N//Union 26' 1 1/2" to Fayette Street ... W w/Fayette 30'... thence to BEGIN--part of parcel given by William Ramsay, **Gentleman,** to Dennis Ramsay [blank] day, [blank] month of 178[blank].
WTT: Jno. Watts, Amas Jackson, Charles Turner, George Ulrick
CMN: John Dundas, Jonah Thompson, James Irvin, **Gentlemen** of [blank], aptd 03Feb76 to examine Jane. Rptd back same day.

16 10 Oct94
Fm Dennis & Jane Ramsay, TwnALX, FfxCo, StVA
To Thomas Richards of   -do-
For £211 cmv, parcel N of King, E of Union:
BEGIN on King 30' E of Unuion--the E line of parcel conveyed by the Ramsays to Thos. Richards ... N w/line //Union 54' 10 1/2"... E//King 30'... S//Union 54' 10 1/2"... thence to BEGIN:
--as above, part of parcel given by William Ramsay, **Gentleman,** to Dennis Ramsay, [blank] day, [blank] month, 178[blank].
WTT: Jno. Watts, Amas Jackson, Charles Turner, George Ulrick

CMN: John Dundas, Jonah Thompson, James Irvin, **Gentlemen** of [blank], aptd 03Feb76 to examine Jane. Rptd back same day.

20 17Feb96
Fm Phoebe Arell, TwnALX, FfxCo, CwlVA
To Peter Loggins of -do-
WHEREAS William Thornton Alexander & wife Lucy 14Sep95 leased to Phoebe a 1/2 acre on W of Washington, N of Wolfe Sts, in an addition made by John Alexander's exxrs, and numbered 12 in the plan of that addition:
BEGIN at int of Wn & Wolf [sic] Sts ... N w/Wn 176' 7"... W//Wolf 123' 5"... S//Washington 176' 7"... thence to BEGIN.
NOW Phoebe leases part of that to Peter Loggins:
BEGIN N side Wolf at W extremity of Lot ... E w/Wolf 20'... N//Wn 65' 7"... S//Wolf 20'... thence to BEGIN.
TERMS: beginning 01Nov96, $10 per annum.
[Peter signs w/mark; clerk spells Peter's name **Loggans**.]
WTT: Henry Moore, Thos. Moore, Thos. Lawrason

24 31Dec95
Fm George Irish, TwnALX, FfxCo, StVA
To Dennis Johnston of -do-, **Mariner**
WHEREAS William Thornton Alexander 23Sep89 leased to Adam Bence a parcel N of Gibbons, E of Ffx:
BEGIN on Gibbons 123' E of Ffx ... W w/Gibbons 60'... N//Ffx 102' 7' to 10'alley ... E w/alley //Gibbons 60'... thence to BEGIN, Bence paying each 01Nov £8.2.6.
--08Apr94 Bence conveyed the parcel to James Keith
--25 Oct94 James & wife Elizabeth Keith conveyed it to George Irish, Irish to continue paying Alexander the annual £8.2.6;
NOW George Irish for £240 cmv conveys it to Dennis Johnston, Johnston now to pay Alexander the annual rent.
WTT: Jonah Isabell, Andrew Taylor, William Moss

28 15Sep95
Fm William Thornton Alexander & wife Lucy, King George Co.
To Charles Simms, TwnALX
WHEREAS exxrs of John Alexander 21Apr85 leased to Simms a 1/2 acre contiguous to ALX, and numbered 11 in a plan of lots laid out and surveyed by Robert Boggess:
BEGIN where N side Wolf [sic] intersects E side Washington St ... N w/Wn 176' 6"... E w/Wolf 123' 5"... S//Wn 176' 6"... and thence to BEGIN--Simms to pay each 01Nov £41.10.0 cmv.
AND WHEREAS on the same day another parcel, W.T.ALXR to Simms:
BEGIN where E side Royal intersects N side Gibbons ... extend Gibbons E 123' 5"... N//Royal 176' 6"... W//Gibbons 123' 5"... thence to BEGIN--Simms to pay each 01Nov £37.10.0 cmv, both this and deed above recorded in FfxCo Court.
NOW the Alexanders for £200 current money remit all further rents from the two parcels.
[Executed by John Taliaferro, Atty in Fact for W.T. Alexander]
WTT: Benj. Grayson Orr, Ja. Keith, Francis Peyton, Jesse Simms

31 04Feb94
Fm William Ramsay   )
   Dennis Ramsay & wife Jane) TwnALX, StVA
   Robert Mease & wife Betty,)
   Robert Allison & wife Ann, Fauquier Co, StVA

Michael Madden & wife Hannah, FfxCo, StVA
Thomas Porter & wife Sarah, TwnALX, StVA
To Alexander Smith, TwnALX, StVA
WHEREAS William Ramsay, **Gentleman,** late of ALX, 23Feb84 conveyed to his daughter Amelia part LOT 54, E of Royal, S of King, fronting 56' on Royal: BEGIN on S line LOT 54, also Richard Arell's lot line ... E w/line 123' 5" to another Richard Arell line as well as LOT 54's E line ... N w/line 56' to 20' alley ... W w/alley 123' 5" to Royal ... thence to BEGIN, as recorded in FfxCo Court.
WHEREAS Amelia since died under 21 and w/o issue, the parcel descended to her brothers and sisters: William & Dennis Ramsay, Betty Mease, Ann Allison, Hannah Madden, Sarah Porter;
NOW for £295 cmv they convey to Alexander Smith a part:
BEGIN on Royal 120' S of King, on S line of a 20' alley ... E w/alley //King 123' 5" to the back line of LOT 54 ... S w/back line //Royal 56'... W//King 123' 5", thence to BEGIN, including the use of the 20' alley.
WTT: James Wilson, Guy Atkinson, Andrew Taylor & Bernard Ghequiere to R.A.; Francis Peyton, James Lawrason & Jno. Wilson to M.M.; *Jonathan Mandeville & Amas Jackson to Mrs. + MM; *Bernard Ghequiere to MM; Robert Mease, James Porter & John Jones to T.P.; *Bernard Ghequiere for Him; *Bryan Hampson & Guy Atkinson to R.M.; *John Wilson & Jonathan Mandeville to Mrs. Mease + R.M.; *Bernard Ghequier & Amas Jackson to Mrs. Mease; Titus Triplett to MM; Robert Allison to D.R. + J.A.; Dennis Ramsay, Lewis Weston & Robt. Brockett to W.R.; M. Madden to [blank]; J. Gilpin to M. Madden. [In the case of the *entries involving the Maddens and Meases, the Clerk's abbreviations are not clear. Also, the "Him" for whom Ghequiere signed may be "RM," not "Him." If these ties are critical to the researcher, the original should be consulted.]
CMN: John Thomas Chunn, William Hale, Lawrence Ashton, **Gentlemen** of Fauquier Co, aptd to examine Ann Allison. Rptd back 11Feb94. John Dundas, Francis Peyton, James Lawrason, **Gentlemen** of TwnALX, aptd 05Jun94 to examine Hannah Madden. [Their return is recorded, but undated.]

39 14Nov95
Fm Elisha Cullen Dick & wife Hannah, TwnALX, FfxCo, StVA
To John Thomas Ricketts AND William Newton of -do-: parcel, 1/2 acre, N of Prince, E of St. Asaph:
BEGIN int Prince & St. A ... N w/St. A 176' 7"... E//Prince 123' 5"... S//St. A 176' 7", thence to BEGIN--granted by John Alexander to Patrick Murray for annual rent of £13.5.0 cmv;
--by certain conveyances vested in Ann Currie and William McKenzie, exxx & exxr of Samuel Ingles;
--McKenzie, Ann Currie and her husband James Currie 15Apr94 conveyed it to E.C. Dick, Dick to pay the annual rent to John Alexander's heir, William Thornton Alexander;
--Ricketts and Newton will now pay Alexander that rent.
WTT: Cleon Moore, John Bennett, William Talbott, T. Lancaster
CMN: John Dundas, Wm. Hickman, Francis Peyton, **Gentlemen** of TwnALX, aptd 03Dec95 to examine Hannah Dick. Rptd same day.

44 08Aug94
Fm Thomas & Ann Richards, TwnALX, FfxCo, StVA
To Francis Peyton of -do-
WHEREAS George & Jane Gilpin 18Nov83 leased to Andrew WaAndrew les a parcel S of Prince, W of Union:

BEGIN on Prince 131' W of Union ... W w/Prince 40'... S//Union & Water Sts 44' 4"... E//Prince 40'... thence to BEGIN, paying Gilpin annually 80 silver $;
--Wales later sold the land to John Short;
--Short sold one part of it to Thomas Richards;
--Short sold the remainder to Samuel Montgomery Brown;
--Richards and Brown each committed to pay [half of] the annual rent: $40 each [suggesting that each had bought half the parcel, as the rent was to be "a due proportion"];
--Richards, having since acquired Brown's portion, now owns the entire parcel that the Gilpins leased to Wales; [no dates given for this or any of the above transactions];
NOW the Richards for £200 cmv fm Francis Peyton convey part:
BEGIN on Prince 131' W of Union ... W w/Prince 20'... S//Union & Water Sts 44' 4"... E//Prince 20'... thence to BEGIN.
WTT: Charles McKnight, Jonah Thompson, John Dundas
CMN: Jonah Thompson, John Dundas, James Laurason, **Gentlemen** of TwnALX, aptd 04 Oct94 to examine Ann. Rptd back same day.

49   10 Oct95
Fm Thomas & Nancy Richards, TwnALX, FfxCo, StVA
To Joseph Riddle AND James Dall, Twn Baltimore, StMD: for £1600 cmv, a parcel N of King, E of Union Sts:
BEGIN int King & Union ... N w/Union 54' 10 1/2"... E//King 30'... S//Union 54' 10 1/2"... thence to BEGIN.
--conveyed by Dennis & Jane Ramsay to Thos. Richards 16Apr94.
ALSO an adjoining parcel:
BEGIN on King 30' E of Union--the E line of the above parcel ... N w/line //Union 54' 10 1/2"... E//King 30'... S//Union 54' 10 1/2", thence to BEGIN.
ALSO another parcel, adjoining the first:
BEGIN on Union 54' 10 1/2" N of King--the N line of the first parcel ... E w/Line //King 30'... N//Union 26' 1 1/2" to Fayette St ... W w/Fayette 30', thence to BEGIN.
--the two additional parcels conveyed by the Ramsays to Richards 10 Oct94.
[Nancy signs herself **Ann**]
WTT: John Dundas, Francis Peyton, John Wise, John Kinnare
CMN: John Dundas, Jonah Thompson, Francis Peyton, **Gentlemen** of TwnALX, aptd 16Dec95 to examine "Nancy Richards." Rptd 17Dec95

54   27Dec94   [Clerk's note for this entry: "acknowledgment on page 400 of Liber H"]
Fm William Thornton Alexander & wife Lucy, King Geo. Co, CwlVA
To Stephen Cook, TwnALX, CwlVA: lease of "the whole of that piece or parcel of Land, to the Southward of the Town of Alexandria commonly called Joneses's Point," about 6 acres.
BOUNDED on N by parcel WTA conveyed to SC 23Jun94 and by the River Potowmack ... on E "by the said River Potowmack"... on S "by Hunting Creek"... on W "by Hunting Creek"
TERMS: on/after 01Jan96 annual rent £19 cmv, and that--on request--Lucy will formally relinquish her dower rights.
[Alexander atty John Taliaferro Junr executes this for them.]
WTT: Charles Simms, Charles Lee, R. West, Thos. Patten
[See also the three entries following.]

57   27Dec94   Memorandum
Taliaferro receives $200 further, over and above the rent, for which the Alexanders "relinquished and assigned to the said Stephen Cooke his heirs and assigns forever all

[their] claims on the United States for the consideration money they may allow for the use of the ground on which they are now erecting a fort." WTT: as above.

57 02Jun95 Memorandum
W.T.Alexander ratifies all the above, in person.
WTT: John Taylor, Senr; G. Swoope; John Taylor, Junr; William Hartshorne, Junr.

57 24Jul95 Memorandum
In court the first three witnesses above swore oaths to the foregoing, but young Hartshorne did it by "affirmation"--apparently a Quaker, or at least as a Quaker would do. [Clerk's note: the Acknowledgement to this deed is in Liber H, page 391.]

58 25Dec94
Fm William Thornton Alexander & wife Lucy, King Geo. Co, CwlVA
To Stephen Cook, TwnALX, CwlVA:
Lease of a parcel contiguous to the town of "Alexandria upon the River Potowmack" [identifying ALX, not the parcel].
BEGIN at int N side King with E side Columbus St ... E w/King 123' 5" to SW corner of 1/2 acre parcel formerly granted Stephen Cooke, now occupied by John Heisler ... N//Washington "to the Fence enclosing the Church burial-ground"... W//King to E side of Columbus, thence to BEGIN.
TERMS: beginning 01Jan95, £8 cmv per annum; and on request Lucy will formally relinquish her dower rights.
[Alexander atty John Taliaferro Junr executes this for them.]
WTT: John Gill, Ch. Simms, Lemuel Bent, Jas. Keith
MEMORANDUM [p.60]: "If Mr. Charles Alexander's Land extends to the Southward of the Church fence, Stephen Cooke claims no further than to his Line, and at any rate, to no Land Northerly of the fence on the south side of the Church-buryingground." [See also the two following entries.]

60 02Jun95
Wm.T. Alexander personally attests to all of the above.
WTT: John Taylor, Senr; G. Swoope; John Taylor, Junr; Wm. Hartshorne, Junr.
[Note also their service at pp. 63-4, 67, 70, 74, 76 and 79 below.]

61 24Jul95
At a Hustings Court session this date the deed and memorandum "were proved by the oath of George Swoope and John Taylor, Junr., and affirmation of William Hartshorne, Junr" to be that of William Thornton Alexander. [Note also their service at pp. 63-4, 67, 70, 74, 76 and 79 below.]

61 25Dec94 [same to same]
Lease of a lot contiguous to ALX:
BEGIN NW corner LOT No. 2 in a plat of 1784 [no ID as to whose plat--surveyor, owner, or seller] on S side King, W side Washington Sts ... W w/King 123' 5" to Columbus St ... S w/Columbus 176' 7"... E//King 123' 5" to SW corner LOT No. 2, thence to BEGIN.
TERMS: from/on 01Jul95 £8 cmv per annum, and on request Lucy will formally relinquish her dower rights.
WTT: Ch. Simms, John Gill, Lemuel Bent, Jas. Keith

63-64 The above proven in court same dates/texts as at 60-61.
[Clerk's note: "Acknowledgement is on page 394 of Liber H."]

64 30May94   [same to same]
Lease of parcel "lying and being near the Town of Alexandria"
BEGIN "on Hunting Creek at high water mark, at the point where the dividing Line of the lots between Fairfax and Royal Streets, when extended, will intersect the said Creek"... Thence up the Creek "to where the dividing Line of the Lots between Royal and Pitt Streets, when extended, will intersect the Creek"... N w/that line //Royal until a right angled line intersecting the Fairfax-Royal line will contain 12 acres ... E at that intersection point until intersecting the Fairfax-Royal line ... thence S to BEGIN.
TERMS: on/after 01Jun95 60 silver $ per annum.
[Alexander atty John Taliaferro Junr executes this for them.]
WTT: Ch. Simms, Joshua Riddle, R.T. Hooe, G. Swoope

67 Proven [same people, dates, texts] as 60-61, 63-4.

67 30May94
[Clerk: Acknowledgment to this deed is on page 396, Liber H.]
Fm William Thornton Alexander & wife Lucy, King Geo. Co, CwlVA
To Stephen Cook, TwnALX, CwlVA:
WHEREAS the William Thornton Alexanders 02May92 leased to Stephen Cooke a Lot contiguous to ALX, known as LOT 2 in a 1784 plat:
BEGIN at int S side King w/W side Washington ... S w/Wn 176' 6"... W//King 123' 5"... N//Wn 176' 6", thence to BEGIN., for an annual rent of £11.5.0 Virginia currency;
ALSO, same date, contiguous to ALX, LOT 1 in the 1784 plat:
BEGIN at int S side King, E side Wn St ... S w/Wn 176' 6"... E//King 123' 5"... N//Wn 176' 6", thence to BEGIN, (same rent);
ALSO, same date, another [no ID] Lot contiguous to Alexandria:
BEGIN at int N side King, E side Wn ... N w/Wn 176' 6"... E to W side of "a Lot let to Mr. Parsons in 1779"...S w/Parson's line 176' 6", thence to BEGIN, (at the same rent);
ALSO, same date, another [no ID] Lot contiguous to Alexandria:
BEGIN at int N side King, W side Wn ... N w/Wn 176' 6"... W//King 123' 5"...S//Wn 176' 6"...thence to BEGIN (same rent);
NOW the Alexanders for £350 Virginia money remit further rent payments by Stephen Cooke.
[Alexander atty John Taliaferro Junr executes this for them.]
WTT: Ch. Simms, Joshua Riddle, R.T. Hooe, G. Swoope

70 The above proven [same people, dates, texts] as 60-61, 63-64, and 67.

71 25Dec94   [same to same]
Lease of parcel contiguous to Alexandria:
BEGIN on W side Ffx St 176' 7" S of NE corner of LOT 36 (formed by int of S side Gibbons w/W side Ffx)... W on W side of Ffx //Gibbons 436' 3" to the middle line between Royal & Pitt ... S w/middle line //Royal to NW corner of the 12-acre parcel lately leased to Stephen Cooke by William Thornton Alexander ... E//Gibbons to W side of Ffx, thence to BEGIN.
TERMS: beginning 01Jul95 £20 Virginia money per annum, and--on request--Lucy will formally relinquish her dower rights.
Executed for the Alexanders by atty John Taliaferro [sic].
WTT: Josiah Watson, Ch. Simms, Elisha C. Dick, Geo. Sweeny
74 The above proven [same people, dates, texts] as 60-61, 63-64, 67, and 70.

74 23Jun94
Fm William Thornton Alexander & wife Lucy, King Geo. Co, CwlVA
To Stephen Cook, TwnALX, CwlVA:

For £274 cmv, parcel "being to the Southward of the Town of Alexandria (in Fairfax County) and adjoining thereto":
BEGIN at SE corner of the 12-acre parcel leased to Cooke by the Alexanders 30May94 ... N w/E boundary of the 12-acre parcel as far as that boundary extends ... E until intersecting at right angles the West edge of Ffx St ... S w/edge "until it strikes or intersects at right angles the north edge or line of the marsh, or low grounds"... E w/the "meanders of the said north edge or line of the marsh or low grounds, into the River Potowmack ... thence--again from BEGIN--E from SE corner of the 12-acre parcel into the River Potowmack ... N w/River until intersecting the 1st line running into the Potowmack.
[Alexander atty John Taliaferro Junr executes this for them.]
WTT: Joseph Riddle, Josa. Riddle, G. Swoope

76 The above proven [same people, dates, texts] as 60-61, 63-64, 67, 70, and 74.

77 30May94
[Clerk's note: acknowledgement on page 392, Liber H.]
Fm William Thornton Alexander & wife Lucy, King Geo. Co, CwlVA
To Stephen Cook, TwnALX, CwlVA:
For £100 current money, 1/2 acre Lot in ALX, bounded by Prince on N, and by Washington on E:
BEGIN at int Wn & Prince Sts ... S w/West line Wn St 176' 7"... W//Prince 123' 5"... N//Wn 176' 7" to S line of Prince ... thence to BEGIN.
Executed for the Alexanders by atty John Taliferro [sic]
WTT: Ch. Simms, Joshua Riddle, R.T. Hooe, G. Swoope

79 The above proven [same people, dates, texts] as 60-61, 63-64, 67, 70, 74, and 76.

80 08Apr94
Fm Adam Bence, TwnALX, FfxCo, StVA
To James Keith of -do-
WHEREAS William Thornton Alexander 23Sep89 leased to Bence a parcel N of Gibbons, E of Ffx:
BEGIN on Gibbons 123' E of Ffx ... W w/Gibbons 60'... N//Ffx 102' 7" to 10' alley ... E w/alley //Gibbons 60'... thence to BEGIN--paying each 01Nov £8.2.6 cmv.
NOW for £160 Bence sells Keith the parcel, Keith to pay the annual rent to William Thornton Alexander.
WTT: John Yost, William Harper, Samuel Keech

83 25 Oct94
Fm James & Elizabeth Keith, TwnALX, FfxCo, StVA
To George Irish, FfxCo, StVA
WHEREAS [the history, metes and bounds of parcel, p. 80]
NOW for £195 CMV the Keiths sell Irish the parcel, Irish to pay the annual rent to William Thornton Alexander.
WTT: George Coryell, Andw. Jamieson, Edward Harper

86 30Apr95
Fm Lewis & Elizabeth Cooke, TwnALX, FfxCo, StVA
To Thomas Tresize AND Richard May of -do-: for £85 cmv part LOT 111, E of Pitt, N of Prince:
BEGIN on Pitt 144' 4" N of int Pitt & Prince ... N w/Pitt 12' 8"... E//Prince 99'... S//Pitt 12' 8", thence to BEGIN.

[The deed goes on to stipulate an annual rent of 25 1/3 Spanish milled $ to John Saunders and his heirs. The deed then notes: John Saunders is now deceased; further, on 19Jul84 he and wife Mary conveyed this property to Lewis Cooke.]
[Both Elizabeth Cooke and Richard May sign w/mark]
WTT: Cleon Moore, Abel Blakeny, Henry Moore
CMN: John Dundas, Francis Peyton, Jonah Thompson, **Gentlemen** of TwnALX, aptd 04Apr95 to examine Elizabeth. Reported same day.

90 01Jun95
Fm Thomas & Nancy Richards, TwnALX, FfxCo, StVA
To Peter Wise   -do-: for £42 cmv, parcel N of King, W of Pitt, part LOT [blank, but w/No. 116 pencilled in]:
BEGIN on King at the line dividing Richards' and Wise's property ... N w/line 176' 7" to the back line of Richards ... E w/back line //King 4'... S//Pitt 176' 7" to King, thence to BEGIN.
--original lot, of which this is part, conveyed by ALX Trustees to Robert Rutherford [no date, no details];
--Rutherford sold to James Hendricks [no date, no details];
--Hendricks conveyed it to [blank] Parker [no date, details;]
--Parker conveyed it to Thos. Richards on [blank] [blank] 1794
[Here Nancy signs herself **Nancy**, unlike p. 49]
WTT: Wm. Allison, James McGuire, James Keating

93 18Apr96   Power of Attorney
Fm Elizabeth Donaldson, late Elizabeth Muir, sister and devisee of John Muir, late of TwnALX, deceased
To William Hartshorne, FfxCo, StVA: For selling real estate and improvements in ALX or elsewhere in Virginia
WTT: William Fitts, John Tracey, Jesse Carpenter, James Cavan

94 10 Oct95
Fm Charles & Frances Alexander, FfxCo, StVA
To Theophilus Harris, TwnALX, FfxCo, StVA: lease 2-acre parcel contiguous to ALX, bounded by W side Washington extended, E side Columbus, N of Pendleton, S of Wythe Sts:
BEGIN at int Wn & Pendleton Sts ... N w/Wn 353' 2" to Wythe ... W w/Wythe 246' 10" to Columbus ... S w/Columbus 353' 2" to Pendleton ... thence to BEGIN.
TERMS: on 25Dec96 60 2/3 silver $; beginning 25Dec97 133 1/3 silver $; and Harris to pay all taxes.
WTT: Francis Peyton, Jesse Simms, James Irvin
CMN: John Dundas, James Irvin, Francis Peyton, **Gentlemen** of TwnALX, aptd 22Apr96 to examine Frances. Rptd back same day.

99 14May95
Fm Alexander & Rachel Smith, TwnALX, FfxCo, StVA
To Joseph Ingle -do-: lease part LOT 54 E of Royal, S of King:
BEGIN on Royal at line dividing LOT 54 from Richard Arell's land ... E w/Arell's line //King-Prince 113' 5"... N//Royal 25'... W//King-Prince 113' 5" to Royal ... thence to BEGIN, for 50 silver $ annual rent beginning 01Apr96.
--conveyed to Smith by William Ramsay and others--heirs of Amelia Ramsay--04Feb94;
--Smith will lay out an alley--from Arell's line--along the E line of this property, through other Smith property, into a 20' alley which runs from Royal through LOT 54 parallel to and 100' S of King. [New alley's width not specified.]

[Rachel Smith signs w/mark]. WTT: none
CMN: John Dundas, Abram [sic] Faw, Francis Peyton, **Gentlemen** of TwnALX, aptd 20Apr96 to examine Rachel. Rptd back 25Apr96.

105 20Apr96
Fm Peter & Sinah Wagener, FfxCo, CwlVA
To George Deneale, TwnALX, FfxCo, StVA
WHEREAS Robert Doughtherty, heir at law of Windsor Browne, deceased, conveyed 23Feb86 to James Lawrason AND Samuel Arell a parcel E of St. Asaph, S of Duke, LOT No. [blank]
--part of Lot conveyed by John Alexander to Windsor Browne AND John Finlay;
--conveyed 24Apr87 by Lawrason AND Arell to Peter Wagener AND George Deneale as tenants in common:
BEGIN on Duke 40' from int of Duke-St. Asaph ... E w/Duke 20'... S//St. A 78'... W//Duke 20'... thence to BEGIN,
--and Wagener has agreed to sell his half to Deneale;
NOW for £345.18.0 current money Wagener conveys to Deneale Wagener's half of the parcel, Deneale now to pay the annual ground rent of $1.04 to Lawrason and Arell.   WTT: Charles Turner, Titus Triplett, Donald Campbell, George McMunn

107 16Sep95
Fm Jacob Cox, TwnALX, FfxCo, StVA
To William Thornton Alexander, King George Co, StVA
WHEREAS Jacob Cox 19Dec92 leased to William Wright a parcel W of Water, N of Wilkes Sts:
BEGIN at int Wilkes-Water Sts ... N w/Water St 50' 2"... W//Wilkes 74'... S//Water St 50' 2", thence to BEGIN--paying each 20Jun 40 1/2 silver $; (this is part of 1/2 acre conveyed to Cox by John Alexander);
NOW in consideration of William Thornton Alexander's remitting this same date annual rent £10.10.0 due from Cox, Cox assigns to Alexander the 40 1/2 silver $ annually due from Wright.
WTT: Jas. Keith; Jas. Keith, Junr; George Slacum

110 22Apr96
Fm Jacob Cox, TwnALX, FfxCo, StVA
To James Keith -do-
WHEREAS Cox 19Jan81 leased to John Sanford parcel W of Water St, N of Wilkes in Lot adjoining LOT 96:
BEGIN on Water St at SE corner LOT 96 ... W w/dividing line between the two lots to SW corner LOT 96 ... S at right angles //Water St 74'... E//first line to Water St ... thence to BEGIN--Sanford paying Cox each 19Jan £4.8.3 cmv;
AND WHEREAS Sanford 24Jul83 sold part to James Keith:
BEGIN on Water St at line dividing of this parcel from LOT 96 ... W w/line 123' 5"... S//Water St 50'... E//Wilkes 123' 5" to Water St ... thence to BEGIN--Keith to pay Cox the annual £4.8.3 each 19 Jan;
NOW for £43 cmv, Cox remits further annual rent from Keith. WTT: none

113 29Dec94
Fm William Thornton Alexander & wife Lucy, King Geo. Co, StVA
To Trustees of Alexandria Academy
WHEREAS exxrs of John Alexander 21Apr85 granted William Hartshorne 1/2 acre Lot adjoining TwnALX, E of Washington, S of Wolfe Sts:

BEGIN at int Wn-Wolfe Sts ... S w/Wn 176' 6"... E//Wolfe 123' 5"... N//Wn 176' 6"... to Wolfe, thence to BEGIN, Hartshorne to pay Wm.T. Alexander £41 current money each 01Nov;
AND WHEREAS 05Sep94 W.T.A. remitted all but £12.3.0 cmv rent;
NOW W.T.A. assigns the £12.3.0 cmv annual rent to the trustees in return for $500 from them.
[Alexander atty John Taliaferro Junr executes this for them.]
WTT: P. Marsteller, John Reynolds, Saml. Davis, J.C. Kempff
WTT to the trustees' payment: P. Marsteller, J.C. Kempff, John Taliaferro, Junr.

117 29Dec94
Fm James & Elizabeth Keith, TwnALX, FfxCo, StVA
To William Thornton Alexander, **Esquire,** King George Co, StVA
WHEREAS exxrs of John Alexander 21Apr85 leased to John Keith 1/2 acre Lot, LOT 19 in a plat laid off and surveyed by Robert Boggess at the exxrs' request, contiguous to TwnALX:
BEGIN at NE corner Washington and Gibbons Sts ... N w/Wn 176' 6"... E//Gibbons 123' 5"... S//Wn 176' 6" ... thence to BEGIN, Keith to pay William Thornton Alexander £35 cmv each 01Nov;
NOW for $1.00 the Keiths convey it back to Wm.T. Alexander.
Executed for the Alexanders by atty John Taliaferro [sic].
WTT: Elisha C. Dick, J.C. Kempff, Saml. Davis, John Reynolds

119 01Aug95
Fm Elisha Cullen Dick & wife Hannah, TwnALX, FfxCo, CwlVA
To Philip Wanton of -do-
WHEREAS William Thornton Alexander & wife Lucy 25Dec94 leased to Dick 2 acres adjacent to TwnALX:
BEGIN at int King-Columbus (S of King, W of Columbus) ... W w/King to Alfred St ... S w/Alfred to Prince ... E w/Prince to Columbus ... N to BEGIN.
NOW the Dicks lease to Wanton 3 parcels in the 2 acres, "numbered in a plan one two and three"
BEGIN W side Columbus 100' from int Columbus-King ... S 66' 7" to 20' alley and its N side where it intersects w/Columbus ... W w/alley 116' to a 14' 10" alley ... N w/alley 26' 7"... E//both first alley and King 24' 3 1/2"... N//Columbus 40'... E//King 91' 8 1/2" to BEGIN, "including all the said Lots number one, two, and three."
ALSO another Lot, part of the 2 acres, numbered 7 in the plan:
BEGIN on S side King 91' 8 1/2" from int King-Alfred ... S//Alfred 140'... E//King 31' 8 1/2"... N 140' to King ... W w/King 31' 8 1/2" to BEGIN, "In which said two last mentioned set of courses are included the said LOTS 1, 2, 3, & 7."
--Wanton paying from 01Jul96 $49.15 per annum.
ALSO: Waton undertakes to build on/before 01Jan98
--on some part of the premises
--a brick house 2 stories high
--not less than 15' wide and 20' long
--and agreeing that neither Wanton, nor his heirs or assigns, nor anyone else shall ever "make any Framed Building on any Front of the said hereby Granted Premises"
WTT: George Drinker, John Watson, Elisha Janney
CMN: John Dundas, Abram Faw, Francis Peyton, **Gentlemen** of TwnALX, aptd 21May96 to examine Hannah. Rptd back same day.

125 01Aug95
[Same] to Elisha Janney, TwnALX, FfxCo, StVA

WHEREAS [title/metes/bounds of the Dicks' 2-acre parcel is recited, as at p. 119, above]; NOW they lease to Janney their LOT 4, in their plan:
BEGIN at int King-Columbus ... W w/King 60'... S//Columbus 100'... E//King 60'... thence to BEGIN--Janney to pay $30 per annum beginning 01Jul96.
ALSO: Janney undertakes to build, same as Wanton, above p.119.
WTT: Philip Wanton, George Drinker, John Watson
CMN: as above, p.119.

130 01Aug95
[Same] to George Drinker, TwnALX, FfxCo, StVA
The Dicks, just as at pp.119, 125 above, lease to Drinker LOTS 10, 11, and 12 in their plan of their 2-acres:
BEGIN on E side Alfred 100' from int of Alfred-King ... S w/Alfred 66' 7" to an alley 20' wide at its intersection w/Alfred ... E w/alley's N side 116' to another alley 14' 10" wide ... N w/alley 26' 7"... W//King and 1st alley 24' 3 1/2"... N//Alfred 40'... W//King 91' 8 1/2" to BEGIN, thus including Dick LOTS 10, 11, 12.
ALSO: Drinker is to pay $33.30 per annum beginning 01Jul96, AND undertakes to build, as Wanton and Janney, (pp.119,125.)
WTT: Philip Wanton, John Watson, Elisha Janney
CMN: John Dundas, Abram Faw, Francis Peyton, **Gentlemen** of TwnALX, aptd 21May96 to examine Hannah. Rptd back same day.

136 24Aug95
Fm John Harper, FfxCo, StVA
To Michael O'Mara, TwnALX, FfxCo, StVA
WHEREAS Harper leased [no date] to Michael Thorn a parcel N of Prince, W of Union Streets:
BEGIN on Prince 88' W of Union ... N//Union 88' "to the line of McRea and Mease being the back line of...John Harper" ... W w/that line 40'... S//Union 88' to Prince ... thence to BEGIN, Thorn paying 100 Spanish milled $ each 01Jul; and
WHEREAS Michael Thorn conveyed part of this to Thomas Vowell:
BEGIN on Prince 109' W of Union ... W w/Prince 19' to W line of parcel ... N w/line 36' 6" to 5' alley ... E w/alley //Prince 19'... thence to BEGIN--Vowell paying Harper $47 1/2 of the $100 rent;
--and on 11Jan94 Thorn conveyed the remainder of the original parcel to Michael O'Mara, O"Mara paying Harper $52 1/2 of the $100 annual rent;
NOW for £180 cmv from O'Mara, Harper remits the $52 1/2 rent.
WTT: Jas. Keith, Cavan Boa, Dennis Foley, Thos. Vowell, Junr.

140 12Jan96
Fm Thomas & Mary Patten, TwnALX, FfxCo, StVA AND
    Joseph & Dorothy May, Town of Boston, St of MASS
To Jonathan Swift, TwnALX, FfxCo, StVA: for £5 cmv, parcel S of King, W of Union Streets:
BEGIN at int King-Union ... S w/Union 40'... W//King 70' to 10' alley ... N w/alley //Union 40' to King, thence to BEGIN--PLUS use of the alley with Valentine Peers; --the parcel is the same as conveyed by Peers to Patten & May 16Apr93.
WTT: Elisha C. Dick, Wm. Herbert, Daniel C. Puppo
CMN: Dorothy May examined 16Feb96 by Joseph Gardner, **1st Justice**, Court of Common Pleas, Boston, Suffolk County. [Judge Gardner's ID attested by Ezekiel Price, **Clerk** of Court]
CMN: William Herbert, Elisha C. Dick, Robert T. Hooe, **Gentlemen** of FfxCo, aptd 13Jan96 to examine Mary Patten. Reported back same day.

146 20Aug95
Fm Dennis Ramsay AND Robert Allison AND Michael Madden, surviving exxrs of William Ramsay [Senior]
To John Gill, TwnALX, FfxCo, StVA
WHEREAS William Ramsay in his last will and testament directed that certain of his real estate be sold to pay debts, and appointed William Ramsay [his oldest son], Dennis Ramsay, Robert Allison, and Michael Madden his executors;
--and William, Dennis, Robert and Michael on the [blank] day of last March offered at public auction (first having advertised in the Alexandria Gazette) a parcel on E side of Pitt and the N side of Cameron:
BEGIN on Pitt 98' N of Cameron--the N line of a 10' alley between Royal and Pitt ... N w/Pitt 72' 6" to a 6' alley also between Royal and Pitt ... E w/this alley 116' to another 14' 10" wide which runs from the 10' to the 6' alley //Royal and Pitt ... S w/the 14' 10" alley //Royal-Pitt 72' 6" to the 10' alley ... W w/that alley to Pitt/BEGIN.
NOW: John Gill being high bidder at £104.10 current money, the surviving exxrs convey the parcel to him.
WTT: Samuel Stone, Bryan Hampson, Samuel Ford, William Newton

150 20Aug95
Fm Dennis Ramsay AND Robert Allison AND Michael Madden, surviving exxrs of William Ramsay [Senior]
To Thomas Richards, TwnALX, FfxCo, StVA
[After the same preamble of "WHEREASES" as above, p. 146, the exxrs identify another parcel, W of Royal, N of Cameron]:
BEGIN on Royal 146' 4" N of Cameron, the N line of a parcel earlier sold by all 4 executors to Richards ... N w/Royal 24' 2" to a 6' alley from Royal to Pitt ... W w/alley //Cameron ... 116' to an alley 14' 10" wide running between the 6' alley //Royal and a 10' alley ... S w/alley //Royal 24' 2" ... thence to BEGIN.
--Richards was high bidder at £98 current money at the auction "since which the said William Ramsay [the son] hath departed this life" and
NOW the surviving exxrs convey the parcel to Richards.
WTT: Samuel Stone, Bryan Hampson, Samuel Ford, William Newton

155 17Sep94
Fm John Harper, FfxCo, StVA
To William Wright, TwnALX, FfxCo, StVA
WHEREAS Harper 11May84 leased Thomas Tobin parcel N of Prince, W of Union:
BEGIN on Prince 168' W of Union ... W w/Prince 20'... N//Union 88' to Harper's back line ... E w/line //Prince 20'... thence to BEGIN--Tobin paying each 01Nov 80 Spanish milled $;
AND WHEREAS Tobin 06Dec85 conveyed the parcel to Wm. Wright, Wright to pay the 80 Spanish milled $ to Harper;
NOW for £200 from Wright Harper remits further rent payments.
WTT: Jas. Keith, Job Greene, Thomas Rogerson, John Reynolds

157 24Sep95
Fm Matthew Franklin Bowne & wife Elizabeth) TwnALX, FfxCo,
    Theodorus James Hamilton & wife Eunice)   StVA
To Joseph Dyson -do-
WHEREAS Richard Marshall Scott & wife Mary 16Apr95 leased to MFB and TJH a parcel S of King, W of Union:
BEGIN on King on W side of all 80' W of Union ... W w/King 40'... S//Union 66'... E//King 40' to the alley, thence to BEGIN, MFB & TJH paying each 01Jun 120 silver $--the rent remittable by paying £400 within 5 years.

NOW for £200 cmv MFB & TJH convey to Dyson the entire parcel, the rent requirement, and the rent remittal option.
[Elizabeth Bowne signs herself **Eliza**]
WTT: Henry Peterson, Baldwin Stith, Daniel C. Puppo
CMN: John Dundas, James Irvin, Francis Peyton, **Gentlemen** of TwnALX, aptd 21Mar96 to examine [blank] [but, judging by the wording, both wives]. Peyton and Irvin reported back 19May96 that they had examined Elizabeth Bowne.

164 16Mar96 Articles of Agreement
   (George Coryell)
between (Robert Brockett) TwnALX, FfxCo, StVA
   (Patrick Burns)
WHEREAS on [blank] day of [blank] 179[blank] William Thornton William Thornton Alexander & wife Lucy conveyed to Coryell a parcel contiguous to TwnALX, bounded by: N side of Duke, extended ... S side of Prince, extended ... W side of Alfred, extended ... E side of Patrick, extended ... "one entire Square of four Lots of ground of one half acre each";
WHEREAS this same date George Coryell & wife Ann conveyed one 1/2-acre lot to Robert Brockett (W side of Alfred, S side of Prince) except those parts to be laid off as alleys "through the said Square for better accommodation of those persons who may settle thereon";
AND on the same date the Coryells conveyed another 1/2-acre lot to Patrick Burns (N side of Duke, E side of Patrick), except those parts reserved for alley ways;
WHEREAS Coryell, Brockett and Burns have "for the better accommodation of that Square, and those persons who may hereafter live thereupon" agreed to make the following improvements and to the following regulations"
--when there are 3 dwellings on each of the 4 lots in the Square, a Well shall be sunk in the center "of the said Court or Alley" described [in the conveyances from Coryell to Brockett, and Burns, below] "at the common Expense of the respective Owners of the said houses and for the common use of all those who may live upon the said Square";
--when there are 6 dwellings on each of the four lots, the several alleys [laid off in the conveyances below] shall be "paved at the joint and common Expense of the respective Owners of the said houses" with:
   --a footway 5' wide on each side of each alley, paved with brick and
   --the remainder of each alley paved with "a proper paving stone according to the town's paving plan as now adopted" and
   --"proper gutters for carrying off the water into the several streets as prescribed by those then directing town paving, and the then Town street regulations" and
   --"no Jut or Bow-Windows projecting into the said Allies...or any Cellar Doors opening into [them] unless such Doors be level with the foot-pavement or square with the Walls of the house to which it may appertain" and
--the three men will write these regulations into any conveyances they, in turn, make to others; to all this they bind themselves to each otheer with a penal sum of [blank] to be paid by "the persons failing to perform to the persons ready and willing to perform...." WTT: none

169 16Mar96
Fm George & Ann Coryell, TwnALX, FfxCo, StVA
To Patrick Burns of -do-
WHEREAS [repeats the Alexander-Coryell 2-acre parcel lease, p.164], Coryell to pay WTA £18 cmv each 01Jul;
NOW the Coryells lease to Burns one 1/2-acre lot--except ground laid off as alleys--in 2 parts:

Part I: BEGIN at int Duke-Patrick ... N w/Patrick 88' to 20' alley ... E w/alley //Duke 113' 5" to another 20' alley ... S w/alley //Patrick 88' to Duke ... W w/Duke 113' 5" to BEGIN.
Part II: BEGIN on Patrick 108' N of Duke and on N line of the first alley ... E w/alley //Duke 100' to an alley or Court 46' 10" wide ... N w/alley or Court //Patrick 70' 4"... W//Duke 100' to Patrick ... S w/Patrick 70' 4" to BEGIN.
TERMS: beginning 15Sep96 Burns to pay £20 cmv per annum
--Burns to erect/cause to be erected "upon some part of the premises," finished and tenantable before 31Dec1801 a brick dwelling "at least two Stories high" [dwelling to be "on some part of the front of the premises"]
--Coryell to open a 20'-wide alley from Patrick, 88' N of Duke
--another, 20'-wide, from Patrick, 88' S of Prince (both alleys to cross the Square //Duke-Prince into Alfred St;
--Coryell to open a third alley 20'-wide beginning on Prince 113' 5" from each of the streets--Patrick and Alfred and
--a fourth alley 20'-wide from Duke, 113' 5" from Patrick and Alfred (the third and fourth alleys to run //Patrick-Alfred from Prince and Duke into the first and second alleys);
--Coryell to open a fifth space 40' 10" wide [clerical error: should be 46' 10"] beginning at the first 20' alley 100' from both Patrick and Alfred, and running parallel to both until intersecting the second 20' alley.
--if Burns should at any time be compelled to pay the £18 Coryell owes William Thornton Alexander, Burns can deduct it from his next payment to Coryell.
WTT: none

176 16Mar96
Fm George & Ann Coryell, TwnALX, FfxCo, StVA
To Robert Brockett, TwnALX, FfxCo, StVA
[Here the Coryells convey the second of four 1/2-acre parcels within their 2-acre Square, beginning with the square's pedigree as at pp. 164 and 169, above.]
NOW the Coryells lease to Brockett land, except ground reserved for alleys, in two parts:
Part I: BEGIN at int Prince-Alfred Sts ... S w/Alfred 88' to 20' alley ... W w/alley //Prince 113' 5" to a second 20' alley ... N w/alley //Alfred 88' to Prince ... E w/Prince to BEGIN.
Part II: BEGIN on Alfred 108' S of prince, on S line of the first 20' alley ... W w/alley //Prince 100' to an alley/Court 46' 10" wide ... S w/Court 70' 4"... E//Prince 100' to Alfred ... N w/Alfred 70' 4" to BEGIN.
TERMS: annual rent and construction terms as for Burns, p.169.
--Coryell to open 20' alley from Alfred, 88' S of Prince,
--and a second, 20' wide, beginning on Alfred 88' N of Duke (both alleys, paralleling Prince-Duke, to run from Alfred across the Square into Patrick St;
--Coryell to open a third, 20' wide, beginning on Prince 113' 5" from both Alfred and Patrick plus
--a fourth, 20' wide, beginning on Duke 113' 5" from both Alfred and Patrick (both alleys to extend parallel to Alfred-Patrick from Prince and Duke until intersecting the first two alleys;
--Coryell to open a fifth space 46' 10" wide from the first 20' alley, 100' from both Alfred-Patrick and parallel to them, into the second 20' alley.
--should Brockett be compelled to pay the annual rent due William Thornton Alexander, he may deduct it from his next rent due Coryell.   WTT: none

183 01Jun95   Tripartite Deed
I-George & Ann Coryell, TwnALX, FfxCo, StVA

II-Elisha Bailey   -do-
III-William Thornton Alexander, King George Co, StVA
WHEREAS Alexander 26Dec94 leased to Coryell a parcel adjoining TwnALX N of Duke extended, W of Columbus, E of Alfred:
BEGIN at int Duke-Columbus ... W w/Duke 246' 10" to Alfred ... N w/Alfred "half the length of the Square between Duke and Prince"--176' 7"... E//Duke 246' to Columbus ... S w/Columbus to BEGIN, paying each 01Jul £12 cmv.
NOW the Coryells lease to Bailey a parcel of the above:
BEGIN on Columbus 102' 4" N of Duke--the N line of a 14' 4" alley from Columbus to Alfred ... W w/alley //Duke 100' to an alley 46' 10"... N w/alley's E line //Columbus-Alfred 40'... E//Duke 100' to Columbus ... S w/Columbus 40' to BEGIN.
TERMS: Bailey to pay 01Jul96 £4 cmv, and beginning 01Jul97 £7.10.0 per annum;
--Coryell to open a 14' 4" alley, beginning on Columbus 88' N of Duke, //Duke, 246' 10" W into Alfred;
--Coryell to open another piece 46' 10" wide beginning on N line of the above alley, 100' from both Columbus-Alfred, running parallel to them N 76' into the center of the Square between Duke and Prince;
--Bailey to have use of the alleys w/Coryell;
--William Thornton Alexander confirms that at no time would he ever ask of Bailey more than £8, which is proportionate to the amount of land Bailey now [here] holds in the larger parcel. [This new clause in such conveyances is not clear. The context suggests a verbal or separately written understanding, such as: if Coryell defaults on his rent to Alexander, Bailey keeps his land but pays Alexander directly, and no more than £8, etc.] WTT: none

188 29Sep95
Fm George & Ann Coryell, TwnALX, FfxCo, StVA
To Amos Alexander, FfxCo, StVA
WHEREAS the Coryells 01Sep95 leased to William Cash, Junr., a parcel contiguous to ALX, N of Duke extended, W of Columbus:
BEGIN on Duke 60' W of Columbus ... W w/Duke 20'... N//Columbus-Alfred 88' to a 14' 4" alley ... E w/alley //Duke 20'... thence to BEGIN, Cash paying each 01Jul £2.5.0 cmv, and having the use of the alley with the Coryells.
NOW the Coryells for £[blank] cmv convey to Alexander both the rental income from Cash, and the parcel. (Coryell re-commits, now to Alexander, to open the two alleys.)
[Signing for Alexander is attorney John Taliaferro, Junr.] WTT: none

191 06Jan96
Fm George & Ann Coryell, TwnALX, FfxCo, StVA
To Amos Alexander, FfxCo, StVA
1. Coryell recites the conveyances to Elisha Bailey at p. 183 above, and that to William Cash in the deed at p. 188 above.]
2. Coryell then notes his 01Sep95 conveyance to John Violet:
BEGIN on Duke 100' W of Columbus ... W w/Duke 22'... N//Columbus 88' to 14' 4" alley ... E w/alley //Duke 22'... thence to BEGIN, Cash paying Coryell each 01Jul £2.10.0 cmv [for which, see also p. 202, below].
3. Coryell recites another, to William Cash, Junr., 01Sep95:
BEGIN on Duke 80' W of Columbus ... W w/Duke 20'...N//Columbus 88' to 14' 4" alley ... E w/alley //Duke 20'... thence to BEGIN, Cash paying Coryell each 01Jul £2.10.0 cmv
4. Coryell, finally, notes a conveyance 29Sep95 to Amos Alexander of a parcel in the same lot and originally granted Coryell by William Thornton Alexander:
BEGIN at int Duke-Columbus ... W w/Duke 60'... N//Columbus 88' to 14' 4" alley ... E w/alley //Duke 60' to Columbus ... S w/Columbus to BEGIN.

NOW, noting that the parcel Amos Alexander leased and the William Cash parcel he acquired make Alexander liable for the £12 annual rent Coryell is supposed to pay William Thornton Alexander, the Coryells--to indemnify Amos from such--place in bond the following rents: the £7.10.0 from Elisha Bailey; the £2.10.0 from William Cash, Junr.; the £2.10.0 from John Violet.   WTT: none

[Clerk: "Look on page 208 for Power of Attorney that refers in some measure to this deed."
198 23Mar95   Tripartite Deed
I-George & Ann Coryell, TwnALX, FfxCo, StVA
II-William Thornton Alexander, King George Co, StVA
III-Susannah Morrison, TwnALX, FfxCo, StVA
[This begins by Coryell reciting the pedigree of the lot from William Thornton Alexander 26Dec94, N of Duke, W of Columbus, E of Alfred, as at p. 191, above.]
NOW the Coryells lease to Susannah part of the lot, a parcel:
BEGIN W side of Columbus at centre of the Square between Duke and prince, 176' 7" N of Duke ... S w/Columbus 16'... W//Duke 100' to Alley or Court 46' 10" wide ... N w/alley/court //Columbus-Alfred 16'... thence to BEGIN--paying 01Jul95 12/ cmv, and on/after 01Jul96 £2.8.0 current money, per annum.
--Coryell to open a space 46' 10" //Columbus & Alfred--from an alley 13' 7" wide laid off by Coryell through his ground from Columbus to Alfred parallel Duke--88' from Duke, to the back/North line of Coryell.
--William Thornton Alexander promises Susannah will never have to pay him more than her proportionate share [£2.8.0] of the annual £12 rent due Alexander from Coryell. [Susannah signs w/mark]
Executed for W.T. Alexander by his atty John Taliaferro, Junr.
WTT: Jas. Keith, Bernard Bryan, William Wright

202 01Sep95   Tripartite Deed
I-George & Ann Coryell, TwnALX, FfxCo, StVA
II-William Thornton Alexander, King George Co, StVA
III-John Violet, FfxCo, StVA
[Coryell recites the pedigree of the 26Dec94 conveyance of the Duke-Columbus-Alfred lot, as at pp. 191 and 198, above--and now leases part of it to Violet:]
BEGIN on Duke 100' W of Columbus ... W w/Duke 22'... N//Alfred-Columbus 88' to 14' 4" alley ... E w/alley //Duke 22'... thence to BEGIN, paying from 01Jul96 £2.15.0 yearly.
--Coryell to open, adjoining this parcel's W line, an alley 2' wide from Duke N w/the property line to the 14' 4" alley;
Coryell to open a 14' 4" alley from Columbus 88' N of Duke //Duke into Alfred.
--William Thornton Alexander promises never to ask of Violet more than his proportionate share [£2.15.0] of the £12 annual rent due Alexander from Coryell.
Executed for Alexander by his attorney, John Taliaferro, Junr.
WTT: Jas. Keith, Bernard Bryan, Wm. Wright

208 22May94   Power of Attorney
   William Thornton Alexander recalls that a parcel of land contiguous to TwnALX was in 1774, 1779 and 1784 leased by the acre to various people for his benefit.
   Wishing to reduce some of the rents and make other adjustments, he now revokes the power of attorney granted to John Taliaferro Brooke, of Fredricksburgh, and empowers instead John Taliaferro, Junr., of King George County.
   He empowers him to sell off yet another parcel contiguous to TwnALX, and to execute penalty clauses on rent contracts in default.

WTT: Francis Fitzhugh, Vincent Doffan, William P. Flood, Thacker Washington, Charles Lee; Gerrard Alexander, Junior   [See following.]

210 26Aug95
   William Thornton Alexander "acknowledges" the power of attorney above in order to record it.
WTT: James Cross, J. Saunders, Francis Fitzhugh, John Daniel

211 Proven in King George Co. Court and certified by C. Smith, **Clerk** of Court.

211 18Feb96
Fm John Crips Vowell & wife Margaret)   TwnALX, FfxCo,
   Thomas Vowell Junr & wife Mary   )   StVA
To Alexander McKenzie of -do-: for £450 cmv, parcel S of Prince, E of Water:
BEGIN on Prince "at that Lot of Ground and Warehouse late the Property of Isaac McPherson but [now] the property of Elisha Janney and George Irish" being 129' E of Water St ... E w/ Water St. 20'[not possible as Water St runs north-south; should be "E w/Prince 20'] ... S//Water St 44' 4"... W//Prince 20'... N//Water St 44' 4" to Prince and BEGIN.
--conveyed to the two male Vowells by Thomas & Ann Richards 05Aug94.
WTT: none
CMN: John Dundas, James Irvin, Alexander Smith, **Gentlemen** of the ALX Corporation, aptd 02Mar96 to examine Peggy [sic] and Mary Vowell. Rptd back same day.

217 15Feb96
Fm George & Jane Gilpin, TwnALX, FfxCo, StVA
To Isaac McPherson -do-
WHEREAS the Gilpins 20Mar86 leased to Daniel McPherson Junr AND Isaac McPherson a parcel S of Prince, W of Union:
BEGIN on Prince 171' W of Union ... W w/Prince 40'... S//Union 44' to line of Jonathan Hall's heirs ... E w/Hall line //Prince 40' ...thence to BEGIN--paying 80 Spanish milled $ each 01Jan, (and since which time Daniel has died, his half passing to Isaac.)
NOW for £240 cmv the Gilpins remit further rent from Isaac.
WTT: Edward Fenwick; John Muncaster to Jane Gilpin; H.K.H. [may be H.Kh.] Smoot

219 01Sep95
Fm George Gilpin, TwnALX, FfxCo, StVA
To Robert Henderson -do- : lease of "that Frame Warehouse lately occupied by...Gilpin as a Store standing upon the East side of Union Street and the North side of a twenty foot alley and contiguous to Gilpin and Harper's Dock" in ALX;
--from today, for 7 years, paying £97 cmv in half yearly payments, first due 01Mar96
WTT: J. Gilpin, Richard Whalley, Thomas Sim[?] [May be Simms/Simen/Simon]

222 17Aug95   Articles of Agreement
John McIver AND Charles Love, TwnALX
--McIver agrees to lease Love the "house on Prince Street...at present occupied by himself [McIver]" for 10 years beginning 01Mar96 and ending 01Mar1806;
--also "the Lot & out-houses at present on the said Lot on which the said Dwelling House stands," the lot to contain a 25' 8" front:
BEGIN at "West corner of...Dwelling House & running back to where the Back fence now stands";

--McIver also agrees to place on the lot a "Good framed Stable to be at least Twelve feet square and to have a Loft sufficient to contain at least One Ton of well cured Timothy Hay, with Racks and Mangers thereto";
--"and also [McIver is] to deliver up at the time aforesaid said Lot & houses in good and sufficient repair, the dwelling House to be completely finished from the Cellar to the Garret";
--"the said McIver also agrees that should he build on the East lots adjoining this said Lot, that the Kitchen nor Dwelling House which may be so built shall not have a Front towards the Lot let to said Love";
--Love agrees he will not let or sublet "to any person of disreputable Character or against whom any reasonable exception can be made";
--Love is to pay £40 per annum in quarterly payments;
--they both agree to post a penalty bond of £1000 in the event either defaults.
WTT: Gurdin Chapin, James McKenna, Jas. Keith
MEMORANDUM: "Note; said Love also agrees that the Houses included in the within Lease shall not, whilst in his Occupation, be allowed to decay in an unreasonable manner, for the want of being duly repainted."

224   04Jun94   Mortgage
Fm Edward Mitchell Ramsay & wife Mary, TwnALX, StVA
To Abraham Usher AND John Wolfenden, Twn Baltimore, StMD
WHEREAS Ramsay owes Usher & Wolfenden £260.7.9 current money of MD "which it is inconvenient for him at present to satisfy"
NOW to secure the note, plus interest, the Ramsays mortgage a parcel S of King, W of Ffx Sts:
BEGIN on King at W line of Benjamin Shreve ... S w/Shreve's line //Ffx 90' to line of George Hunter ... W w/Hunter's line //King 20'... thence //Ffx 90' to King ... thence to BEGIN--plus use of a 4' alley on the parcel's W side.
--this parcel conveyed to Ramsay by Richard & Eleanor Arell [blank date] for an annual payment of 1000 lbs. crop tobacco
--if Ramsay pays principal plus interest on/before 04Dec94 this conveyance is void.
WTT: Jas. Keith, Rob. Hamilton, Benjn. Weir

229   23Dec95
Fm Bushrod & Ann Washington, Henrico Co, StVA
To Robert Hamilton, TwnALX:
For 5/ a lot or 1/4-acre in ALX on Wolfe St:
BEGIN on S side Wolfe at junction of LOT 152 or LOT 102 at NE corner of LOT 152 ... W w/Wolfe 61' 8 1/2"... S//St. Asaph across LOT 152 176' 7"... E//Wolfe along line of LOT 152 61' 8 1/2"... N//St A along E line LOT 152 to BEGIN.
--purchased by Bushrod from John & Margaret Chew [no date] and having annual rent due Jesse Taylor [no date] of £3.3.0.
ALSO 1/2-acre lot adjoining, purchased by Bushrod from Ludwell Lee, but conveyed to Bushrod by Francis L. Lee to whom it was conveyed by ALX Trustees John Muir and Harry Piper 15Jan65--bounded by Wolfe and Pitt Sts.   WTT: none
MEMO: 24Dec95 Andrew Dunscomb, **Mayor** of Richmond, attests that Bushrod Washington personally appeared and confirmed the above.
CMN: John Pendleton, Roger Gregory, John Naye, **Gentlemen Justices** of Henrico Co, aptd to examine Ann Washington. Reported back same day.

233   26Mar96
Fm Thomas & Nancy Richards, TwnALX, FfxCo, StVA
To Jesse Greene, Sussex Co, State of Delaware: for £300 cmv part LOT 40, W of Royal, N of Cameron:

BEGIN on Royal 122' 2" N of Cameron ... N w/Royal 48' 4" to a 6' alley ... W w/alley //Cameron 116' to 14' 10" alley ... S w/alley //Royal 48' 4" ... thence to BEGIN.
--part of LOT 40, half the part conveyed by the exxrs of William Ramsay to Thomas Richards 19Jun94;
--the other half of this part conveyed by same to same 20Aug95
--this includes use of the alleys mentioned.
WTT: Luke Shortill [also written Shortle], Richard Wren, Peter Tartspaugh [also Tartzbaugh]
CMN: Jonah Thompson, John Dundas, Abraham Faw, **Gentlemen** of the Corporation of ALX, aptd 28Mar96 to examine Ann. Reported back same day.

238 01Jan96
Fm Isaac McPherson, TwnALX, FfxCo, StVA
To Elisha Janney AND George Irish of -do-
WHEREAS this same day McPherson conveyed to Janney & Irish parcel S of Prince, W of Union:
BEGIN on Prince 171' W of Union ... W w/Union 40' [should be Prince] ... S//Union 44' to land of the late Jonathan Hall, dec'd ... E w/Hall's line //Prince 40'... thence to BEGIN;
AND WHEREAS McPherson by an indenture 18Jun93 used this parcel as collateral to secure payment of £610.7.3 cmv to his daughters Jane and Elizabeth McPherson;
NOW, to indemnify Janney & Irish from loss should the 18Jun93 mortgage be foreclosed, McPherson puts in trust to Janney & Irish a parcel W of St Asaph, N of Duke:
BEGIN on St. A at centre of Square in Duke and Prince ... W//Duke-Prince 123' 5"... S//St A. 88' 3 1/2"... E//Duke and Prince 123' 5" to St. A ... thence to BEGIN, sold to Isaac 01Nov93 by Samuel & Mary Hanson.
WTT: Edward Fenwick, Abram [sic] Hewes, Jas. Keith [See below]

243 01Jan96
[Same to same] [This is the parcel referred to above, p.238]
--conveyed to Daniel & Isaac McPherson by George & Jane Gilpin
--subject to annual rent 80 Spanish milled $ to the Gilpins
--since which time Daniel died, the property passed entirely to Isaac, and Isaac paid to have the rent remitted.
WTT: as above

246 07Mar96
Fm James Wilson, Junr & wife Elizabeth, TwnALX, FfxCo, StVA
To Bryan Hampson of -do-: for £360 cmv, a parcel N of King and E of Water Sts:
BEGIN on King 120' E of Water St ... E w/Water St [should be King, as Water St runs N-S] ... 30'... N//Water St 81' to Fayette St ... W//King 30' ... thence to BEGIN.
--conveyed 01Nov94 by James Kennedy to James Wilson, Junr;
--and 15' "the residue thereof" being that piece conveyed by Thomas & Sarah Porter to Wilson 03Nov94. [Elizabeth signs herself **Eliza** Wilson]
WTT: James Kennedy, Daniel Henry, James Miller
CMN: Jonah Thompson, John Dundas, Abm. Faw, **Gentlemen** of TwnALX, aptd 08Mar96 to examine Elizabeth. Rptd back 21Mar96.

251 02May96
Fm Jacob Cox, TwnALX, FfxCo, StVA
To John Crips Vowell -do-:
For £400 cmv parcel N of Wilkes, W of Water Sts:

BEGIN on Wilkes 74' W of Water St ... W w/Wilkes 22'... N//Water St 32'... W//-Wilkes 1' 9"... N//Water St 70' 7" to John Saunder's line ... E//Wilkes w/Saunder's line 23' 9"... S//Water St 102' &' to BEGIN.
--part of lot conveyed to Cox by John Alexander [blank]Dec74, subject to annual rent of £10.10.0, since remitted by William Thornton Alexander--son and devisee of John, 16Sep95;
--Cox will lay off a 3' 6" alley along this parcel's W line, beginning on Wilkes and running 32' //Water St.
WTT: Washer Blunt, Richard Warren, John Clegg, Thos. Vowell, Jr.

254 11Mar96
Fm Jacob Cox, TwnALX, FfxCo, StVA
To Henry Stanton Earle -do-: for £480 cmv, part LOT 66 W of Ffx and S of Prince Streets:
BEGIN on Ffx 73' 6" S of Prince at NE corner of ground once conveyed by George & Mary Kyger to William Hunter ... W w/Kyger-Hunter line 90' //Prince-Duke ... N//Ffx 20'... E//Prince-Duke 90' to Ffx ... thence to BEGIN.
--part of LOT 66, conveyed 23 Oct75 by the Kygers to Cox, subject to an annual rent of £6.6.8;
--the Kygers sold the rent to Josiah Watson [blank]day of [blank] 179[blank], and Watson remitted the rent 18Dec93.
WTT: William Newton, George Slacum, John Bennett

258 12May96
Fm Abraham Faw AND Joseph M. Perrin--Commissioners aptd by   FfxCo. Court to sell ground late the property of John Baptist Petit of TwnALX, dec'd
To Jesse Taylor, TwnALX, FfxCo, StVA
WHEREAS James & Elizabeth Parsons 08Nov84 leased to John Baptist Petit AND Michael Simon Blondelet part LOT 180, N of King and W of St. Asaph:
BEGIN on King 59' W of St A ... W w/King 38' 6"... N//St A 34' to a 6' alley ... E//King 38' 6"... thence to BEGIN, w/use of the alley, and paying each 25Jun £19.5.6 cmv;
--later divided by Petit and Blondelet, each paying part of the annual rent, and WHEREAS Michael Simon Blondelet & wife Jane 03Jul88 conveyed their portion to Petit, Petit then subject to the entire rent;
--later Petit became indebted to Henry Didier and mortgaged the parcel to secure the debt, and soon thereafter died not having paid the debt;
--whereupon Didier brought suit in Chancery in FfxCo Court against John James Neblon & wife Margaret, she being daughter and heir of Petit;
--and the Court found for Didier, appointing Faw and Perrin commissioners to advertise in the <u>Alexandria Gazette</u> 4 weeks for disposing of the parcel at public auction, subject to the dower rights of Petit's wife, Margaret. Didier was awarded the sum £236 cmv + interest from 23Nov93 plus $7.40 court costs;
--4 advertisements were duly placed for a sale 05May, on which day Taylor was high bidder at £271 cmv.
NOW, for that sum, the commissioners convey Taylor the parcel.
WTT: Jas. Keith, Achd. J. Taylor, Jno. White

263 19Jul96
Fm John Harper, FfxCo, StVA
To James Murray, TwnALX, FfxCo, StVA: for £215 cmv, part of LOT 38 W of Ffx, N of Cameron Sts:
BEGIN on Ffx 117 1/2' N of Cameron ... N w/Ffx 23' to William Herbert's line ... W w/line //Cameron 123' 5" to LOT 38's W line ... S//Ffx 23'... thence to BEGIN--sold to Harper by William Hodgson [no date, details].   WTT: none

266   21Jul96
Fm Abraham & Mary Ann Faw, TwnALX, StVA
To Lewis Tristler -do-, **Blacksmith**: lease the parcel [no ID]:
BEGIN 176' 7" S of SW corner King-St. Asaph ... W//King 80'... N//St A 34'... E//King 80' to St A ... thence to BEGIN, for annual rent of $68 beginning 01Nov96.
WTT: Jona. Faw, Abel Blakeny, Samuel Cooper
CMN: John Dundas, James Irvin, Francis Peyton, **Gentlemen** of [blank], aptd 20Jul96 to examine Mary Ann̲e Faw. Rptd same day.

271   16Jul96
Fm Abraham & Mary Ann Faw, TwnALX, StVA
To William Hartshorne) Exxrs of John Saunders,
   John Butcher   )   late of ALX,
   Mary Wanton   )   dec'd
WHEREAS Saunders in his last will and testament 13May90 directed the sale of sufficient real estate to satisfy indebtedness and
WHEREAS Abraham Faw in Saunders' lifetime conveyed 18Jan83 to Saunders a parcel, part LOT 111, which Faw had bought from William Carlin:
BEGIN on Pitt 119' N of corner of Prince ... N w/Pitt 58' to SW corner of Henry McCabe's lot ... E//Prince 99'... S//Pitt 58' ... thence to BEGIN, subject to an annual rent equal to that owed by Faw to William Thornton Alexander for a lot in ALX on the SW corner of King and St Asaph;
AND WHEREAS for £400 Virginia currency FAW has agreed to remit and release Saunders' exxrs from further rent, so that they may convey it clear to someone else: NOW for that £400 the Faws do so convey them the parcel.
[Mary Ann signs her own name w/o an "e"]
WTT: W. McKnight, Samuel Cooper, Jona. Faw, Philip Wanton
CMN: John Dundas, James Irvin, Francis Peyton, **Gentlemen** of [blank] aptd 16Jul96 to examine Mary Ann. Rptd back 21Jul96.

276   17Jun96   Articles of Agreement
between John Sullivan AND wife Honora, TwnALX, FfxCo, StVA:
WHEREAS "both parties with a firm consideration having unanimously agreed upon to live more comfortable asunder from each other"
--John "out of natural affection" conveys to his children Nelly, Mary and Bethsy [sic] that house 16' on St. Asaph and 24' deep, for their life--their mother, Honora, to live there with them, but giving up all claim to it;
--Honora to pay all ground rent, taxes, and half the paving costs "whenever the said Street should be paved" but the house will revert to John should the children predecease him;
--John and Honora have elected Lanty Crowe, "as a good and trusty Citizen of this Town," as guardian and trustee for the children and the property;
--each party binds to a £500 penal bond, made to the other
[Honora signs w/mark]
WTT: J.C. Kempff, Dennis Foley

277   04Jul94
Fm Daniel & Jane Roberdeau, TwnALX, FfxCo, StVA
To Archibald McClean -do-:
For £120 cmv, parcel E of Water St, S of Wolfe:
BEGIN on Water St 97' S of Wolfe ... S w/Water St 24'... E//Wolfe 125' to Potowmack Street "and binding thereupon 25'"... thence W w/"streight Line" to BEGIN:
--part of LOT [blank] conveyed by ALX Trustees to John Hughs, and by Hughs to Roberdeau;

--Roberdeau will lay off 2' along the N line of this parcel for an alley from Water St to Potowmack St;
--McClean will lay off an adjoining 2' strip.
WTT: Jas. Keith, Leml. Bent, James Muir
CMN: [names of Commissioners not written in], **Gentlemen** of TwnALX, aptd 09Jul94 to examine Jane. Report returned 14 Oct94 by Robert Mease and John Dundas.

283   05May96   Articles of Agreement
between Thomas AND Mary Fitzpatrick   [no ID]
Having agreed to live "asunder":
--Thomas grants Mary for her lifetime "all that house and premises situate on Duke St" in ALX with all its "furnitures," it "being the house dwelling in it" [sic];
--Thomas will pay ground rent and taxes, and half the paving costs "if ever the said Street should be paved"
--each binds to the other for an £800 penal bond
[Thomas signs w/mark]
WTT: J.C. Kempff, John Sullivan, Dennis Foley

284   28Mar96
Fm John Thomas Ricketts & wife Mary)   TwnALX, FfxCo,
       William & Jane Newton   )   StVA
To John Woodrow -do-: Lease parcel E of St Asaph, N of Prince:
BEGIN on St A at center of Square formed by Prince & King ... E//Prince-King 123' 5"... S//St A 42 1/2'... W//Prince-King 123' 5" to St. A ... thence to BEGIN:
--part of lot leased by John Alexander to Patrick Murray [blank]Dec1774 for £13 cmv per annum;
--since when the lot has passed to Ricketts and Newton;
--Woodrow to pay beginning 01Apr98 £21.5.0 cmv per annum
--Woodrow to lay off a 5' 6" alley along the S line from St A to the parcel's E line;
--should Woodrow be compelled to pay the Murray-Alexander rent, he may deduct same from his rent to Ricketts & Newton;
--Ricketts & Newton will lay off a 5' 6" alley space adjoining Woodrow's, and another from that along the E line of Woodrow's parcel into Prince St.
WTT: William Halley, Wm. Talbott, J. Lancaster
CMN: John Dundas, Francis Peyton, James Irvin, **Gentlemen** of TwnALX, aptd to examine Mary Ricketts and Jane Newton. Reported back 10May96.

291   01Aug95
Fm Elisha Cullen Dick & wife Hannah, TwnALX, FfxCo, CwlVA
To John Simpson, FfxCo, CwlVA
WHEREAS William Thornton Alexander & wife Lucy 25Dec94 leased to E.C. Dick 2 acres in FfxCo, adjoining TwnALX:
BEGIN at int King-Columbus, S of King and W of Columbus ... W w/King to Alfred ... S w/Alfred to Prince ... E w/Prince to Columbus ... N w/Columbus to BEGIN.
NOW the Dicks lease Simpson a parcel, part of the 2 acres, LOT No. 8 in their plan:
BEGIN S side of King, 60' E of King-Alfred ... S//Alfred 100'... E//King 31' 8 1/2"... N//Alfred 100' to King ... thence to BEGIN, paying $15.83 per annum, beginning 01Jul96.
--Simpson to build a two-storey brick house on/before 01Jan98, not less than 15' wide and 20' long;
--neither Simpson nor anyone else will build a frame building on the front of this parcel.
WTT: John Watson, Thomas Triplett

CMN: Francis Peyton, James Irvin, John Dundas, **Gentlemen** of [blank], aptd 21May96 to examine Hannah. Rptd back same day.

297 18Jul96
Fm William & Agnes Hepburn, TwnALX, FfxCo, StVA
To Nathan Hatherly -do-: lease a parcel [no ID]:
BEGIN W of St Asaph, 140' 7 1/2" N of Princess ... S w/St A 37'... W//Princess 63'... N//St A 37'... thence to BEGIN, paying per annum 41 Spanish milled $ at 6\ each, or the equivalent in specie, beginning 01May97;
--Hatherly neither to remove nor alter nor destroy any standing structures or those to be built.
WTT: Robert Allison, George Darling, James Chamberlin

301 08Mar96
Fm James & Mary Ann Patton)   TwnALX, FfxCo,
    James & Latitia Kennedy)   StVA
To Mungo Dykes -do-
WHEREAS David & Eleanor Steuart 18Jun91 conveyed to Patton & Kennedy a parcel S of Prince, W of St Asaph:
BEGIN at int Prince-St A ... W w/Prince 123' 5"...S//St A 50'... E//Prince 123' 5"... thence to BEGIN, Patton & Kennedy paying every 05Aug to Wm.T. Alexander £5.18.4 VA currency.
NOW for £300 the Pattons & Kennedys convey it to Dykes, Dykes now to pay the rent to William Thornton Alexander.
[Latitia signs her name **Letitia**]
WTT: Charles McKenna, Jas. Dykes
CMN: Jonah Thompson, Francis Peyton, John Dundas, **Gentlemen** of TwnALX, aptd 09Mar96 to examine Mary Ann Patton & Letitia Kennedy. Reported back 31Mar96.

307 09Apr96   Deed of Trust
Fm Dennis Foley, TwnALX
To Cavan Boa -do-
For the use by Dennis' wife Elizabeth, for her separate support and maintenance: "1 Black milch Cow, and all...the household & kitchen furniture contained in the List hereto annexed" [list not included in this deed book]. See also p.308, below.
WTT: Michl. Cleary, Wm. Hoye, Patk. Byrne

308 24Mar96   Mortgage
Fm Dennis Foley, TwnALX
To Cavan Boa -do- : for 6/ a mortgage to secure annual payment of £20 to Boa for the separate support and maintenance of Dennis' wife, Elizabeth, of a parcel on Duke and St Asaph:
BEGIN at int Duke-St Asaph ... N w/St A 100'... E//Duke 28'... S//St A 100'... thence to BEGIN, void if payments made on time
WTT: Ch. Simms, Steph. Cooke, Townshend Stuart Dade, Patrick Byrne. [See also above, p. 307.]

310 29 Oct95   Power of Attorney
Fm Peter Blake, New York City, **Merchant**
To John Coates, -do- , **Merchant**
WTT: James Woods, Charles Ridel
ATTEST: Sworn to 28Apr96 by James Woods before Richard Varick, **Mayor** of New York

312   13Jul96   Deed of Trust
Fm Stephen & Phoebe Moore, TwnALX, FfxCo, CwlVA
To George Slacum, -do-
WHEREAS William Thornton Alexander & wife Lucy [blank]Sep95 leased to Phoebe, then Phoebe Arell, widow of David Arell, a 1/2-acre lot W of Washington St, N of Wolfe--LOT No. 12 in the Alexander plan:
BEGIN at int Wn-Wolfe ... N w/Wn 176' 7"... W//Wolfe 123' 5"... S//Wn 176' 7"... thence to BEGIN--part of which Phoebe 17Feb96 conveyed to Peter Loggens;
AND WHEREAS "the said Stephen Moore hath since his marriage with the said Phoebe laid out and expanded upon [the remaining part of the 1/2-acre] considerable sums of Money in Buildings and Repairs in consideration whereof, and of the Love and Affection which...Phoebe hath and doth bear to her...Husband Stephen It is her sincere Wish and Intention that after her Life [these same ungranted premises] shall be so directed that they may vest in...Stephen";
NOW for 5/ Stephen and Phoebe convey the property to Slacum in trust, for Phoebe's benefit while she lives, for Stephen's when she dies. The ungranted part of the 1/2-acre is "at this time in the occupation of the said Stephen Moore and Phoebe his wife." [Phoebe signs herself **Phebe**]
WTT: Cleon Moore, A.Faw, Jacob Leap, Henry Moore
CMN: Abraham Faw, James Irvin, Alexander Smith, **Gentlemen** of the Corporation of ALX, aptd 13Jul96 to examine Phoebe. Reported back same day.

318   21Sep95   Tripartite Deed
I-William & Mary Patton)   TwnALX, FfxCo
   John & Ann Butcher   )   StVA
II-Oliver & Jane Price of   -do-
III-John Stewart   -do-
WHEREAS the exxrs of John Alexander conveyed 05Aug79 to Oliver Price a 1/2-acre lot contiguous to TwnALX and "described in the Plan of Lotts adjoining to the said Town by the Number (178)" on N side Prince, W side St Asaph "opposite to the W side of a Lot adjoining the W line of the LOT 112 in TwnALX":
BEGIN on W side St A where a line from the SW corner of LOT 112 (drawn parallel w/the lot's southern line and Prince) meets the W side of St A ... N w/St A 176' 7"... W//Prince 123' 5"... S//St A 176' 7"... thence to BEGIN, Price paying William Thornton Alexander each 05Aug £22.3.0 cmv.
AND WHEREAS the Prices 16Jul83 conveyed to Peter Wise a parcel:
BEGIN NE corner LOT 178 ... W w/N line of lot 123' 5"... S//St A 46'... E//first line 123' 5"... thence to BEGIN, Wise paying annual rent [no date] of £6.3.0 cmv, thus reducing the Prices' rent for the remainder of the 1/2-acre to £16;
AND WHEREAS William Thornton Alexander 16Sep95 assigned to Paton & Butcher the £16 rent due annually from the parcel not conveyed to Wise;
AND WHEREAS the Prices 21Jul83 conveyed to John Stewart a parcel:
BEGIN on Prince 60' from SE corner of LOT 178 ... W w/Prince along the lot's S line to the lot's NW [sic][NW?] corner ... N//St A along the lot's W line 130' 7"... E//Prince across the lot to St A ... S w/St A 30'... W//Prince 60'... S//St A 100' 7" to BEGIN, Stewart paying each 05Aug £16 to Price;
AND WHEREAS John Stewart conveyed to William Hough 11Jan84 parcel:
BEGIN on St A 100' 7" N of int St Asaph-Prince ... N w/St A 30'... W//Prince 81'... S//St A 30'... thence to BEGIN, Hough paying each 05Aug £5 to Stewart;
AND WHEREAS John & Cicily Stewart conveyed this same day [21Sep95] [to whom is not here stated, but see below, p. 325] a parcel:
BEGIN on Prince 60' W of St A ... W w/Princve 21'... N//St A 100' 7"... E//Prince 21'... thence to BEGIN.

NOW [!] for £120 cmv the Patons and the Butchers remit John Stewart's rent obligation for what Stewart got from Price and did not later convey to Hough--AND the Prices release Stewart from any obligation in the matter of £16 annual rent once due William Thornton Alexander, since assigned by Alexander to Paton and Butcher.
WTT: John Janney, Charles Bennett, John Muncaster, Jonathan Butcher
CMN: none

325 21Sep95
Fm John & Cicily Stewart, TwnALX, FfxCo, StVA
To William Paton AND John Butcher of -do- as tenants in common
for £60 cmv, part of LOT 178, N of Prince and W of St Asaph:
BEGIN on Prince 60' W of St A ... W w/Prince 21'... N//St A 100' 7"... E//Prince 21'... thence to BEGIN, part of a parcel conveyed to Stewart by Oliver Price 21Jul83
[Cicily signs w/mark]. WTT: same as above

329 17Sep95 Tripartite Deed
I-Oliver & Jane Price, TwnALX, FfxCo, StVA
II-William & Mary Paton) TwnALX, FfxCo,
   John & Ann Butcher)   StVA
III-Walter Pomery Junior) TwnALX, FfxCo,
   Jonah Isabel Junior)   StVA
HEREAS the exxrs of John Alexander 05Aug79 conveyed to Oliver Price LOT 178 [text same as at p. 318, above]] for rent due each 05Aug of £22.3.0;
--part of which parcel Price leased to Peter Wise for £6.3.0 of the annual rent;
--the £16.0.0 balance of the annual rent being assigned 16Sep95 by William Thornton Alexander (John Alexander's heir) to Paton and Butcher;
NOW for £60 cmv the Prices convey to Pomery & Isabel a parcel
BEGIN on St Asaph 100' 7" N of Prince ... S w/St A 23' 1"... W//Prince 35'... S//St A 7"... W//Prince 25'... N//St A 30' 1" ... thence to BEGIN.
WTT: Lewis J. [may be Lewis I.] Marsteller, Siedr. Albers, Jno. Beatty, Wm. Hepburn, Jonathan Butcher; Charles Jones and Alexr. McConnell to Jane Price

336 17Sep95 Tripartite Deed
I-Oliver & Jane Price, TwnALX, FfxCo, StVA
II-William & Mary Paton) TwnALX, FfxCo,
   John & Ann Butcher)   StVA
III-Joseph Saul, TwnALX, FfxCo, StVA
WHEREAS [the text repeats the history of LOT 178 as above, at pp. 318 and 329]
NOW the Prices for [sum left blank] cmv convey to Saul parcel:
BEGIN on Prince 35' W of St. A ... W w/Prince 25'... N//St. A 70' 6"... E//Prince 25'... thence to BEGIN.
WTT: Lewis J. [possibly Lewis I.] Marsteller, Siedr. Albers, Jno. Beatty, John Gretter, Wm. Hepburn; Matth. Clarkson and Wm. Mease to Jane Price

342 20Jul95
Fm John Harper, FfxCo, StVA
To Benjamin Shreve, TwnALX, FfxCo, StVA: for £95 cmv, a parcel S of Duke and E of Washington Sts:
BEGIN on Duke 100' E of Wn ... E w/Duke 23' 5"... S//Wn 176' 7" to the centre of the Square between Duke-Wolfe Sts ... W//Duke 23' 5"... thence to BEGIN--part of 1/2-acre conveyed by exxrs of John Alexander to Harper for an annual rent later remitted by William Thornton Alexander.
WTT: Wm. Summers, Ja. Keith Junr, John Reynolds, James Lawrason

[Clerk's marginal note: "Del'd to Capt. Bayne by H.Gates"]
345 07Mar96
Fm John Harper, FfxCo, StVa
To Henry Bayne, Prince George's Co, StMD: for £73 cmv, a parcel S of Duke and E of Washington Sts:
BEGIN on Duke 28' E of Wn ... E w/Duke 24'... S//Wn 100' to 10' alley ... W w/alley //Duke 24'... thence to BEGIN--part of a 1/2-acre lot conveyed to Harper by exxrs of John Alexander;
--Harper will lay off for Bayne a 10' alley from Wn, 100' S of Duke, running east and parallel Duke 100'
WTT: Ja. Keith; Ja. Keith Junr; Jno. McCallmont

349 14Sep95
Fm William Thornton Alexander & wife Lucy, King Geo. Co, StVA
To James Lawrason, TwnALX, FfxCo, StVA
Lease of two 1/2-acre lots contiguous to TwnALX, bounded by S side of Duke extended, W side Alfred, N side Wolfe extended:
BEGIN at int Duke-Alfred ... W w/Duke 123' 5"... S//Alfred 353' 2"... E w/Wolfe 123' 5" to Alfred ... N w/Alfred to BEGIN;
--Lawrason, beginning 13Sep96, to pay £22 cmv annual rent.
[Alexander atty John Taliaferro Junr executes this for them.]
WTT: Jesse Simms, Wm. Paton, Robert Fulton, Samuel Keach, J. Gilpin
CMN: [Clerk's note: "The commission is recorded in Lib.K, No.2, page 591."]

353 16Sep95
[Same] to William Paton AND John Butcher, TwnALX, FfxCo, StVA
WHEREAS [history of LOT 178: exxrs of John Alexander to Oliver Price, Price conveying a part to Peter Wise, as at pp. 318, 329, and 336 above.]
NOW for £300 cmv the Alexanders assign to Paton & Butcher the annual £16 rent still due from Price.
[Alexander atty John Taliaferro Junr executes this for them.]
WTT: J. Gilpin, Robert Fulton, Samuel Keach, Benjn. Shreve, Jesse Simms

358 14Sep95
Fm William Thornton Alexander & wife Lucy, King Geo. Co, StVA
To Benjamin Shreve AND James Lawrason, TwnALX, FfxCo, StVA
WHEREAS the exxrs of John Alexander 05Aug79 conveyed to Thomas Wilkinson a 1/2-acre S of Duke, W of St Asaph, LOT 175, opposite W side of a lot which adjoined the W side of LOT 106:
BEGIN W side St A at the end of a line extended from NW corner of the lot adjoining LOT 106, the line parallel with the lot's N line and with Duke ... S w/W side St A 176' 7"... W//Duke 123' 5"... N//St A 176' 7"... thence to BEGIN, Wilkinson paying each 05 Aug £14.10.0 cmv;
--William Thornton Alexander later [no date] conveying the property to Shreve and Lawrason, they to pay the rent.
NOW for £300 cmv the Alexanders remit and release Shreve and Lawrason from any further rent payments.
[Alexander atty John Taliaferro Junr executes this for them.]
WTT: Jesse Simms, Wm. Paton, Robert Fulton, Samuel Keech [sic; see above], J. Gilpin, Jesse Simms [yes;Jesse is listed twice].

362 14Sep95
[Same] to Benjamin Shreve, TwnALX, FfxCo, StVA: lease two 1/2-acre lots contiguous to TwnALX, S of Duke, N of Wolfe, E of Patrick:

BEGIN at int Duke-Patrick ... E w/Duke 123' 5"... S//Patrick 353' 2" to Wolfe ... W w/Wolfe 123' 5" to Patrick ... N w/Patrick to BEGIN, Shreve to pay beginning 13Sep96 £20 cmv per annum.
[Alexander atty John Taliaferro Junr executes this for them.]
WTT: as above, but Jesse Simms here listed only once.
[Clerk's note: "Acknowledgement in Liber K, No.2, page 593."]

366 06May95 Tripartite Deed
I- Robert & Mary Ann Fulton, TwnALX, FfxCo, StVA
II-William Thornton Alexander, King George Co, StVA
III-Samuel Keech, TwnALX, FfxCo, StVA
WHEREAS Alexander 23Sep89 leased to Robert Fulton a parcel E of Ffx and N of Gibbons (part of a lot numbered 37 in the plan of the 1784 addition made by the exxrs of John Alexander):
BEGIN on Ffx 20' from NW corner LOT 37 ... S w/Ffx 44' to a 10' alley ... E w/alley 123' 5"... N//Ffx 44'...thence to BEGIN;
--Fulton paying each 01Nov £9.2.9 Virginia currency.
NOW for $1 (one dollar) the Fultons convey to Keech a parcel:
BEGIN on Ffx at N line of the alley ... E w/alley 103'... N//Ffx 24'... W//alley and Gibbons 103' to Ffx ... thence to BEGIN, Keech to pay beginning 01Nov95 £5.10.0 Virginia currency per annum to William Thornton Alexander;
--Fulton will lay off an alley 4' 5" wide //Ffx from the end of this parcel at the 10' alley, along the parcel's E line for the length of that line.
[Mary Ann Fulton signs w/mark.]
Executed for Alexander by his attorney John Taliaferro, Junr.
WTT: John Wise, Edmund J. Lee, Charles Harper
CMN: John Dundas, Abraham Faw, Francis Peyton, **Gentlemen** of TwnALX, aptd 18Apr96 to examine Mary Ann. Rptd back same day.

375 25Jan95 Bill of Sale
Fm Jesse Taylor, TwnALX, StVA
To Benjamin Shreve & James Lawrason -do-:
For £50 cmv, the negro boy slave George Harle, for a term of six years from this date. To be manumitted thereafter.
WTT: Gerrard Briscoe, Peter Wise, Henry S. Earl
[Clerk's note: "Delivered to George Harle."]

376 15Apr95 Bill of Sale
Fm Henry Bayne, TwnALX, StVA
To Daniel Moxley -do-:
For £84 cmv, Negro boy Benjamin for a term of seven years from this date. Thereafter to be manumitted.
WTT: Ja. Keith, Junr; J. Gilpin, James Lawrason
[Clerk's note: "Delivered to Negro Ben."]

378 08Jun96
Fm Stephen & Catharine Cooke, TwnALX, FfxCo, StVA
To William Cash Junior -do-:for £60 cmv parcel W of Washington, S of Prince:
BEGIN on Wn 48' 7" S of Prince ... S w/Wn 22'... W//Prince 60'... N//Wn 22'... thence to BEGIN.
WTT: William Bowrie, Daniel Bishop, Simon Thomas
CMN: Francis Peyton, James Irvin, John Dundas, **Gentlemen** of Corporation of ALX, aptd 09Jun96 to examine Catharine. Rptd back same day.

382 21Jul95
Fm Benjamin & Susanna Shreve, TwnALX, FfxCo, StVA
To James Lawrason -do- : parcel S of Duke, W of St Asaph:
BEGIN on Duke 100' W of St A ... W w/Duke 20'... S//St A 88' 3 1/2" "to equal the length of the line of...James Lawrason upon [St A] where the division Line between the Ground of... Shreve and...Lawrason commences"...E//Duke 20'... thence to BEGIN--part of a 1/2-acre lot conveyed by exxrs of John Alexander to Thomas Wilkinson, by Wilkinson to Shreve and Lawrason, and by them partitioned
--this being a part of Shreve's portion of their partitioned property;
--Shreve to lay off a 6' 10" alley along the W line of this parcel from Duke the full length of the line.
WTT: Wm. Summers, Ja. Keith Junior, John Reynolds, John Janney

386 01Aug95
Fm Elisha Cullen Dick & wife Hannah, TwnALX, FfxCo, CwlVA
To David Davey -do-
WHEREAS William Thornton Alexander & wife Lucy 25Dec94 leased to Dick 2 acres of land in FfxCo adjacent to ALX:
BEGIN at int King-Columbus, S side King, W side Columbus ... W w/King to Alfred ... S w/Alfred to Prince ... E w/Prince to Columbus ... thence to BEGIN.
NOW the Dicks lease to Davey a parcel within the 2 acres, numbered 9 in their plan:
BEGIN at int King-Alfred ... S on E side of Alfred 100'... E//King 60'... N//Alfred 100'... thence to BEGIN, Davey to pay beginning 01Jul96 $30 per annum;
--Davey to build on/before 01Jan98 a 2-storey brick house not less than 15' wide and 20' long "upon some part of the said premises";
--neither Davey nor anyone else to "make any framed Building on any front belonging to the said...premises."
[David Davey signs w/mark.]
WTT: John Watson, Thomas Triplett
CMN: Abram [sic] Faw, Alexander Smith, Francis Peyton, **Gentlemen** of [blank], aptd 20Jul96 to examine Hannah. Rptd back 22Jul96.

391 15Jul93
Fm Thomas Cunningham, Jefferson Co, District of Kentucky
To Phillip Marsteller, TwnALX, FfxCo, StVA
WHEREAS 01 Oct84 Cunnigham and James Adams (also of Jefferson Co) gave George Hunter [no ID] their note for £550.12.0 cmv due six months later;
--Cunningham, considering the distance between them and Hunter, gave to Hunter 7 survey plats made by the Jefferson Co surveyor, authorizing Hunter to get the patents from the Register's Office; and
--Cunningham 01 Oct84 gave Hunter power of attorney to sell 12 months hence enough property to recover the principal plus interest due at that moment, the P/Atty being filed in the Hustings Court of Alexandria; and
--Hunter did get a patent for a survey dated 02Dec85 for 600 acres of land:
BEGIN at Hiccory & Beech at S side of the Beech Fork on the bank of the fork at the upper end of the first bottom below the mouth of Harding's Creek ... thence w/meanders of the fork N74W 80 poles ... S68W 130 poles ... S50W 50 poles ... N85W 80 poles to a Hoopash and Buckeye ... S9E 292 poles to two Walnut Trees ... N81E 320 poles to white Oak and Ash ... N9W 277 poles to BEGIN.

ALSO for a 21Mar86 survey for 400 acres:
BEGIN at 4 Hiccories and white Oak corner to Hart's Preemption ... S70E 141 poles to 2 sugar trees in Coombs's Line ... N20E w/the line 316 poles to Coombs's corner (two Hiccories) ... N 232 poles to Dogwood & Hiccorie ... S8W 65 poles to a Walnut

& White oak ... S20W 46 [poles] to a Poplar & Dogwood, corner to Hart's Preemption ... thence w/Hart's line 495 poles to BEGIN.

ALSO a 21Mar86 survey for 409 1/2 acres:
BEGIN at a Sugar Tree and blue ash corner to his 300 acre survey on the North side of Beech Fork ... thence up the Fork's meanders S15W 52 poles ... S40W 103 poles ... S13W 98 poles ... S35E 62 poles ... S80E 50 poles ... N55E 340 poles to a Poplar and Mulberry Tree standing on the side of a small hill ... N39W 108 poles to an ash & poplar in a cleft of rocks ... N88W 195 poles to BEGIN.

ALSO a 21Mar86 survey for 688 acres:
BEGIN at 3 Gum trees near 2 miles from mouth of Hardin's Creek on N side of the Beech-Fork on the side of a small ridge ... W 470 poles to two black oaks in a small glade on N side of Bear Creek ... S 234 1/4 poles to a Mulberry & Sugar tree ... E 470 poles to 3 sugar trees on E side of a small Branch emptying into the Beech Fork below the mouth of Hardin's Creek ... N 234 1/4 poles to BEGIN.

ALSO a 21Mar86 survey for 200 acres lying upon Murray's Run--a Branch of Cox's Creek--adjoining the lands of George Hart, William Combs and Osburn Sprigg:
BEGIN at a Poplar & Dogwood ... N20E 47 poles to a Walnut and White Oak ... S78E 65 poles to a Hiccorie & Dogwood in Combs's Line ... thence w/his line N 115 poles to a Poplar in Sprigg's line ... thence w/Sprigg's Line N82W 184 poles to 2 white Oaks ... S34W 164 poles to a white oak & Honey Locust in George Hart's Line ... thence w/Hart's line S70E 172 poles to BEGIN.

ALSO a 09Jun86 survey for 288 acres:
BEGIN at a Hiccorie & Sugar trees on N side of Beech Fork at mouth of Bear Creek ... thence up meanders of the Fork S13W 189 poles ... S75E 58 poles ... S65E 80 poles ... S46E 50 poles to a Sugar & a blue ash tree ... N89E 60 poles to a Cedar & a white Oak ... N5 1/2 W 270 poles to a Walnut & blue ash tree on Bear Creek ... S89W [blank] poles to BEGIN.

ALSO a 09Jun86 survey for 700 acres "upon Mill Creek Waters of [Clerk has overwritten: Back or Beech] Fork:
BEGIN at NE corner of Isaac Davis's 500 acre survey ... N15E 194 poles to a sugar tree, white oak & Dogwood ... S75E 579 poles to a Sugar & 2 Dogwoods in a Briar Patch ... S15W 194 poles to a Mulberry, White Oak & Elm ... N75W 579 poles to BEGIN.

WHEREAS neither Cunningham nor Adams have paid any part of the note; on 10 Oct89 at the Vendue Store in ALX the Vendue Masters --Thompson & Peyton--put all the above land up for sale by public auction, by the hundred acre increment, first having advertised 2 successive weeks in the <u>Alexandria Gazette</u>;
--Philip Marsteller was high bidder at £5.6.0 per 100 acres

NOW Thomas Cunningham, for £165.1.9 from Marsteller, conveys to Marsteller all the above land.
Executed for Cunningham by his attorney, George Hunter.
WTT: Jonathan Swift, John Taylor, James Kerr

399   26Sep95
Fm Walter Pomery, Junior, & wife Elizabeth, TwnALX, FfxCo, StVA
   AND Jonah Isabel   -do-

To William Mendenhall -do-: For £110 cmv, a parcel W of St Asaph, N of Prince: BEGIN on St A 100' 7" N of Prince ... S w/St A 23' 1"... W//Prince 35'... S//St A 7'... W//Prince 25'... N//St A 30' 1"... thence to BEGIN--part LOT 178, conveyed by exxrs of John Alexander to Oliver Price 05Aug79 for an annual rent;
--rent remitted by William Paton and John Butcher, in whom the rent was vested 17Sep95.
WTT: Wm. Hepburn, Lawrence Hoof, Cha. McKnight, George Darling

402 13Jun96
Fm Joseph & Mary Saul, City of Philadelphia, StPA
To William Mendenhall, TwnALX, FfxCo, StVA: for £90 cmv, a parcel N of Prince, W of St Asaph:
BEGIN on Prince 35' W of St A ... W w/Prince 25'... N//St A 70' 6"... E//Prince 25'... thence to BEGIN--conveyed to Saul by the Prices, Patons and Butchers 17Sep95.
WTT: William A. Harper, Joshua Jacobs, A. Faw
CMN: Abraham Faw, John Dundas, James Irvin, **Gentlemen** of TwnALX, aptd 13Jun96 to examine Mary Saul. Rptd same day.

406 21Jul96
Fm Abraham & Mary Anne Faw, TwnALX, StVA
To David Davey, TwnALX, **Merchant**: parcel SW corner King-St A.
BEGIN 90' from King on W line of the whole lot, the line dividing the lot from Stephen Cooke's lot ... S w/division line 20'... E//King 20'... N//St Asaph 20'... W//King 20' to BEGIN--Davey to pay beginning 01Nov96 $10 per annum.
[Davey signs w/mark.]
WTT: Jona. Faw, Abel Blakeny, Samuel Cooper
CMN: John Dundas, James Irvin, Francis Peyton aptd 20Jul96 [N.B. this is the day before the deed] to examine Maryann [sic] Faw. Reported back 21Jul96.

410 30 Oct 95
Fm David Davey, TwnALX, FfxCo, CwlVA
To Abraham Faw   -do-
WHEREAS 01Aug95 Elisha Cullen Dick & wife Hannah leased to David Davey a parcel in FfxCo, adjacent to ALX:
BEGIN at int King-Alfred ... S on E side Alfred 100'... E//King 60'... N//Alfred 100' to King ... thence to BEGIN.
NOW David Davey & wife Mary lease to Faw all the above parcel:
--Faw to pay E.C. Dick beginning 01Jul96 annual rent of $30;
--Faw to build on/before 01Jan98 a 2-storey brick house at least 15' wide and 20' long.
[Both David & Mary Davey sign w/marks.]
WTT: James Kennedy, Henry F. Lowe, Thomas Peake
CMN: John Dundas, James Irvin, Francis Peyton, **Gentlemen** of [blank], aptd 20Jul96 to examine Mary. Reported back 21Jul96.

416 16May96
Fm Oliver & Jane Price, TwnALX, FfxCo, StVA
To John Limrick -do-
WHEREAS Richard & Eleanor Arell 16Jun73 conveyed to Angel Hart Couter part LOT 48 W of Ffx, N of King:
BEGIN on Ffx 120' N of SE corner LOT 48 or to N of King and on the North line of the parcel granted by Richard Arell to William McCleary and John Allison ... N w/Ffx 30'... W//King 60'... S//Ffx 30' to the line or corner of McCleary & Allison ... E w/their line 60' to BEGIN, Couter paying Arell each 01 Oct $25;

--Couter and his wife Catharine 27 Oct79 conveying the property to Christian Langmarch, still subject to the annual $25 to Arell;
--Langmarch, by his last will and testament devising the property to Oliver Price; NOW for £350 cmv the Prices convey it to John Limrick, Limrick to continue the annual $25 to the Arells. WTT: Elisha C. Dick, Philip G. Marsteller, Ellis Price

420 22Jun96 Deed of Trust
Fm Elisha Cullen Dick & wife Hannah, TwnALX, FfxCo, StVA
To William Hartshorne, FfxCo, StVA
WHEREAS Dick owes Elizabeth Donaldson £455 cmv by a note of [blank] [blank] 1796, "negotiable at the Bank of Alexandria," and due 28 Oct96; and
ALSO £1111.10.0 cmv to Elizabeth Donaldson to be paid £555.15 on/before 27 Apr97 AND £555.15 on/before 27 Oct97;
NOW to secure payment of these sums, the Dicks deed in trust:
a parcel, part of LOT 84, S of Duke, W of Royal, E of Pitt:
BEGIN on Duke 115' 3" W of Royal on E line of 10' alley ... E w/Duke 115' 3" to Royal ... S w/Royal 177' 1" (half the Square formed by Duke-Wolfe) ... W//Duke-Wolfe 255' 3" to Pitt ... N w/Pitt 57' 1 1/2" to an 18' alley ... E w/alley //Duke 140' to E line of the 10' alley ... thence w/alley //Royal-Pitt 120' to BEGIN, conveyed by Elizabeth Donaldson to Dick the day before this.
WTT: Jonah Thompson, Francis Peyton, Jas. M. McCrea
CMN: Jonah Thompson, Francis Peyton, James Irvin, **Gentlemen** of the Corporation of ALX, aptd 16May96 to examine Hannah. Reported back same day.

426 16May96
Fm Elizabeth Donaldson, late Elizabeth Muir, sister & devisee of John Muir, TwnALX, deceased
To John Janney. TwnALX, FfxCo, StVA: for £700 cmv, a parcel N of King, E of Royal Streets:
BEGIN on King at W line of 21' alley, 109' 5" E of Royal ... W w/King 35'... N//Royal 95' to 5' alley ... E w/alley //King 35' to the 21' alley ... S w/alley //Royal 95' to BEGIN.
--part of LOT [blank] conveyed by ALX Trustees to Benjamin Sebastian, and by various conveyances eventually to John Muir, who willed it to his sister Elizabeth Donaldson;
--Elizabeth will lay off a 5' alley beginning at the 21' alley 95' from King and running //King the length of this parcel's N line, for the common use of the Janneys and Elizabeth.
Executed for Elizabeth by her atty Wm. Hartshorne as per her Power of Attorney letter of 18Apr96. WTT: Ja. Keith

430 16Apr96 Power of Attorney
Fm John Taliaferro, Jr., King George Co, StVA
To James Keith, TwnALX, StVA
For/on behalf of William Thornton Alexander to recover rents in arrears due from property conveyed by exxrs of John Alexander to Tobias Zimmerman--£20.18.0 due each 05Aug--payable to John Alexander's son and heir, Wm.T. Alexander.
(Taliaferro is William Thornton Alexander's lawyer.)
WTT: John Gill, Jesse Simms, John Wise

431 20Jul96
Fm John Simpson, FfxCo, StVA
To Thomas Richards, TwnALX, FfxCo, StVA
WHEREAS Elisha & Hannah Dick 01Aug95 leased to Simpson a parcel S of King, E of Alfred, contiguous to TwnALX:

BEGIN on King 60' E of Alfred ... S//Alfred 100'... E//King 31' 8 1/2"... N//Alfred 100'... thence to BEGIN, Simpson paying Dick each 01Jul $15.83;
--Simpson to erect on some part of the parcel before 01Jan98 a brick house not less than 15' wide, 20' long;
--no one to erect any frame dwellings fronting on the street;
--and all the property, rents and covenants since assigned by Dick to Francis Peyton; NOW for £6 cmv Simpson conveys all the parcel to Richards, with Richards now responsible to Peyton for the rent and for satisfying the covenants.
WTT: Jno. Stewart, Junr; Joseph Fullmer, Hiram Chapin

436 06May95   Tripartite Deed
I-Robert & Mary Anne Fulton, TwnALX, FfxCo, StVA
II-William Thornton Alexander, King George Co, StVA
III-Charles Harper, TwnALX, FfxCo, StVA
WHEREAS Alexander 23Sep89 conveyed to Fulton parcel E of Ffx, N of Gibbons, part of a Lot in an addition made by the exxrs of John Alexander in 1784, in the addition plan LOT No. 37:
BEGIN on Ffx 20' S of NW corner LOT 37 ... S w/Ffx 44' to 10' alley ... E w/alley 123' 5"... N//Ffx 44'... thence to BEGIN, Fulton paying Alexander each 01Nov £9.2.9 Virginia currency;
NOW for £100 cmv, the Fultons convey part to Harper:
BEGIN on Ffx 44' N of N line of the alley ... N w/Ffx 20'... E//Gibbons 103'... S//Ffx 20'... thence to BEGIN, Harper to pay William Thornton Alexander each 01Nov £3.12.9 cmv;
--Fulton will lay out an alley 4' 5" wide //Ffx from this parcel's N line south to the 10' alley.   [Executed for Alexander by his atty, John Taliaferro, Junr.]
WTT: John Wise, Edmund J. Lee, Samuel Keech
CMN: John Dundas, Abraham Faw, Francis Peyton, **Gentlemen** of TwnALX, aptd 16Apr95 to examine Mary Anne. Rptd back 18Apr96.

443 21Jun96
Fm Elizabeth Donaldson, the former Elizabeth Muir, sister and devisee of John Muir, TwnALX, deceased
To Elisha Cullen Dick, TwnALX, FfxCo, StVA
WHEREAS Elizabeth gave power of attorney to William Hartshorne 18Apr96 to dispose of real estate:
NOW for £2169 cmv, she conveys to Dick a parcel S of Duke, W of Royal, E of Pitt:
BEGIN on Duke 115' 3" W of Royal, on E line of 10' alley ... E w/Duke 115' 3" to Royal ... S w/Royal 177' 1" (half the Square in Duke-Wolfe) ... thence //Duke-Wolfe 255' 3" to Pitt ... N w/Pitt 57' 1 1/2" to an 18' alley ... E w/alley //Duke to E side of the 10' alley--about 140'... N w/alley //Royal-Pitt 120' to BEGIN, on Duke;
--parts of the lots or half-acre parcels numbered 84 and [blank] conveyed by the ALX Trustees to John Muir 18Jul58 and [blank] day of [blank] 176[blank], and willed to Elizabeth by her brother John Muir;
--Elizabeth to lay off a 10' alley from Duke, 115' 3" W of Royal, running 120' to the south;
--and a second alley, 18' wide, from Pitt 102' S of Duke and running eastward //Duke 130' to W line of the 10' alley.
Executed for Elizabeth by her atty, William Hartshorne.
WTT: Jonah Thompson, Francis Peyton, Jas. McCrea

448 08 Oct95   Tripartite Deed
I-George & Ann Coryell, TwnALX, FfxCo, StVA
II-William Thornton Alexander, King George Co, StVA

III-Leonard Doucher, TwnALX, FfxCo, StVA
WHEREAS William Thornton Alexander & wife Lucy 26Dec94 leased to the Coryells a parcel contiguous to ALX, N of Duke extended, W of Columbus, E of Alfred:
BEGIN at int Duke-Columbus... W w/Duke 246' 10" to Alfred ... N w/Alfred 178' 4" (half the Duke-Prince Square)... E//Duke 246' 10" to Columbus ... thence to BEGIN, Coryell to pay each 01Jul £12 cmv;
NOW the Coryells lease to Doucher a part of their parcel:
BEGIN on Alfred 18' S of center of Duke-Prince Square (160' 4" N of Duke) ... S w/Alfred 18'... E//Duke 100' to an "Alley or Court" 46' 10" wide ... N w/alley-court //Alfred 18'... thence to BEGIN, Doucher to pay Coryell beginning 01Jul96 £3.12.0 cmv per annum;
--Coryell will lay off a 14' 4" alley from Columbus 88' N of Duke, running //Duke, west 246' 10" to Alfred, and
--also another, 46' 10" wide, from the N side of the 1st alley--100' E of Alfred and 100' from Columbus--to run N and parallel to Columbus-Alfred 76' to the center of the Duke-Prince Square.
[Executed for Alexander by his atty, John Taliaferro, Junr.]
[Leonard Doucher signs w/mark.]
WTT: Ja. Keith, Bernard Bryan, Wm. Wright

454   08 Oct95   Tripartite Deed
I-George & Ann Coryell, TwnALX, FfxCo, StVA
II-William Thornton Alexander, King George Co, StVA
III-Ignatius Crawford, TwnALX, FfxCo, StVA
WHEREAS [text relates the history, metes, bounds, as at p.448, of which the Coryells are leasing a part to Crawford]:
BEGIN on Alfred at centre of Duke-Prince Square (178' 4" N of Duke) ... S w/Alfred 18'... E//Duke 100' to "Alley or Court" 46' 10" wide ... N w/alley-court //Alfred 18'... thence to BEGIN, Crawford to pay from 01Jul96 £3.12.0 cmv per annum.
--Coryell to lay out the two spaces--the 14' 4" alley and the 46' 10" alley/court--as for Doucher, above at p. 448.
[Executed for Alexander by his atty, John Taliaferro, Junr.]
WTT: as above

459   01Sep95   Tripartite Deed
I-George & Ann Coryell, TwnALX, FfxCo, StVA
II-William Thornton Alexander, King George Co, StVA
III- William Cash, Jr., TwnALX, FfxCo, StVA
WHEREAS [same text as above, pp. 448, 454.]
NOW the Coryells lease to Cash a parcel:
BEGIN on Duke 60' W of Columbus ... W w/Duke 20'... N//Columbus 80' to 14' 4" alley ... E w/alley //Duke 20'... thence to BEGIN, Cash to pay from 01Jul96 £2.5.0 per annum;
--Coryell to lay out the 14' 4" alley as described in the leases to Doucher and Crawford, above.
W.T. Alexander is signed for by his atty, John Taliaferro, Jr.
WTT: as above

465   01Sep95   Tripartite Deed
All three parties as above, p. 459. Reciting the same preamble, the Coryells lease Cash another parcel:

BEGIN on Duke 80' W of Columbus ... W w/Duke 20'... N//Columbus 88' to 14' 4"
alley ... E w/alley //Duke 20'... thence to BEGIN, Cash to pay fm 01Jul96 £2.10.0 cmv
per annum
--Coryell commits to laying our the 14' 4" alley as in the Doucher-Crawford-Cash
leases, above. [Executed for Alexander by his atty, John Taliaferro, Junr.]
WTT: Ja. Keith, Bernard Bryan, Wm. Wright

470 22Feb96
Fm Peter Caverly, guardian of Richard Arell--son and devisee of David Arell of
TwnALX, deceased
To James Grimes, TwnALX, FfxCo, StVA
WHEREAS Peter by his power of attorney has authorized David's mother--Phebe
Arell--to handle Richard Arell's estate,
NOW Peter Caverly leases to Grimes a "parcel of ground with the buildings &
improvements thereupon" E of Ffx, N of Wilkes:
BEGIN on Ffx 88' 3 1/2" N of Wilkes ... N w/Ffx 22'... E//Wilkes 98' 5"... S//Ffx 22'...
thence to BEGIN.
--conveyed by David Arell in his lifetime to George Mason;
--sold by Mason to William Bromley with an annual rent payable to David Arell; on
non-payment of rent by Bromley, Peter Caverly (on behalf of Phebe) re-entered and
seized the property which he now conveys to Grimes;
--Grimes leases from this 19Feb for 14 years, paying each 18Feb £8.10.0 cmv.
WTT: Daniel Minor, Thomas Davis, James Middleton

473 13Feb96
Fm John & Susannah Rawlins [no ID]
To Peter Pile [no ID]: a lease of part of Lot contiguous [in 1784] to ALX, the Lot
numbered No. 2 in the 1784 plan:
BEGIN SW corner LOT 2 ... N w/Washington 20'... E//King 123'... S//Wn 20'... thence
to BEGIN, Pile to pay from 01Jun93 [yes:1793] £6 Virginia currency per annum to
Stephen Cooke "the original conveyer to the said Rawlins."
WTT: Henry Walker, Jacob Resler, Andrew Reintzel
CMN: Abraham Faw, Francis Peyton, James Irvin, **Gentlemen** of TwnALX, aptd
15Aug96 to examine Susannah. Rptd back same day.

477 14Sep96
Fm William Summers & wife Isabella--the former Isabella Elton, widow of John
Elton of ALX, deceased
To Joseph Cary, TwnALX, FfxCo, StVA: lease parcel [one of several of John Elton,
the text notes] N of Wolfe, E of Ffx:
BEGIN on Wolfe 103' 5" E of Ffx ... E w/Wolfe 20'... N//Ffx 100' to 10' alley ... W
w/alley //Wolfe 20'...thence to BEGIN. --the term is for the rest of Isabella's life,
Carey to pay 20 silver $ each 31Dec. WTT: none
MEMO: the parties to the above later [no date] agree the rent is to be paid each 13th
September.
CMN: Francis Peyton, John Dundas, James Irvin, Alexander Smith, **Gentlemen** of
[blank], aptd 19Sep96 to examine Isabella. Reported back 23Sep96.

482 02Aug96
Fm William & Sarah Herbert, TwnALX, FfxCo, StVA
To Lanty Crowe: parcel W of Ffx, N of Cameron:
BEGIN on Ffx 141' 1" N of Cameron ... N w/Ffx 35' 6" to center of the Queen-
Cameron Square ... W//Cameron-Queen 123' 5" to center of the Ffx-Royal Square ...
S//Ffx-Royal [35' 6"] ... thence to BEGIN, Crowe to pay beginning 01Aug97 £30 cmv
in specie, per annum;

--conveyed to Herbert by Robert Adam 29Jul83;
--rent remittable any time w/in 15 years by paying £500 cmv in specie; or, rent reducable proportionately with payments of not less than £50.   WTT: Francis Peyton
CMN: John Dundas, James Irvin, Francis Peyton, **Gentlemen** of Corporation of ALX, aptd 01Sep96 to examine Sarah. Reported back 23Sep96.

487   17Jun96
Fm George & Elizabeth McMunn, TwnALX, FfxCo, StVA
To Jonathan Pancas -do-: lease parcel S of Prince, W of Royal:
BEGIN on Prince 39' W of Royal, at George Spangler's line ... E w/Prince 17'... S//Royal 78'... W//Prince 17' to Spangler's line ... N w/line to BEGIN, Pancas to pay beginning 01May97 50 silver $ per annum;
--part of parcel conveyed by John & Jane Fitzgerald 01May95 to George McMunn;
--McMunn will lay off a 4' alley beginning on Royal 74' S of Prince, parallel w/Prince, to E line of this parcel;
--Pancas may "lay off the Gavel [end] Wall of any House" he builds on the premises 4 1/2" on McMunn's land, the wall to be a common partition wall. Should McMunn later build against this wall, he will pay half its cost. [See entry following.]
["Pancas" signs his name **Pancoast**, and the clerk's entry noting this deed recorded also refers to him as **Pancoast**.]
WTT: Isaac Sittler [or Littler], John Lemoine, Henry Polkinhorn, Robert McMunn

491   17Jun96   Articles of Agreement
George Spangler and Jonathan Pancas, TwnALX, StVA
[The text refers to the deed above, p. 487.]
--Pancas intends to build a brick house;
--Spangler says Pancas may come 4 1/2" onto Spangler's land to build the "Gavel wall;"
--this will be a common partition wall, should Spangler later build. In that event, Spangler will reimburse Pancas by half.
[As above, "Pancas" signs his own name **Pancoast**, but this time the clerk's note names him Pancas.]

493   24Aug96
Fm Andrew & Margaret Wales, TwnALX, FfxCo, StVA
To Jesse Simms   -do- : for £600 cmv, a parcel E of Union, N of Prince;
BEGIN on Union on N line of parcel conveyed by the Wales to McCrea & Mease-- and now in possession of Jesse Simms--132' 5 1/4" N of Prince ... N w/Union 38' 1 3/4" to 12' alley ... E w/alley //King into the R
River Potomack ... S//Union 38' 1 3/4"... thence to BEGIN.
--"part of the ground and wharf made and extended by...Andrew Wales into the River Potomack from that piece of Ground...conveyed unto him by Robert Adam saving...-unto... Wales...the right and privilege at his...expense of extending the trunks communicating with the River Potomack and the Brew House of the said Andrew Wales, whatever distance the said Jesse Simms...may at any future day extend the wharf hereby granted into the River"
--Simms will not intentionally stop up the Trunk, the "communication" from the Brew House to the River. [See below, p. 499]
WTT: Abraham Faw, Alexander Smith, Tho. Crandall
CMN: Abraham Faw, Alexander Smith, Jonah Thompson, **Gentlemen** of TwnALX, aptd 24Aug96 to examine Margaret. Rptd 25Aug96.

499   09Sep96
Fm Jesse Simms, TwnALX, FfxCo, StVA

To John Crips Vowell AND Thomas Vowell Junr of -do-:
For £700 Simms sells to the Vowells the same parcel he bought from Wales 24Aug96 [see above, p. 493.] The Vowells agree to the stipulations and covenants of the Wales-Simms conveyance.
WTT: B. Dade, Washer Blunt, Alexr. MacKenzie

502 02Auug96 Power of Attorney
Fm John Allison, late of TwnALX, CwlVA, now of Wilkes Co, StGA
To "my friends Robert Allison of Alexandria, **Merchant**, and Robert McCrea of Wilkes Co, Georgia
For selling a parcel in ALX, part of LOTS 14 & 8, purchased from Mr. Thomas West by John Allison & William Hunter (deceased) as tenants in common:
South Bounds--by the part of LOT 14 "purchased and possessed by Messrs. Hepburn & Dundas";
--North Bounds--land of Jesse Taylor;
--West Bounds--"by Water Street and extending from thence eastward and crossing Union Street into the River Potomack including the wharf made and extended into the River by the said Hunter and Allison";
--"Having a front on Water Street, and Union Street of one hundred and five feet nearly"
WTT: Garland Wingfield Panacott, Wilkes County Sct [sic]
ATTESTED: by Edward Butler, **Judge** of Inferior Court of Wilkes Co.; and Butler's entry by Edwin Mounger, **Clerk** of that court.

504 15May95
Fm William Hodgson, TwnALX, FfxCo, CwlVA
To John Fitzgerald -do-: for £36 cmv parcel, part of piece "lately conveyed by Valentine Peers to...Hodgson," both part of a 1/2-acre Lot numbered [blank] on S side of King St:
BEGIN S of King adjoining a parcel let by Fitzgerald to William Anderson "on which a brick house now stands"... E w/King 4'... thence //Ffx 82' to a 12' alley ... W//King 4'... thence to BEGIN.
WTT: Geo. Clementson, B. Rawlings, John Ritchie, Vincent Gray

506 10May96
Fm Philip Godhelp Marsteller & wife Christiana, TwnALX, FfxCo, StVA
To Alexander McKenzie -do-: for £44 cmv parcel S of Prince, E of Water Streets:
BEGIN on line dividing property lately George Gilpin's from that of the heirs of Jonathan Hall--44' 4" S of Prince and at a point on the line 130' E of Water St ... E w/line //Prince 20'... S//Water St 22' 2" to the line of Faulkner who married one of Jonathan Hall's daughters ... W w/Faulkner's line //Prince 20'... thence to BEGIN.
--part of the ground sold to Marsteller by George Gilpin.
WTT: Jonah Thompson, Jas. Keith, Leml. Bent, A. Faw
CMN: Jonah Thompson, Francis Peyton, Abraham Faw, **Gentlemen** of TwnALX, aptd 19May96 to examine Christiana. Rptd back 24May96.

510 13May96
Fm Philip Godhelp Marsteller & Christiana, TwnALX, FfxCo, StVA
To Elisha Janney AND George Irish, -do-: for £96.16.0 cmv a parcel S of Prince, E of Water Streets:
BEGIN on the line dividing property formerly that of Gilpin, and Hall's heirs' [as above, p.506] 44' 4" S of Prince and on that line 86' E of Water St ... E w/line 44' to the line of parcel sold by the Marstellers to Andrew McKenzie [above] ... S w/that line

// Water St 22' 2" to Faulkner's line [see above] ... W w/Faulkner //Prince 44'... thence to BEGIN.
--part of ground sold to the Marstellers by George Gilpin;
--the Marstellers will lay off a 4' alley from the ex-Gilpin ground "and immediately joining the Alley laid off by him and Robert Hamelton [sic] from Prince St to that line, to the line of...Faulkner."
WTT: Jonah Thompson, Jas. Keith, Lemuel Bent, A. Faw
CMN: Jonah Thompson, Francis Peyton, Abraham Faw, **Gentlemen** of the Corporation of ALX, aptd 19May96 to examine Christiana.
Reported back 24 [blank] 1796.

End of Book G

ALEXANDRIA HUSTINGS COURT

Deed Book H   1795-1797

1 27Aug96
Fm Lemuel & Betsey Bent, TwnALX, FfxCo, StVA
To Thomas Patten -do-
WHEREAS Robert & Ann Adam 24May85 leased to Robert Evans a parcel on W side of an alley "which falls into Princess Street upon the South side" and in center of Square of Water & Union:
BEGIN on W side of the alley, 94' S of Princess ... W//Princess 52'... S//Water St 23 1/2' to Richard Conway's line ... E w/Conway's line //Princess 52' to the alley ... thence w/alley 23 1/2'to BEGIN, paying £14.2.0 cmv each 25Dec;
--and 01Mar94 Robert & Drusilla Evans AND Thomas & Betty White conveyed the parcel to Lemuel Bent;
NOW for £30 cmv the Bents convey it to Thomas Patten, Patten to pay the Adam family the £14.2.0 each 25Dec.
WTT: K. Hurst, John Callemloy, Alexr. Smith
CMN: Alexander Smith, Abraham Faw, Francis Peyton, Alexander
Gentlemen of TwnALX, aptd 15Sep96 to examine Betsey. Rptd back 16Sep96.

6 04May96
Fm Morris & Elizabeth Worrell--late Elizabeth Sewell, widow of William Sewell, deceased--TwnALX, FfxCo, StVA
To Dennis Ramsay, Robert Allison AND Michael Madden--surviving exxrs of William Ramsay "the elder", all TwnALX, FfxCo, StVA
WHEREAS William Sewell owned LOT 61, N of Prince and W of Royal, and mortaged it to secure a debt, dying w/o satisfying the indebtedness;
--his creditors then sued in Chancery in FfxCo Court, the court ruling the lot be sold to pay the debts; but
--the court excepted, as Elizabeth Sewell's dower right, one parcel of the property for the rest of her life:
BEGIN on Royal 19' S of NE corner of LOT 61 ... W//Prince 83' 5"... S//Royal 157' 6" to Prince ... E w/Prince 34' 5"... N//Royal 133' 6"... E//Prince 49' to Royal ...thence to BEGIN.
--FfxCo Sheriff Thomas Pollard auctioned the lot, minus her parcel; William Ramsay the Elder being high bidder, Pollard conveyed the lot to him 20May82.

NOW for $1 the Worrells convey title to the surviving Ramsay exxrs of part of Elizabeth's dower parcel:
BEGIN on Prince 49' W of Royal ... thence w/E line of the dower parcel 127' 6" "ending six feet short of or to the Southward of the Dwelling House of...Morris...and Elizabeth" ... thence W parallel to the "broad side of the said House" 34' 5" to the parcel's W line ... thence w/W line S to Prince ... thence w/Prince 34' 5" to BEGIN.
WTT: Andrew Reintzell, James Balfour, Samuel Simmons [Simmons signs w/mark, a reversed "3"] See also following entry.

9 04May96 Articles of Agreement
Ramsay, Allison and Madden--surviving exxrs of William Ramsay [see p. 6, above] post bond for £300 cmv to Morris & Elizabeth Worrell, stating:
--Elizabeth's dower right parcel lies on the W of Royal and N of Prince, both streets having been directed to be paved, by authority of the ALX Mayor and Commonalty. Likewise the Mayor and Commonalty directed that the ground adjoining the streets be raised enough to carry water run-off into the streets;
--the Worrell parcel's ground level "requiring to be raised considerably," the parties disputed at whose cost it should be done, as well as who was to pay a proportionate share of the paving;
--the Worrells now having conveyed part of their parcel to the Ramsay exxrs, the exxrs now take responsibility for all the Worrells' LOT 61 land: to raise the sunken parts, and to pave the streets and footways fronting on those parts;
--the £300 bond is void if the exxrs make good on their land fill and paving commitments. WTT: as above

11 16Sep95
Fm William Thornton Alexander & wife Lucy, King Geo. Co, StVA
To Jacob Cox, TwnALX, FfxCo, StVA
WHEREAS 19Dec74 John Alexander conveyed to Cox a 1/2-acre lot then contiguous to ALX, adjoining S side of 1/2-acre LOT 96:
BEGIN at SE corner LOT 96 ... W w/lot to SW corner LOT 96 ... S at right angles 176' 7"... E//first line for same distance ... thence to BEGIN, Cox paying each 19Dec £10.10.0 cmv, this rent devised by John Alexander in his will to Wm.T. Alexander;
NOW in return for a conveyance of this same date by which Cox assigns to William Thornton Alexander the annual $41 1/2 Cox receives from William Wright, Alexander remits Cox's £10.10.0
[Alexander atty John Taliaferro Junr executes this for them.]
WTT: John Wise, Ch. Simms, Ja. Keith

13 17Jun96
Fm Elizabeth Donaldson [no ID]
To William McKnight AND Charles McKnight [no ID]
WHEREAS the ALX Trustees conveyed to Benjamin Sebastian (now deceased) the 1/2-acre LOT 49 on N side King, E side Royal Sts:
--and on 22Mar65 he conveyed it to his son, Benjamin, excepting a parcel "fifty feet one way and forty-two feet another way" and
--both men and their wives 22Feb68 conveyed all their interest in the lot to John Muir, who by his will dated [blank] December 1789 conveyed it to his sister, Elizabeth Muir;
--John died, and after his death Elizabeth married Robert Donaldson, who has also since died;
--Elizabeth 18Apr96 gave power of attorney to William Hartshorne to sell all her Alexandria and Virginia real estate;

NOW Elizabeth for £701 cmv paid to Hartshorne by the two McKnights conveys two parts LOT 49 as follows:
I: BEGIN on E side Royal at line dividing LOT 49 from the "Court House Square"... E w/that line //King 111' to a 21' alley ... S w/alley 25' 7" to a line by William Hartshorne which, in his plan of division, divides this parcel from the other ... West w/that line //King 111' to Royal ... N w/Royal 25' 7" to BEGIN;
II: BEGIN 25' 7" S of the LOT 49-Court House Square line ... E 111' to the alley ... S w/alley 25' 6"... W 111' to Royal ... thence to BEGIN.
WTT: Cleon Moore, Jonathan Mandeville, Caleb Earp, Henry Moore

16 17May96
Fm Dennis Ramsay)   (Surviving executors of
  Robert Allison)   (William Ramsay the Elder,
  Michael Madden)   (all TwnALX, FfxCo, StVA
To Joseph Cary -do-: for £182.8.0 cmv, part LOT 61, N of Prince, W of Royal Sts: BEGIN on Prince 49' W of Royal ... W w/Prince 34' 5"... N//Royal 88' to 6' alley ...E w/alley 34' 5", thence to BEGIN.
--LOT 61 sold and conveyed by FfxCo Sheriff to Wm. Ramsay the elder 20May82, subject to the dower of Elizabeth Sewell, widow of William Sewell, who has since released her right to the exxrs on [blank] May 1796 [see p. 6, above].
WTT: Jesse Wherry, George Coryell and James Jobson to DR & MM; Robert McMunn, George Painter, Isaac Sittler, Isaac Davis, James Jobson

19 29Nov85   [This is a 1785 conveyance.]
Fm Baldwin & Catharine Dade, TwnALX, FfxCo, CwlVA
To Henry Lee, Junr, **Esquire**, Westmoreland Co, CwlVA
WHEREAS the John Alexander exxrs leased to David & Samuel Arell 09 Oct80 a 1/2-acre lot contiguous to ALX:
BEGIN on E side of Water St as extended by the exxrs, South 176' 7" from int Water-Wilkes (the beginning point being SW corner of the lot granted William Hartshorne & Josiah Watson ... S w/Water St 176' 7"... E//Wilkes to River Potowmack ... thence w/"meanders of the River" to line of Hartshorne & Watson ... thence to BEGIN, the Arells paying beginning 01Nov81 1000 lbs. crop tobacco per annum;
--the conveyance was witnessed by Philip Thornton Alexander, Charles Jones and Philip Stuart. P.T. Alexander having died before the conveyance was proved (although Jones and Stuart did swear to it), the deed has not been admitted to record;
--on 03Jun85 David & Phoebe Arell, and Samuel Arell, for £750 conveyed half this lot to Baldwin Dade.
NOW the Dades for £750 from Henry Lee, convey the half lot they got from the Arells to Lee, Lee to pay half the rent the Arells must pay each 01Nov to the Alexanders.
WTT: D. Arell, Wm. Herbert, A. Skinner, Cleon Moore, William Stuart, John Fitzgerald, Benja. G. Orr
CMN: David Arell and William Herbert, **Gentlemen** of Corporation of ALX, aptd to examine Catharine. Reported back 29Nov85.

25 16Apr96
Fm Francis & Sarah Peyton, TwnALX, FfxCo, StVA
To Jonathan Mandeville -do-: lease parcel N of King St extended, E of Alfred: BEGIN on King 60' E of Alfred ... E w/King 43' 5"... N//Alfred 100' to 15' alley ... W w/alley 43' 5"... thence to BEGIN.
--part of parcel leased by William Thornton Alexander to George Gilpin for annual rent of $20, later conveyed by Gilpin to Peyton subject to the annual rent [no dates given);

--Mandeville to pay begin 15Apr97 £13.6.0 per annum to Peyton;
--Mandeville to erect w/in 9 months hence a dwelling house at least 20' long by 16' wide w/brick or stone chimney;
--Peyton to lay off 15' wide alley from Alfred, 100' N of King, to run parallel to King the length of this lot.
WTT: Daniel Macleod, Lewis Beckwith, William Follin, Liston Temple

29 28Mar96
Fm Francis & Sarah Peyton, TwnALX, FfxCo, StVA
To Daniel Macleod, TwnALX, FfxCo, StVA: lease of parcel
BEGIN N of King 123' 5" W of Columbus ... W w/King 20'... N//Columbus 100' to 15' alley ...E//King 20', thence to BEGIN.
--part of lot George Gilpin & wife conveyed [blank date] to Peyton, conveyed to Gilpin by William Thornton Alexander & wife Lucy [date blank];
--Macleod to pay beginning 28Mar97 $20 per annum to Peyton;
--Macleod to erect w/in 9 months a "Kitchen on any part of the...premises, except the front."   WTT: Liston Temple, William Follin, Jonathan Mandeville, Jeremiah Rinker

31 20Mar94
Fm Stephen & Catharine Cooke, TwnALX
To William Wright -do- : for $500, a parcel:
BEGIN on Water St 132' 5 1/4" S of Gibbon's [sic] St ... S w/Water St 44'... E//Gibbon's 123'... N//Water St 44'... thence to BEGIN.
WTT: Joseph Riddle, James Chrisheylen, Joshua Riddle, Archd. J. Taylor

33 08Apr93
Fm Stephen & Catharine Cooke, TwnALX
To William Wright -do- :
For £168.6.0 part lot contiguous to ALX, N of King, E of Wn:
BEGIN on N side King, 60' 5" E of int N side King-E side Wn... E w/ King 36'... N//Washington 90'... W//King 36'... thence to BEGIN.
WTT: Samuel Vowell, James Kennedy, James Russell

34 02Jun96
Fm Stephen & Catharine Cooke, TwnALX
To Cavan Boa, TwnALX: parcel, part of lot in ALX "known by No. 6 according to a plat of Lands demised in 1784":
BEGIN at corner formed by int S side Prince-W side Washington ... S//Wn 48' 7"... W//Prince 42' 5"... N//Wn 48' 7"... thence to BEGIN.
WTT: Jams. Butler, Henry S. Earl, Ephraim Evans

36 17Aug96
Fm Jesse Simms, TwnALX, FfxCo, CwlVA
To Richard Marshall Scott -do-
WHEREAS 20Dec84 the late William Ramsay conveyed to his daughter Amelia a parcel N of King, W of Water Sts:
BEGIN at int King-Water ... W w/King 34' 4"... N//Water St. 81' to Ramsay's Alley ... E w/alley 34' to Water St ... thence to BEGIN--but Amelia died w/o issue before she was 21, and the property thus passed to her brothers and sisters: William and Dennis; Betty Mease; Ann Allison; Hannah Madden; Sarah Porter;
--brother William "also departed this Life without Issue or making any bequest of the same" and they [the survivors] conveyed the parcel 03May96 to Jesse Simms, "they" then being: Dennis & Jane Allen Ramsay; Robert & Betty Mease; Robert & Ann Allison; Michael & Hannah Madden; Thomas & Sarah Porter;

NOW Jesse Simms for £900 cmv conveys the parcel to Scott.
WTT: Cleon Moore, J. D. Orr, Aug. J. Smith

39 03Aug96
Fm Thomas & Mary Patten, TwnALX, FfxCo, StVA
To John Crips Vowell AND Thomas Vowell junior   -do-
WHEREAS the Pattens on [blank day/blank month] 1795 leased to James Kenner parcel S of Princess, W of Washington Sts:
BEGIN at int Princess-Wn ... W w/Princess 79' 5"... S//Wn 75'... E//Princess 79' 5"... thence to BEGIN, Kenner paying from 01Jan96 £40 cmv per annum in quarterly installments; and
WHEREAS the Pattens leased to Kenner 24Apr96 another parcel:
BEGIN on Princess 103' 5" W of Wn ... E w/Princess 24'... S//Wn 75'... W//Princess 24'... thence to BEGIN, Kenner paying from 22Apr97 24 silver $ per annum;
NOW for £350 cmv the Pattens assign both rents to the Vowells.
WTT: Alexr. Smith, Abraham Faw, William Savage
CMN: Abraham Faw, Alexander Smith, Jonah Thompson, **Gentlemen** of TwnALX, aptd 03Sep96 top examine Mary. Reported same day.

44 08Jun96
Fm Thomas & Anstis Rogerson, TwnALX, FfxCo, StVA
    AND John Bass Dabney & wife Roxa   -do-
To Thomas Patten -do- : for £450 cmv, parcel W of Washington and S of Duke Sts:
BEGIN on Wn 132' 6" S of Duke ... S w/Wn 22'... W//Duke 92' 7"... N//Wn 54'... E//Duke 30' 10"... S//Wn 32'... E//Duke 61' 9" to BEGIN;
--part of ground conveyed 08Jun93 to Rogerson & Dabney by Aaron & Mary Hewes, and by William Cunningham.
WTT: George Gilpin, R.T. Hooe, Leml. Bent
CMN: George Gilpin, Robert T. Hooe, Wm. Herbert, Richard Conway, Gentlemen Justices of FfxCo, aptd 27Jun96 to examine both Anstis and Roxa. Reported back same day.

49 08Jun96
Fm John Bass Dabney & wife Roxa, TwnALX, FfxCo, StVA
To Thomas Patten   -do-
WHEREAS the late Thomas Fleming owned a lot on S side of Duke and the "West and East Sides of Union Street and a narrow Slip thereof extending into the River Potowmack" No. 77 in the Town Plan; and
--ALSO a piece demised to him by the Trustees for a Term of years "adjoining to a part" of LOT 77; and
--ALSO part of another lot W side of Water St and S side of Wolfe (No. 96 in the Town Plan):
BEGIN at int Water-Wolfe ... W w/Wolfe 80' to a 12' alley ... S w/alley 100'... E//-Wolfe 80' to Water St ...thence to BEGIN.
WHEREAS 16Dec83 Fleming leased to Samuel Montgomery Brown a parcel, part LOT 96, W side of Water St and S of Wolfe, Brown paying each 04Nov £34.4.0;
--with the above real estate and the rents from Brown, Fleming made his will, bequeathing the residue of his estate after taxes and debts being paid to his five daughters: Bridget Kirk; Betty, since married to Eli Valette; Catharine; Sarah; Ann; his wife Betty and his friend George Hunter as exxx/exxr;
--Betty has since died and Hunter, to satisfy Fleming debts, conveyed part LOT 77 and a part of the adjoing Trustee-demised land to Robert Townshend Hooe;

--Eli & Betty Valette 09Apr94 conveyed to John Lockwood 1/5 of both LOT 77 and
the adjacent Trustee-demised land; 1/5 of the ground W of Water and S of Wolfe Sts;
1/5 of the S.M. Brown annual payment of £34.4.0;
--John Lockwood 11Jun94 conveyed these holdings to Dabney;
NOW for £450 cmv the Dabneys convey the 3 holdings to Patten.
WTT: George Gilpin, R.T. Hooe, Leml. Bent
CMN: George Gilpin. Robert T. Hooe, Wm. Herbert, Richard Conway, **Gentlemen Justices** of Ffx Co, aptd to examine Roxa Dabney. Reported back same day.

55 23May96
Fm Alexander & Rachel Smith, TwnALX, FfxCo, StVA
To George Gilpin -do-: for £283.10.0 cmv a parcel S of King, W of Water Sts:
BEGIN on King 29' E of E line of property conveyed by John Fitzgerald to William
Anderson "upon which there is a Brick dwelling House now in the seizin of Dedrick
Sheckle"... E w/King 31' 6"... S//Water St 82' to 12 1/2' alley running from Ffx to
Water St ... W w/alley 31' 6"... thence to BEGIN.
--part of land conveyed by William Hodgson to Alexander Smith 06Jan96.
[Rachel Smith signs w/mark.]   WTT: none
CMN: Jonah Thompson, Francis Peyton, John Dundas, **Gentlemen** of TwnALX, aptd
01Jun96 to examine Rachel. Rptd back same day.

59 24Sep96   Non-Importation Compliance
John Watts swore to a certificate about slave importation [text not given] before
acting Court of Hustings **Magistrate**, John Dundas.

59 30Aug96   Non-Importation Compliance
George Collard "late of the City of Washington" took an oath about slave
importation [no details] before James Irvin, "one of the Commonwealth's **Justices**"
for the Corporation of Alexandria.

60 20Aug96   Non-Importation Compliance
Joseph R. Neale took an oath regarding slave importation in the case of: "Negro
Stephen, about fifteen years old, who I brought with me [into Virginia] being imported from Africa or the West India Islands." Sworn before Robert Townshend
Hooe. [No Hooe ID]

60 26May96   Non-Importation Compliance
Nicholas Voss took an oath before Jonah Thompson, **Justice** for TwnALX,
regarding slave importation in the cases of: George, Isreal, Anthony, Thomas, James,
Cate, Dolly, Bello, Maria, Mildred.

61 29Jul96   Non-Importation Compliance
George Singleton took an oath before A. Faw, **Justice of the Peace** for ALX,
regarding the importation of unnamed slaves.

61 05May96   Non-Importation Compliance
John Muncaster took an oath before R.T. Hooe, one of the acting **magistrates**
of the Hustings Court, regarding slave importation into Virginia. He particularly cited
the case of a Negro man Peter, brought from Charles Co, MD, into VA; Peter was
born in Charles Co.

62 01Apr96
Fm Stephen & Catharine Cooke, TwnALX
To Henry Walker, **Schoolmaster**, TwnALX: a lease:

BEGIN E side Columbus "at the centre between King and Prince Sts"... N w/Columbus 24'... E//King 100'... S//Columbus 24' ... thence to BEGIN, Walker to pay beginning 01Apr96 £6 Virginia currency "in Gold or Silver" per annum.
WTT: Will. Armistead, Hiram Chapin, James Brandon, Jno. Hughes
MEMO: If Walker pays $200 or £60 Virginia money within 5 years, rent will be remitted and title conveyed.

64 02Jan96
Fm Philip Richard Fendall & wife Mary, TwnALX, FfxCo, StVA
To Alexander Smith -do-: for £2400 cmv, a parcel on E side Union, S of King:
BEGIN on Union on N line of 12' alley on N side of Andrew Wales' land, 170' 7" S of King ... N w/Union 67' to 30' alley ... E w/alley 112' to river Potowmack ... S w/river [67'] to the 12' alley ... W w/alley to BEGIN;
--with use of the 12' alley together w/Andrew Wales;
--with use of the 30' alley together w/John Fitzgerald;
--with the privilege of extending a pier into the river;
--this is the property sold by Valentine Peers to Philip Richard Fendall, "except six feet thereof appropriated towards the forming of the said twelve foot Alley."
WTT: Jno. Hughes, John W. Lewis, Lucy Lee, A. Faw, James Irvin
CMN: John Dundas, A. Faw, James Irvin, **Gentlemen** of TwnALX, aptd 23Sep96 to examine Mary. Reported back same day.

68 03May96
Fm Dennis & Jane Allen Ramsay
   Robert & Betty Mease   [all five couples] TwnALX, FfxCo, StVA
   Robert & Ann Allison
   Michael & Hannah Madden
   Thomas & Sarah Porter
To Jesse Simms -do-: for £300 cmv, parcel N of King, W of Water Sts, originally conveyed by William Ramsay to his daughter Amelia, now both dead. For the parcel's metes and bounds, and the chain of title, see p. 36 above where Jesse Simms sells it all to Richard Marshall Scott.
WTT: Michael Madden; P. Marsteller, Francis Peyton, John Dundas to M.M.; Francis Peyton to R.M., R.A. and T.P.; A. Faw and S. Lowe to R.M., R.A., T.P.
CMN: John Dundas, James Irvin, Alexander Smith, **Gentlemen** of [blank], aptd 23Sep96 to examine Jane Allen Ramsay. Reported back 24Sep96.
CMN: John Dundas, Abram [sic] Faw, Francis Peyton, **Gentlemen** of TwnALX, aptd 02May96 to examine Ann Allison, Hannah Madden, Sarah Porter and Betty Mease. Reported back 03May96.

73 21May96
Fm John Crips Vowell & wife Margaret
   AND Thomas Vowell, Junior & wife Mary   [No ID, either couple]
To Alexander Smith [No ID]: for £1345 cmv, two parcels:
I-parcel E of Pitt, S of King:
BEGIN on King at NE corner of John Dundas' land, which extends 6 1/2" into the land formerly Robert Allison's ... "Eastwardly with the Brick house erected upon the said piece of Ground to the East end thereof"--30' 11 1/2"... S//Pitt 176' 7" to the back property line ... W//King 31' 6" to John Dundas' line ... N w/Dundas' line //Pitt until it is 34' from King ... E//King 6 1/2"... N//Pitt 34' to BEGIN;
--this is the ground (except a strip 6 1/2" wide from King south for 34' sold to Dundas by William Hodgson) sold by Robert Allison to Forrest and Stoddart;
--F & S then sold it to Peter Casanave, PC sold it to William Hodgson, and WH sold it to the two Vowells.

II-parcel on E of Pitt, N of Prince:
BEGIN on Pitt at center of Square formed by King and Prince ... S w/Pitt 20'... E//King-Prince 100'... N//Pitt 20'... thence to BEGIN;
--this was sold to the Vowells by William Hodgson plus half the partition wall "between the Brick house of John Dundas and the Brick house upon the premises hereby granted"
WTT: Washer Blunt, Jno. G. Ladd, Alexr. Greer
CMN: Jonah Thompson, John Dundas, Francis Peyton, **Gentlemen** of TwnALX, aptd 27May96 to examine Margaret and Mary. Reported back same day.

77 13Apr96
Fm William & Ann Wright, TwnALX, FfxCo, StVA
To Bernard Bryan -do- : for £147.10.0 a parcel N of King, E of Washington Streets:
BEGIN on King 60' 5" E of Wn ... E w/King 36'... N//Wn 90'... W//King 36'... thence to BEGIN--sold by Stephen & Catharine Cooke to Wright 08Apr93.
WTT: Ja. Keith, Archd. McLean, John Morris

79 23Aug96 Manumission
Fm Aaron Hewes of TwnALX, for the Negro woman Sylvia
WTT: G. Deneale, Wm. Summers

80 09Jan96 Mortgage
Fm Archibald & Mary Dobbin, TwnALX, FfxCo, StVA
To Henry Rozer, PG Co, StMD as exxr of John Casey, PG Co, StMD
WHEREAS 08Jan96 Dobbin acknowledged £360 owed to Casey, to be repaid £15 cmv each 01Nov 1796-7-8-9;
--to secure this Dobbin hereby mortgages a 1/2-acre lot in ALX, W of Washington, N of Prince Sts, in the addition made by John Alexander's exxrs 1784, numbered in their plan No. 4:
BEGIN at int Wn-Prince ... N w/Wn 176' 6"... W//Prince 123' 5"... S//Wn 176' 7"... thence to BEGIN--conveyed to Dobbins by Rozer 08Jan96;
--if Dobbins repays per schedule, this conveyance is void.
WTT: Ben. Weir, Fns. H. Rozer, James Moore, Wm. Cannon

82 16Aug96
CMN: Abraham Faw, John Dundas, James Irvin, **Gentlemen** of TwnALX, aptd 16Aug96 to examine Sarah Peyton. Reported back same day. [Conveyance is in Liber F, p. 515.]

84 12Sep96
Fm Joseph & Hannah Dyson, TwnALX, FfxCo, StVA
To John Lumsden AND Daniel McLeod -do-
WHEREAS Richard Marshall Scott & wife Mary 16Apr95 conveyed to Matthew Franklin Bowne AND Theodorus James Hamilton a parcel S of King and W of Union Streets:
BEGIN on King, on W line of 10' alley, 80' W of Union ... W w/King 40'... S//Union 66'... E//King 40' to the alley ... thence to BEGIN, Bowne & Hamilton to pay annually each 01Jun 120 silver $ to Scott;
--Bowne & Hamilton later [no date given] conveyed the land to Joseph Dyson, Dyson to pay Scott the annual rent.

NOW the Dysons will rent to Lumsden & McLeod a parcel, for £100 cmv plus an annual rent:
BEGIN on King 20' W of the 10' alley ... W w/King 20'... S//Union 66'... E//King 20'... thence to BEGIN;
--including "one half of the Frame now standing upon the piece of ground and of the Stone and Scantling lying thereupon";
--Lumsden & McLeod to pay beginning 01Jun97 60 silver $ yearly
WTT: Thos. Breillat, Patk. Byrne, James McHenry

86 16May96
Fm Joseph & Hannah Dyson, TwnALX, FfxCo, StVA
To John Lumsden -do-
[Dyson here leases another part of the property he got from Bowne & Hamilton (see above, p. 84) on King and Union.] Lumsden is to make a one-time payment of £150 cmv plus annual rent beginning 01Jun97 of 60 silver $:
BEGIN on King on W line of the 10' alley ... W w/King 20'... S//Union 62'... E//King 20'... thence to BEGIN;
--plus "half of the Frame erected upon the aforesaid piece of ground, and of the Stone & Scantling now lying upon it...."
--Dyson will lay off as an alley the space of ground between this parcel's S line and the property of Bowne & Hamilton.
WTT: Patrick Byrne, John Barber, William Bradley, Wm. Hoye

90 13Apr96
Fm Michael & Hannah Madden, FfxCo, StVA
To William Pomery, TwnALX, FfxCo, StVA: for £80 cmv a parcel N of Cameron, W of Pitt Streets:
BEGIN on Cameron 51' 5" W of Pitt ... W w/Cameron 24'... N//Pitt 100' &" to a 10' alley ... W w/alley 24'... thence to BEGIN, part of LOT 120 granted by the Trustees 21 Oct65 to the then Hannah Ramsay, [since married to Michael Madden];
--the Maddens will lay off a 10' alley beginning on Pitt 100' 7" n of Cameron, to run parallel to Cameron across LOT 120.
WTT: P. Marsteller, Jesse Simms, John Dundas
CMN: Francis Peyton, John Dundas, James Irvin, **Gentlemen** of TwnALX, aptd 13Apr96 to examine Hannah. Reported back 03May96.

93 13Apr96
Fm Michael & Hannah Madden, FfxCo, StVA
To John White, TwnALX, FfxCo, StVA: for £80 a parcel N of Cameron, W of Pitt:
BEGIN on Cameron 75' 5" W of Pitt ...W w/Cameron 24'...N//Pitt 101' 7" to a 10' alley... E w/alley 24'... thence to BEGIN.
--as at p. 90, above, this is part of LOT 120, and the Maddens will lay out the alley as described above. Wtt: as above
CMN: John Dundas, Francis Peyton, James Irvin, **Gentlemen** of TwnALX, aptd 02May96 to examine Hannah. Reported back 03May96.

97 13Apr96
[Same] to Thomas Richards, TwnALX, FfxCo, StVA: for £73 cmv a parcel N of Cameron, W of Pitt:
BEGIN on Cameron 99' 5" W of Pitt ... W w/Cameron 24'... N//Pitt 101' 7" to 10' alley ... E w/alley 24'... thence to BEGIN, another part LOT 120.
--as at pp. 90, 93 above, the Maddens will lay out a 10' alley as described above.
WTT: as above

CMN: Francis Peyton, John Dundas, James Irvin, **Gentlemen** of TwnALX, aptd 13Apr96 to examine Hannah. Reported back 03May96.

101 21Jul96
Fm Alexander & Rachel Smith, TwnALX, FfxCo, StVA
To Jesse Simms -do-: for £1200 cmv, two parcels:
I: S of King, W of Water Sts:
BEGIN at int King-Water Sts ... W w/King 42'... S//Water St 82' to 12' alley which divides this from John Fitzgerald ... E w/alley 42'... thence to BEGIN;
--sold to Smith by John Harper 09Jul94.
       AND
II: adjoining Parcel I, above:
BEGIN on King 42' W of Water St at above parcel's W line ... W w/King 21' 9" to land sold by the Smiths to George Gilpin ... thence w/Gilpin's line 82' to the 12' alley ... thence w/alley 21' 9" to the first parcel ... thence N to BEGIN;
--sold to Smith by William Hodgson 06Jan96. [Rachel Smith signs w/mark]
WTT: A. Faw, John Dundas, Jno. Horsburgh
CMN: Francis Peyton, Abraham Faw, John Dundas, **Gentlemen** of TwnALX, aptd 15Aug96 to examine Rachel. Reported same day.

105 24Aug96
Fm Jesse Simms, TwnALX, FfxCo, StVA
To Bernard Ghequiere -do-: for £1300 Virginia currency Simms sells Parcels I & II just bought from the Smiths, p. 101, above.
WTT: Moses Coates, Thomas Shreve, Alexr. Greer, Dennis Ramsay

107 04 Oct96
Fm Alexander & Rachel Smith, TwnALX, FfxCo, StVA
To Jonathan Swift -do-: for £4000 cmv, a parcel E of Union, S of King:
BEGIN on Union on N line of 12' alley on N side of John & Thomas Vowell's land, recently Wales', 170' &" S of King ... N w/Union 67' to a 30' alley ... E w/alley 112' to the river ... S w/river [67'] to the 12' alley ... thence to BEGIN;
--plus the use of the 12' alley with the Vowells, and the 30' alley w/John Fitzgerald;
--plus the right to extend a pier into the river;
--this is land sold by Valentine Peers to Philip Richard Fendall (except 6' appropriated toward forming the 12' alley); sold by Philip & Mary Fendall 01Jan96 to Alexander Smith.
[The clerk does not, this time, show Rachel signing w/mark]
WTT: Robert Young, James Brandon, David Henderson
CMN: John Dundas, Abram [sic] Faw, James Irvin, **Gentlemen** of [blank], aptd 06 Oct96 to examine Rachel. Reported same day.

111 05 Oct96
Fm John Robert Wheaton & wife Elizabeth, City of New York
To James McClenachan, TwnALX, FfxCo, StVA: for £500 cmv a parcel N of Wolfe, E of Ffx Sts, part of LOT 89:
BEGIN on Wolfe 63' E of Ffx ... E w/Wolfe 40'... N//Ffx 100' to 10' alley ... W//Wolfe w/alley 40'... thence to BEGIN.
--conveyed by Samuel & Sarah Harper to Wheaton 31Aug89
Executed for Wheaton by his attorney Robert Murray.
WTT: Jos. Barrett, Philip Ammidon
ATTEST: Robert Murray swore to the above 13 Oct96 before Richard Varick, **Mayor** of New York

114 01Apr96   Power of Attorney
William Thornton Alexander of King George Co. refers to his letter of 22May94 giving power of attorney to John Taliaferro, Jr. WTA now gives Taliaferro the right to appoint substitutes to collect rents due, or to take action on unpaid rents.
WTT: Joseph Fullmer, Jno. Helms, Simon Pearson, George Swann

115 12Jul96
Fm William Thornton Alexander & wife Lucy, King Geo. Co, StVA
To Joseph Fullmer, TwnALX, FfxCo, StVA
WHEREAS exxrs of John Alexander 05Aug79 conveyed to Tobias Zimmerman 1/2-acre lot contiguous to ALX on S of Prince, W of St Asaph, opposite W side of lot adj. LOT 100 [? must be 110]:
BEGIN on W side St A at termination of line drawn from NW corner of lot adjoining LOT 100 [110?], the line parallel w/lot's N line and Prince, drawn to W side of St Asaph ... S w/W side of St A 176' 7"... W//Prince 123' 5"... N//St A 176' 7"... thence to BEGIN, Zimmerman to pay William Thornton Alexander, heir of J. Alexander, £20.18 current money yearly;
WHEREAS Zimmerman and his wife Elizabeth later conveyed parts of the lot to others, subject to annual rent, and the Zimmermans having now failed to pay the full amount, the Alexanders authorized their attorney (J.T.,Jr.) 22May94 to prosecute lapsed rental agreements incident to lots leased in 1774, 1779 and 1784;
--and the Alexanders further authorized Taliaferro 01Apr96 to appoint substitutes for this purpose, whereby James Keith was appointed to act in the Zimmerman case;
--and Keith, on 09Jul96, demanded payment of the back rent: £239.14.8. Getting no response, he ordered the Deputy Sergeant of the TwnALX to levy the amount on goods and chattels on the property, but the sergeant could find none.
NOW the Alexanders for £84 cmv and a rental agreement convey to Joseph Fullmer a part of the lot:
BEGIN on W side St A 50' from int St Asaph-Prince ... S w/St A 42'... W//Prince 123' 5"... N//St A 42'... thence to BEGIN, Fullmer to pay beginning 03Apr97 £8.8.0 cmv per annum. Executed for the Alexanders by John Taliaferro, Jr.
WTT: Jno. Holmes, Simon Pearson, George Swann
CMN: John Taliaferro, Senior and Junior, and John Pollard, **Gentlemen** of King George Co, aptd 24Sep96 to examine Lucy. Reported back 26Sep96.

123 04 Oct96   Manumission
Lillburn Williams "(commonly known by the name of Anthony Williams)" of Prince William Co., in return for £120 cmv from Negro slave Anthony, manumits Anthony, wife Sophia, and sons John, Tom and Lewis.
WTT: Walter Dodson, John Stewart Junr, <u>Wm. Summers</u>

124 27Feb96   Deed of Trust
Fm George Spangler, TwnALX, FfxCo, StVA
To James Keith -do-
WHEREAS John & Jane Fitzgerald 15May95 conveyed to Spangler a parcel S of Prince, W of Royal:
BEGIN on Prince at E line of ground conveyed by the Fitzgeralds to Lodowick Trisseler ... S w/line 78'... E//Prince 20'... N//Royal 78'... thence to BEGIN, Spangler paying rent each 25May of £14.10.0 cmv;
WHEREAS George McMunn of the same place has advanced sums to Spangler (£60 cmv), Spangler wishes to secure repayment to McMunn. Spangler now puts the property in trust to Keith until 27Feb97, when the £60 is supposed to be repaid.
WTT: James Jobson, Thomas Holmes, Jonah Isabell

127 21Apr96
Fm Richard Marshall Scott & wife Mary, TwnALX, FfxCo, StVA
To Philip Richard Fendall -do-: for £90 lawful money of VA, a 1/2-acre lot, part of land conveyed 29Dec85 by Henry Lee to Baldwin Dade, and by Dade 18Apr89 to Scott:
BEGIN at NW corner of the 10 acre tract conveyed by Lee to Dade ... E w/line of Charles Alexander to land sold by Baldwin & Catharine Dade to Philip Richard Fendall AND Charles Lee ... S w/Fendall-Lee line "to a Corner of their land"... W w/a 2nd Fendall-Lee line "to another corner thereof"... N to BEGIN.
WTT: Thomas Darne Junr, Alexr Smith, A. Faw
CMN: Abraham Faw, Francis Peyton, Alexander Smith, **Gentlemen** of TwnALX, aptd 12May96 to examine Mary. Reported same day.

130 04Jul96
Fm Elizabeth Donaldson [nee Muir, sister and heir of the late John Muir of
    TwnALX, FfxCo, StVA]
To Mordecai Miller, TwnALX, FfxCo, StVA: for £415 cmv a parcel S of King, W of Royal Sts:
BEGIN on King at W line of land which James Kirk owned at his death ... W 1/4 of the length of LOT 113 to line of ground recently Robert Allison's, now Alexander Smith's ... S//Royal & Pitt to S line of LOT 113: 178' 4"... E w/line //King the length of the first course, to Kirk's land ... N w/Kirk's land to BEGIN;
--sold by Robert & Marianne Alexander to Charles Turner 15Dec66 and, when Turner died intestate, the land was escheated to Thomas, Lord Fairfax;
--Lord Fairfax granted the land to Robert Muir 06Feb77 and, when Muir died intestate, the land passed to his brother John;
--John Muir rented the land for a term yet unexpired, following which the renter may remove any buildings he erects during his tenure; [neither renter nor rent terms given];
--John Muir devised the land in his will to sister Elizabeth, who later married Mr. Donaldson.
[Elizabeth appointed William Hartshorne her atty 18Apr96 to sell real estate inherited from her brother. This conveyance executed for her by Hartshorne.]
WTT: Thomas Shreve, Saml. Stansbury, William Smith

134 23Jul96
Fm Thomas & Nancy Richards, TwnALX, FfxCo, StVA
To Samuel Craig -do-: for £2150 cmv, N of King, W of Pitt: BEGIN on King 4" to E of the center of the Pitt-St Asaph Square ... E w/King 23' 9" to the E line "of the Brick house lately built by...Thomas Richards upon the premises intended to be hereby granted"... N//Pitt-St A 119'... W//King the length of first line ... S 119' to BEGIN;
--part of the 1/2-acre conveyed by Richard Parker to Richards.
WTT: Jno. Stewart Junr, Walter Pomery Junr, Daniel Foush
CMN: James Irvin, Abraham Faw, Francis Peyton, **Gentlemen** of TwnALX, aptd 23Jul96 to examine Nancy. Reported back same day.

137 01Nov96
Fm Francis & Sarah Peyton, TwnALX, FfxCo, CwlVA
To Thomas Jacobs -do-: lease parcel adjoining TwnALX:
BEGIN N side Prince 68' W of Columbus ... N//Columbus 89' to an alley ... W w/alley //Prince 19'... S//Columbus 89' to Prince ... thence to BEGIN, Jacobs to pay beginning 01Nov97 $23.75 in gold or silver per annum.   WTT: none

CMN: Jonah Thompson, John Dundas, Abram [sic] Faw, **Gentlemen** of [blank], aptd 21Dec96 to examine Sarah. Rptd back same day.

141 01Sep96
Fm Francis & Sarah Peyton, TwnALX, FfxCo, CwlVA
To Peter Tetespaugh, TwnALX, FfxCo, CwlVA: lease a parcel on N side of Prince between Columbus and Alfred:
BEGIN on N side Prince 87' W of Columbus ... N//Columbus 89' to 11' 7" alley ... W//Prince 30'... S//Columbus 89'... thence to BEGIN, Tetespaugh to pay from 01Sep97 30 silver $ per annum
[Peter signs his name **Tartsbaugh**]. WTT: none
CMN: Jonah Thompson, John Dundas, Abraham Faw, **Gentlemen** of [blank], aptd 10Dec96 to examine Sarah. Reported back 21Dec96.

144 19Dec96
Fm James Irvin, TwnALX, FfxCo, StVA
To John Potten -do-: for £40 cmv parcel E of Wn, N of Cameron
BEGIN on Washington at S line of land conveyed by Irvin to Susannah Hamilton--159' N of Cameron ... S w/Wn 19' 6"... E//Cameron 100'... N//Wn 19' 6"... thence to BEGIN--part of 1/2-acre conveyed to Irvin by Charles & Frances Alexander [blank] [blank] 179[blank. WTT: none

147 20 Oct96
[Same] to Richard Wren, TwnALX, FfxCo, StVA: for £40 cmv another part of above parcel, p. 144:
BEGIN on Wn 120' N of Cameron ... N w/Wn 19' 6"... E//Cameron 100'... S//Wn 19' 6"... thence to BEGIN--part of 1/2-acre leased to Irvin by Charles Alexander for £25 cmv per annum. WTT: none

149 19Dec96
[Same] to Samuel Collard, TwnALX, FfxCo, StVA: for £[blank] cmv, parcel S side Queen, E of Washington Sts:
BEGIN on Queen 123' 5" E of Wn ... W w/Queen 26'... S//Wn 87' 8" to the line of ground conveyed by Irvin to Joseph & Samuel Harper [no date] ... E w/line 26'... thence to BEGIN--part of 1/2-acre lot conveyed by Charles & Frances Alexander to Irvin 12Dec94. WTT: none

152 19Dec96
[Same] to Richard Wren, TwnALX, FfxCo, StVA: lease another part of same lot above, p. 149:
BEGIN at int Washington-Queen ... E w/Queen 65'... S//Wn 45'... W//Queen 65'... thence to BEGIN
--and "also that frame house now used and occupied by Mr. Thomas Swann as an Office";
--Wren to pay beginning 25Dec97 £14 cmv in specie per annum;
--Irvin will lay off as an alley "all that space of Ground upon Queen Street, lying between [this] and the frame house belonging to...Irvin, now in the occupation of Thomas Swann; and will extend the same with the Line of the said House and the ground thereto belonging; and the Line of the premises hereby granted, until it intersects...the North Line [extended] of the new Brick House built by...Irvin." [The alley will run parallel Queen to the land of the frame house.]
--Irvin will also lay off as an alley "all that space...between the premises hereby granted upon Washington Street and [Irvin's new] Brick house," extending E until intersecting the first alley;

--when the rent is due, Wren will pay £12.10.0 to Charles Alexander and deduct that from Wren's rent due to Irvin. WTT: none

157   16Nov96
Fm Richard & Mary Conway, TwnALX, FfxCo, StVA
To William Wilson   -do-
   William Hepburn   -do-
   Roger Coltart   -do-
Part of "all that Slip of ground" adjoining E side of Water Street, S side of LOT 20: BEGIN on Water St at S end of LOT 20 ... E w/lot line into the River ... thence //Water St 117' to Queen ... W w/Queen to Water St ... thence w/Water St to BEGIN, and "the Waters and water courses Landings Profits and Commodities to the same belonging," conveyed to Conway 20Sep91 by Thomas West.
NOW the Conways for 5/ convey to Wilson, Hepburn & Coltart:
BEGIN on Water St 50' S of LOT 20's S line ... E//Queen into the River ... S//Water St 67' to Queen ... W w/Queen to Water St ... N w/Water St 67' to BEGIN.
WTT: Wm. Herbert, Ja. Keith, Jas. Kennedy, John McIver; A. Faw AND James Irvin to Mrs. Conway
CMN: Jonah Thompson, James Irvin, Abraham Faw, **Gentlemen** of Corporation of ALX, aptd 24Nov96 to examine Mary. Rptd 25Nov96

162   20Sep96
Fm Francis & Sarah Peyton, TwnALX, CwlVA
To Ann Peyton -do-: for £100 current money, a parcel "on Columbus Street":
BEGIN on Columbus 122' 7" N of Prince ... W//Prince 113' to 20' 10" alley ... N//Columbus 44' to a 20' alley ... E w/alley //Prince 113' to Columbus ... thence S w/Columbus 44' to BEGIN.
WTT: Edward M. Ramsay, Nathan Hatherly, Lewis Beckwith
CMN: Jonah Thompson, John Dundas, Abraham Faw, **Gentlemen** of [blank], aptd 21Nov96 to examine Sarah. Reported back 21Dec96

169   12Sep96
Fm "Francis Peyton and [blank] his wife" TwnALX, FfxCo, StVA
To John Richter -do-: for £70 cmv plus rent a parcel contiguous to ALX, S of King St. extended, W of Alfred:
BEGIN at int King-Alfred ... W w/King 49' 5"... S//Alfred 100' to 15' alley ... E w/alley //King 49' 5" to Alfred ... thence to BEGIN, Richter to pay beginning 01 Oct97 £19.15.4 cmv in specie, per annum;
--part of land granted Peyton [blank] [blank] 1795 by William Thornton Alexander & wife Lucy, subject to annual rent of £20 cmv due [date left blank].
WTT: Liston Temple, William Cash Junr, Lewis Davis, Lewis Beckwith
CMN: Jonah Thompson, Abram [sic] Faw, John Dundas, **Gentlemen** of [blank], aptd 15Dec96 to examine Sarah Peyton. Rptd 21Dec96

175   26Nov96
Fm Francis & Sarah Peyton, TwnALX, FfxCo, StVA
To William Cash Jr -do-: lease parcel contiguous to ALX, N side of Prince extended, E side Patrick Sts:
BEGIN at int Prince-Patrick ... E w/Prince 60'... N//Patrick 100'... W//Prince 60' to Patrick ... thence to BEGIN, Cash to pay beginning 01Apr98 60 silver $ per annum.
WTT: none
MEMO: Cash is to "erect upon some part of this lot" a flour shed at least 20x40 feet square within 8 months. Failure to do so means loss of lot.

CMN: Jonah Thompson, Abraham Faw, John Dundas, **Gentlemen** of TwnALX, aptd 28Nov96 to examine Sarah. Reported back 21Dec96.

181 22Sep96
Fm Dennis Ramsay   The three surviving exxrs of William Ramsay, **Gent.**,
   Robert Allison   (William Ramsay the younger
   Michael Madden   having died.)
To William Summers, TwnALX, FfxCo, StVA: for £90 cmv a parcel part LOT 61, W of Royal, N of Prince:
BEGIN on Royal 94' N of Prince--the N line of a 6' alley ... W w/alley //Prince 83' 5" to the line of ground sold by them to John Horner ... N w/line // Royal 18'... E//Prince 83' 5" to Royal ... thence 18' to BEGIN;
--part LOT 61, which lot was conveyed by Ffx Co. Sheriff Thomas Pollard to William Ramsay 20May82, excepting that part reserved during her life to Elizabeth Sewell Worrell, part of which she and Morris Worrell have released to the Ramsay exxrs
--the exxrs commit to the 6' alley running from Royal to John Horner's line.
WTT: Tho. Waller to Robert Allison; Donald Campbell, L. [**Lewis**, as per mention on page 185] Summers

186 23Jun96   Quadripartite Deed
I-John Harper, FfxCo, StVA
II-Edward Harper
   Charles Harper   [All 4 men:
   William Hartshorne   TwnALX, FfxCo, StVA]
   James Keith
III-Mary Vowell (nee Harper, daughter of John Harper, TwnALX, FfxCo, StVA)
IV-Aloysius Boone AND Joseph Boone [no ID]
WHEREAS on 10Apr93 John Harper deeded in trust to Group II, for the benefit of Mary, a parcel E of Water St, N of Prince:
BEGIN at int Water-Prince Sts ... E w/Prince 40' to 10' alley ... N w/alley 22'...
W//Prince 40' to Water St ... thence to BEGIN, John reserving the right to lease the property while he lived, the rents to be disposed of after his death according to the trust provisions he set up;
NOW John will lease to the Boones the above described parcel:
--the Boones to pay per annum beginning 01Jul97 £40 cmv in Spanish milled dollars at 6/ each; "half-Johannes's" weighing 9 pennyweight at 48/ each; or any other gold or silver coins at prevailing values;
--this rent is payable to Mary during her life, then to her surviving children after she dies;
--payable to other heirs of John should Mary have no surviving children;
--the Boones commit to building w/in 3 years a "Brick Dwelling House three stories high"
WTT: Joseph Coleman, Wm. Wright, Thomas Lock [whose name in an entry on p. 196 is spelled **Lockie**], John Lloyd

196 01Aug95
Fm Elisha Cullen Dick & wife Hannah TwnALX, FfxCo, StVA
To Jesse Wherry -do-
WHEREAS William Thornton Alexander & wife Lucy 25Dec94 leased to Dick a 2-acre parcel in FfxCo, adjacent to ALX:
BEGIN at int King-Columbus Sts, S of King and W of Columbus ... W w/King to Alfred ... S w/Alfred to Prince ... E w/Prince to Columbus ... thence to BEGIN.
NOW the Dicks lease to Wherry two parcels in the 2-acre piece, numbered 5 and 6 in their plan of the 2-acres:

BEGIN 60' S of int King-Columbus, S side King ... S//Columbus 100'... W//King 31' 8 1/2"... S//Columbus 40'... W//King 31' 8 1/2" by the "North end of a Short Alley ten feet wide"... N// Columbus 140' to King ... thence w/King E 63' 5" to BEGIN, which includes both Nos. 5 & 6;
--Wherry to pay beginning 01Jul96 $31.71 per annum;
--Wherry to build "on some part of the said premises" on or before 01Jan98 a brick house 2 stories high not less than 15' wide and 20' long;
--Wherry will not erect any framed building on any front of this property.
WTT: Francis Peyton, Thomas Triplett, Thomas Simmes
CMN: John Dundas, James Irvin, Abram [sic] Faw, **Gentlemen** of TwnALX, aptd 01Aug96 to examine Hannah. [Clerk first wrote the date as **January**, but then used August in the text. August appears to be correct; see following:] Reported back 23Sep96.

203 23Jun96 Quadripartite Deed
I-John Harper, FfxCo, StVA
II-Edward Harper
   Charles Harper   [All 4 men:
   William Hartshorne   TwnALX, FfxCo, StVA]
   James Keith
III-Frances Rush Riddle (nee Frances Rush Harper, dau of John Harper) [no ID]
IV-Aloysius Boone AND Joseph Boone [no ID]
WHEREAS 10Apr93 John put into trust with Group II for the future benefit of his daughter Frances parcel E of Water, N of Prince Streets:
BEGIN on Water St 44' S of line of McRea & Mease ... E//Prince 40' to 10' alley ... S w/alley 22'... W//Prince 40' to Water St ... thence to BEGIN, John reserving the right to rent or lease the property, the rents after his death to go to Frances
NOW he does so lease, to the Boones;
--the Boones pay beginning 01Jul97 annual rent £22 cmv in Spanish milled $ at 6/ each; half-Johannes of 9 pennyweight at 48/ each; or other gold or silver coins at prevailing rates;
--payable to John while he lives, to Frances when he dies, to her children when she dies, or to other John Harper heirs if Frances leaves no children.
[The clerk notes, pp. 213-214, that the name **Peggy Vowell** has in 14 places been erased, and that of Frances Rush Riddle written in its place.]
WTT: Joseph Coleman, Wm. Wright, Thomas Locke, John Lloyd

215 30Sep96
Fm James Irvin, TwnALX, FfxCo, StVA
To Joseph Harper AND Samuel Harper -do-:for £750 cmv plus a lease, parcel E of Washington, S of Queen Sts:
BEGIN on Wn 87' 8" S of Queen ... S w/Wn 86' 6"... E//Queen 123' 5"... N//Wn 86' 6"... thence to BEGIN, the Harpers to pay beginning 25Dec95 $41 2/3 per annum;
--part of 1/2acre conveyed by Charles & Frances Alexander to Irvin 12Dec94;
--"and all Houses Buildings--and that part of the Necessary which opens into [these] premises";
--Irvin will lay off as an alley the spaces between this and the "South Gavel of the brick House lately built by...Irvin," from Washington Street E for 40';
--the Harpers have the right to join the second story of any brick house they may build here to the brick wall of Irvin's recently built brick house--over the alley, leaving the alley clear up to the second story of the Harpers' new house.
WTT: Ja. Keith, Saml. Collard, Ja. Keith Junr.

221 30Sep96
Fm James Irvin, TwnALX, FfxCo, StVA
To Joseph Harper AND Samuel Harper -do-:
WHEREAS 04Apr91 Charles Alexander leased to Irvin ground contiguous to TwnALX on S side of Queen extended and "to the Westward of a Line drawn from the Steeple of the Episcopal Church northwardly so as to intersect the said Street": BEGIN at int of the steeple line and Queen ... W w/Queen 1200'... S//steeple line 90'... E//Queen 1200' to steeple line ... thence to BEGIN, for 20 years, Irvin to pay each 30Jun 100 Spanish milled $ or the equivalent in silver or gold coins;
--Irvin allowed to remove structures built during the lease if Alexander did not want them, or if independent evaluations of them were unacceptable;
--"upon which...Ground...Irvin both erected a Rope Walk, with all necessary Inclosures Buildings and Implements & Machines necessary for executing, conducting and carrying on the Business of Rope making"
NOW Irvin for £750 cmv conveys to the Harpers the unexpired portion of the lease, the buildings and equipment of the rope walk, (for which the Harpers are to take up paying Alexander the annual 100 silver $ rent), and from Irvin to them Negroes:
- Will, "a Slave for and during his natural life"
- Guss, to serve from this day until 3 years from 25Dec next
- James Bull to serve -do- until 5 years from 25Dec next
- Harry to serve -do- until 14 years from 25Dec next
WTT: Ja. Keith, Saml. Collard, Ja. Keith Junr.

226 01May96
Fm Robert Townshend Hooe, TwnALX, FfxCo, CwlVA AND
   Richard & Ann Harrison, City of Philadelphia, StPENNA but "formerly of said Town, County and State"
To John Muncaster, TwnALX, FfxCo, CwlVA: for £411.9.2 cmv plus rent, parcel "on Water and Duke Streets...numbered in the Plan of the said Town [blank]" [number not filled in]:
BEGIN on S line of Bernard Mann's lot on Water St 180' from int Duke-Water Sts ... S w/Water St 20' "to include the house thereon built by James Grimes"... E//Duke and Mann's lot 90' to a 6' alley ... N w/alley //Water St 20' to line of Mann's lot ... W 90' to BEGIN, together w/use of the alley;
--also use of an 8' alley "described in Bernard Mann's Deed, in common with George Chapman" of FfxCo;
--Muncaster to pay beginning 01May 97 £13.16.0 per annum in gold or silver
WTT: Philip Wanton, Robert Young, Jesse Wherry to RTH and JM; Jno. Steele, David Easton, B. Dandridge to the Harrisons
CMN: Matthew Clarkson, **Mayor** of Philadelphia was commissioned 01May96 to examine Ann Harrison, and did so 08 Oct96.

233 19Apr96
Fm John Harper, FfxCo, StVA
To Robert Henderson, TwnALX, FfxCo, StVA: lease of a parcel N of Prince, E of Union belonging to Harper. [No metes and bounds; whoever drafted the lease--probably John Harper himself--did not use the standard format. This individualistic approach shows in Harper's other conveyances, as well.]
--"together with the Pier and Dock thereunto appertaining";
--and all the houses and buildings thereon., except that Thomas Patten & Company has the privilege of removing the frame warehouse they erected there;
--term to run from 14 Oct97 for 7 years;
--Henderson to pay an annual rent of £160 cmv in quarterly installments, the first due 13Jan98;

--if Harper cannot purchase the Patten warehouse, he will reduce Henderson's rent by £40 per annum.
WTT: Ja. Keith, Thomas Sim, Edward P. Ball

237 09Nov96
Fm Robert Henderson, TwnALX, FfxCo, StVA
To John Barber -do-: lease of a parcel--"part of Harper's Pier and Wharff lying" N of Prince, E of Union Sts:
BEGIN on Prince on a line "corresponding with the West Gavel of the Frame Warehouse built upon the said Pier by Thomas Patten"... N w/line and West gavel of warehouse to the dividing line between Harper and Watson ... E w/Harper-Watson line to the "end of the Pier and all the Ground lying to the Southward of the said dividing Line the end of the said Pier and a Line drawn from the said dividing Line along the West Gavel of the said Warehouse to the edge of the Dock and the whole of the Dock...of John Harper"
--part of the land leased by Harper to Henderson for 7 years from 14 Oct next;
--Barber's lease to run from 14 Oct next for 6 years, 9 months, paying $235 per annum in quarterly payments beginning 13Jan98.
WTT: Ja. Keith, Daniel Campbell, Charles Fras. his + mark Butler

241 17 Oct96
Fm Dennis & Jane Allen Ramsay, TwnALX, FfxCo, StVA
To James McGuire -do-: for £165 cmv a parcel E of Royal, S of Queen:
BEGIN at center of Square formed by Queen and Cameron, the line of ground formerly Stroman's, but now William Smith's ... N w/Royal 32'... E//Queen & Cameron 123' 5"... S//Royal 32' ... thence to BEGIN--granted to Dennis by William Ramsay.
WTT: A. Faw, John Dundas, Matthw. Sexsmith
CMN: John Dundas, Abraham Faw, James Irvin, **Gentlemen** of the Court of Hustings, aptd 22 Oct96 to examine Jane. Faw and Dundas reported back, but the date of reporting is not given.

247 23 Oct94
Fm Thomas & Mary Patten, TwnALX, StVA
  AND Joseph & Dorothy May, Twn Boston, StMASS
To John Walter Fletcher, TwnALX, StVA
WHEREAS 05Jun86 Charles Lee conveyed to John McClenachen part LOT 110 S of Prince, W of Pitt:
BEGIN on Prince 51' 5" W of Pitt ... W w/Prince 24'... S//Pitt 100' to 9' alley running //Prince through LOT 110 ... E w/alley 24'... thence to BEGIN, McClenachen paying Lee each 05Jun 56 silver $, and McClenachen conveying the parcel 13Mar94 to the Pattens, they to pay Lee that same rent;
NOW the Pattens for £604 cmv plus annual rent convey the parcel to Fletcher, Fletcher to pay Lee that annual rent.
[Dorothy May signs herself **Dolly**.]
WTT: Jonah Thompson, James Lawrason, Alexr. McConnell
CMN: Dorothy examined 16Feb96 by **Chief Justice**, Court of Common Pleas, Suffolk Co., MASS: Joseph Gardner. Gardner certified 22Feb96 as being Chief Justice by **Clerk** of Court Ezekiel Price.
CMN: James Lawrason, Jonah Thompson, **Gentlemen** of TwnALX, aptd 16Jul95 to examine Dorothy May. Reported back 17Jul95.

255 19 Oct96
Fm William Newton, TwnALX
To William Summers -do-: for £10 cmv part LOT 126, S of Princess and W of Pitt:

BEGIN 93' 3" S of int Princess-Pitt ... S w/Pitt 36' 3 1/2"... W 123' 5"... N 36' 3 1/2"... thence to BEGIN.
--conveyed to Newton 07May88 by Thomas Williams and Joseph Carey [sic, but Cary below, p. 258], terming the property an "Indefeasible Estate of Inheritance."
WTT: none

258 10Nov96 Mortgage
Fm Joseph Cary [sic; see p. 255, above] TwnALX, FfxCo, StVA
To James McClenachan -do-: parcel N of Wolfe, E of Ffx Sts:
BEGIN on Wolfe 63' 5" E of Ffx ... E w/Wolfe 40'... N//Ffx 100' to 10' alley ... W w/alley 40'... thence to BEGIN--originally sold 17 Oct96 by McClenachan and wife Ann to Cary;
--now mortgaged by Cary to McClenachan to secure Cary's $583.24 to McClenachan due 01 Oct97;
--if debt paid on time, this deed is void.
WTT: George Darling, A. Faw, Alexr. Smith

262 10Nov96 Same to same
[On the same date, under the same terms, Cary mortgages the same property to secure a second debt to McClenachan of $610.92 due 01 Oct98. Same witnesses.]

266 10Nov96 [As above at pp. 258, 262, this time for a third debt of $597.07, due 01Apr98.]

269 22Dec96 Non-Importation Compliance
Aloysius Brown [no ID] swears before George Gilpin, Justice of FfxCo, as to his compliance with the 1788 slave importation act. "The negroes Benjn. Maide & Lewis are for my own use--said negroes I brought with me..."

270 12Dec96
Fm John B. Murray, City of New York, StNY
To Thomas Porter, TwnALX, FfxCo, StVA
WHEREAS John Spann Conway & wife Susannah, Robert & Mary Conway, Cuthbert & Mary Elliston, Hannah Webb, and Joseph Conway [no IDs] conveyed 11Dec84 to Murray and Porter part LOT 110, W of Pitt and S of Prince:
BEGIN on Pitt 109' S of Prince on S line of a 9' alley ... W w/alley //Prince 123' 5"... S//Pitt 45'... E//Prince 123' 5" to Pitt ... thence to BEGIN;
AND WHEREAS James & Ann Rattle 10Apr88 conveyed to Murray and Porter part LOT 110, a parcel S of Prince, W of Pitt:
BEGIN at int Prince-Pitt ... W w/Prince 51' 5"... S//Pitt 100' to a 9' alley ... E w/alley 51' 5"... thence to BEGIN;
NOW Murray and Porter will divide the parcels.
I - Murray's share of the 1st parcel:
BEGIN on Pitt at S line of the alley ... W w/alley 123' 5"... S//Pitt 22' 6"... E//Alley 123' 5"... thence to BEGIN;
--and one half of the stable they built on the whole property
--Murray to allow Porter a 9' cartway from the alley into his part of the property, along the East end of the stable while it stands. When it "shall fall to decay or be removed," the cartway will run along the West line of the property.
II - Murray's share of the 2nd parcel:
BEGIN at int Prince-Pitt ... W w/Prince 24'... S//Pitt 100' to 9' alley ... E w/alley 24'... thence to BEGIN;
AND as Murray's portions are worth more he will pay Porter $50
III - Porter's part of the 1st parcel:

BEGIN on Pitt 133' 6" S of Prince ... W//Prince and the alley 123' 5"... S//Pitt 22' 6"...E//Prince 123' 5", thence to BEGIN
IV - Porter's part of the 2nd parcel:
BEGIN on Prince 24' W of Pitt ... W w/Prince 27' 5"... S//Pitt 100' to the 9' alley ... E w/alley 27' 5"... thence to BEGIN.
WTT: John McIver, Francis Peyton, Steph. Cooke
ATTEST: Murray attested to this 09Jan97 before Richard Varick, **Mayor** of New York City.

278   08Feb96   Power of Attorney
　　　William Hodgson gives p/atty to George Clementson, both of TwnALX, to collect debts; to draw Bills of Exchange on Robinson, Sanderson & Rumney of Whitehaven; to contract for shipping; to dispose of real estate by sale or lease.
WTT: Wm. Bowness, Wm. Graham, Chr. Robinson
MEMO: on 04Mar96 Hodgson further empowers Clementson to act in matters of "Copartnery." [Same witnesses.]

283   14Apr96
CMN: John Taliaferro Senr, John Pollard and John Taliaferro Junr, **Gentlemen** of King George Co., aptd to examine William Thornton Alexander's wife Lucy in the matter of a conveyance 14Sep95 from the Alexanders to Phebe Arell of a 1/2 acre lot (No. 12 in the Alexanders' plan) W of Washington, N of Wolfe. Rptd 26Sep96.

285   08Jun98   Bill of Sale
Fm Lemuel Bent, TwnALX, StVA
To Elisha Janney AND George Irish of -do-: for $3000
　　　1/3 of ship Paragon of Boston, 300 tons burthen;
　　　1/3 of her rigging, fittings, etc.;
　　　1/3 of proceeds of voyage being/about to be made.
--the Paragon is a British ship sold by her owner in France to John Bass Dabney, Calvin Ellis of Boston, and Samuel P. Broome of New York;
--1/3 of the ship sold by Dabney to Bent
--and now by Bent to Janney & Irish as a bond to guarantee the original buyers' and seller's stipulation: "that the said ship shall trade between France and Neutral ports only, until the present War in Europe ceases, and then the said Ship shall retake the French Flag."
WTT: Thomas Rogerson, Jno. G. Ladd

287   26Sep96
Fm James Irvin, TwnALX, FfxCo, StVA
To Hanson Davis -do-: parcel W of St. Asaph, N of Cameron:
BEGIN on Cameron on line of ground granted Mial [sic] Dorsey by Irvin, 151' N of Cameron ... N w/St A 25'... W//Cameron 123' 5"... S//St A 25'... thence to BEGIN.
--part of land granted Irvin by Charles Alexander [blank] day of [blank] 1795;
--Davis to pay per annum beginning 25Dec96 £7 cmv in specie.
[Davis signs w/mark.]   WTT: none.

292   25 Oct96   Deed of Trust
Fm Dennis Foley, TwnALX, FfxCo, StVA
To Peter Wise -do-
WHEREAS Arthur Lee 21Feb88 granted to Maurice Herlihy a parcel N of Duke, E of St. Asaph:
BEGIN at int Duke-St. A ... E w/Duke 28'... N//St A 100' to 10' alley ... W w/alley 28'... thence to BEGIN, Herlihy paying each 01Apr 60 silver $;

--and Herlihy 11Jun93 conveyed it to Foley, Foley then paying the rent to Lucinda Leiper (to whom Lee had devised it);
AND WHEREAS "the said Dennis Foley was, by the **Reverend** James Muir, duly married unto Elizabeth Dunn, the widow of a certain William Dunn, by whose aid and assistance, care and attention the said Dennis Foley hath been enabled to acquire an handsome living, a part of which he is desirous of securing unto [her] ...as a just Retribution for her great Care and Attention, Aid and Assistance in acquiring the same...."
NOW Foley conveys in trust to Wise, for Elizabeth, part of the Herlihy parcel:
BEGIN on St. A at the "Southern Gavel of the Brick House" on it ... E//Duke 28' to the E line of the parcel ... N w/line to alley ... W w/alley 28' to St. A ... thence to BEGIN;
AND ALSO the slaves Kate and Lucy ["Lucy" below becomes **Susey**] and their increase.
TERMS of this trust:
--Elizabeth is to have Cavan Boa release an earlier trust Dennis set up with Boa for her;
--she is to have the rents from the property during her life, as well as the benefits of the slaves;
--Elizabeth is to pay half the rent due each year;
--when she dies, the property and slave Susey [listed above as **Lucy**] go to her son, James Dunn (James to pay the half-rent thereafter); the slave Kate goes to daughter Martha Dunn;
--Elizabeth is to turn over to Dennis the "Goods, Chattels, Wares amd Merchandize" of which she is now possessed (or this deed of trust is void).
WTT: Ja. Keith, Geo. Wise, Joseph Fullmer
MEMO: On 26 Oct96 Foley refers to this deed of trust, and certfies he has received Elizabeth's goods, chattels, etc.
MEMO: On 25 Oct96 Cavan Boa refers to the deed of trust, and delivery of goods, and releases the [same] parcel of property; Foley had put it in trust to him 04Mar96 to secure a £20 annual income to Elizabeth.

303 16Dec96
Fm Jesse & Elizabeth Taylor, TwnALX, FfxCo, StVA
To Robert Hamilton -do-
WHEREAS William & Sarah Carlin 22May81 conveyed to Jesse Taylor the 1/2-acre LOT 152 S of Duke, E of St. Asaph, adjoining the W side of LOT 102:
BEGIN at NW corner LOT 102 ... S w/LOT 102 to its SW corner ... thence //Wolfe 123' 5" to St. A ... N//first line w/St. A to Wolfe ... E w/Wolfe to BEGIN;
--granted by John Alexander to William Carlin for £6.6.0 per annum each 23Dec;
--since then [no date] the Taylors conveyed half the lot to John Mills, Mills to pay half the annual rent when due;
--since that transaction the Mills' half has passed to Robert Hamilton [no date];
NOW the Taylors for £375 cmv plus the rent convey to Hamilton part of the original Carlin 1/2-acre lot:
BEGIN at int Wolfe-St. Asaph ... E w/Wolfe 61' 8 1/2" to Hamilton's line ... S w/line 176' 7"... W//Wolfe 61' 8 1/2" to St. A ... thence to BEGIN--Hamilton to pay beginning 23Dec97 to William Thornton Alexander (heir to John Alexander) annual rent of £3.3.0 cmv.
WTT: Jonah Isabell, Walter Pomery, R.T. Taylor

308 21Mar96   Tripartite Deed
I - William Wilson, TwnALX, StVA
    Roger Coltart, Twn Fredericksburg, StVA

II - Elizabeth Kirkpatrick, alias Cutler, widow
　Catharine Kirkpatrick, alias Coltart, widow
　Henrietta Kirkpatrick
　(all sisters/co-heirs of Thomas Kirkpatrick, late of ALX)
III-Samuel Simmons, TwnALX, StVA
WHEREAS in his will Thomas Kirkpatrick placed his real estate, to be disposed of for the benefit of his sisters, in the hands of his exxrs: Alexander Henderson; Robert Adam, now dead; Robert McRea; John Muir, now dead; John Gibson; William Hunter, Jr., now dead;
AND WHEREAS Henderson, McCrea and Gibson 14Sep95 conveyed their responsibilities to William Wilson and Roger Coltart; and on 28Sep91 the sisters gave Wilson and Coltart power of attorney to handle their real estate matters;
NOW Wilson & Coltart for £139 cmv convey to Simmons a part LOT 100, S of Wolfe and W of Royal:
BEGIN on Wolfe 75' 5" W of Royal ... W w/Wolfe 48'... S//Royal 101' 6 1/2" to a 9' alley ... E w/alley 48'... thence to BEGIN
--the sellers to keep open a 9' alley from Royal, 101' 6 1/2" S of Wolfe, W and //Wolfe, across LOT 100 "of which lot [these premises] are a part."
[William Wilson signed, as attorney, for the three sisters.]
WTT: Wm. Summers, John Longden, Richd. Weightman, Andrew Zelefro, Andrew Reintzell, Joseph Ingle

318　31May96
Fm Thomas & Ann Richards, TwnALX, FfxCo, StVA
To Walter Pomery AND Jonah Isabell -do-: for £70 cmv a parcel N of Cameron, W of Pitt:
BEGIN on Cameron 99' 5" W of Pitt ... W w/Cameron 24'... N//Pitt 101' 7" to a 10' alley ... E w/alley 24'... thence to BEGIN--part of a 1/2-acre lot sold by the ALX Trustees to Hannah Ramsay Madden, and then by Michael & Hannah Madden to Thomas Richards 13Apr96.
WTT: George Darling, James Irvin, Cary Pratt, Alexr. Smith, Francis Peyton

323　04Nov96
Fm Gurden Chapin, TwnALX, FfxCo, CwlVA
To Philip Magruder -do-: a parcel, part of LOT [blank], part of the parcel Josiah & Jane Watson 29Nov94 conveyed to Gurden Chapin as recorded in FfxCo Court:
BEGIN on N side Duke 100' 5" from St. Asaph ... E w/Duke 23'... N//Pitt & St. A 117' 7"... W//Duke 23'... thence to BEGIN, for 5 years from this date, paying in quarterly installments an annual rent of £90 cmv, beginning 04Feb97;
--rent remitted and title given if Macgruder pays £800 cmv within a year from this date.　WTT: J.A. [possibly T.A.] Sutton, Charles Love, James McKenna

332　30Nov96　[verbatim transcript]
　　Town of Alexandria. William Payne the Surveyor of Fairfax County is requested in conjunction with George Gilpin and Thomazin Ellzey to have the original plan of the Town of Alexandria inserted in the record book for the Corporation and Town aforesaid, together with the minutes of the surveyors relative to the said Town.
　　Done in Council the 30th November 1796
　　Oliver Price　Clerk of the Council
[Copy of map/plan inserted here, as per explanation on p. 333]

333　[verbatim transcript, continued from p. 332 above.]
Each regular and compleat lott contains half an acre or eighty square perches. The courses of Royal, Fairfax, and Water Streets is N12E and S12W.

The courses of Duke, Prince, King, Cameron, Queen, Princess and Oronoko Streets are N78W and S78E all the Streets except Water Street are 66 feet wide and Water Street is 50 feet wide
All regular lotts 5 Chains 17 1/2 links by 3 Chains 37 links is the measure.

Fairfax County July the 18th 1749
    By virtue of an Act of the General Assembly made at the College in the City of Williamsburg in the twenty second year of the Reign of our Sovereign Lord George the second, by the Grace of God of Great Britain, France, and Ireland King defender of the faith &ca and in the year of our Lord one thousand seven hundred and forty eight, Entitled an Act for erecting a Town at Hunting Creek Warehouses in the County of Fairfax.
And persuant to the directions and order of Richard Osborne Lawrence Washington William Ramsay, John Carlyle, Gerrard Alexander and Hugh West Gentlemen, by the said Act appointed Trustees for the said Town to be called Alexandria, I the subscriber did Survey and lay of sixty acres of land to be for the said Town and divided the same into lotts Streets &ca as per the plan thereof
        Jno. West Jr. Depy SFC

A true Copy by Daniel Jennings
Memo. The Genl. Assembly in which
the Act was made began the 27th day
of October 1748

                                Alexandria March 27th 1797
    In Obedience to a request of The Corporation of the Town of Alexandria to us directed as will appear of record in Folio 332 in this book, We the subscribers have copied from the Surveyors Book of the County of Fairfax from Folio 29 in the said book that plan which we have inserted in the 332 Folio of this Book of Records belonging to the Said Town. Which with the notes above, Contain a just and full Copy of the plans and the notes which belong to the plan of the said Town, to the best of our knowledge and belief. /s/ W Payne SFC
                          /s/ George Gilpin
                          /s/ Tz Ellzey

333 27 Oct96
Fm John & Honora Sullivan, TwnALX, CwlVA
To William Pomery AND John Walker, ALX: for £60 cmv a parcel on South of Prince Street:
BEGIN on Prince, S side, 101' 5" W of int of S side Prince-W side Washington Sts ... W w/Prince 22'... S//Wn 132'... E//Prince 22'... thence to BEGIN, part of LOT 6 in a 1784 plan [no further ID of the plan.]   [Honora signs w/mark.]
WTT: Alex. Smith, A. Faw, Wm. Isabel, Walter Pomery Junr.
CMN: Abram [sic] Faw, Alexander Smith, James Irvine, **Gentlemen** of TwnALX, aptd 27 Oct96 to examine Honora. Rptd back same day.

337 20Apr96
Fm John & Mary Woodrow, TwnALX, FfxCo, StVA
To William Halley -do-: for £12 a parcel N of Prince, E of St. Asaph Streets:
BEGIN on N line of this 1/2-acre lot 103' 5" E of St. A ... E w/the line to the E lot line ... S w/that line 37' to an 11' alley ... W w/alley //Prince 20'... thence to BEGIN-- conveyed to Woodrow 28Mar96 by John Thomas Ricketts and William Newton as part of a larger parcel, for annual rent of £21 cmv.
WTT: John Thomas Ricketts, Tho. Lancaster, Wm. Talbott.

CMN: Abram [sic] Faw, John Dundas, Francis Peyton, **Gentlemen** of TwnALX, aptd 24Feb96 to examine Mary. Rptd back same day.

341 17 Oct96
Fm John Harper, TwnALX, FfxCo, StVA
To John Woodrow -do-: for £71 cmv a parcel S of Duke, E of Washington Streets:
BEGIN on Duke 52' E of Wn ... E w/Duke 24'... S//Wn 100' to 10' alley ... W w/alley 24'... thence to BEGIN.
--part of a 1/2-acre leased to Harper by John Alexander's exxrs subject to annual rent paid to William Thornton Alexander (since remitted by William Thornton Alexander for payment [amount/date not specified] by Harper);
--Harper will lay off a 10' alley beginning on Wn 100' S of Duke, for a distance of 100' and parallel to Duke.   WTT: Jacob Cox, Ch. Douglas, Joseph Coleman, Ja. Keith

344 20 Oct96
Fm John Harper, TwnALX, FfxCo, StVA
To William Wright -do-: for £20 cmv a parcel S of "Wales's Alley which is to the Northward of Prince Street and extends from Water to Union Street":
BEGIN on the alley on the E line of ground sold by McRea and Mease to Harper, 121' 1 1/2" E of Water St ... W w/alley 4'... S//Water & Union Sts 39' 7 3/4" to BEGIN [metes and bounds, as incomplete as they seem, are as transcribed by the clerk.]
WTT: Ja. Keith

348 24May96
Fm John & Mary White, TwnALX, FfxCo, StVA
To William Pomery AND John Walkom -do-: for £80.10.0 cmv a parcel part LOT 120, N of Cameron, W of Pitt:
BEGIN on Cameron 75' 5" W of Pitt ... W w/Cameron 24'... N//Pitt 101' 7" to 10' alley ... E w/alley 24'... thence to BEGIN--part of LOT 120 sold by the ALX Trustees to Hannah Ramsay Madden, then by Hannah & Michael Madden to White 13Apr96. [Mary signs her last name as **Whigt**]
WTT: Chrisr. Gird, Alexandr. Smith, P. Marsteller
CMN: Abraham Faw, Alexander Smith, James Irvine aptd 25May96 to examine Mary. Reported back same day.

353 3Nov96
Fm William Cash junior & wife Mary, TwnALX, FfxCo, StVA
To Amos Alexander, FfxCo, StVA
WHEREAS George & Ann Coryell 01Sep95 conveyed to William Cash junior parcel N of Duke, W of Columbus Sts:
BEGIN on Duke 60' W of Columbus ... W w/Duke 20'... N//Columbus 80' to 14' 4" alley ... E w/alley 20'... thence to BEGIN, paying Coryell each 01Jul £2.5.0 cmv, since which time the Coryells transferred the rents paid to Amos Alexander;
NOW the Cashes for £100 cmv convey the parcel to Alexander.
WTT: Francis Peyton, A. Faw, Ja. Keith
CMN: Jonah Thompson, Frances Peyton, Abraham Faw, **Gentlemen** of TwnALX, aptd 28Nov96 to examine Mary. Rptd back 07Feb97.

357 03Nov96
Fm William Cash junior & wife Mary, TwnALX, FfxCo, StVA
To Amos Alexander, FfxCo, StVA
WHEREAS George & Mary Coryell 01Sep95 conveyed to William Cash junior a parcel N of Duke, W of Columbus [exactly as at p.353]

with Cash paying Coryell each 01Jul £2.10.0 cmv [although at p. 353 the rent is listed as £2.5.0];
NOW the Cashes for £35 cmv plus rent convey this parcel to Amos Alexander, Alexander to pay Coryell 25/ cmv 01Jul97, and from 01Jul98 rent of £2.10.0 [unlike p. 353] cmv per annum. WTT: as above; also CMN as above.

363 25Jan97
Fm William Cash junior & wife Mary, TwnALX, FfxCo, StVA
To John Gibory -do-
WHEREAS Stephen & Catharine Cooke 08Jun96 conveyed to William Cash a parcel W of Washington, S of Prince Streets:
BEGIN on Wn, W side, 48' 7" S of Prince ... S w/Wn 22'... W// Prince 60'... N//Wn 22'... thence 60' to BEGIN;
NOW the Cashes for £20 cmv convey to Gibory a parcel:
BEGIN at beginning of final course of the above parcel, which will be 60' W of that parcel's beginning ... E//Prince 19'... S//Wn 22'... W//Prince 19'... N//Wn 22' to BEGIN
WTT: Henry Moore, Cleon Moore, Ax. Henderson [Henderson's name is followed by (possibly): "ygt." Perhaps "the younger."]

366 15 Oct96
Fm Thomas & Mary Patten, TwnALX, FfxCo, StVA
To Alexander Vietch -do-: lease of parcel W of Water St, N of Gibbons St.:
BEGIN on Water St. 113' 9" N of Gibbons--the N line of a 10' alley ... N w/Water St 62' 10"... W//Gibbons 105' 5"... S//Water St 62' 10" to the alley ... thence to BEGIN.
--part of 1/2-acre conveyed to Patten 29Dec94 by William Thornton Alexander & wife Lucy for annual rent of £25 cmv due [blank] day of [blank] each year;
--Vietch is to pay the Pattens, beginning 01Jan98, £23.11.3 per annum [but the next sentence says the rent begins 01Jan97]
--the Pattens will lay off a 10' alley beginning on Water St 103' 9" N of Gibbons, running from Water St 123' 5", parallel to Gibbons.
WTT: John Barber, Thomas Clark, William Savage
CMN: Jonah Thompson, Abm. Faw, Francs [sic] Peyton, **Gentlemen** of TwnALX, aptd 16Feb97 to examine Mary. Rptd back same day.

372 16Sep96   Tripartite Deed
[Clerk's marginal note: Commission in Liber L, page 363.]
I - George & Ann Coryell, TwnALX, FfxCo, CwlVA
II - George Bailey -do-
III - William Thornton Alexander, King George Co, CwlVA
WHEREAS 29Dec94 William Thornton Alexander & wife Lucy leased to George Coryell a 1-acre parcel in FfxCo, adjacent to ALX:
BEGIN at int Columbus-Duke, N side Duke, W side Columbus ... N w/Columbus 176' 5" "or half a Square"... W w/Prince extended 246' 10" to Alfred ... thence at right angles w/W line, parallel to Alfred, until intersecting Duke St extended ... thence w/N edge of Duke to BEGIN;
--and William Thornton Alexander "hath verbally promised and agreed to and with George Coryell" regarding non-payment penalties [stated, but not here abstracted];
NOW the Coryells will lease to Bailey a parcel:
BEGIN on E of Alfred, 102' 4" N of int Duke-Alfred, on N side of alley where it intersects Alfred St ... E 100' to "open square space of ground" 46' wide left there by agreement between Coryell and Samuel Davis ... N w/that space's line 40'... W//first line and Duke 100' to Alfred ... S w/Alfred 40' to BEGIN, Bailey to pay beginning 01Jul97 $25 per annum. WTT: Cleon Moore, Henry Moore, John Alton

376 13Aug96
Fm George & Ann Coryell, TwnALX, FfxCo, StVA
To John Alton -do-
WHEREAS William Thornton Alexander & wife Lucy 06Dec94 conveyed to Coryell 2 acres in FfxCo, adjacent to ALX:
BEGIN at int Alfred-Prince, S of Prince and W of Alfred ... W and parallel until intersecting Patrick St ... S w/Patrick until intersecting Duke ... E w/Duke until intersecting W line of Alfred ... N w/Alfred's W line to BEGIN;
NOW the Coryells lease to Alton a parcel:
BEGIN on N side Duke 56' 2" from int Duke-Alfred ... N w/Alfred 88' to 20' alley ... W//Duke 18'... S//Alfred 88' to Duke ... thence 18' to BEGIN, Alton to pay beginning 26Jan97 £14.19.0 cmv per annum.
WTT: Cleon Moore, George Bayly, Henry Moore

380 12 Oct96
Fm Dennis & Jane Allen Ramsay, TwnALX, FfxCo, StVA
To Hugh Smith -do-: for £270 cmv parcel N of King, W of Union
BEGIN on King 45' W of Union ... W w/King 30' to Charles Page's line ... N w/Page's line 81' to Fayette St ... E w/Fayette 30'... thence to BEGIN--part of ground given Dennis by William Ramsay 20Dec84.
WTT: John Dunlap, Thomas Irwin, Peter Murray, Francis Peyton, A. Faw
CMN: Abraham Faw, James Irvin, Francis Peyton, **Gentlemen** of [blank], aptd 12 Oct96 to examine Jane. Rptd back [blank] Oct96.

385 05Apr95   Deed of Trust
Fm John Lemoine, TwnALX, StVA
To John Mandeville, John Foster AND George Clementson of -do-
[Lemoine is in debt to the creditors below, and places his assets in trust to the trio to sell, apportioning the proceeds among the creditors. In a memo following the signed deed, Elisha C. Dick declares that it is the intent of the group of creditors that Lemoine continue to ply his trade with the stock, tools and furniture hereby placed in trust.]
WTT: Wm. Gunnell, H. Sutton

Schedule of Creditors and Amounts owed:
Messers Hodgson & Nikolson   £157.11.9 1/2
Mr. John Mandeville   56.16.0
Mr. Wm. Hodgson   49.13.0
Messrs Fosters & May   46.16.0
Mr. Bernard Ghequiere per order for Mr. Tiernan   60. 0.0
and his Brothers of Baltimore
Mr. George Hunter   14.13.0
Messrs. Patton & Butcher   31.10.0
Mr. Eliza [sic] Dick   15. 0.0
Messrs. Lansdall & Hodges in Upper Malbrough [sic]   18. 9.0
Mrs. [sic] Fletcher & Otway   18. 0.0
Messrs. Polkinhorne & Andrew   16. 0.0
Mr. Piere [sic] Adoni   Baltimore   27. 0.0
Mr. John Gibory   14. 0.0
Mr. John Aubrier   12. 0.0
Mr. George Spangler   9. 0.0
Mr. George Meeme [sic]   Winchester   18. 0.0
Mrs. Catharine Lutz   18. 2.0

Mr. Benjamin Carry   13.10.0
                    [Sub total] 623.2.9 1/2
        [Less this amount, not explained] 27.0.0
                          [TOTAL] 596.2.9 1/2

A List of John Lemoine's Property of every description, vizt.
15 saddles ready made
25 Saddle trees ready plated
7   ditto ditto naked
20 Blind Bridle ready made
5 Cart-Saddles
1 Martengail
2 pairs of Galleses
10 Saddle Cloaths
10 Buckskins leather
4 Pairs of plated Stirrups
28 Yards of Velverett
4 Turkey Straps
8 Hair Brushes
5 Pieces of wasted webb [possibly wusted or wosted]
2 1/2 dozen of Bridle Bitts
1 ditto of Snaffles
7 pieces of Binding
5 yards of prince of Wales check
4 large Glasses Cases
3 Waggon whips
30 sets of plated nails
1 dozen of staples and plates
1 ten-plate stove
1 Con_   [sic]
3 Beds, 6 Blankets, 4 pairs of Sheets
3 Rugs, one Desk, one Clothes Press, 4 Tables
3 Bedsteads, 6 Chairs, one Looking-Glass
10 Pictures
2 large tea canisters
1 Stand, 6 Candlesticks, 3 Iron pots, 2 Dutch ovens
1 frying pan, 1 dozen of plates, 1 Tureen, 4 Dishes
1 Gridiron, 1 Collender, 3 flat-irons, 1 Kitchen Table
4 Tubs, 3 Piggens, 6 Knives & Forks, 6 pewter spoons
One third part of Stage Waggon and Harness in company
      with John Johnson and John Bryan.

[N.B.: the following eight entries are all commissions arising from conveyances by William Thornton Alexander & wife Lucy to Stephen Cooke.]

391 [blank] day of [blank] 1795   [A Commission]
John Taliaferro, John Taliaferro Junr and Mich. Wallace, **Gentlemen** of King George Co., aptd to examine Lucy Alexander regarding the parcel W of Columbus and S of King conveyed to Stephen Cooke 25Dec94. Reported back 12Nov96.

392 As above, p. 391, except here regarding 1/2-acre lot N of Prince, E of Washington Sts. Rptd back [blank] [blank] 1796.

394 As above, pp. 391-2, except here regarding a 30May94 conveyance of 12-acre parcel between Fairfax and Pitt, bounded by Hunting Creek on the South. Reported back 12Nov96.

396 As above, pp. 391-2-4, except here regarding the 30May94 conveyance of rents from four lots on W + E side of Washington, and S + N sides of King. Reported back 12Nov96.

397 As above, pp. 391-2-4-6, except here regarding the 05Dec94 conveyance of 1/2-acre lot W of Columbus, N of King Streets. Reported back 12Nov95. [Note that other reporting dates in this series are 12Nov 179<u>6</u>.]

399 As above, pp. 391-2-4-6-7, except here regarding the 25Dec94 conveyance of 4-acre parcel W of Ffx St and adjoining LOT 36. Reported back 12Nov96.

400 As above, pp. 391-2-4-6-7-9, except here regarding the 27Dec94 conveyance of 6-acre parcel on Jones Point. Reported back 12Nov 179[blank].

402 As above, pp. 391-2-4-6-7-9 and 400, except here regarding the 23Jun94 conveyance of a parcel "to the Southward of the Town of Alexandria." Reported back 12Nov96.

404 12Nov96
Fm Charles & Frances Alexander, FfxCo, StVA
To Hugh Smith, TwnALX, FfxCo, StVA: lease of 2-acre parcel contiguous to ALX, W of Washington, E of Columbus, N of Wythe, S of Madison Streets:
BEGIN at int Wn-Wythe ... W w/Wythe 246' 10" to Columbus ... N w/Columbus 353' 2" to Madison ... E w/Madison 246' 10" to Wn ... S w/Wn to BEGIN, Smith to pay rent 01Jan98 of 71 2/3 silver $; beginning 01Jan99, 143 1/2 silver $ per annum.
WTT: Wm. Hepburn, William A. Harper, Thomas Cook
CMN: John Dundas, Francis Peyton, **Gentlemen** of [blank], aptd 09May97 to examine Frances Alexander. Reported back same day.

409 06Feb97
Fm Francis & Mary Patten, TwnALX, FfxCo, StVA
To Dennis McCarty Johnston -do-
WHEREAS William Thornton Alexander & wife Lucy 29Dec94 leased to the Pattens 1/2-acre lot in ALX:
BEGIN at int Gibbons-Water Sts, N of Gibbons, W of Water St ... N w/Water st 176' 7"... W//Gibbons 123' 5"... S//Water St 176' 7"... thence to BEGIN, the Pattens paying each 01Jan £25 lawful money of Virginia;
AND WHEREAS Francis Patten 15 Oct96 leased to Alexander Veitch: BEGIN on Water St. 113' 9" N of Gibbons, on N side of 10' alley ... N w/Water St 62' 10"... W//Gibbons 105' 5"... S//Water St 62' 10" to the alley ... thence to BEGIN, Veitch paying Patten each 01Jan £23.11.3 cmv;
AND WHEREAS Francis Patten 04Feb97 leased to Negro Craigy: BEGIN on N side of 10' alley 105' 5" W of Water St ... W w/alley 18'... N//Water St 62' 10"... E//Gibbons 18'... thence to BEGIN, Craigy paying Patten each 01Jan £5.8.0 cmv;
NOW the Pattens for £312 cmv plus rent convey to Johnston:
BEGIN at int Gibbons-Water Sts ... N w/Water St 103' 9" to 10' alley ... W w/alley, parallel Gibbons, 123' 5"... S//Water St 103' 9"... thence to BEGIN.

--assigning to Johnston the £23.11.3 annual rent from Veitch, and the £5.8.0 annual rent from Negro Craigy;
--Johnston now to pay William Thornton Alexander each 01Jan the annual rent of £25 cmv. WTT: Dennis McCarty, Thomas Irwin, William Savage
CMN: [names left blank], **Gentlemen** of TwnALX, aptd 07Feb97 to examine Mary. On 16Feb97 Jonah Thompson and Francis Peyton reported they had done so.

417 04Feb97
Fm Thomas & Mary Patten, TwnALX, FfxCo, StVA
To Negro Craigy -do-: lease of the parcel W of Water St, N of Gibbons, as detailed in the lease above, p. 409.
[Craigy signs w/mark]
WTT: William Savage, Thomas Irwin, Dennis McCarty Johnston for Craigy, Alexander Veitch for Craigy, Robert Fulton.
CMN: Jonah Thompson, Abm. Faw, Francis Peyton aptd 16Feb97 to examine Mary. Reported back same day.

422 06Dec96
Fm Stephen & Catharine Cooke "of Alexandria"
To John Gibbory "of the same Town": for £80 Virginia money a parcel on S side of Pince, W of Washington Streets:
BEGIN at NE corner of the lot sold to Lewis Cook ... E w/Prince to the lot sold to Cavan Boa, 39'... S//Wn 48' "as far as Cavan Boa's lot extends southerly"... W//Prince 19' "to within 20 feet of the east line of Lewis Cook's lot"... S//Wn 32'... W//Prince 20'... N//Wn to BEGIN.
WTT: James Muir, Jno.Thos.Ricketts, Daniel Woods, John Bowsall

423 20Jan97
Fm Charles Alexander, **Gentlemen**, FfxCo & wife Francis
To Daniel McLeod AND John Lumsden, TwnALX: lease of 2 full 1/2-acre lots adjoining ALX, between Oronoko, Columbus, Pendleton and Alfred Streets:
I - BEGIN at NW corner of int Oronoko-Columbus Sts ... N w/Columbus 176' 7"... W//Oronoko 123' 5"... S//Columbus 176' 7" ... thence to BEGIN.
II - BEGIN at SE corner Pendleton and Alfred Sts ... S w/Alfred 176' 7"... E//Pendleton 123' 5" to NW corner of Lot I, above ... thence //Alfred 176' 7"... thence to BEGIN, McLeod & Lumsden to pay, beginning 01May98, 71 2/3 silver $ per annum;
--McLeod, Lumsden and Alexander agree to pay proportionately to make three alleys: two to parallel Pendleton and Oronoko, each 15' wide, the third to parallel Columbus through the center of the Square, 26' 10" wide. [The deed refers to a plat showing this, but the plat is not entered in the deed book.]
WTT: John Bogue, Charles Alexander Junr, James Davidson
CMN: John Dundas, Francis Peyton, Alexander Smith, **Gentlemen** of TwnALX, aptd 09May97 to examine Frances Alexander. Reported back same day.

428 04 Oct96
Fm Robert & Elizabeth Lyle, TwnALX, FfxCo, StVA
To Duncan Nevin -do-: for £226 cmv part LOT 23, W of Ffx, S of Princess Sts:
BEGIN on Ffx on line dividing LOT 23 and LOT 28 ... N w/Ffx 31'... W//Princess 123' 5" to W line of LOT 23 ... S w/line 31' to the Dividing line ... thence to BEGIN.
ALSO part LOT 24, E of Royal, S of Princess:
BEGIN on Royal at line dividing LOT 24 and LOT 29 ... N w/Royal 31'... E//Princess 123' 5" to E line of LOT 24 ... S w/line 31' to the Dividing line ... thence to BEGIN.
--these are the parcels conveyed 10May96 to Robert Lyle by Philip Marsteller and Peter Wise.

WTT: Lanty Crowe, Andrew Fleming, Thos. Stewart

431   25Apr97   Mortgage
Fm Levi Reynolds, TwnALX, StVA
To William Reynolds [no ID but possibly of Maryland, because of the currency involved]: for £41 current money of MD owed and payable w/in 3 years from now:
WHEREAS George Coryell and George McMunn leased to Levi a parcel on S side Prince and E of Pitt, with the privilege of removing when the lease was up any building Levi might erect,
AND "upon which piece of Ground I have built a Nailor's Shop"
NOW to secure payment of that £41, Levi mortgages to William:
--"that house built by me" and "one pair of Smith's bellows now in the said Shop" and "4 Steaks and Hammers for making Nails" and 4 pair Smith's Tongs and 15 nail Tools. (The deed is void if the debt is paid on time.)
WTT: Ja. Keith, John Weylie

433   28Jan97   Non-Importation Compliance
   Thomas Marshall [no ID] swears to his compliance with the slave non-importation act before William Deneale, **Justice of the Peace** for FfxCo. [No slave ID, dates, nor slave source.]

433   30Sep96
Fm Thomas & Anne Richards, TwnALX, StVA
To Charles Lee, City of Philadelphia
WHEREAS Richards 11Apr96 leased to John McIver for 5 years from 30Mar96 at £90 cmv per annum, in half yearly payments, the first payment due 29Sep97, a house--on N side of King and E side of an alley, fronting 24' on King ... with the Kitchen, Smoke-house, Necessary and Yard to the Fence ... "being part of the House built by James Hendricks and which he,...Thomas Richards, lately occupied himself"... and the use of the alley together with others who opened on it ... and a Stable and Loft on [blank] Street "adjoining the Stable occupied by Doctor Rose";
NOW the Richardses for $1000 from Lee assign the McIver indenture and the £90 annual rents to Lee.
WTT: Edmund J. Lee, A. Faw, Francis Peyton
CMN: Francis Peyton, Abran [sic] Faw, James Irvin, **Gentlemen Justices** for Alexandria, aptd 16 Oct96 to examine Anne. Rptd back 26 Oct96.

437   12Apr97
Fm Roger Coltart, Twn of Fredericksburg, StVA
To John Dundas, TwnALX, StVA
WHEREAS William Wilson AND Roger Coltart, as agents for:
--Elizabeth Kirkpatrick Cutler
--Katharine Kirkpatrick Coltart
--Henrietta Kirkpatrick   [see p. 443, below]
on 27Sep96 sold to William Hepburn [no ID for any of these]:
water property E of Water St which fronts on LOT 26--the residue of a 99-year lease to the ground under the river bank fronting LOT 26 (from the S corner of LOT 26, N along Water St 117' 7 1/8", and into the Potomac on the flats to the channel edge), the lease having been granted to John & Thomas Kirkpatrick by the ALX Trustees--Hepburn also paying Wilson & Coltart £50 cmv for some landfill to be done;
AND WHEREAS 30Sep96 Hepburn sold to Wilson & Coltart two thirds of these premises--Wilson & Coltart to pay Hepburn 2/3 of the £50 cost of the landfill to be done; and

WHEREAS 16Nov96 Hepburn and Wilson sold to Richard Conway part of this ground "under the bank" which Hepburn had just bought, and then conveyed 2/3 back to Coltart & Wilson;
AND WHEREAS 20Sep91 Thomas West sold to Richard Conway "all that Slip of Ground lying and adjoining upon the East side of Water Street and the South side of ... LOT 20":
BEGIN on Water St at s line of LOT 20 ... E w/lot line into the River ... thence //Water St 117' to Queen ... W w/Queen to Water St ... thence to BEGIN, plus "the waters, water courses and Landings";
AND WHEREAS 16Nov96 Richard & Mary Conway sold to Wilson, Hepburn & Coltart part of the parcel Conway bought from West:
BEGIN on Water St 50' S of S line of LOT 20 ... E//Queen = LOT 20's S line into the river ... S//Water St 67' to Queen ... W w/Queen to Water St ... N w/Water St. 67' to BEGIN, plus "waters water courses Landings and Beaches";
NOW Roger Coltart for £250 cmv sells to John Dundas:
--half of what Hepburn sold to Wilson & Coltart (that being 1/3 of what Wilson and Coltart [as agents for the Kirkpatrick heirs] sold to Hepburn);
--PLUS 1/3 of the parcel sold by Conway to Wilson, Hepburn & Coltart
WTT: Ja. Keith, Geo. Darling, John Gordon, Thos. Cook

443 27Sep96
Fm William Wilson, TwnALX, StVA AND Roger Coltart, Twn of Fredericksburg, StVA--as agents for:
--Widow Elizabeth Kirkpatrick Cutler   [All 3 are Sisters and Co-
--Widow Katharine Kirkpatrick Coltart   Heiresses of
--Henrietta Kirkpatrick   Thomas Kirkpatrick]
To William Hepburn, TwnALX, StVA
WHEREAS "it appearing by an Entry made in the Books of the Trustees [of ALX] 1st September 1760 that the Trustees had, previous to their exposing any Lotts of Ground to Sale in the said Town, made a declaration which was at the Sale made public that any person purchasing a Lot of ground upon the West Side of Water Street should have all the Benefit and privilege of the water joining upon that Street and extending Improvements into the River as the purchaser might think proper notwithstanding the intervention of [Water street] between the Lot...and the water";
WHEREAS Alan McRea bought LOT 26 of the W side of Water St and the N of Queen, later sold by McRea and by various contracts vesting in Thomas Kirkpatrick; however, when Alan McRea died without having made proper conveyance of it, LOT 26 passed to his son and heir, John McRea;
WHEREAS 17Mar70 the Trustees leased to John & Thomas Kirkpatrick the ground "under the River Bank opposite to their Lot No. 26..."--from the S lot line up Water St 117' 7 1/8" and from the E side of Water St into the River--from 01Dec68 for 99 years, the lease passing entirely to Thomas when his brother John Kirkpatrick died;
--when Thomas died his will directed his properties be placed in trust for his sisters to Alexander Henderson, Robert Adam, Robert McCrea, John Muir, John Gibson and William Hunter, jr--since which time Adam, Muir and Hunter have died;
AND WHEREAS Alan McRea's son and heir, John, conveyed in two indentures to the heiresses of Thomas Kirkpatrick and their trustees:
--on 20Sep86 the lot bought by his father but--by error--calling the lot 20 instead of 26, and
--on 12Sep95 the water rights to the lot (as announced by the Trustees prior to the lot's sale;
AND WHEREAS 14Sep95 Henderson, Robert McRea and Gibson (as surviving trustees of Thomas Kirkpatrick) conveyed their trusteeship to William Wilson and Roger Coltart and

--on 28Sep91 the sisters/heiresses had given power of attorney to Wilson and Coltart, as recorded in FfxCo Court;
NOW Wilson & Coltart for £280 cmv from William Hepburn convey to him all the Water property fronting LOT 26, E of Water St, by virtue (in concert) of the Trustees' pre-sale declaration, the deeds from John McRea, and the legacies of Thomas Kirkpatrick including the unexpired 99-year lease;
--Hepburn to pay an additional £50 cmv to Wilson and Coltart "to fill up that space of Water lying between the wharf of Richard Conway and the wharf of Herbert, Wilson & Potts when the same is completed." [Context suggests the money is to be paid when the landfill is completed, not when the H,W & P wharf is completed.]
WTT: Ja. Keith, George Darling, John Gordon, John Dundas

451 20Apr97 Mortgage
Fm John Harper, TwnALX, FfxCo, StVA
To William Harper -do-
WHEREAS John owes William £240 cmv, to secure payment of same he conveys to William parcel N of Prince, E of Ffx:
BEGIN on Prince [blank feet] E of Ffx--at the W line or "gavel of that 3-story brick house lately built by the said John Harper which is now in the occupation of Thomas Williams"... E w/Prince "and the front line of the said house...to the Eastern line or Gavel of the said House"... N//Ffx to John Harper's back line ... W w/line the distance of the first line ... thence to BEGIN.
--the debt is payable 20Apr99; if paid on time, this is void.
WTT: Benjn. Shreve, Saml Davis, Isaac Gibson

451 30Dec96
Fm John Harper, TwnALX, FfxCo, StVA
To Charles Harper -do-: for £446 cmv, two parcels:
I - N of Prince, E of Water St:
BEGIN on Prince at E line of ground granted by John to William Wright--91' 1 1/2" E of Water St ... E w/Prince 20'... N//Water St 88' 3 1/2"... W//Prince 20'... thence to BEGIN--part of parcel conveyed to John Harper by John Hough;

II - An ajoining parcel:
BEGIN at N end of the W (last) line of the above parcel--88' 3 1/2" N of Prince ... N//Water St 39' 7 3/4" to "Wales's Alley"... W w/alley 26'... S//Water St same as first line to ground recently William Wright's, now Joseph Dyson's ... W//Prince "and the said Alley" 26' to BEGIN--part of parcel conveyed to John Harper by Robert & Nancy McRea AND Robert & Betty Mease.
WTT: William Harper, Edward Harper

457 15 Oct96
[Clerk's note: "N.B. Acknowledgement on page 301, Liber K."]
Fm Robert & Esther Hamilton, TwnALX, FfxCo, StVA
To John Hill -do-: for £120 cmv parcel W of Pitt, S of Wolfe:
BEGIN on Pitt 110' S of Wolfe on S line of 10' alley ... S w/Pitt 22'... W//Wolfe 80' to alley 8' 8" wide ... N w/alley, parallel Pitt, 22' to first alley ... thence to BEGIN.
--part of parcel conveyed to Hamilton by Bushrod & Mary Washington on [date left blank];
--Hamilton to keep open a 10' alley beginning on Pitt 100' S of Wolfe, running west for 94'
--Hamilton also to keep open an 8' 8" alley beginning on S line of the first alley, 80' W of Pitt, running S//Pitt 66'
WTT: Ja.Keith, Jas. Hamilton, Geo.Jeffreys, Theophilus Randell

460 19Mar96
Fm Corbin & Hannah Washington, Westmoreland Co.
To Charles Lee, TwnALX: for £300 lawful money of VA, a 1/2-acre lot in ALX, "in the Parish of Ffx and the County of Ffx"
--devised by Arthur Lee **Esquire** in his last will and testament to Hannah;
--sold to Arthur Lee by Henry Lee, Jr;
--sold to Henry Lee, Jr. by Baldwin Dade;
--sold to Baldwin Dade by Thomas West who received the land as heir-at-law of George Carlyle;
--the lot is "in the occupation of" William Merchant, Beale Howard and Jacob Heineman except 1/6 of it, now vacant:
BEGIN at int Washington-Oronoko on W of Wn, S of Oronoko ... W w/Oronoko 123' 5"... S//Wn 176' 7"... E//Oronoko 123' 5"... thence to BEGIN.
WTT: Sally Lee, Harriot [sic] Turberville, Geo. Richard Lee Turberville, Edm. J. Lee, John Potts, Chas. Alexander as [to] C.W.
CMN: Charles Alexander, John Potts, Charles Little, **Gentlemen** of Ffx Co, aptd 17Apr97 to examine Hannah. Rptd back same day.

464 01Sep96
[This deed, unlike all its predecessors, begins "This Conveyance" rather than "This Indenture."]
Fm Francis & Sarah Peyton, TwnALX, FfxCo, StVA
To Luke Shortill -do-: lease of parcel between Columbus and Alfred on N side of Prince:
BEGIN N side of Prince 42' W of Columbus ... W//Prince 26'... S//Columbus 89'... thence to BEGIN, Shortill to pay beginning 01Sep97 26 silver $ per annum.
WTT: none
CMN: Jonah Thompson, John Dundas, Abraham Faw, **Gentlemen** of [blank], aptd 20Dec96 to examine Sarah. Reprted back 21Dec96.

468 02Jan97
Fm George & Jane Gilpin, TwnALX, FfxCo, StVA
To George Slacum -do-
WHEREAS 18Feb83 the Gilpins leased to Michael Madden a parcel S of Prince, W of Union:
BEGIN on Prince 51' W of Union ... W w/Prince 40'... S//Union 44' 4" to the land of Jonathan Hall's heirs, "now belonging to Francis Peyton"...E w/that line, parallel Prince, 40'...thence to BEGIN, Madden to pay each 31Dec 80 silver $;
NOW the Gilpins for £240 cmv assign Slacum the Madden rents.
WTT: P. Marsteller "by G. Gilpin"; Jno. Lewis Marsteller; Leml. Bent
CMN: Jonah Thompson, Abm. Faw, Francis Peyton, **Gentlemen** of TwnALX, aptd 23Jan97 to examine Jane. Reported back 27Jan97.

473 13Jul96   Mortgage
Fm William & Mary Bushby, FfxCo, StVA
To Benton Riggen -do-
WHEREAS Bushby owes Riggen £62.8.6, to secure payment of same he mortgages part of a lot in ALX:
BEGIN on Ffx 53' 2" N of the Presbyterian Church yard ... N w/Ffx 18'... W//Duke 11' to Chapel Alley ... S w/alley 18'... thence to BEGIN--if debt is paid by 6 months from now, this deed is void.
WTT: Joseph Emmit, Wm. Summers, Sally Adams; Mary [her + mark] Bushby, Jno. Dalton

475 14Feb97
Fm Patrick & Margaret Byrne, TwnALX, FfxCo, StVA
To Charles Douglas -do-
WHEREAS Michael & Hannah Madden 08Jul93 leased to Byrne a parcel S of Prince, W of Union:
BEGIN on Prince 51' W of Union ... W w/Prince 22'... S//Union 44' 4" to ground formerly the heirs of Jonathan Hall, now of Francis Peyton ... E//Prince 22'... thence to BEGIN, Byrne paying to George Gilpin each 31Dec 44 silver $, thus fulfilling an obligation of Michael Madden to Benjamin Shreve and James Lawrason--this parcel being part of the ground leased by the Gilpins to Michael Madden 18Nov83 for an annual rent of 80 silver $;
NOW the Byrnes for £241 cmv convey to Douglas the entire parcel leased from the Maddens, Douglas to pay Gilpin 31Dec97 38 1/2 silver $, and beginning 31Dec98 44 silver $ per annum. [Margaret Byrne signs w/mark.]
WTT: Jonah Thompson, Francis Peyton, Abraham Faw, **Gentlemen** of TwnALX, aptd 14Feb97 to examine Margaret. Rptd back same day.

481 29Mar96   Quadripartite Deed
I - David Ridgway & wife Martha, widow & exx of Daniel McPherson
   PLUS Isaac McPherson AND Edward Beeson, exxrs of Daniel McPherson
II - Isaac McPherson
III - David & Martha Ridgway
IV - Henry McGough, TwnALX, FfxCo, StVA [No IDs for the others]
WHEREAS the **Honorable** James Mercer **Esquire** 22May87 conveyed to Daniel & Isaac McPherson three parcels of land in LOT 80, shown in Mercer's plat of LOT 80 as parcels 2,3 and 5;
WHEREAS Daniel died before he and Isaac had divided or sold Parcel 3, and Daniel's will directed it be sold;
--and his heirs and exx (see above) with Isaac on 11Apr91 put it up for public sale, at which James Wilson, Jr., was high bidder at £70.10 cmv;
--and on 13Apr91 Martha, Isaac and Edward conveyed to Wilson what "they supposed to be the piece of Ground exposed by them to Auction" but on examining the deed find it describes Parcel 2, which had already been conveyed by Daniel and Isaac to John Murray;
--and James Wilson had sold his "parcel 3" to Henry McGough, and needs a clear title;
NOW the exx and exxrs of Daniel McPherson for £35.10 cmv already paid them by Wilson, plus £69 current money also paid to Wilson by McGough, convey to McGough Parcel 3 of LOT 80:
BEGIN on Duke 67' 10" W of Water St ... W w/Duke 27' 10"... S//Water St 91' 6" to 10' alley ... E w/alley 27' 10" ... thence to BEGIN, plus the use of LOT 80's alleys.
WTT: Ja. Keith, Edward Fenwick, H. Kh. Smoot, Daniel McPherson

488 30Mar97
Fm Valentine Peers, Prince William Co, StVA
To George Rutter, TwnALX, StVA
WHEREAS Peers on [dates left blank] leased to Rutter a parcel in ALX with a 20' front on Union St, for an annual rent of £16 currency, remittable within [blank] years on payment of £176 currency;
NOW Peers, for £176 current money, conveys the land to Rutter
WTT: Jno. Thos. Ricketts, Samuel Harper, Thomas Irwin

489 01Feb97
Fm Elisha Cullen Dick & wife Hannah, TwnALX, FfxCo, StVA

To Alexander Smith -do-: for £360 cmv a parcel E of Pitt, S of Duke Streets:
BEGIN on Pitt "at the Center of the Square formed by Duke and Wolfe Streets"--
177' 1 1/2" from each of the streets ... N w/Pitt 57' 1 1/2" to an 18' alley ... E w/alley
130' to the corner of a 10' alley ...S//Pitt 57' 1 1/2"...thence to BEGIN
--part of property conveyed 21Jun96 by Elizabeth Donaldson to Elisha Cullen Dick
WTT: Ann Price, Jonah Thompson, A. Faw
CMN: Jonah Thompson, Abraham Faw, Francis Peyton, **Gentlemen** of [blank], aptd
02Feb97 to examine Hannah. Rptd back same day.

493 27Jan97
Fm Jesse Simms, TwnALX, FfxCo, StVA
To Alexander Smith -do-: for £600 cmv, a parcel N of King and W of Union Streets:
BEGIN at int King-Union ... W w/King 45' to property conveyed by Dennis & Jane
Ramsay to Hugh Smith ... N w/line 81' to "Fayette Street or Alley"...E w/Fayette
45'...thence to BEGIN--conveyed by the Ramsays to Simms 08Dec96.
WTT: Dennis Ramsay, Charles Dodson Junr, Ja. Keith

End of Book H

INDEX

Abert
  Jno. 80
  John 60, 96, 104
Accomack Co., VA 79
Adam
  Ann 29, 41, 49, 185
  Jacob 90
  James 2, 3
  Jane 92, 132, 137, 148
  John 92, 132, 137, 148
  Mary Adam Barry 138
  Robert 2, 4, 25, 29, 36, 40-42, 49, 53, 58, 64, 79, 92, 100, 107, 116, 121, 132, 137, 148, 182, 185, 206, 215
  Robert: his estate sale 58
Adams
  Jacob 97
  James 175
  John 109
  Sally 217
Adamson
  Anthony 85
Adoni
  Piere 210
Albers
  Ludwell 118, 126
  Siedr. 172
Alderson
  Thomas 17
Alexander
  Alexander-West property line 33
  Alexanders' property line 34
  Amos 162, 163, 208
  Catharine 43
  Charles 57, 61, 93, 104, 114, 118, 131, 133, 138, 145, 155, 196, 197, 200, 201, 204, 212, 213, 217
  Charles Jr. 213
  Frances 104, 114, 131, 133, 155, 197, 200, 212, 213
  Gerard/Gerrard 5, 43, 207
  Gerrard Jr. 164
  John 5, 9-16, 19, 25, 28, 44, 51, 53, 54, 56, 63, 67, 86, 95, 96, 105, 111, 119, 122, 141, 143, 150, 156, 157, 167, 169, 171-175, 177, 178, 186, 187, 192, 195, 205, 208
  Lucy 19, 49-51, 54, 72, 105-108, 1-17, 118, 119, 125, 126, 135, 136, 140, 149, 151-154, 156, 157, 160, 169, 171, 173, 175, 180, 186, 188, 195, 198, 199, 204, 209-211, 212
  Marianne 196
  Mary 5, 43
  Philip 5, 43
  Philip Thornton 187
  Robert 9, 196
  William 10-14
  William Thornton 10-14, 19, 40, 44, 49, 50, 51, 54, 59, 70, 72, 94-96, 105, 106-108, 117-119, 125, 126, 129, 135, 136, 140, 141, 144, 145, 149, 150, 151-154, 156, 157, 161-163, 167-175, 178-181, 186-188, 195, 198, 199, 204, 205, 208-212
Alexandria
  Act of Incorporation 131
  Common Council 81
  County court house approved for town use 81
  currency 1
  Deputy Town Sergeant 195
  Mayor & Commonalty 14, 51, 81, 104, 130, 186
  Powder House 104
  Town & county record office 81
  Town lands & survey 62
  Town line 3
  Town line (old) 33
  Town Plan 189, 201, 206
  Town school house 81
  Town Sergeant 109, 138
  Trustees 2-6, 15, 33, 36, 38, 40, 43, 53, 57, 62, 84, 99, 121, 130, 155, 165, 168, 178, 186, 189, 193, 206, 207, 208, 215, 216
  Vendue Master 32, 33, 176
  Vendue Store 176
Alexandria Academy 156
Alexandria Aldermen:
  Marsteller, P. 131
  Marsteller, Philip 104
  Mease, Robert 104, 131
  Porter, Thomas 82
  Ramsay, Dennis 82
  Taylor, Jesse 82, 104, 131
  Thompson, Jonah 131
Alexandria Commissioner:
  Conway, Richard 45
Alexandria Councilmen:
  Duvall, William 52
  Hickman, William 104, 131

Hoof, Lawrence 104, 131
Hunter, William 82
Longdon, John 52
Mease, Robert 82
Paton, William 52, 82, 104, 131
Porter, Thomas 104, 131
Reynolds, John 52
Saunders, John 52
Shreve/Shreeve, Benjamin 52, 104, 131
Wise, Peter 82, 104, 131
Alexandria Gazette 33, 58, 73, 83, 87, 89, 103, 109, 110, 131, 135, 139, 159, 176
Alexandria Hustings Court 109, 125, 175
Alexandria Recorders:
  Dundas, John 104, 131
  Taylor, Jesse 82
Alexandria Trustees:
  Muir, John 99, 165
  Piper, Harry 99, 165
Alexandria, addition to:
  D. Griffith's 20-24, 76, 80
  J. Alexander's 4, 10, 11, 13, 15, 25, 28, 72, 74, 96, 119, 136, 137, 141, 149, 171, 172, 174, 179, 186, 187, 192, 195
  leased by ALX for powder house 104
  W. Ramsay's 76
  W.T. Alexander's 59, 107
Alleys, named:
  Allison's 4, 30, 39, 49, 87
  Chapel/Chappel 109, 217
  Jamieson's 132
  Ramsay's 16, 76, 128
  Ramsay's, formerly Fayette St. 123, 124
  Ramsay's, now Fayette St. 71, 84, 97, 133, 136
  Swift's 117, 127
  Thompson's, formerly Wales' [?] 143
  Wales' 208, 216
  Wales', now Thompson's [?] 143
Allison 31
  Ann 4, 16, 30, 39, 76, 77, 83, 97, 121, 122, 123, 133, 136, 149, 188, 191
  Ann Ramsay 123
  Elizabeth 35
  Hunter & Allison 59

John 8, 15, 18, 31, 37, 41, 44, 61, 80, 177, 183
Mary 93
Patrick 93
Rebecca 80
Robert 3, 4, 16, 18, 30, 32, 39, 72, 76, 83, 87, 96, 97, 119, 121-123, 127, 133, 136, 149, 159, 170, 183, 185, 187, 188, 191, 196, 199
William 35, 73, 86, 93, 155
Alton
  John 209, 210
Ammidon
  Philip 194
Anderson
  Colbert 69, 83
  Elizabeth 35
  Margareth 61
  Ninian 24, 61, 94
  Robert 76, 148
  William 28, 29, 35, 37, 58, 183, 190
Andrew
  Polkinhorne & Andrew 210
Annapolis, MD 53
Antigua 42
Arell
  Christiana 39, 101
  David 13, 18, 25, 39, 69, 95, 101, 105, 106, 129, 130, 171, 181, 187
  Dolly 59
  Eleanor 39, 91, 132, 139, 142, 165, 177
  Phoebe 101, 136, 149, 181, 187, 204
  Phoebe Arell Moore 171
  Richard 2, 39, 91, 108, 132, 139, 142, 146, 150, 155, 165, 177, 181
  Richard Jr. 101
  Samuel 1, 16, 51, 54, 55, 59, 66, 70, 74, 99, 101, 105, 108, 125, 129, 130, 137, 139, 156, 187
Arell [?Earl?]
  Richard 62
Armistead
  Will. 191
Articles of Agreement:
  Coryell-Brockett-Burns 160
  Dennis & Elizabeth Foley marital separation 170
  Harper-Watson 65
  Herbert-Roberdeau 46
  John & Honora Sullivan marital separation 168
  McIver-Love 164
  Spangler-Pancas/Pancoast 182

221

Thomas & Mary Fitzpatrick marital separation 169
W. Ramsay exxrs-W. & E. Worrell 186
Ash
  William 123
Ashton
  Laurence 76
  Lawrence 84, 150
  R.W. 15
Atkinson
  Guy 60, 83, 97, 134, 150
  William 60
Attorney, Power of:
  Blake to Coates 170
  Boden to Taylor 40
  Bowdon to Hollins, Marsteller & Thompson 38
  Caverly to P. Arell 181
  Cunningham to Hunter 175
  Cutler, Coltart & Kirkpatrick to Wilson & Coltart 70, 206
  D. Hunter, MacKenzie & partners to W. Hunter 45
  Dixon, Littledale, Piper to Hooe 24
  Donaldson to Hartshorne 155, 178, 179, 186, 196
  Finlay to Patton 118, 133
  Griffith to Greenup 47
  Hadfield to Barry 114
  Hamilton to Wilson 42
  Harrison to Hooe 17, 24
  Hartshorne to Gibb 79
  Hicks to Wilson 85
  Hodgson to Clementson 204
  J. Allison to R. Allison & R. McCrea 183
  Lockhart & Campbells to Ballendine, Adam & Hunter 2
  McCrea to Mease 69, 95
  McCrea to R. Mease 144
  Merian to Hesshuyson 60
  Mounsher to Porter 44
  Ownbread to Korn & Wisemiller 71
  Paterson, Campbell & Gemmill to Wilson 43
  Robinson, Sanderson, Rumney to Hodgson 55
  Rumney to Hodgson 44
  S. Williams to T. Williams & Cary 31
  Semple to Deneale 70
  T. Hamilton relatives to H. Hamilton 44
  Taliaferro to Keith 178
  Taylor to Watson 39
  W. T. Alexander revokes P/atty of J. T. Brooke 163
  W. T. Alexander to J. Taliaferro, Jr. 163
  W. T. Alexander to J. Taliaferro, Jr.: for substitutes 195
  W.T. Alexander to J.T. Brooke 51
Attorneys:
  Brooke, John T. 49-51, 72, 106
  Brooke, John Taliaferro 163
  Clementson, George 204
  Coltart, Roger 206
  Harper, William 140
  Hartshorne, William 178, 179, 196
  Henderson, Alexander 43
  Hunter, George 176
  Murray, Robert 194
  Porter, Thomas 44
  Suckley, George 73
  Taliaferro, John 105, 107, 108, 118, 125, 149, 157
  Taliaferro, John Jr. 117, 135, 137, 151, 152-154, 157, 162, 163, 173, 174, 178-181, 186, 195
  Wilson, William 206
Aubrier
  John 210
Augusta Co., VA 90
Ayr (Scotland) 2, 42
B_bltt_
  K. 39
Backers [Bakers]:
  Scheckel, Diedrick 112
  Thornton, Joseph 112
Bading
  John Baptist 106
Bagot
  C. 60
Bailey
  Elisha 162, 163
  George 209
Baillice
  Andrew 90
Bakehouse 148
Baker
  William 136
Bakers:
  Eichenbrade, William 56
  Korn, John 43
Balfour

James 186
Ball
   Edward P. 202
Ballendine
   John, of Nomini 2
Baltimore Co., MD 93
Baltimore Gazette 58
Baltimore Town 18, 27, 28, 38, 60, 62, 64, 91, 93, 97, 105, 114, 116, 117, 124, 127, 135, 136, 143, 151, 165, 210
Bank of Alexandria 80, 178
   ground of 100, 116
Banking out:
   Lot 46, by W. Ramsay 123, 124
Barber
   John 193, 202, 209
Barclay
   Ann 120
   Reynolds & Barclay 41
   Thomas 7, 16, 17, 32, 120
Barns
   Henry 55
Barr
   Hugh 22, 24
Barr (Scotland) 2
Barrett
   Jos. 194
Barry
   Daniel 138
   James 114
   Mary Adam 138
   Thomas 138
Bayly
   Elisha Thom. 128
   George 210
   George Wm. 128
Bayne
   Henry 173, 174
Beal
   William Murdoch 13
Bealer/Beeler/Beelor
   Christopher 1, 2, 63, 109, 110, 116
   Henrietta Wilhemina 109, 110
Beall
   Brooke 68
   John 106
   Thomas 68
Bealle
   John 73
Bear Creek 176
Beatty
   Jno. 172
Beaufort Co., NC 17, 42

Beckwith
   Lewis 146, 188, 198
Bedinger
   Jacob 46, 56
Beech Fork 175
Beeson
   Edward 60, 218
Beideman
   Charlotte 129
   Harry 13
   Henry 129
   [first name not given] 130
Bell
   Anna 73
Bence
   Adam 94, 141, 148, 149, 154
Benedict, MD 60
Bennett
   Charles 172
   John 150, 167
Bent
   Betsey 83, 185
   Lemuel 83, 96, 103, 118-120, 130, 152, 169, 183, 185, 189, 190, 204, 217
Bentz
   [first name not given] 130
Berkley Co., VA 4, 38, 69, 83
Beveridge
   Innes 69
Biddle
   Charles 99
Bill of Sale:
   Anderson's Negroes Grace, Nancy, Ellsey 94
   Bayne's Negro Benjamin 174
   household effects 16
   household effects & store merchandize 45
   ship "Paragon" w/rigging and voyage proceeds 204
   sloops 16
   store goods, household effects, conveyances, slaves 26
   Taylor's Negro George Harle 174
   Taylor's Negroes Charity, Bob, Jacob 79
   Thomas' Negro Henry 19
   Ward's Negro Andrew 121
   Watson's Negro Will 28
Bird
   Catharine 84, 113, 133
   Catharine Dalton 84
   William 15, 84, 113, 133

Biscuit Bakers:
  Korn, John 56, 64
  Wisemiller, Jacob 56, 64
Bishop
  Daniel 127, 174
Black
  William 25
Blacksmiths:
  Merchant, William 9
  Tristler, Lewis 168
Bladensburg Town 4, 29, 38, 47, 129
Blake
  Peter 170
Blakely
  Abel 140
Blakeny
  Abel 155, 168, 177
Blass
  Adam 58
Blondelet/Blondeley
  Jane 54, 167
  Michael Simon 54, 86, 91, 167
  Simon Michael 143
Blount
  Washer 137
Bluehill
  William Coltart of 70
Bluehill (Scotland) 70
Blunt
  Washer 39, 92, 99, 122, 167, 183, 192
Boa
  Cavan 128, 158, 170, 188, 205, 213
Boden
  George 40
Bogert
  D. Ritzema 35
Boggess
  Henley 111
  Robert 10, 11, 13, 15, 149, 157
Bogue
  John 138, 213
Bohrer
  Peter 40
Boling
  Samuel 121
Boling/Bowling
  John 139
Bonds:
  punitive, Arell to McLeod 146
  Searcher, Port of ALX 31
  Sergeant of the Court 31, 46
Bontz
  Valentine 13

Boone
  Aloysius 199, 200
  Joseph 199, 200
Boston, MA 45, 103, 142, 158, 202, 204
Botetourt Co., VA 73
Bott
  Jacob 38, 130
Bowdon
  Kirk & Bowdon 38
Bowen
  Obediah 26
Bowling
  Peggy 93
Bowne
  Elizabeth 159
  Matthew F. 115
  Matthew Franklin 135, 159, 192
Bowness
  William 44, 58, 113, 204
Bowrie
  William 174
Bowsall
  John 213
Boyce
  John 26
Boyd
  John 18
Boyer
  Henry 137
  John 88, 89, 95, 103, 119
Bradley
  William 193
Braehead (Scotland) 43
Brander
  Joseph 68
Brandon
  James 191, 194
Breden/Bredin
  John 2, 22
Breillat
  Thomas 193
Brent
  John 39
  Lemuel 83, 87
Brewery
  Wales' Brew House & its trunks 182
Bright
  Windle 39
Briscoe
  Gerrard 105, 174
Bristol (England) 40
Broad
  Thomas 93
Broadwater

Charles 103
Brockett
  Robert 56, 71, 92, 94, 121, 138, 150, 161
Bromley
  William 181
Bronaugh
  William 59
Brooke
  Francis 20-23, 46
  John Taliaferro 49-51, 163
Brooks
  John Turpin 127
Broom
  Jaco. 43
Broome
  Samuel P. 204
Brown
  Aloysius 203
  Catharine 75
  John 98, 103, 117
  Mary 27, 28, 44
  Samuel Montgomery 7, 22, 27, 28, 41, 42-44, 79, 94, 102, 151, 189
  W. 4
  William 1, 17, 39, 56, 75, 99
  Windsor/Winsor 16, 55, 66
Browne
  Acquila 19
  Windsor 156
Brownell
  John 122, 130
Brumley
  Reuben 62
  William 25
Bryan
  Bernard 83, 87, 128, 134, 135, 138, 163, 180, 181, 192
  Charles 69, 124
  John 67, 72, 211
Bryce
  Hannah 28
  John 3, 28, 67, 73, 88
  Nicholas 28, 67, 73
  Robert 67, 73
Bryson
  William 22
Buchan
  Alexander 25, 38, 41
Building, right to remove:
  Brockett's new buildings 92, 138
  from J. Harper's pier, by builder T. Patten & Co. 201
  Hodgson's improvements, at lease end 132
  Jamieson & Anderson's new buildings 148
  Jamiesson's new buildings 76
  Levi Reynold's new building 214
  may not remove/alter/destroy present/future buildings 170
  old Ffx Co. Court House 82
  on Fleming lot/wharf 19
  on Kirk lot 71
  on Muir lot, renter's new construction 196
  R. T. Hooe's improvements 108
  structures built during lease, at lease end 201
  warehouse by Hunter 81
Bullitt
  Cuthbert 70
Bumill
  John [possibly Burnill] 135
Burke
  John 96
Burnes/Byrne
  Patrick 137
Burnett
  Charles 18
  George 18
  Mary 18
Burney
  Michael 26
Burnill
  John [possibly Bumill] 135
Burns
  Patrick 160
Burying ground
  Episcopal Church 152
  Quaker 3
Bushby
  Joseph 73
  Mary 73, 109, 217
  William 73, 95, 109, 217
Business firms:
  Abraham Morehouse & Co. 115
  Adam Morehouse & Co. 99
  Carlyle & Dalton 110
  Carson & Muir 53
  Colin Dunlap & Son & Co. 53
  Colin Dunlap Son & Co. 7
  Dixon & Littledale 24
  Edward K. Thompson & Co. 27
  Fletcher & Otway 210
  Fosters & May 210
  Gurden Chapin & Co. 27

Hepburn & Dundas 41, 183
Hodgson & Nikolson 210
Innes Beveridge & Co. 69
Isaac Littledale & Co. 24, 47
James Hendricks & Co. 41
James Wilson & Sons 42
John Murray & Co. 142
John Sutton & Co. 27
Jonathan Swift & Co. 27
Joseph Janney & Co. 97
Kirk & Bowdon 38
Lansdall & Hodges 210
Messrs. Perrin & Brothers 60
Patton & Butcher 210
Polkinhorne & Andrew 210
Reynolds & Barclay 41
Robinson, Sanderson & Rumney 44, 75, 204
Robinson, Saunderson & Rumney 55
Saunderson & Rumney 39
Thomas Patten & Co. 201
William Lowery & Co. 135, 136
Butcher
  Ann 139, 171, 172, 177
  John 3, 7, 34, 53, 54, 139, 168, 171, 172, 173, 177
  Jonathan 53, 172
  Patton & Butcher 210
Butchers:
  Mattart, Jacob 114
  Miller, Godfrey 8
Butler
  Charles Fras. 202
  Edward 183
  James 188
Butt
  Adam 90
  Jacob 90, 129
Byrne
  Margaret 218
  Patrick 92, 170, 193, 218
Byrne/Burnes
  Patrick 137
Byrnes
  Patrick 128
Cabinet makers:
  McKnight, William 56, 63
Cadiz (Spain) 14, 17, 18
Calhoun
  James 93, 105
  James Jr. 93
Callemloy
  John 185

Camock
  James 105, 124
Campbell
  Bruce 43
  Daniel 202
  Donald 147, 156, 199
  James 62, 67
  Jean 2
  John 2
  Marian 2
  Matthew 2
Canada 42
Cannon
  William 192
Captains:
  Bayne [first name not given; Henry?] 173
  Clark, Joseph 92
  Conway [first name not given] 132
  Harper, John 67
Carey
  Joseph 57
Carey/Cary
  Joseph 203
Carlin
  Sarah 1, 205
  William 1, 168, 205
Carlyle
  Carlyle & Dalton 110
  George 217
  John 57, 72, 121, 123, 124, 207
Carpenter
  Jesse 155
Carry
  Benjamin 211
Carson
  Carson & Muir 53
  John 60
  Thomas 79
Cartlish
  Charles 106
Cary
  Joseph 31, 37, 43, 47, 62, 89, 141, 181, 187
  Williams & Cary 86, 93
Casanave
  Peter 67, 68, 113, 191
Casey
  Daniel 56, 72, 99
  John 11, 94, 113, 192
Casey/Cassey
  John 72
Cash
  Mary 208

William Jr. 162, 163, 174, 180, 198, 208
Casson
   John 136
Castmill
   John 73
Catharine 5
Caton
   Joseph 146
Cavan
   James 143, 155
Cavens
   James 132
Caverly
   Ann 25
   Joseph 12, 19, 25, 71, 75, 136
   Peter 25, 181
Cecil Co., MD 5
Certificates
   military 4
Chamberlin
   James 170
Chambersburgh, PA 128
Chancery suits:
   [-unk- v. Sewell estate/exxrs] 185
   [Didier v. Neblon et ux] 167
   [Hepburn v. Gretter] 48
   [Jones v. Alexander] 20
   [McCaughen v. Wales] 109
Chapel
   Nightengale Lane, Middlesex Co. 119
Chapin
   Benjamin 19, 142
   Gurden 2, 19, 27, 68, 70, 142, 206
   Gurdin 132, 165
   Hiram 2, 19, 76, 142, 179, 191
   Margaret 142
Chapman
   George 70, 110, 125, 201
   Martha 43
Charles Co., MD 38, 58, 90, 190
Charlton
   Richard 34
Cheapside, London (England) 45
Chernin [?Chewin?]
   P. A. 96
Chew
   John 165
   Margaret 165
   Roger 2, 4, 35, 61, 63
Chichester
   Richard 103
Chief Justice, 5th District of MD:
   Beall, W. M. 115
Chief Justice, Court of Common Pleas, Suffolk Co.:
   Gardner, Joseph 202
Chief Justice, Supreme Court, NY:
   Morris, Richard 62
Chrisheylen
   James 188
Christie
   James Jr. 93
Chunn
   John Thomas 76, 84, 150
Claims
   by S. Cooke on U.S. re: Jones Point 117
Clark
   John 70
   Joseph 92
   Thomas 24, 209
Clarke
   Michael 8
   Richard 16, 28
Clarkson
   Matthew 70, 92, 110, 172, 201
Cleary
   Michael 170
Clegg
   John 167
Clements
   George 40, 53
Clementson
   George 44, 58, 75, 111, 113, 132, 183, 204, 210
Clerke
   Joseph (see Clark) 92
Clerks:
   Beall, Brooke 68
   Gibson, William 93, 105, 117
   Griffith, David 3, 21, 33, 34, 47, 76
   Mounger, Edwin 183
   Price, Ezekiel 142, 158, 202
   Price, Oliver 206
   Ritchie, William 115
   Smith, C. 164
   Turner, Jno. B. 90
   Wagener, Peter 31
Clifford
   Nehemiah 59
Clinton
   George 62
Coates
   John 170
   Moses 194
   Samuel 7, 110

William 99
Cohagen
  John 122
Coleman
  Joseph 91, 199, 200, 208
Coles
  Edward 6
  John 6, 7
Collard
  Samuel 197, 200, 201
Collateral:
  Foley to Boa: livestock, household effects 170
  Lemoine to creditors: 1/3 Stage Waggon & harness 211
  Lemoine to creditors: saddlery effects, household effects 211
  Ramsay to Taylor: slaves, household effects, articles 74
  Reynolds to Reynolds: nailor's shop & fittings 214
Coller
  Thomas 70
Collins
  James 90
Colonels:
  Carlyle, John 72, 121, 123, 124
  Hooe, Robert Townshend 131
  Mercer, George 32
  Powell, Levin 47
Coltart
  Catharine Kirkpatrick 70, 206
  Katharine Kirkpatrick 214, 215
  Roger 70, 198, 205, 214, 215
  William 70
Colvill
  Elizabeth 34
Combs
  William 176
Commissioners, duties of 4
Commissioners, Ffx Co. Court:
  Faw, Abraham 167
  Perrin, Joseph M. 167
Commissioners, VA Court of Chancery:
  Dundas, John 74
  Harris, Richard 75
  Herbert, William 74
Commissioners:
  Allison, John 86
  McKnight, William 86
  Wise, Peter 86
Commonwealth Justice for the Corporation of ALX:

Irvin, James 190
Condon
  Mary 107
  Richard 107
Conn
  Amelia Thame 97
  Casina 77
  Cassina 123
  Gerrard Trammell 61, 97
  Philip 90, 141
  Robert 30
  Thomas 30, 35, 77, 90, 123, 125
Construction covenants:
  build new flour shed or forfeit leased lot 198
  earth fill between wharves of Conway, Herbert-Wilson-Potts 216
  earth fill space adj County Wharf 52
  fill dirt for new wharf 48
  may alter/build; must leave new structures 115
  may build above alley 29
  may build above alley onto adj house 30
  may build half the gavel wall's thickness on adj property 36, 37, 125, 182
  may build onto adj lot/building 109
  may build onto Simms' adj brick house wall 97
  may build shared wall partly on each other's land 46, 48, 137
  may build stables in Swift's alley 127
  may convert distillery to brewery; must leave conversion intact 115
  may extend/build stories above alley 112
  may join to adj building at 2nd story level, above alley 200
  may join to adj wall, then raise it as common partition 113
  may keep new-built structures 106
  may not build any framed building on front of premises 157, 158
  may not build frame building on front of these premises 169
  may not build framed building on front of premises 200
  may not build framed buildings on front of premises 175
  may not build framed dwellings fronting on the street 179
  may not destroy/remove new construction 140

may not remove/alter/destroy structures to be built 170
may purchase new additions at lease end 138
may raise a common partition wall 113, 125
may remove improvements at lease end 132
neither dwelling nor kitchen to front on adjoining lot 165
new construction of stone/brick 99
no building, to keep Lumley Point passage open 15
no encumbrances of Point West/-County warehouse alley 52
no jut/bow windows projecting nor doors opening into alley 160
not to build new house adj intersection/existing house 114
provision of well, paved alleys & sidewalks, gutters 160
single gavel wall on two properties becomes common partition 182
to erect a kitchen, but not on the lot front 188
to leave new buildings intact at lease end 73
Conway
  Capt. [first name not given] 132
  John 6, 7, 103
  John Span 6
  John Spann 203
  Joseph 6, 7, 32, 203
  Lucy 32
  Mary 1, 6, 7, 103, 122, 130, 198, 203, 215
  Richard 1, 24, 29, 32, 39, 45, 62, 92, 96, 120, 122, 130, 138, 185, 189, 190, 198, 215
  Robert 6, 7, 103, 203
  Susannah 6, 7, 103, 203
  Thomas 6, 7, 32, 36
Cook
  Lewis 213
  Thomas 212, 215
Cooke
  Catharine 73, 107, 118, 127, 140, 174, 188, 190, 192, 209, 213
  Elizabeth 154
  Lewis 154
  Stephen 73, 107, 108, 117-119, 126, 127, 129, 136, 140, 151-154, 170, 174, 177, 181, 188, 190, 192, 204, 209, 211, 213
Coombs
  William 175
Cooper
  Elizabeth 147
  Joel 109
  Samuel 147, 168, 177
Copper
  Cyrus 6, 69
Cordwainers:
  Holliday, James 4
Corn
  John 52, 55
  [see also: Korn] 52
Corporation of ALX, Gentlemen:
  Murray, John 67
  Ramsay, Dennis 67
  Taylor, Jesse 67
Coryell
  Ann 160-163, 179, 180, 208-210
  George 48, 71, 95, 119, 121, 125, 140, 148, 154, 160-163, 179, 180, 187, 208, 209, 210, 214
Coryll
  John 87
Cotter
  James 24
Court House Square 187
Court of Chancery, StVA 74
Court of Common Pleas, Boston, MA 158
Court of Hustings 61
Court of Hustings Magistrates:
  Dundas, John 190
  Hooe, Robert Townshend 190
Court of Hustings, Gentlemen:
  Marsteller, Philip 85
  Mease, Robert 85
  Taylor, Jesse 85
Court of Hustings:
  Marsteller, Philip 56, 57
  Ramsay, Dennis 56, 57
  Winsor, Olney 56, 57
Courtney
  William 37
Couter
  Angel Hart 177
  Catharine 178
Cox
  George 25, 40
  Jacob 27, 36, 40, 63, 91, 92, 112, 122, 126, 141, 156, 166, 167, 186, 208
Cox's Creek 176
Crabb
  George 84

Craig
  Adam 129
  George 70
  James 98
  Samuel 74, 115, 120, 138, 196
Craigy
  Negro Craigy 212
Craik
  Doctor 89
  James 58, 90, 143
  James Jr. 16
  William 115
Crammond
  William 144, 145
Cramphin
  Richard 139
Crandall
  Thomas 182
Crandel
  Thomas 119
Crandle
  Thomas 95
Crawford
  Ignatius 180
  Isabella Hamilton 45
  John 45
  Mary 45
  William 45
Cross
  John 164
Crowe
  Lanty 51, 70, 80, 84, 96, 100, 120,
    168, 181, 214
Cumberland Co., (England) 24, 55, 85
Cunningham
  Thomas 175
  William 96, 189
Curacao 120
Currie
  Ann 150
  James 150
Cutlar
  Elizabeth Kirkpatrick 70
  Roger 70
Cutler
  Catharine 25
  Elizabeth 25
  Elizabeth Kirkpatrick 206, 214, 215
Cuttar
  James Reedston 134
Dabney
  John B. 46, 57, 58
  John Bass 83, 96, 189, 204
  Roxa 83, 189

Dade
  Baldwin 3, 4, 7-9, 12, 22, 33-36, 43,
    55, 61, 76, 77, 99, 125, 132, 135,
    136, 183, 187, 196, 217
  Behethland 12
  Catharine 3, 4, 7-9, 12, 33, 35, 61, 76,
    99, 136, 187, 196
  Elizabeth 8, 12
  Margaret 12
  Parthenia 12
  Townshend Stuart 170
Dall
  James 117, 127, 151
Dalrymple
  John 65
Dalton
  Carlyle & Dalton 110
  Catharine 84
  Jane 84, 133
  Jane Dalton Herbert 133
  Jno. 217
  John 84, 86, 93, 133
  William 38
Dandridge
  B. 201
Daniel
  John 164
Daniell
  Thomas 68
Dark/Dartz
  John B. 35
Darling
  George 3, 59, 93, 109, 112, 124, 170,
    177, 203, 206, 215, 216
  Jos. 49-51
  Joseph 41, 55
Darmstat
  Joseph 60
Darne
  Robert 146
  Thomas Jr. 196
Daugherty
  Robert 16, 55, 66
Davey
  David 175, 177
  Mary 177
Davidson
  James 213
Davies
  William 62
Davis
  Benjamin 63
  Hanson 204
  Isaac 176, 187

Lewis 198
Mary 139, 140
Samuel 139, 140, 157, 209, 216
Thomas 181
Davison
  Pl[?]iercy 26
Deblois
  George 142
  James S. 142
  Lewis Jr. 26, 142
  Lydia 142
Dedier
  Henry 91
Delarue
  Augustus 42, 79
Deneale
  G. 8, 139, 145, 192
  George 28, 30, 55, 66, 70, 83, 90, 91, 98, 100, 136, 156
  William 27, 28, 214
Dent
  George 90
Devilbiss
  Christian 12
  Mary 12
Devilby
  [first name not given] 130
Dick
  Elisha C. 118
  Elisha Cullen 28, 77, 106, 126, 145, 150, 153, 157, 158, 169, 175, 177, 178, 179, 199, 210, 218
  Hannah 150, 157, 169, 175, 177, 178, 199, 218
Didier
  Henry 167
Digges
  Francis 10-14
Distillery, complete 115
Dixon
  John 18, 24
Dobbin
  Archibald 126, 192
  Mary 192
Doctor in Divinity
  Griffith, David 34
Doctor of Physic:
  Dick, Elisha Cullen 28
Doctors:
  Baker, William 136
  Craik, James 143
  Dr. Rose [first name not given] 214
Dodson
  Charles Jr. 219

Walter 195
Doerhy
  William 146
Doffan
  Vincent 164
Dominica 42
Donaldson
  Elizabeth 178, 186, 219
  Elizabeth Muir 155, 178, 179, 196
  Robert 84, 186
Donegal (Co.), Ireland 45
Donnell
  John 65
Dooish, Rye Parish, Donegal 45
Dorsey
  Mial 204
Dorsheimer
  Jacob 27
Doucher
  Leonard 180
Doughlass
  John 45
Doughtherty
  Robert 156
Douglas
  Ch. 208
  Charles 218
Douglass
  James 115
Dover
  John Jr. 35
Dowdall
  John 35, 40, 57
Downman
  William 96, 99, 100, 116
Doyear
  John 30
Drinker
  George 157, 158
Drumbarnett, Rye Parish, Donegal 45
Duff
  John 110
Duffey
  Bartholemew 72
Dulany
  Benjamin 74, 96
Dumfries, VA 116, 126, 136
Dundas
  Agnes 59
  Hepburn & Dundas 41, 67, 68, 93, 183
  John 17, 30, 57, 59, 74, 93, 95, 97, 104, 110, 111, 113, 114, 116, 120, 121, 123, 127, 129-131, 133, 135,

137, 139, 141, 144-146, 148--
151, 155-158, 160, 164, 166,
168-170, 174, 177, 179, 181,
182, 190-194, 197, 198, 200,
202, 208, 212-217
Dunlap
  Colin 7, 53
  James 69
  John 38, 94, 111-113, 138, 210
  Robert 69
Dunlop
  John 5, 26
Dunn
  Elizabeth 205
  James 205
  Matty 141
  William 141, 205
Dunscomb
  Andrew 165
  Aw. 62
Duplessis
  Peter LeBarbier 60
Duvall
  Ann 96, 100, 116
  Nancy 80
  William 1, 2, 7, 52, 57, 61, 68, 80, 96, 99, 100, 116
Dwellings to be built:
  by A. & J. Boone 199
  by A. Faw 177
  by D. Davey 175
  by D. Pancoast 16
  by D. Ramsay 36
  by E. Janney 158
  by G. Drinker 158
  by Herlihy 44
  by J. Boling/Bowling 140
  by J. Bryan 73
  by J. Dalton 84
  by J. Harper 89
  by J. Irvine (2) 114
  by J. Mandeville 188
  by J. Simpson 169, 179
  by J. Thompson 64
  by J. Wherry 200
  by Jones 20, 21
  by Lanphier 23
  by Lyles 26
  by Mann 22
  by Miller 8
  by Moxley 23
  by Orpwood 23
  by P. Burns 161
  by P. Furneau 140
  by P. Wanton 157
  by Reed 22
  by Rozer 44
  by Stiever 22
  by Thorn 25
  by Trout 22
  by W. & J. Hickman 36, 37
  By W. Hartshorne (2) 106
  by Wilkinson 22
Dwellings, existing:
  at Prince & Union 89
  of A. & J. Swoope 38
  of A. Jamieson 75
  of A. Wales 109
  of Anderson/Sheckle 190
  of B. Chapin 19
  of B. Kirk 71
  of B. Mann/J. Grimes 201
  of C. Simms 97
  of Conn/Simms 97
  of D. Arell 101
  of D. Arell/Doyle 101
  of D. Arell/L. Weston 101
  of D. Easton/J. Harper 143
  of D. Foley [?] 205
  of D. Young 35, 87, 90
  of E. Gretter 98
  of Fitzgerald/Anderson 183
  of G. Conn 97
  of H. McCue 78
  of H. Strowman 55
  of Hannah Bryce 28
  of Harper/Craik 89
  of Harper/Gill 88
  of J. & H. Dyson 193
  of J. B. Nickolls 140
  of J. B. Petit: of brick on King St.; of frame on King 68
  of J. B. Petit: on Ffx St 68
  of J. C. Vowell/T. Vowell, Jr. 192
  of J. Caverly 132
  of J. Craik 143
  of J. Dalton 84
  of J. Dundas 113, 192
  of J. Dundas/R. Allison [?] 191
  of J. Faxon [?] 144
  of J. Gretter 65
  of J. Harper 88, 122, 124
  of J. Harper/T. Williams 216
  of J. Hawkins 97
  of J. Heineman 125
  of J. Hendricks/T. Richards/J. McIver 214
  of J. Hess 97

of J. Hess (2): on Ffx St.; residence on King St. 90
of J. Irvin 197, 200
of J. Irvin/T. Swann 197
of J. Jackson 143
of J. Jolly 86
of J. Kidd 72
of J. McIver 164
of J. Orr/J. Keating 128
of J. Steel/E. Shaw 38
of John Bryce, dec'd 67
of John/Honora Sullivan 168
of Jolly/Williams & Cary 93
of Korn & Wisemiller 106
of M. Lewis 110
of M. Thorn [?] 25
of M. Worrell 186
of McIver/Love 144
of N. Mooney 56, 63
of P. Casanave 68
of P. Murray 24
of R. Adam 148
of R. Evans 107
of R. Lyle 75
of R. T. Hooe 18
of S. & P. Moore [?] 171
of S. Arell 101
of S. M. Brown 27
of T. Conn 35
of T. Richards 196
of Thomas/Mary Fitzpatrick 169
of U. Forrest 67
of W. Bird 84
of W. Cunningham 96
of W. Duvall 80
of W. Duvall (2) 96, 99
of W. Hepburn (2) 48
of W. Hodgson 89
of W. Miller 70
of W. Reynolds 109
of W. Summers 143
of Wise/Saunderson/Rumney 39
[dwellings ?] of John Murray & Co. 142

Dyer
  Thomas B. 128
Dykes
  James 170
  Mungo 81, 170
Dyson
  Hannah 192
  Joseph 159, 192, 216
Earl
  Henry S. 139, 174, 188

Earl [?Arell?]
  Richard 62
Earle
  Henry Stanton 167
Earp
  Caleb 57, 59, 69, 77, 109, 124, 134, 187
Easton
  David 120, 143, 201
Edmonds
  Edmond 70, 96, 100
Edward
  Thomas 6
Edwards
  Thomas 7
Eichenbrade
  Magdalena 52
  Magdalina 56
  William 52, 56
  Wm. "under the name of Ownbread" 56
  [see also: Ownbread] 52
Eigenbrode
  Magdalena 63
  William "under the name of William Ownbread" 63
Elliott
  Frank 83
Ellis
  Calvin 204
Elliston
  Cuthbert 6, 7, 103, 203
  Cuthbert Jr. 6
  Mary 6, 7, 103, 203
Ellzey
  Thomazin 206, 207
  W. 8, 54
Elton
  Isabel Shaw 36
  Isabella Elton Summers 181
  John 181
Emmit
  Joseph 61, 217
  Josiah 109
Episcopal Church
  burial ground 152
  burying ground 117
  fence 152
  steeple 201
Escheated property 6, 7
Escheators:
  Ross, H. of FfxCo. 6, 53
Eskridge
  Charles 104

Esquire:
  Adam, Robert 53
  Alexander, John 67
  Alexander, William Thornton 157
  Bullitt, Cuthbert 70
  Clarkson, Matthew 110
  Clinton, George 62
  Conway, Richard 45
  Duplessis, Peter LeBarbier 60
  Gibb, William 79
  Gilpin, George 43
  Greenup, Christopher 47
  Hunter, William Jr. 38
  Johnson, Joshua 119
  Keith, James 13
  Lee, Arthur 217
  Lee, Henry Jr. 187
  Marsteller, Philip 89
  May, Thomas 43
  Mercer, George 33
  Mercer, James 218
  Ramsay, Dennis 47
  Ramsay, William 7, 16, 53, 66, 71, 84
  Randolph, Beverly 46
  Randolph, Edmund 31
  Ross, Hector 53
  Wagener, Peter 81
  Wormley, Ralph 65
Europe
  present war in 204
Evans
  Drusilla 185
  Ephraim 121, 188
  John 57
  Robert 107, 185
  Thomas 128
Everingham
  Benjamin 31
Ewell
  Leroy 141
Ewing
  Thomas 93
Excavation rights:
  from Lots 93-94-95 48
  from Wilkes St 15
  on Fleming lot/wharf 19
  sand & dirt from adj land 71
Fairfax
  George William 36
  Thomas, [6th] Lord Fairfax 196
Fairfax Co. Justice of the Peace:
  Herbert, William 45
Fairfax County Court House
  approved for TwnALX use 81
Fairfax County Sheriffs:
  Pollard, Thomas 83, 87, 185, 199
  Turner, Charles (Deputy) 121
  Wren, James 121
  [Pollard, Thomas] 187
Fairfax Parish 217
Falconar/Falconer
  Abraham 105, 116
  Sarah 105, 116
Farmers:
  Crawford, John 45
  Hamilton, William of Gortree 45
Faulkener
  Abraham 147
  [wife of Abraham; unnamed] 147
Faulkner
  [first name not given] 183
Fauquier Co., VA 59, 76, 83, 149
Faw
  Abraham 90, 156-158, 166-168, 171, 174, 175, 177, 179, 181-183, 185, 189, 190-192, 194, 196-198, 200, 202, 203, 207-210, 213, 214, 217, 219
  Jona. 177
  Jonathan 168
  Mary Ann 168, 177
Fawsfarm (Loudoun Co.) 2
Faxon
  Joseph 98, 144
  Josiah 101
Fendall
  Mary 191, 194
  Philip Richard 61, 80, 95, 191, 194, 196
Fenley
  John B. 14
Fenwick
  Edward 164, 166, 218
Ferno
  Philip 66
Ferry/ferry landing
  West's, West's Point 41
Field/Feild
  John 5
Finlay
  Amelia 118, 119, 132, 136
  David 25, 41, 85, 106, 118, 119, 132, 136
  John 156
Finley
  David 84, 96, 97
  Hugh 4, 5, 16, 37, 67, 69, 83, 137

John 5, 16, 67, 111, 137
John B. 16
Susanna 4, 5
Susannah 16, 37, 83
First Justice, Court of Common Pleas, Boston, MA:
  Gardner, Joseph 158
Fisher
  Miers 29
Fitts
  William 155
Fitzgerald
  Jane 29, 60, 104, 127-129, 182, 195
  John 4, 8, 12, 15, 17, 29, 34, 38, 44, 48, 58, 60, 64, 84, 85, 87, 99, 104, 112, 115, 117, 122, 127-129, 182, 183, 187, 190, 191, 194, 195
Fitzgeralds & Peers Lotts
  Town Lots 56-57-58 (formerly Pattersons) 100
Fitzhugh
  Francis 164
  Giles 87, 90
  Mordeca C. 135
Fitzpatrick
  Mary 169
  Thomas 128, 169
Flannery
  Michael 49-51, 142, 145
Fleming
  Andrew 78, 147, 214
  Ann 189
  Betty 3, 18, 95, 103, 110, 131, 189
  Betty Junior 3
  Catharine 189
  Sarah 189
  Thomas 3, 15, 18, 71, 95, 103, 109, 130, 189
Fletcher
  Fletcher & Otway 210
  James 66
  John Walter 59, 105, 106, 202
  Mary 105
Flood
  William P. 164
Flynn
  Michael 42
Foley
  Dennis 141, 158, 168-170, 204
  Elizabeth 170
  Elizabeth Dunn 141, 205
Follin
  William 188
Footways, pedestrian 186

Forbes
  William 60
Ford
  John B. 5, 16
  John Edward 37, 40, 68
  Samuel 159
Forrest
  Rebecca 68
  Uriah 47, 67
  [first name not given] 191
Fortnay
  David 29
Fortney
  Joseph 112
Foster
  John 97, 106, 111, 112, 210
Fosters
  Fosters & May 210
Foush
  Daniel 196
France
  Philip 22
France: 204, 207
Francis
  Sarah 187
Frazer
  Mary 57
  William 57
Frederick Co., MD 3, 12, 114, 146
Frederick Co., VA 67, 73, 83, 137
Frederick Town, MD 12, 60, 114
Fredericksburg, VA 60, 65, 163, 205, 214, 215
  District Court 51
Fullmer
  Joseph 106, 179, 195, 205
Fullmore
  Joseph 23, 40, 80
Fulton
  Mary Ann 174
  Mary Anne 179
  Robert 15, 173, 174, 179, 213
Furneau
  Philip 140
Furtney
  Jacob 93, 110
Gardner
  Henry 41
  Henry Jr. 42
  Joseph 30, 158, 202
  Samuel 45
Garvey
  Ann 1
  Lucas 1

235

Gemmill
  John 43
General Assembly of VA:
  Act to found Alexandria 130, 207
  an act of, to lay off Oronoko St. 134
  emitter of paper money 34
  J. Mercer applies to 33
Gentlemen Justices for Alexandria:
  Faw, Abraham 214
  Irvin, James 214
  Peyton, Francis 214
Gentlemen Justices of ALX:
  Fitzgerald, John 17
  Herbert, William 17
  Kirk, James 17
  Marsteller, Philip 59
  Ramsay, Dennis 59
  Winsor, Olney 59
Gentlemen Justices of FfxCo.:
  Conway, Richard 189, 190
  Gilpin, George 189, 190
  Herbert, William 189, 190
  Hooe, Robert Townshend 189, 190
Gentlemen Justices of Henrico Co.:
  Gregory, Roger 165
  Naye, John 165
  Pendleton, John 165
Gentlemen Justices of TwnALX:
  Marsteller, Philip 59
  Ramsay, Dennis 59
  Winsor, Olney 59
Gentlemen of ALX:
  Hickman, William 142
  Mease, Robert 107
  Peyton, Francis 142
  Thompson, Jonah 107, 142
Gentlemen of Botetourt Co.:
  Bealle, John 73
  Castmill, John 73
  Skillern, George 73
Gentlemen of Corporation of ALX:
  Arell, David 187
  Dundas, John 182
  Faw, Abraham 198
  Herbert, William 187
  Irvin, James 182, 198
  Peyton, Francis 182
  Thompson, Jonah 198
Gentlemen of Fairfax Co.:
  Alexander, Charles 217
  Broadwater, Charles 103
  Brown, William 99
  Chichester, Richard 103
  Dick, Elisha Cullen 158
  Gilpin, George 99
  Herbert, William 158
  Hooe, Robert Townshend 158
  Little, Charles 217
  Mason, Thompson 103
  McCarty, Daniel 103
  Potts, John 217
Gentlemen of Fauquier Co.:
  Ashton, Lawrence 84, 150
  Chunn, John Thomas 150
  Hale, William 150
  Harrison, John P. 84
Gentlemen of Hampshire Co.:
  Johnson, Oke 63
  Johnston, Oke 91
  Johnstone, Abraham 112
  McCarty, Edward 63, 91, 112
  Wheeler, Ignatius 63, 91
Gentlemen of King George Co.:
  Hooe, William 125
  Pollard, John 125, 195, 204
  Taliaferro, John 211
  Taliaferro, John Jr. 195, 204, 211
  Taliaferro, John Sr. 195, 204
  Wallace, Mich. 211
  Wallace, Michael 125
Gentlemen of Loudon Co.:
  Eskridge, Charles 104
  Orr, John 104
Gentlemen of Prince William Co.:
  Boling, Samuel 121
  Brown, John 103, 117
  Faxon, Josiah 98
  Grant, William 121
  Lawson, John 116, 126, 136
  Lethgow, Alexander 116, 121
  Lithgow, Alexander 126, 136
  Love, John 98, 103, 117
  McCrea, John 116
  Smith, James 126, 136
  Tyler, Charles 117
Gentlemen of the ALX Corporation:
  Dundas, John 164
  Irvin, James 164
  Smith, Alexander 164
Gentlemen of the Corporation of ALX:
  Dundas, John 166, 174
  Faw, Abraham 166, 171, 184
  Irvin, James 171, 174, 178
  Peyton, Francis 174, 178, 184
  Smith, Alexander 171
  Thompson, Jonah 166, 178, 184
Gentlemen of the Corporation [ALX]:

Dundas 139
Irvin, James 139
Peyton, Francis 139
Gentlemen of the Court of Hustings:
  Dundas, John 202
  Faw, Abraham 202
  Irvin, James 202
Gentlemen of TwnALX:
  Conway, Richard 96
  Dulany, Benjamin 96
  Dundas, John 95, 110, 111, 114, 116, 120, 121, 127, 135, 141, 145, 146, 150, 151, 155-158, 160, 166, 169, 170, 174, 177, 179, 190-192, 193, 194, 199, 200, 208, 213
  Duvall, William 57
  Faw, Abraham 156-158, 166, 174, 177, 179, 181-183, 185, 189, 191, 192, 194, 196, 199, 200, 207-209, 217
  Herbert, William 96
  Hickman, William 141, 143, 150
  Irvin, James 127, 135, 143, 155, 160, 169, 177, 181, 191-194, 196, 200
  Irvine, James 207
  Laurason, James 151
  Lawrason, James 101, 103, 109, 111, 112, 123, 141, 150
  Marsteller, Philip 64, 69, 92, 96, 102
  McKnight, Charles 151
  Mease, Robert 95, 100, 101, 103, 109, 111, 112, 114, 116, 120, 141, 169
  Murray, John 64
  Peyton, Francis 100, 103, 109, 112, 120, 123, 135, 141, 145, 146, 150, 151, 155-158, 160, 169, 170, 174, 179, 181, 183, 185, 190, 192-194, 196, 208, 209, 213, 217
  Porter, Thomas 69
  Ramsay, Dennis 57, 64, 92, 94-96, 102
  Smith, Alexander 182, 185, 189, 196, 207, 213
  Taylor, Jesse 57, 69, 92, 96, 102
  Thompson, Jonah 100, 109, 111, 114, 116, 120, 121, 123, 127, 141, 143, 146, 151, 155, 166, 170, 182, 183, 189, 190, 192, 199, 208, 209, 213, 217
Gentlemen:
  Adam, Robert 41
  Alexander, Charles 114, 133, 213
  Alexander, Gerrard 207
  Alexander, John 5, 9, 15
  Brown, William 56
  Carlyle, John 207
  Chunn, John Thomas 76
  Dundas, John 131, 148, 149, 168, 170, 177, 181, 191, 194, 197, 198, 212, 217
  Faw, Abraham 175, 194, 197, 198, 210, 217, 219
  Fitzgerald, John 4, 8
  Gilpin, George 56
  Harper, John 36
  Harrison, John P. 76
  Herbert, William 4, 48
  Hickman, William 134
  Hicks, George 85
  Irvin, James 134, 148, 149, 168, 170, 177, 181, 191, 194, 210
  Johnston, Oke 91
  Keith, James 4, 8, 17, 48
  Kirk, James 17
  Lawrason, James 101
  Marsteller, Philip 56, 57, 85, 94
  McCarty, Edward 91
  McCrea, Robert 54
  Mease, Robert 76, 77, 81, 85, 93, 101, 110
  Murray, John 67
  Osborne, Richard 207
  Peyton, Francis 101, 134, 168, 170, 175, 177, 181, 191, 210, 212, 219
  Potts, John 56
  Ramsay, Dennis 56, 57, 67, 77, 85
  Ramsay, William 2, 83, 96, 97, 99, 100, 108, 110-112, 116, 123, 127, 128, 133, 134, 136, 148, 150, 207
  Ross, Hector 53
  Shackley, W. 119
  Smith, Alexander 175, 181
  Taylor, Jesse 54, 67, 76, 77, 81, 85, 93
  Thompson, Jonah 94, 131, 134, 148, 149, 197, 198, 217, 219
  Washington, Lawrence 207
  West, Hugh 207
  Wheeler, Ignatius 91
  Wilson, James 76
  Wilson, William 76
  Winsor, Olney 56, 57
George II [king] 207
George Town, MD 47, 68, 69, 120
Georgia, state of 95, 143
Ghequiere

Bernard 91, 95, 97, 99, 144, 150, 194, 210
Ghequire
  Bernard 120
Gibb
  William 79
Gibbory
  John 213
Gibory
  John 209, 210
Gibson
  Isaac 146, 216
  John 5, 25, 43, 55, 206, 215
  William 93, 117
  Wm. 105
Gill
  John 71, 118, 126, 135, 136, 152, 159, 178
  Thomas 134
Gillespie
  Martha 45
Gilpin
  George 27, 28, 39, 40, 43, 47, 56, 82, 92, 99, 101, 102, 105, 116, 120, 126, 137, 139, 150, 164, 166, 183, 187, 188-190, 194, 203, 206, 207, 217, 218
  J. 79, 111, 132, 150, 164, 173, 174
  Jane 39, 43, 47, 101, 102, 120, 137, 150, 164, 166, 188, 217, 218
  John 111
  Joseph 56
Gird
  Chrisr. 208
Gist
  John 130
Glasgow (Scotland) 42
Glass
  William 14
Glasscock
  William 138
Glassford
  John 5, 43
Glentown, Taboyne Parish, Donegal (Co.) 45
Gloucester Co., VA 126
Goode
  George 69
Goodes
  George 25
Gordon
  David 91, 96, 99, 100, 116
  John 32, 215, 216
  Sarah 91, 100

[blank] 72
Gortree (Ireland) 44
Goulding
  Mary Goulding Gretter 98
Governors:
  of NY: George Clinton 62
  of VA: Beverly Randolph 46
  of VA: Edmund Randolph 31
  of VA: Thos. Jefferson 53
Graham
  James 105
  John 11, 14, 109, 110, 120
  William 204
Granada 42
Grant
  William 121
Gray
  Vincent 76, 80, 127, 129, 183
Green
  Job 63, 71, 74, 83, 119
  Lydia 63
Greene
  Jesse 165
  Job 125, 159
Greenup
  Christopher 47
Greenway
  Joseph 17, 30, 39, 69
  Rebecca 39
Greer
  Alexander 192, 194
Gregory
  Robert 165
Gretter
  Ann Hoof 98
  Elizabeth 48, 65
  John 2, 65, 98, 172
  Margaret 98
  Mary Goulding 98
  Michael 18, 28, 29, 35, 48, 65, 76, 90, 98
  Michael Jr. 98
Griffith
  David 3, 4, 20-24, 33, 34, 47, 76, 80
  Hannah 20-24, 34, 80
  Reverend David 12
Grimes
  James 35, 146, 181
Ground
  under the river bank adj Lot 26 214, 215
Ground, raising for drainage 186
Ground: "made ground":
  adjoining Fleming's Lot 77 110

adjoining Ramsay's Lot 46 123
by Peers & Fitzgerald adj LOT 52
   58
by Wales, from his Brew House
   182
piece "known as Kirks Wharf" 132
Guadaloupe 42
Gunnell
   William 210
Hackleroad/Hachleroad
   John 26
Hadfield
   Joseph 114
Hagerty
   Patrick 46
Hague
   [first name not given] 139, 142
Hale
   George 96
   William 150
Hall
   Elizabeth 105
   Elizabeth Hall Massey 105, 116
   Francis 22
   Jonathan 39, 43, 47, 82, 101, 102,
      105, 116, 120, 137, 139, 164, 166,
      183, 217, 218
   Sarah 105
   Sarah Hall Falconar 105
   Sarah Hall Falconer 116
   William 70, 141
   William James 142
Halladay
   James 30
Halley
   Esther 113
   William 79, 113, 169, 207
Hallowell
   John 29
Hamelton
   Robert 184
Hamilton
   Esther 216
   Eunice 159
   Gilbert 42
   Hans of Gortree 44
   Isabella 45
   James 131, 216
   Jennett 45
   John Garner 4, 5, 67, 137
   Robert 101, 102, 111, 112, 132, 136,
      165, 205, 216
   Susanna 70
   Susannah 197

Theodore James 135
Theodorus James 159, 192
Thomas 44
William of Gortree 45
Hamp/Hampe
   Augustus 91
   Benjamin 19, 26, 106
   Benjamin Augustus 38, 96, 132
Hampshire Co., VA 63, 91, 112
Hampson
   Bryan 64, 65, 97, 111, 112, 117, 120,
      121, 148, 150, 159, 166
Hanson
   Mary 95, 166
   S. [or L.] "of Saml/Taml" 39
   Samuel 95, 166
   Samuel of Samuel 44
Harding's Creek 175
Harman/Harmon
   Jacob 17, 18, 28, 124
Harper
   Charles 87-89, 140, 174, 179, 199,
      200, 216
   Edward 32, 39, 67, 87-89, 154, 199,
      200, 216
   Elizabeth 88
   Frances Rush 88, 89, 200
   John 4, 11, 13, 25, 26, 30, 36, 37, 45,
      49, 50, 51, 55, 65, 67, 69, 73, 87-89,
      90, 92, 94, 95, 116, 119, 122-124,
      128, 141-143, 146, 158, 159, 167,
      172, 194, 199-201, 208, 216
   John Weathers 35, 90
   Joseph 197, 200, 201
   Mary 88, 142
   Mary Harper Vowell 199
   Peggy 88
   Samuel 24, 49, 142, 194, 197, 200,
      201, 218
   Sarah 194
   William 14, 15, 87, 94, 154, 216
   William A. 177, 212
Harrington Town (England) 24
Harris
   Richard 75
   Theophilus 155
Harrison
   Ann 201
   Barbara Hess 90
   John P. 76, 84
   Joseph 66, 68
   Joseph White 14, 17, 109
   Nathaniel 40
   Richard 14, 17, 18, 24, 62, 201

Sally 7
Samuel 64, 90
Vilinda 90
Harrow
　Gilbert 29
Hart
　George 175, 176
Hartshorne
　Susanna 1, 28, 70, 110
　William 1, 10, 14, 28, 63, 70, 79, 87, 88, 89, 101, 105, 106, 110, 119, 129, 132, 142, 155, 156, 168, 178, 179, 187, 199, 200
　William Jr. 129, 152
Harwood
　Rachel 53
　Risdon B. 53
Hatcher
　Isaac 59
Hatherly
　Nathan 170, 198
Hawkins
　Eleanor 81
　John 61, 81, 97
Hay_ _ _
　Andrew 39
Hayes
　Andrew 105
Headley
　Henry 91
Headley/Headly
　George 91, 100
　Henry 100
　Sarah 91
　Sarah Gordon 100
Heale
　George 96
Hedrick
　Thomas 24
Heineman
　Jacob 125, 217
　Maria 125
Heisler
　John 117, 152
Helms
　Jno. 195
Henderson
　Alexander 5, 25, 43, 55, 206, 215
　Archibald 5, 43
　Ax. [followed by--possibly--ygt. ?the younger?] 209
　David 194
　Robert 132, 164, 201, 202
Hendricks

James 2, 4, 28, 32, 41, 99, 155, 214
John 114, 115
Kitty 99
Henley/Henly
　David 62, 96
Henrico Co., VA 165
Henry
　Daniel 166
　James 104
Hepburn
　Agnes 2, 3, 59, 145, 170
　Ann 40
　Hepburn & Dundas 41, 67, 68, 93, 183
　William 2-4, 22, 28-30, 35, 40, 48, 57, 59, 65, 93, 123, 145, 170, 172, 177, 198, 212, 214-216
Herbert
　George 25, 48
　Herbert & Potts 26, 38
　Herbert, Potts & Wilson 84, 133
　Jane 94
　Jane Dalton 84, 133
　Jenny 113
　Michael 14
　Sarah 5, 36, 42, 146, 181
　Thomas 84, 94, 113, 133
　William 4, 5, 8, 15, 17, 24, 34, 36-38, 39, 42-44, 48, 58, 74, 79, 83, 96, 146, 158, 167, 181, 187, 189, 190, 198
Herlihy
　Maurice 122, 130, 204
　Morris 44
Herredsburg, KY 90
Hess
　Barbara 98
　Barbara Hess Harrison 90
　Jacob 90, 97
Hewes
　Aaron 12, 14, 63, 88, 96, 116, 136, 142, 189, 192
　Abraham 83, 166
　Mary 96, 189
Hewes/Hughes
　Aaron 143
Hewett
　Thomas 75
　William 61
Hewitt
　Richard 125
Hews
　Aaron 64
Hickman
　John 4, 5, 25, 36, 37, 111, 137

Mary 137
Rebecca 146
William 104, 131, 134, 137, 141-143, 146, 150
William Jr. 16, 19, 25, 32, 36, 37
Hicks
George 85
Priscilla 85
William 85
Hill
John 71, 216
Hineman
Ann 86, 87
George 18, 86
Nancy 86, 90
Hodges
Lansdall & Hodges 210
Hodgson
Hodgson & Nikolson 210
Joseph 68, 75
William 37, 43, 44, 55, 58, 61, 68, 75, 84, 89, 113, 120, 122, 132, 167, 183, 190, 191, 194, 204, 210
Hoge
Isaac 26
Holliday
James 4, 39
Hollingsworth
George 2
Jesse 116
Holmes
Jno. 195
Thomas 195
Honeff
Joseph 65
Honorable:
Mercer, James 33, 218
Hooe
James H. 54
Robert Townshend 4, 14, 17, 18, 24, 31, 41, 53, 62, 98, 107-109, 124, 130, 131, 153, 154, 158, 189, 190, 201
Seymour 19
William 125
William Townshend 118
Hoof
Ann Hoof Gretter 98
Lawrence 41, 65, 95, 96, 98, 100, 104, 116, 131, 177
Horner
John 83, 87, 125, 199
Horsburgh
Jno. 194

Hough
John 53, 216
Sarah 53
William 171
Howard
Beal 9
Beale 217
William 8
Hoye
William 122, 128, 137, 170, 193
Hubball
John 145
Hughes
Aaron 37
James 34, 38
Jno. 191
Hughes/Hewes
Aaron 143
Hughs
John 115, 168
Hull
John 32
Hunter 31
Christiana 1, 8, 40, 66, 68
Duncan 45
George 103, 109, 130, 131, 135, 165, 175, 189, 210
Hunter & Allison 59
Ichabod 20, 38, 44, 58
James 45
John 7, 54, 111
Joseph 41
Kitty 8, 69
Nathaniel Chapman 116, 121, 126, 136
Robert 30
Sarah Ann 116, 126, 136
Sarah Anne 121
William 1, 2, 8, 55, 82, 91, 167, 183
William Jr. 7, 8, 20, 25, 38, 40, 42, 47, 51, 53, 55, 58, 61, 65, 75, 79, 81, 94, 206, 215
William Sr. 16, 39, 40, 66, 68, 69
William the younger 45
Hunting Creek 107, 108, 117, 118, 153, 207, 212
Hurst
K. 185
Hynman/Hyneman
Jacob 9
H[?]ickey
Francis 27
Ingle
Joseph 155, 206

Ingles
  Samuel 150
Inglish
  Ann 24
  Samuel 24
Ingraham
  Nath. 58
Inheritance rights:
  Catharine Brown's 75
Ireland 207
  John Mease of 76
Irfmeizer [?]
  Johan 49
Irish
  George 147, 149, 154, 164, 166, 183, 204
Ironmasters:
  May, Thomas 5
Irvin
  James 127, 130-132, 134, 135, 137, 138, 139, 143, 145, 148, 149, 155, 160, 164, 168-171, 174, 177, 178, 181, 182, 191-194, 196-198, 200, 201, 202, 204, 206, 210, 214
  John 177
  William 81
Irvin, James 168
Irvine 17
  James 57, 92, 98, 114, 207, 208
  Thomas 98
Irving (Scotland) 43
Irwin
  Thomas 121, 210, 213, 218
Isabel
  Jonah 176
  Jonah Jr. 172
  William 207
Isabell
  Jonah 149, 195, 205, 206
J-i-b-o [?]
  (clerk's name "sketch") 90
Jackson
  Amas 148, 150
  Henry 6, 7
  Joseph 143
  William 143
Jacob
  Moses 60
Jacobs
  Joshua 177
  Thomas 87, 196
Jameson
  Andrew 24
Jamesson

Robert B. 72, 79
Jamieson
  Andrew 70, 71, 75, 99, 148, 154
  James B. 104
Jamison
  Robert Brown 27, 28, 42
Janney
  Elisha 82, 116, 157, 158, 164, 166, 183, 204
  John 5, 106, 172, 175, 178
  Joseph 97, 117
Jeboe
  Mr. 97
Jefferson Co., KY 175
Jeffreys
  George 216
Jenkes
  Crawford 60
  John 60
  Joseph 26, 60
Jennings
  Daniel 207
  Thomas 19
Je[?]rmingham
  Henry 26
Jobson
  James 110, 187, 195
Johnson
  John 211
  Joshua 114, 119
  Leonard William 114
  Oke 63
Johnston
  Abraham 112
  Dennis 149
  Dennis McCarty 212, 213
  Elizabeth 124
  George 105, 116
  Oke 91
  Samuel 124
  William 113
Johnstone
  Gerrard 25
Jolly
  John 37, 57, 66, 68, 86, 89, 93, 135
  Rachel 37, 89, 135
Jones
  Charles 19, 81, 93, 172, 187
  David 20, 21, 23, 76, 77
  John 150
  Sarah 93
Jones Point 117, 212
  constructing fort on 117
  lease of 151

Judge
   Andrew 28, 35
Judge, Inferior Court, Wilkes Co.:
   Butler, Edward 183
Justice for TwnALX:
   Thompson, Jonah 190
Justice of the Peace for ALX:
   Faw, Abraham 190
Justice of the Peace for FfxCo.:
   Deneale, William 214
Justice of the Peace for Wilmington:
   Broome, Jaco. 43
Justice of the Peace of ALX:
   Dundas, John 129
   Peyton, Francis 129
Justices of Ffx Co.:
   Deneale, William 27, 28
   Gilpin, George 27, 28, 203
Justices of the Peace for Gloucester Co.:
   Lewis, Thomas 126
   Whiting, J. 126
Justices of the Peace for Montgomery Co., MD:
   Magruder, Sam. W. 68
   Thompson, Richard 68
Justices of the Peace of Baltimore Co., MD:
   Calhoun, James 105
   Presbury, George Gouldsmith 117
   Salmon, George 105, 117
Justices of the Peace of Charles Co., MD:
   Baillice, Andrew 90
   Dent, George 90
Justices of the Peace of Suffolk Co.:
   Cooper, Samuel 142
   Minot, George Richards 142
Justices of the Peace, Frederick Co., MD:
   Luckett, William 115
   Scott, George 115
Justices of the Peace, Philadelphia Co., PA:
   Sowess, Joseph 99
Keach
   Samuel 173
Keatch/Keech
   Samuel 141
Keating
   James 128, 147, 155
Keech
   Samuel 154, 174, 179
   William 65
Keech/Keatch
   Samuel 141
Keimhoff/Kleiŋhoff
   John 83
Keith
   Elizabeth 141, 149, 154, 157
   James 4, 6, 8, 12, 13, 17, 18, 20-23, 25, 26, 27, 32, 34, 36, 38-40, 42, 45, 47, 48-51, 63-66, 71-73, 75, 79-81, 85, 87-89, 91-96, 98-103, 107, 110, 112, 113, 114, 116, 118-120, 122, 124, 125-129, 131, 132, 135, 138, 139, 141-145, 147-149, 152, 154, 156, 157-159, 163, 165-167, 169, 173, 178, 180, 181, 183, 186, 192, 195, 198-202, 205, 208, 214-216, 218, 219
   James Jr. 39, 66, 100, 120, 141, 156, 172, 173-175, 200, 201
   Jno. 66
   John 30
   John Contee 39, 49-51, 67
   Smith 139
Kemech
   Samuel 173
Kemp
   Johann Christian 129
Kempff
   C.B. 41
   J.C. 157, 168, 169
   Johan Christian 61, 68, 69, 74, 112, 125
   Johann Christian 35
   John C. 157
   John Christopher 90
   Jonathan Christian 55
Kennedy
   Dr. 88
   James 37, 83, 96, 97, 110, 111, 118, 121, 123, 133, 136, 142-144, 166, 170, 177, 188, 198
   Laetitia 121
   Letitia 111, 143, 170
Kenner/Kennor
   Hannah 73
   James 67, 73, 189
Kenney
   James 107
Kenny
   Richard 60
Kentucky land, of D. Griffith 47
Kentucky, District of 175
Kerr
   James 107, 176

Keyger [See also Kyger]
  George 1, 2
  Mary 1, 2
Khun/Keen
  Khun/Keen & Risberg 27
Kidd
  James 72, 94
Killbarchen (Scotland) 2
Kilmarnock (Scotland) 42, 43
King
  William 53
King George Co., VA 10-14, 49, 50, 54, 70, 86, 105-108, 117-119, 125, 126, 135, 149, 151-154, 156, 157, 162, 163, 173, 174, 178, 195, 204, 209, 211
Kinnare
  John 151
Kinzey
  Ezra 126
Kirckcudbright Co., (Scotland) 70
Kirckcudbright Town (Scotland) 70
Kirk
  Bridget 70, 75
  Bridget Fleming 189
  James 3, 17-19, 29, 70, 75, 146, 196
  Kirk & Bowdon 38
  Kirk's lott 72
  Robert 70, 75
Kirkpatrick
  Catharine Kirkpatrick Coltart 206
  Elizabeth Kirkpatrick Cutler 206, 214, 215
  Henrietta 25, 70, 206, 214, 215
  John 214, 215
  Katharine Kirkpatrick Coltart 214, 215
  Thomas 25, 70, 206, 214, 215
Kleinhoff
  John 4
Kleinhoof
  John 69, 94, 97, 100
Knight
  John 119
Korn
  John 43, 56, 63, 71, 96, 102, 106
  Korn & Wisemiller 106
  Rosannah/Rosina 102
Kuhn
  John 60
Kyger
  George 63, 91, 112, 167
  John 63, 91
  Mary 63, 91, 112, 167

L'Orient city (France) 18, 24
Lacost
  Steven 60
Ladd
  Jno. G. 192, 204
Lamphier
  Gowen/Going 23
  Gowing 77
Lancaster
  J. 169
  T. 150
  Thomas 207
Lane
  Joseph 59
Langmarch
  Christian 178
Langphier
  Robert Going 59
Lankphier
  Going 77
Lansdall
  Lansdall & Hodges 210
Lanston
  Benjamin 139
Laurason
  James 123
Lawrason
  Alice 55, 66
  James 5, 16, 25, 33, 34, 55, 66, 69, 81, 99, 101-103, 109, 111, 112, 120, 137, 141, 150, 151, 156, 172-175, 202, 218
  Shreeve & Lawrason 26
  Thomas 149
Lawson
  John 116, 121, 126, 136
Leap
  Jacob 129, 146, 171
Lear
  Jao. 70
Lee
  Arthur 44, 80, 204, 217
  Charles 3, 6, 28, 36, 61, 70, 76, 103, 117, 151, 164, 196, 202, 214, 217
  Edmund 76
  Edmund J. 105, 106, 174, 179, 214, 217
  Francis L. 165
  Henry 3, 77, 80, 104, 196
  Henry Jr. 34, 35, 61, 187, 217
  Lucy 191
  Ludwell 165
  Sally 217
  Theodorick 39

Tom 120
Lefewick
  Thomas 90
Leiper
  Lucinda 205
LeMesurier
  Paul 119
Lemoine
  John 182, 210
Lethgow
  Alexander 116, 121
Lewis
  Hannah 110
  John W. 191
  Jos: 54
  Joseph Jr. 24
  Mordecai 28, 110, 142
  Thomas 110, 126, 131
Lightfoot
  Daniel 74
Liles
  Zacharias 122
Limrick
  John 147, 177
Linendrapers:
  Williams, Stephen 31
Lingan
  Js. McCubbin (see also Linglar) 5
Linglar
  Jo. McCubbin (see also Lingan) 5
Lintch
  Daniel 87
Lithgow
  Alexander 126, 136
Little
  Charles 31, 217
Littledale
  Isaac 24, 47
Littler
  Isaac [or Sittler] 182
  Nathan 67, 83
Liverpool (England) 38
Lloyd
  John 199, 200
Lock/Lockie
  Thomas 199
Locke
  Thomas 145, 200
Lockhart
  Marian 2
Lockwood
  John 83, 96, 189
Loggens
  Peter 171
Loggins
  Peter 149
Lomax
  John 1-3, 16, 20, 21, 42, 55, 78, 122, 130
  Rachel 42, 122, 130
London (England) 31, 33, 44, 45, 69, 114, 118
Londonderry city, (Ireland) 45
Long Ordinary Lot, The 42, 147
Longden
  John 206
  Ralph 48
Longdon
  Elizabeth 30
  John 30, 52, 69, 81, 82, 87, 108
  Ralph 52, 78
Loudon/Loudoun Co., VA 2, 53, 54, 59, 84, 98, 103, 130
Love
  Charles 132, 206
  Charles Jr. 81
  John 98, 103, 117
Lowe
  Henry 18
  Henry F. 48, 147, 177
  S. 191
  Samuel 75
Lowery
  Olivia 136
  William 136
Lownes
  James 11, 14, 36, 37
  Sarah 37
Lowrie
  James 6
Luckett
  William 115
Lumley/Point Lumley
  Oct 1780 lease of 14
  Trustees' lease to Fleming 130
Lumsden
  John 192, 213
Lunt
  Henry 119
Lutz
  Catharine 210
Lyle
  Elizabeth 213
  Jane 75
  Martha 24, 75
  Robert 14, 39, 54, 58, 61, 75, 147, 213
  Robert Jr. 24, 25

Robert Sr. 24
Robert the elder 75
William 75
Lyles
　Henry 41
　Sarah 26, 121
　William 33, 38, 41, 115, 121
　William Jr. 26, 48, 115
Lynn
　Adam 2, 4, 51, 81, 95, 96, 105
　Mary Lynn Webster 81
Lyon
　Walter 133
MacHarg
　Anthony 2
MacIver
　Colin 8, 15, 19, 32
MacKenzie
　Alexander 144, 183
　John 45, 144
Macleod
　Daniel 188
MacRea
　W. 76
Madden
　Hannah 17, 22, 32, 47, 77, 85, 97, 106, 110, 111, 137, 139, 150, 188, 191, 193, 218
　Hannah Ramsay 193, 206, 208
　Michael 7, 17, 18, 22, 32, 47, 53, 77, 83, 97, 106, 110, 111, 127, 137, 138, 150, 159, 185, 187, 188, 191, 193, 199, 206, 208, 217, 218
Magistrates of ALX:
　Duvall, William 61
　Porter, Thomas 120
　Ramsay, Dennis 61, 120
　Taylor, Jesse 61
　Winter, William Jr. 94
Magruder
　Philip 85, 206
　Sam. W. 68
Maguire
　Thomas 15
Manchester, VA 60
Mandeville
　John 187, 210
　Jonathan 69, 150, 187, 188
　Joseph 5
Mann
　Bernard 22, 80, 201
　Bernhard 125
　Johanna 125
Manning
　Jacob H. 73
Manumission:
　A. Hewes' slave Sylvia 192
　C. Noland's slave Dennis 129
　E. Hawkins' slave Celia 81
　J. Caverly/J. Hunter's slave Peter 111
　J. Gist's slave George 130
　L. Williams' slaves Anthony, Sophia, John, Tom, Lewis 195
　W. Johnstone's slave Milly 113
　W. Rhodes' slave Rachel and her issue 136
　W. Summers' slave Henry 145
Mariners:
　Boden, George 40
　Green, Job 63
　Johnston, Dennis 149
　Speake, Josias Milburne 147
　Tarbuck alias Scott, John 17, 42
Marshall
　Benjamin Jr. 105, 106
　George 45
　R. 112
Marsteller
　Christiana 126, 141, 183
　Ferdinand 90
　Jno. Lewis 217
　Lewis J. [may be I.] 172
　Magdalena 43, 102
　Magdelena 102
　P. 30, 53, 54, 56, 64, 71, 73, 126, 131, 157, 191, 193, 208, 217
　P. Jr. 56
　P.G. 71
　Peter 83
　Philip 33, 43, 52, 56, 57, 59, 62, 64, 66, 69, 82, 85, 89, 90, 92, 94, 96, 97, 101, 102, 104, 116, 141, 175, 176, 213
　Philip G. 98, 125, 126, 130, 139, 142, 178
　Philip Godhelp 5, 126, 183
　Philip Jr. 43
Martin
　Robert 60
Mason
　George 181
　J. 80
　John 72, 86
　Stes. Thon. 61
　Thompson 103
Mason Co., KY 91
Massey
　Elizabeth 105, 116

Joseph 105, 116
Masterson
  Sarah 7
Mattart/Medtart/Mettart
  Jacob 114, 115
  Magdalena 115
May
  Dolly/Dorothy 202
  Dorothy 158
  Fosters & May 210
  Joseph 103, 158, 202
  Richard 154
  Sarah 5, 43
  Thomas 5, 43
Mayer
  Christian 62
Mayfield (Scotland) 43
Mayors:
  of ALX: D. Ramsay 52, 104, 131
  of ALX: Jesse Taylor 76
  of ALX: P. Marsteller 82
  of ALX: R.T. Hooe 14
  of Annapolis: J. Price 53
  of George Town: T. Turner 120
  of George Town: Thomas Beall 68
  of London: J. Sanderson 114
  of London: P. LeMesurier 119
  of New York: R. Varick 170, 194, 204
  of Phila.: M. Clarkson 70, 92, 110, 201
  of Richmond: A. Dunscomb 165
McCabe
  Henry 168
McCallmont
  Jno. 173
McCarty
  Daniel 103
  Dennis 213
  Edward 63, 91, 112
McCaughen
  Hugh 109
McCauley
  William 37
McCausland
  Marcus 64, 67
McClain
  Daniel 112
McClanachan
  Ann 103
  John 103
McClean
  Archibald 115, 116, 122, 168
McCleary

William 177
McClenachan
  Ann 203
  James 194
  Joseph 203
McClenachen
  John 202
McClish
  James 61
McConnel
  Andrew 103
McConnell
  Alexander 98, 112, 125, 137, 172, 202
  Mary 112
McCormick
  James 69
McCrea
  Agness 64
  Allan 25
  Ann 18
  James 110, 179
  James M. 18, 178
  James Mease 31
  John 25, 53, 116
  McCrea & Mease 88-90, 98, 119, 122, 124, 182
  Nancy 25, 62, 69, 95, 143
  Robert 15, 16, 18, 25, 38, 51, 54, 62, 64, 65, 69, 81, 85, 95, 100, 124, 143, 183, 215
McCready
  James 137
McCue
  Henry 78, 122
McGough
  Henry 218
McGuier
  James 127
McGuire
  James 155, 202
McHenry
  James 48, 93, 122, 130, 193
McIver
  Charles 39
  Colin 144
  John 32, 144, 145, 198, 204, 214
  Margaret 144, 145
McKenna
  Charles 143, 170
  James 57, 132, 142, 165, 206
McKensie
  William 76
McKenzie
  Alexander 145, 164, 183

247

William 150
McKinzey
  William 24
McKnight
  Charles 73, 100, 109, 124, 151, 177, 186
  W. 66
  William 8, 30, 53, 56, 61, 63, 73, 124, 168, 186
MClanachan
  John 47
McLean
  Archibald 99, 192
McLellan
  Daniel 70
McLeod
  Daniel 192, 213
  James 3
  Robert 3, 146
McLish
  James 94
McMahan
  Ann 41
  Michael 41
McMasters
  Andrew 28
McMunn
  Elizabeth 182
  George 127, 129, 156, 182, 195, 214
  Robert 182, 187
McPherson
  Daniel 33, 58-60, 82, 101, 218
  Daniel Jr. 19, 164
  Elizabeth 82, 166
  Isaac 19, 33, 34, 58-60, 63, 82, 95, 101, 105, 164, 166, 218
  Jane 82, 166
  Jonas 61
  Martha 58, 60
McRea
  Alan 215
  Jn. 61
  John 215
  McCrea & Mease 158
  McRea & Mease 208
  Nancy 216
  Robert 206, 215, 216
McReady
  James 23, 28
McWhir
  William 18
Mease
  Betty 95, 121, 143, 149, 188, 191, 216

Betty Steuart 124
  John 76
  Mathew 85
  Matthew 64, 65, 95, 100, 144
  McCrea & Mease 88-90, 98, 119, 122, 124, 182
  McRea & Mease 158, 208
  Robert 16, 18, 25, 38, 62, 64, 65, 69, 76, 77, 80-83, 85, 93, 95, 99-101, 102-104, 107-112, 114, 116, 120, 121, 124, 125, 131, 135, 141, 143, 149, 150, 169, 188, 191, 216
  William 172
Meazarvey/Measervey
  Thomas 103
Meazowy/Mezewey
  Thomas 98
Meeme
  George 210
Mellum [?]
  [illegible] 24
Mendenhall
  William 177
Mercer
  Colo. George 32
  George 33, 121
  James 32-34, 38, 58, 61, 121, 218
Merchant
  William 9, 217
Merchants:
  Adam, Robert 2
  Allison, Robert 3, 4, 16, 183
  Ballendine, John 2
  Barry, James 114
  Black, William 25
  Blake, Peter 170
  Bowen, Obediah 26
  Carson, Thomas 79
  Coates, John 170
  Coltart, Roger 70
  Dade, Baldwin 3, 35
  Davey, David 177
  Deblois, George 142
  Dixon, John 24
  Dundas, John 93, 133
  Dunlap, John 112
  Dunlop, George 2
  Field/Feild, John 5
  Finlay, David 118
  Gemmill, John 43
  Hadfield, Joseph 114
  Hall, William james 142
  Harper, John 11, 13
  Hartshorne, William 10, 110

Henley, David 62
Hepburn, William 93
Herbert, William 5, 8, 15, 79
Hesshuyson, Lewis D. 60
Hunter, Duncan 45
Hunter, William 1, 2, 55
Hunter, William Jr. 40, 42
Janney, John 5
Kennedy, James 118
Kirkpatrick, Thomas 25, 70
Lewis, Mordecai 28, 110
Littledale, Isaac 24, 47
Lyle, Robert the elder 75
MacKenzie, John 45
Marshall, George 45
McCrea, Allan 25
McCrea, Robert 69
McPherson, Daniel 33
McPherson, Isaac 33
Mease, Robert 69
Merian, Samuel 60
Miller, James 76
Miller, Joseph 146
Miller, William 76
Muir, James 79
Munford, John 26
Murray, John 26
Patton, James 118
Pleasants, Samuel 5
Ramsay, Dennis 3
Ramsay, Edward Mitchell 91
Reynolds, John 13
Robinson, Christopher 55
Robinson, Sanderson & Rumney 75
Roome, Henry 34
Rumney, John 55
Sanderson, Robert 55
Semple, William 70
Smith, James the younger 91
Taylor, Jesse 36, 40, 52
Thorn, Michael 16
Tobin, Thomas 14
Watson, Josiah 40, 110
Wheeler, Israel 146
Wilson, William 70
Merian
   Samuel 60
Merryman
   Joshua 26
Methodist Church 109
Meyler
   James 4
Mezarvey
   Thomas 147
Middlesex Co. (England) 132
Middlesex Co., VA 80
Middleton
   James 181
Mifflin
   Thomas Jr. 110
Military certificates 4
Mill Creek 176
Miller
   Godfrey 8
   James 76, 166
   Jane 70
   Joseph 146
   Mordecai 116, 130, 196
   Mordechai 74
   William 70, 76
Millers:
   Nichols, Isaac 59
Mills
   John 17, 205
Minchin
   J. 97
Ministers:
   Campbell, John 2
   Griffith, David 34
   Knight, John 119
   Muir, James 94, 205
Minor
   Daniel 181
Mitchell
   Hugh 32, 108
   William 139
Mittchell
   Hugh 22
Montgomery Co., MD 67, 68
Montgomery Co., PA 43
Mooney
   Mary 8
   Neal 8
   Neil 36, 53, 56, 63, 148
Moore
   Cleon 16, 27, 28, 31, 42, 44, 55, 56, 63, 78, 91, 93, 122, 130, 134, 140, 150, 155, 171, 187, 189, 209, 210
   Henry 149, 155, 171, 187, 209, 210
   James 192
   Jesse 130
   Phoebe Arell 171
   Stephen 171
   Thomas 149
Morehouse
   Abraham 115
Morris

John 135, 192
Richard 62
Morrison
  Susannah 163
Mortgage, deed of: 4, 67, 69, 73, 76, 90, 91, 94, 99, 112, 128, 135, 165, 170, 192, 214, 216, 217
Mosely
  William 145
Moss
  John 36
  William 149
Mounger
  Edwin 183
Moxley
  Ann 134
  Daniel 134, 174
  Thomas 23
Muir
  Carson & Muir 53
  Elizabeth Muir Donaldson 155, 178, 179, 186, 196
  James 42, 79, 94, 169, 205, 213
  John 18, 25, 72, 132, 155, 178, 179, 186, 196, 206, 215
  Robert 72, 196
Muncaster
  John 110, 124, 131, 164, 172, 190, 201
  Zachariah 118, 124
Munford
  John 26
Murdoch
  George 13
Murray
  Elizabeth 59
  George W. 59
  James 167
  John 6, 26, 32-34, 58, 59, 63, 64, 67, 105, 218
  John B. 203
  Margaret 24
  Patrick 24, 81, 150, 169
  Patty 59, 105
  Peter 58, 112, 210
  Robert 194
Murray's Run 176
Myler
  Elizabeth 29
  James 28, 29
Nailors:
  Reynolds, Levi 214
Nallette [See also Valette]
  Elie 15

Nassau Island, Queens Co., NY 34
Naye
  John 165
Neale
  Joseph R. 190
Neblon
  John James 91, 167
  Margaret Petit 167
Negro Craigy 212
Negroes:
  of A. Brown: Benjamin, Maide, Lewis 203
  of A. Hewes: Sylvia 192
  of A. Thomas: Harry 19
  of C. Noland: Dennis 129
  of C. Page/A. Craig: Arianna 129
  of Capt. J. Clark/Clerke: Maria 92
  of D. Foley: Kate, Lucy [also Susey] 205
  of D. Ramsay: Ismael, Ellis, Daniel, Sall, William, Dennis 74
  of E. Hawkins: Celia 81
  of H. Bayne: Benjamin 174
  of J. B. Petit: Mely 68
  of J. Fitzgerald: Jack & Matt 115
  of J. Graham: Sam & Linder 120
  of J. Harper: Esther 89
  of J. Harper: Kitt 88
  of J. Harper: Lucy 89
  of J. Harper: Mary 88
  of J. Heard: Orwell 90
  of J. Irvin/Rope Walk: Will, Guss, James Bull, Harry 201
  of J. Meyler: Sarah & Jack 38
  of J. Meyler: Sarah, Moses, Jack 4
  of J. Muir. Kate 94
  of J. Muncaster: Peter 190
  of J. Parsons: Janey 86
  of J. R. Neale: Stephen 190
  of J. Taylor: Charity, Bob, Jacob 79
  of J. Taylor: George Harle 174
  of J. Wise: Ramey 39
  of L. Crowe: Mima, William, Eleanor 120
  of L. Williams: Anthony, Sophia, John, Tom, Lewis 195
  of M. Swoope: Jane, Jude 27
  of N. Anderson: Grace, Nancy, Ellsey 94
  of N. Anderson: Isaac & Forester 61
  of N. Anderson: Mary, Grace, Sampson, Charlotte, Nancy 61
  of N. Voss: Cate, Dolly, Bello, Maria, Mildred 190

of N. Voss: George, Isreal, Anthony, Thomas, James 190
of P. Bowling & S. Shreve: Mary, Ann, Elizabeth, Daphne, John 93
of P. Poyer: unnamed boy 129
of R. Adam: Bravo & Bristow 58
of R. Croke: James, Silvia, Amelia, Stace 73
of T. Lee/D. Easton: Prince 120
of T. W. Watson: Will 28
of W. Halley: Nace 113
of W. Johnstone: Milly 113
of W. Oden: Mint & Mary 129
of W. Rhodes: Rachel 136
of W. Summers: Henry 145
of W. Ward: Andrew 121
Neil
  William 108
Neill
  John 117
Neilson
  Hugh 24
Nell
  W. 119
Nelson
  Alexander 60
Nevin
  Duncan 213
New Town, Nassau Island, Queens Co., NY 34
New York city 26, 34, 170, 194, 203, 204
Newton
  Jane 169
  William 43, 89, 109, 140, 150, 159, 167, 169, 202, 207
  Wm. 140
  [first name not given] 142
Nicholl
  James 26
Nicholls
  Scudamore 83
Nichols
  Isaac 59
  Samuel 59
Nickolls
  Isaac 120
  James B. 140
Nikolson
  Hodgson & Nikolson 210
Nisbett
  John Maxwell 15
Nivien

Dun. 62
Nixon
  George 26
Noble
  William 124
  William [?S.] 134
Non-Importation Compliance:
  by Aloysius Brown 203
  by Capt. J. Clark 92
  by Charles Page 129
  by David Easton 120
  by George Collard 190
  by George Singleton 190
  by George Slacum 76
  by Horatio Ross 83
  by James Graham 120
  by John Edward Ford 68
  by John Heard 90
  by John Muncaster 190
  by John Parsons 86
  by John Watts 92, 190
  by Joseph R. Neale 190
  by L. Crowe 120
  by Nicholas Voss 190
  by Philip Poyer 129
  by Rev. James Muir 94
  by Richard Croke 73
  by Thomas Marshall 214
  by Walter Lyon 76
  by William Olden 129
Northumberland Co., VA 6, 7, 32
Notary and Tabellion Publick:
  Broome, Jaco. 43
Notary Public:
  Robson, Robert 114, 118
  Younger, Peter How 55
Notary, Tabellion Public, Interpreter:
  Duplessis, Peter LeBarbier 60
Noyes
  Samuel 58
O'Mara
  Michael 92, 158
Oden
  William 129
OKelly
  John B. 29
Oliphant
  Jno. 24
Oneil
  J. H. 145
Orange Co., NC 4, 5, 37
Orpwood
  John 23
Orr

Benjamin G. 187
Benjamin Grayson 149
J. D. 189
John 104
John D. 128
John Dalrymple 135
Lucinda 128
Orraland
  Roger Cutlar of 70
Orraland (Scotland) 70
Osborne
  Richard 207
Otway
  Fletcher & Otway 210
Outbuildings:
  bake house & associated structures 148
  bake house & ovens 71
  distillery's 115
  flour shed, to be built 198
  Gill's ground fenced as garden 71
  Heineman's [unnamed] 125
  kitchen 15, 17, 188, 214
  kitchen & garden 84
  necessary 80, 200, 214
  on J. Harper's pier/dock [unspecified] 201
  out-houses [unspecified] and fence 164
  rope walk [unspecified] 201
  scale house 15
  shed 128
  shed kitchen 71
  smoke house 15, 214
  stable 17, 76, 127, 203, 214
  stable [to be built] 165
  woodyard 71
  woodyard, enclosed 75, 115
Ownbread
  Magdalena 63
  Mary 41
  William 41, 63, 71
Packard
  Samuel 59
Page
  Charles 127, 129, 210
Painter
  George 187
Panacott
  Garland Wingfield 183
Pancas
  Jonathan 182
Pancoast
  David 11, 16

  Jonathan 182
Parker
  Richard 98, 99, 196
  [first name not given] 155
Parrott
  Richard 137
Parsons
  Elizabeth 61, 167
  James 6, 54, 86, 91, 167
  James, estate 61
  John 61, 86, 143
  Mr. [first name not given] 153
Parton
  Thomas 98
Paterson
  William 43
Paton
  Mary 139, 172, 177
  William 3, 15, 34, 52-54, 82, 104, 131, 139, 172, 173, 177
Patten
  Francis 212
  Mary 158, 189, 202, 209, 212, 213
  Thomas 76, 77, 117, 125, 151, 158, 185, 189, 202, 209, 213
Patterson
  David 60
  John 38, 117
  Susanna 53
  Thomas 18, 35
  William 17, 27, 28, 42, 53
Pattersons Lotts
  Town Lots 56-57-58 100
Patton
  James 8, 25, 32, 38, 84, 96, 97, 106, 118, 133, 136, 144, 170
  Mary 171
  Mary Ann 97, 133, 170
  Patton & Butcher 210
  Robert Jr. 97, 137
  Thomas 103
  William 171
Payne
  W. 104
  William 7, 31, 206, 207
Peake
  Thomas 177
Pearson
  Mr. [no first name given] 107
  Simon 195
Pedestrian footways 186
Peers
  Eleanor 98, 103, 117

Valentine 15, 38, 44, 58, 64, 84, 98, 103, 112, 117, 120, 122, 135, 158, 183, 191, 194, 218
Peltz
  John 13
Pendleton
  John 165
Pens
  Jacob 13
Perrin
  Jh. M. 51, 91
  Joseph M. 108, 119, 126, 167
  Joseph Mr. 77
  Mathrin. 119
  Mathurien/Matzurin 77
  Mathvin. 126
  Messrs. Perrin & Brothers 60
Peter
  Robert 69
Peterkin
  Thomas 58
Peterson
  Henry 160
Petit
  John 86, 143
  John Babtist 90
  John Baptist 68, 167
  Margaret 68
  Margaret Petit Neblon 167
Pettit
  John 54
Peyton
  Ann 198
  Francis 32, 59, 100-103, 105, 108, 109, 111, 112, 120, 123, 125-127, 129, 134, 135, 137, 139-142, 144, 145, 146, 147, 149-151, 155-157, 158, 160, 168-170, 174, 175, 177, 178, 179, 181-183, 185, 190-192, 193, 194, 196-198, 200, 204, 206, 208, 209, 210, 212-214, 217-219
  Sarah 127, 145, 147, 192, 196-198, 217
Philadelphia city 5, 15, 19, 28, 35, 60, 70, 76, 91, 98, 110, 144, 146, 177, 201, 214
Physicians:
  Brown, William 1
  Dick, Elisha Cullen 28
  Ramsay, William 101, 106
  Townshend, Platt 62
Pile
  Peter 181
Pinkney

  Jona. of Robt. 53
  Robert 53
Piper
  Anthony 24
  Harry 24
Plat
  J. Mercer's 7 lots 32
  J. Parson's estate 61
  original Alexandria Town Plan 206
Pleasants
  John L. [or S.] 39
  Samuel 5
Polk
  Charles 25
Polkinhorn
  Henry 182
Polkinhorne
  Polkinhorne & Andrew 210
Pollard
  John 125, 195, 204
  Thomas 83, 87, 185, 199
Pomery
  Elizabeth 176
  Walter 206
  Walter Jr. 172, 176, 196, 207
  William 193, 205, 207, 208
Port Tobacco, MD 71
Porter
  James 84, 150
  Sarah 84, 108, 111, 150, 166, 188, 191
  Sarah Ramsay 108
  Thomas 6, 37, 38, 44, 58, 69, 72, 82, 84, 104, 108, 111, 120, 131, 150, 166, 188, 191, 203
Potomac River 5, 8, 10, 13, 15, 19, 20, 29, 41, 50-52, 55, 62, 73, 81, 84, 96, 108, 117, 119, 128, 130, 131, 133, 135, 140, 148, 151, 152, 154, 182, 183, 187, 189, 194, 214, 215
Potomack River 131
Potomack Street 46, 50, 51
Potten
  John 197
Potts
  Herbert & Potts 26, 38
  Herbert, Potts & Wilson 84, 133
  John 56, 217
  John Jr. 5, 15, 20-23, 43, 80
Powell
  B. 15
  Burr 20-23
  Leven 33, 38, 47, 61, 145
  Leven [possibly Leven Jr.] 146
  Levin 59

William H. 33
Poyer
  Philip 129
Pratt
  Cary 206
Presbury
  George Gouldsmith 117
Presbyterian Church
  parsonage house 109
  yard 73, 109, 217
Prescott
  R. 47
Preston
  Thomas 142
Price
  Ann 219
  Ellis 178
  Ezekiel 142, 158, 202
  James 53
  Jane 54, 171, 172, 177
  Mary 115
  Oliver 29, 52-54, 57, 82, 104, 131, 139, 171-173, 177, 206
  Thomas 114, 115
  William 23
Prince George's Co., MD 4, 11, 29, 59, 94, 113, 121, 173, 192
Prince William Co., VA 10-14, 25, 70, 96, 99, 100, 103, 116, 117, 121, 126, 136, 195, 218
Proprietor, Northern Neck of VA 72
Protonotary of Court of Common Pleas, Philadelphia Co.,PA:
  Biddle, Charles 99
Puppo
  Daniel C. 158, 160
Quadripartite Deeds: 98, 199, 200, 218
Quakers
  burying ground 3
Quebec 42
Queen Ann Co., MD 116
Queens Co., NY 34
Quinquepartite Deeds: 101
Raeberry
  Thomas Kirkpatrick of 70
Raeberry (Scotland) 70
Ralston
  Jennett Hamilton 45
  Robert 45
Ramsay
  Amelia 150, 155, 188, 191
  Ann 2, 3, 7, 123
  Ann Junior 4
  Ann Ramsay Allison 123
  Betty Ramsay Steuart 124
  Dennis 3, 7, 15, 22, 24, 36, 47, 52, 56, 57, 59, 61, 64, 66, 67, 72, 77, 82, 83, 85, 87, 92, 94-96, 99, 102, 104, 110, 120, 121, 123, 124, 127, 128, 131, 134, 135, 136, 138, 148, 149, 151, 159, 185, 187, 188, 191, 194, 199, 202, 210, 219
  Edward 5, 19, 66, 126, 142
  Edward Mitchell 91, 132, 165, 198
  Hannah Ramsay Madden 193, 206, 208
  Jane 47, 99, 100, 148, 149, 151, 219
  Jane Allen 128, 134, 188, 191, 202, 210
  John 16, 22, 76
  Mary 91, 132, 165
  Sarah 7, 22, 32, 112
  Sarah Ramsay Porter 108
  Thomas 24, 35, 76
  William 1-4, 7, 15, 17, 19, 37, 44, 47, 53, 66, 71, 76, 83, 84, 87, 96, 97, 99, 100, 108, 110-112, 116, 123, 124, 127, 128, 133, 134, 136, 142, 144, 148, 149, 155, 159, 166, 188, 191, 202, 207, 210
  William (Doctor) 101, 106
  William the elder 127, 185, 187, 199
  William the younger 199
  William, natural son of Dr. Wm. Ramsay 101
  William, son of William 15, 159
Randell
  Theophilus 216
Randolph
  Beverly 46
  Edmund 31
Ratcliff
  Richard 7, 57, 95
Rather
  Thomas 81
Rattle
  Ann 203
  James 6, 203
Rawlings
  B. 113, 183
Rawlins
  John 73, 181
  Susannah 181
Re-entry, deed of 130
Rea
  William 8
Reardon

William 80
Redman
　Thomas 78, 105
Redmon
　Thomas 129
Reed
　Elizabeth 28
　Thomas 3, 22, 28, 35, 80
Reeds
　William 14
Reintzel
　Andrew 181
Reintzell
　Andrew 186, 206
Release, deed of:
　Harper: Lyles to build frame vice brick dwelling 26
　Ownbread's lot to Korn & Wisemiller 71
　Sydebotham, of Meyler's negroes 38
Renwick
　William 85
Resler
　Jacob 126, 181
Rester
　Jacob 141
Reverends:
　Muir, James 205
Reynolds
　John 5, 7, 13-16, 33, 34, 41, 52, 67, 69, 83, 125, 157, 159, 172, 175
　Levi 214
　Michael 15
　Reynolds & Barclay 41
　Sarah 67, 69, 83
　William 109, 214
Rhodes
　John 102
Rice
　Frederick William 87
Richards
　Ann 109, 126, 139, 150, 164, 206, 214
　George 6, 20, 21, 32, 39, 54
　Nancy 155, 165, 196
　Nancy [Ann] 127
　Nancy/Ann 151
　Thomas 39, 94, 98, 99, 109, 126, 139, 147, 148, 150, 151, 155, 159, 164, 165, 178, 193, 196, 206, 214
Richmond Co., VA 44, 91, 100
Richmond, VA 44, 60, 75
Richter
　John 198
Ricketts
　John Thomas 109, 123, 150, 169, 207, 213, 218
　Mary 169
　[first name not given] 142
Riddle
　Frances Rush Harper 200
　Josa. 140
　Joseph 84, 108, 117-119, 127, 128, 140, 151, 154, 188
　Joshua 107, 108, 153, 154, 188
　Samuel 128
Ridel
　Charles 170
Ridgway
　Daniel 26
　David 218
　Martha McPherson 218
Riggen
　Benton 217
Right
　Israel 37
Rinker
　Jeremiah 188
Rirbre [?]
　Migal [?] 41
Risberg
　Khun/Keen & Risberg 27
Ritchie
　John 132, 183
　William 115
Roach
　Milly 35
　William 35, 40
Roads:
　the old Georgetown 3, 33, 34
　the present Georgetown 3, 33
Roberdeau
　Daniel 45, 47, 99, 115, 168
　Jane 47, 115, 168
Robinson
　Chr. 204
　Christopher 55
　John 3
　Matthew 112, 116
　Robinson, Sanderson & Rumney 75, 204
Robson
　Robert 114, 118
Rodgers
　Joseph 55
Roe/Wroe
　Absalom 101

Rogers
  John 6, 32
Rogerson
  Anstis 189
  Thomas 26, 57, 67, 96, 120, 125, 159, 189, 204
Roome
  Henry 34
Rope Walk
  built by James Irvin 201
  Negroes belonging to 201
Rose
  Dr. [first name not given] 214
Ross
  David 139
  Hector 6, 53
  Horatio 83
Royal Exchange (London) 114, 119
Rozer
  Eleanor 28
  Frs. H. 192
  Henry 28, 44, 192
Rumney
  John 37, 38, 43, 44, 55
  Robinson, Sanderson & Rumney 75, 204
Russell
  James 119, 188
Rutherford
  Robert 2, 3, 99, 155
Rutter
  George 218
  [first name not given] 104, 112
Rye Parish, Donegal (Co.) 45
Sadler
  Henry 44
Sadlers:
  Bryan, John 72
  Kidd, James 72
Saint Lucia 42
Salkeld
  Henry 79, 93, 100
Salmon
  George 93, 105, 117
Sanderson
  James 114
  Robert 55
  Robinson, Sanderson & Rumney 75, 204
Sanford
  Edward 5, 99
  John 156
  Lawrence 1
Saul
  Joseph 121, 172, 177
  Mary 177
Saunder
  John 68, 167
Saunders
  Hannah 66
  J. 164
  John 5, 6, 17, 18, 52, 66, 70, 155, 168
  Joseph 19, 66, 142
  Mary 70, 155
Savage
  William 189, 209, 213
Schahel/Shahel/Schabel
  Dederick 29
Scheckel
  Diederich 90
  Diederick 69
  Diedrick 112
Schess/Schiess
  Sebastian 62
Schoolmasters:
  Walker, Henry 190
Scot
  James 59
  Wm. 57
Scotland 45
Scott
  Charles R. 49-51, 58, 97, 133
  Charles Robert 133, 136
  David Marshall 55
  George 115
  James 59
  Mary 135, 137, 159, 192, 196
  Richard Marshall 61, 66, 135, 159, 188, 191, 192, 196
  Wm. 59
Scott, John (see Tarbuck) 17, 42
Sebastian
  Benjamin 178
  Benjamin the elder 186
  Benjamin the younger 186
Semple
  William 70
Sergeant of TwnALX:
  Summers, William 138
Servat
  Nicholas M. 58
Sewall
  William 83
Sewell
  Elizabeth 187
  Elizabeth Sewell Worrell 185, 199
  William 87, 185, 187
Sexsmith

Elizabeth 128
Mathew 128
Matthew 134, 135, 138, 141, 202
Shackley
   W. 119
Shakespear
   [first name not given] 101
Shakle
   Dedrick 55, 56
Sharlock
   [first name omitted] 79
Shaw
   Eleanor 110
   Elizabeth 36
   William 14, 36, 76, 110
Sheckle
   Dederick 145
   Dedrick 190
Shekle
   Diederk 134
   Diedrik 145
Shepard
   Daniel 91
Ship Carpenters:
   Caverly, Joseph 12
   Piper, Anthony 24
   Weston, Lewis 12
Ship Masters:
   Lunt, Henry, of the "Peggy" 119
   [?] Lee, Tom, of Brig "Cornwallis" 120
Ships:
   "Paragon" of Boston 204
   "Peggy" 119
   Brig "Cornwallis" 120
   Sloop "Industry" 16
   Sloop "William" 16
Shoemakers:
   Halladay, James 30
Shop-keepers:
   White, Thomas 70
Short
   Anne 39
   Elizabeth 13
   John 4, 17, 39, 151
Shortill/Shortle
   Luke 166, 217
Shreeve/Shreve
   Benjamin 7, 64, 111, 216, 218
   Samuel 93
   Shreeve & Lawrason 26
   Susannah 111
Shreve
   Thomas 194, 196
Shreve/Shreeve
   Benjamin 52, 104, 120, 121, 126, 131, 132, 137-139, 141, 165, 172-174, 175
   Susanna 126, 175
Shuck
   Jacob 130
Shugart
   Michael 38
   Zachariah 49
Shum
   Adam 102
Silversmiths:
   Mason, John 72
Sim
   Thomas 202
Simmes
   Thomas 200
Simmonds
   Jane 87
   Samuel 30, 87
   Simon 87
Simmons
   Samuel 36, 90, 186, 206
Simms
   Charles 10-14, 29, 32, 34, 38, 47, 53, 97, 107, 108, 117, 118, 126, 127, 135, 136, 149, 151-154, 170, 186
   Jesse 7, 72, 105, 106, 119, 121, 126, 142, 149, 155, 173, 178, 182, 188, 191, 193, 194, 219
Simpson
   Elizabeth Gretter 65
   French 113
   John 169, 178
   William 65
Sim[?]
   Thomas [may be Simms/Simen/Simon] 164
Singer
   Abraham 70
Singleton
   George 190
Sittler
   Isaac 187
   Isaac [or Littler] 182
Skillern
   George 73
Skinner
   A. 187
Slacum
   George 33, 34, 53, 69, 73, 103, 122, 124, 147, 156, 167, 171, 217
Slade

Charles Jr. 135
Slimmer
  Ch. 56
  Christian 1, 17, 18, 27, 29, 38, 43, 88, 89, 119, 128
  Christina 16
  Mary 2, 17
Smaw
  John 17
Smith
  Alexander 17, 22, 32, 41, 46, 64, 77, 85, 95, 116, 122, 136, 150, 155, 164, 171, 175, 181, 182, 185, 189, 190, 191, 194, 196, 203, 206-208, 213, 219
  Aug. J. 189
  Ezekiel 59
  Hugh 210, 212, 219
  James 35, 36, 41, 126, 136
  James the younger 91
  John 22, 24, 80
  Rachel 155, 190, 194
  Samuel 29
  William 74, 93, 128, 145, 196, 202
Smoot
  H. Kh. 218
  H.K.H. [may be H. Kh.] 164
Snow
  Gedion 58
  Gideon 44
Soho, Middlesex Co. (England) 118
Somerset Co., MD 6, 7
Sowess
  Joseph 99
Spangler
  Baltzer 62
  George 127, 128, 182, 195, 210
Speake
  Josias Milburne 147
Spencer
  Samuel 59
  William 93
Spiers
  John 2
Spilman
  Merryman 14
Spinsters:
  Crawford, Mary 45
Spotsylvania Co., VA 33
Sprigg
  Osburn 176
St. Mary's Co., MD 85
Stabler
  Edward 130

Stafford Co., VA 10-13, 15, 63
Stallcup
  William 59
Stansbury
  Samuel 196
Stark
  Ebenezer 38, 97
Steeber
  Michael 139
Steel
  John 38
Steel/Steile
  Peter 45
Steele
  Jno. 201
Steiber
  Michael 129
  Richard 142
Steiver
  Michael 21
Sterling
  Andrew 45
  James 45
  John 45
Steuart
  David 170
  Eleanor 170
  James 76
  William Gibbons 10-14
Steuart/Stewart
  Betty 71, 124
  Betty Ramsay 124
  James 71, 84, 97, 123
  James Montgomery 71
  William Ramsay 71
Stewardson
  Thomas 99
Stewart
  Andrew 15
  Betty 7
  Cicily 171, 172
  David 15
  Jno. Jr. 179, 196
  John 6, 7, 71, 139, 171, 172
  John Jr. 195
  Thomas 94, 110, 147, 214
Stieber
  Michael 80
Stith
  Baldwin 66, 100, 115, 160
Stoddart
  George 47
  [first name not given] 191
Stone

Samuel 159
Stonemasons:
  Mooney, Neal 8
Store:
  L. Reynolds' nailor's shop 214
  of G. Gilpin 164
  of J. Gill 88
  of Saunderson & Rumney 39
  of W. Hartshorne 19
  of Wm. Hepburn 48
Storekeepers:
  Marsteller, Philip 43
Streets privately laid out:
  (possibly) by S. Cooke 108
  Abingdon, now Gibbons 19
  by C. Alexander [streets unnamed] 133
  covenant by W.T. Alexander 59
  Fairfax, Gibbons, Pitt, Royal by J. Alexander's exxrs 10
  Fayette by W. Ramsay 123, 124
  King, Prince, Duke, Wolfe, Wilkes, Gibbons by W.T. Alexander 50, 55
  Oronoko by Dade 8, 9, 27
  Oronoko by Griffith 20
  Princess by Dade 9
  Princess by Griffith 22
  Queen by Dade 9
  St. Asaph by Griffith 20, 22
  St. Asaph, Washington, Water by J. Alexander's exxrs 10
  Washington by Dade 3, 8, 9, 27
  Washington by J. Alexander 9
  Washington, St. Asaph, Pitt, Royal, Fairfax by W.T. Alexander 50, 55
  Water St. by W.T. Alexander 50, 55
  [Columbus] by Dade 12, 27
Streets, laid out:
  Oronoko, by an Act of Assembly 134
Streets, paving of 186
Stroman
  Elizabeth 69
  Henry 69, 127, 145
  [first name not given] 202
Strowman
  Henry 55
Stuart
  James 133, 136
  Philip 187
  William 187
  William Jr. 93

Suckley
  George 73
Suffolk Co., MA 142, 158, 202
Sullivan
  Bethsey 168
  Honora 168, 207
  John 168, 169, 207
  Mary 168
  Nelly 168
Summers
  Francis Jr. 86, 93
  George 31
  Isabel 143
  Isabella 57
  Isabella Elton 181
  Lewis 199
  William 40, 43, 46, 52, 57, 82, 86, 93, 97, 104, 109, 129, 131, 136, 138, 139, 143, 172, 175, 181, 192, 195, 199, 202, 206, 217
Supreme Court...NY
  Chief Justice R. Morris 62
Surveyors:
  Boggess, Robert 10, 11, 13, 15, 149, 157
  Copper, Cyrus 69
  Payne, W.--of Ffx Co. 104, 206, 207
  West, George 29
  West, George--of Ffx Co. 3
  West, John 84
  West, John Jr.--of Ffx Co. 207
Sussex Co., DE 165
Sutton
  H. 210
  J. A. [may be T. A.] 206
  John 27
Swann
  George 195
  Thomas 10-14, 19, 24, 29, 34, 38, 197
Sweeney
  George 118
Sweeny
  George 75, 153
Swift
  Jonathan 27, 114, 117, 122, 158, 176, 194
Swoope
  Adam Simon 26, 37, 38
  Eve 38
  G. 107, 140
  George 152-154
  Jacob 26, 37, 38
  Michael 26, 37, 38
Swope

G. 108, 119, 129
Sydebotham
   William 4, 29, 38, 47, 138, 139
Taboyne Parish, Co. Donegal, Ireland 45
Tait
   Henry 24
Talbott
   William 150, 169, 207
Taliaferro
   John 118, 211
   John Jr. 117, 178, 180, 181, 186, 195, 204, 211
   John Sr. 195, 204
Tallbutt
   Conny 36
   McKinsey 36
Tandy
   Moses 39
Tarbuck
   Ann 53
   John 53
Tarbuck alias Scott
   John 17, 42
Tartsback
   Peter 146
Tartsbaugh
   Peter [also Tetespaugh] 197
Tartspaugh/Tartzbaugh
   Peter 166
Tartzback/Tertzback
   Peter 74
   Susanah/Susannah 74
Tartzpaugh
   Peter 146
Tate
   Benjamin 70
Tavern Keepers:
   Ward, William 55
Taylor
   Andrew 40, 57, 149, 150
   Archibald 105
   Archibald J. 74, 93, 167, 188
   Charles 144
   George 64, 65, 100
   James 79, 121, 126
   Jesse 4, 36, 40, 52, 54, 57, 58, 61, 66, 67-69, 76, 77, 80-82, 85, 92, 93, 96, 102, 104, 127, 131, 139, 165, 167, 174, 183, 205
   Jesse Andrew 61
   Jesse Jr. 62, 69, 81
   John 37, 81, 85, 176
   John Jr. 129, 152
   John Sr. 129, 152
   R.T. 205
   Robert 105
   Taylor 205
   Thomas 122
Taylors:
   Harper, John Weathers 35
Temple
   Liston 188, 198
Tetespaugh
   Peter [also Tartsbaugh] 197
Therie
   Lewis 60
Thomas
   Alexander 19
   Jos. 91
   Joseph 66, 68
   Rachel 68
   Samuel S. 146
   Simon 174
Thompson 131
   Ann 40
   Edward Kinnicut 26, 27
   Edward Kinnicutt 142
   James 40, 57
   Jonah 20, 29, 33, 34, 38, 41, 64, 65, 67, 69, 83-85, 89, 94, 97, 99, 100, 107, 108, 109, 111, 112, 114, 116, 120, 121, 123, 127, 131-134, 136, 137, 141-143, 146-149, 151, 155, 166, 170, 178, 179, 182, 183, 189, 190, 192, 197, 198, 202, 208, 209, 213, 217, 219
   Margaret 12, 85
   Richard 68
Thorn
   Michael 14, 16, 25, 92, 95, 158
Thorne
   Michael 15
Thornton
   Joseph 112
Tiernan
   [first name not given] & Brothers 210
Tobacco 3, 4, 16, 19, 29, 38, 132, 165, 187
Tobin
   John 14
   Thomas 11, 14, 159
Townshend
   Piatt 62
Tracey
   John 155
Trade

between France and neutral ports, only, specified 204
Treasury warrants 47
Tresize
 Thomas 154
Tressler
 Lodowick 129
Tripartite Deeds: 93, 96, 119, 123, 124, 130, 135, 137, 161, 163, 171, 172, 174, 179, 180, 205, 209
Triplett
 Thomas 169, 200
 Titus 66, 87, 90, 91, 104, 132, 139, 147, 150, 156
Trisseler
 Lodowick 195
Trissler
 Lodowick 128
Tristler
 Lewis 168
Trout
 Paul 22
Trust, deed of: 170, 171, 178, 195, 204, 210
Tumbler
 George 130
Turberville
 George Richard Lee 217
 Harriet 217
Turner
 Charles 53, 77, 99, 121, 128, 139, 148, 156, 196
 Jno. B. 90
 Thos. 120
Tyler
 Charles 117
U.S. Consul:
 Port of London: J. Johnson 114, 119
Ubrich
 George 120
Uhler
 Catharine 29, 112
 Valentine 29, 112
Ulrick
 George 148
Upper Marlborough, MD 210
Usher
 Abraham 165
Valette [See also Nallette]
 Betty Fleming 189
 Elie 189
Vallette
 Elie 24

Vanersdel
 Lucas 90
Varick
 Richard 170, 194, 204
Veitch
 Alexander 212, 213
 Richard 133, 136
Vendue Master 133
Vendue Master of ALX:
 Marsteller, Philip 32, 33, 89
 Thompson & Peyton 176
Vendue Store, Alexandria 176
Vietch
 Alexander 209
Violet
 John 162, 163
Voss
 Nicholas 190
Vowell
 Ebenezer 73
 Jno. C. 143
 John 194
 John C. 120, 143
 John Crips 113, 164, 166, 183, 189, 191
 Margaret 164, 191
 Mary 191
 Mary Harper 199
 Peggy 200
 Peggy [Margaret] 164
 Samuel 74, 188
 Thomas 60, 73, 88, 92, 158, 194
 Thomas Jr. 73, 98, 113, 158, 164, 167, 183, 189, 191
Waddell
 Henry L. 110
Wade
 Benjamin 53, 56
Wagener
 Andrew 69
 P. 131
 Peter 31, 55, 66, 81, 82, 156
 Sinah 156
Wagoner
 Andrew 83
Wailes/Wales
 Andrew 12, 14, 25, 29, 39, 40, 58, 64, 75, 84, 85, 95, 100, 103, 109, 117, 118, 127, 144, 147, 150, 182, 191, 194
 Margaret 14, 40, 64, 67, 85, 95, 100, 109, 144, 147, 182
Walker
 Henry 66, 139, 181, 190

John 207
Richard 135
Robert 102
Walkom
　John 208
Wallace
　James 83, 90
　Mich. 211
　Michael 125
Waller
　Thomas 199
Wanton
　Mary 168
　Philip 53, 61, 111, 157, 158, 168, 201
War, now in Europe 204
Ward
　Enoch 61
　William 2, 3, 8, 38, 41, 55, 63, 65
Warden
　William 42
Warehouse:
　Hooe's 110, 131
　Hunting Creek 207
　of Capt. Conway 132
　of D. Roberdeau 99
　of G. Gilpin 164
　of Hunter & Allison 81
　of J. Green 119
　of J. Harper 128
　of J. Kirk 75
　of McPherson, now Janney & Irish 164
　of R. Adam, on his pier 132
　of T. Patten & Co., on J. Harper's pier/dock 201, 202
　of W. Hartshorne 19
　public tobacco 3
　the County 52
　to be built by Morehouse & Co. 99
Warren
　Richard 167
Washington
　Ann 165
　Bailey Jr. 63
　Bushrod 61, 165, 216
　Corbin 217
　George Augustine 61
　Hannah 217
　Lawrence 207
　Mary 216
　Thacker 164
　Washington John 118, 126, 127
Washington Co., VA 97

Water passage
　to drain back yard 117
Waterfront rights granted:
　by ALX Trustees: water & improvements into the river 215
　communication w/Prince St. 66
　extending north & east from Point Lumley 130
　ferry & wharfing out 41, 81
　general privileges 8, 148
　may extend a pier into the river 191
　new or extended wharves 19
　Point West mooring 52
　Simms may extend wharf 182
　to extend into the Potomac on the flats to the channel 214
　Wales may extend brewery trunks into the Potomac 182
　water and extending into the river 215
　water, landing places 15, 198, 215
Watermen:
　Clarke, Richard 16
Watson
　James 79, 85, 92, 97, 112, 127
　Jane 85, 91, 206
　Jean 92
　John 157, 158, 169
　Josiah 32, 36, 37, 40, 54, 63-65, 85, 91, 92, 97, 110, 118, 119, 142, 143, 153, 167, 187, 206
Watts
　Jno. 117, 148
　John 92
Weaver
　Frederick 14
Webb
　Hannah 6, 103, 203
　John 6
Webster
　Elizabeth 87
　John Stone 81
　Mary Lynn 81
　Philip 30, 34, 81, 87, 110
Weightman
　Richard 66, 68, 206
Weightmen
　Richard 142
Weir
　Benjamin 165, 192
West
　Alexander-West property line 33
　Ann 30
　George 3, 29

Hugh 31, 135, 207
Hugh the elder 2, 3, 40
John 84
John Jr. 207
John Jr., son of Hugh the elder 62
R. 117, 151
Roger 58
Sybil 8, 31
Sybil, dau of Hugh 41
Sybil, wife of Hugh 41
Thomas 3, 8, 30, 33, 35, 41, 78, 81, 99, 106, 122, 130, 183, 198, 215, 217
Thomas, son of J. West Jr. 62
West's Point/Point West
  ferry & ferry landing 81
  irregular lot adjoining 62
  Jan90 partial lease 52
Westmoreland Co., VA 2, 80, 187, 217
Weston
  Lewis 12, 16, 46, 54, 101, 150
Weylie
  Ephraim 86
  John 214
Whalen
  Dennis 86, 93
Whalin
  Dennis 57
Whalley
  Richard 164
Wharf/pier:
  Conway 107, 216
  Fairfax County 52
  Fitzgerald distillery 115
  Fleming 19
  Fleming & Caverly 19
  Gilpin and Harper's 164
  Harper & Watson 66
  Herbert, Wilson & Potts 216
  Hooe & Harrison 19
  Hunter & Allison 81, 183
  J. Fitzgerald 60
  J. Harper's 201, 202
  Kirk's 75, 132
  known as "Adam's Pier" [R. Adam] 132
  Lumley Point 15
  Peers & Fitzgerald 84
  R. Adam 107
  Ramsay/Richards 99
  Roberdeau 116
  Wales' Brew House site 182
Wheaton

Elizabeth 120, 194
John 26
John R. 103, 142
John Robert 120, 194
Wheeler
  Ignatius 63, 91
  Israel 146
Wherry
  Jesse 108, 187, 199, 201
Whitacre
  Caleb 59
  Phebe 59
  Robert 7, 13, 15
White
  Betty 185
  Jno. 167
  John 99, 100, 112, 116, 193, 208
  Mary 208
  Miles 55
  Thomas 70, 109, 185
Whitehaven (England) 24, 47, 55, 75, 85, 204
Whitford
  Samuel 28
Whiting
  J. 126
  Mary 126
  Thomas 17, 18, 126
Wilkes Co., GA 183
Wilkinson
  Jane 74
  John 28
  Thomas 22, 80, 173, 175
Williams
  James 53
  Jeremiah 16
  John 31
  Lillburn (commonly: Anthony) 195
  Stephen 31
  Thomas 31, 37, 43, 57, 68, 89, 141, 203, 216
  Williams & Cary 86, 93
Williamsburg, VA 60, 207
Willson
  Cumberland 42
  James the elder 42
  James the younger 42
  William 42
Wilmington, DE 43
Wilson
  Eleanor 85
  Elizabeth/Eliza 166
  George 16
  Herbert, Potts & Wilson 84, 133

James 47, 67, 75, 76, 81, 150
James Jr. 42, 43, 60, 111, 166, 218
James Wilson & Sons 42
Jno. 150
John Jr. 111
Thomas 43
William 7, 53, 58, 62, 67, 70, 73, 75, 76, 77, 198, 205, 214, 215
Winchester, VA 210
Windsor
  O. 67
Winsor
  Olney 26, 56, 57, 59, 60
Winterberry
  John Jr. 123
Winterbury
  John Jr. 137
Wise
  Elizabeth 39, 122, 130
  George 205
  John 2, 3, 39, 47, 78, 90, 122, 130, 135, 142, 151, 174, 178, 179, 186
  Peter 61, 68, 77, 82, 87, 98, 104, 113, 131, 155, 171-174, 204, 213
  Peter Jr. 129, 137
Wisemiller
  Jacob 41, 52, 56, 63, 71, 83, 102
  Korn & Wisemiller 106
Wolfenden
  John 165
Woodrow
  John 169, 207, 208
  Mary 207
Woods
  Daniel 213
  John 45, 170
Wormley
  Ralph 65

Worrell
  Elizabeth Sewell 185, 199
  Morris 185, 199
Wren
  John 68
  Richard 166, 197, 198
Wright
  Ann 76, 122, 192
  William 76, 122, 124, 141, 144, 156, 159, 163, 180, 181, 186, 188, 192, 199, 200, 208, 216
Writers:
  MacHarg, Anthony 2
  Spiers, John 2
Wroe/Roe
  Absalom 101
Yost
  Jesorn/John 67
  John 91, 141, 154
  John Jr. 67
Young
  Charles 112, 129
  Charles Jr. 63, 91, 119, 142
  David 29, 35, 77, 86, 87, 90
  David the elder 30
  Jacob 13
  James 107
  Robert 94-96, 103, 129, 148, 194, 201
  William 29, 30
Younger
  Peter How 55
Zelefro
  Andrew 206
Zimmerman
  Elizabeth 195
  Henry 125
  Tobias 25, 178, 195
Zrillmuller [?]
  Iomor [?] 43